Praise for *Asian American History*

"This is an excellent introduction to Asian Americans. It is thorough and thoughtful, especially because it includes the diversity of the many communities who make up this fast-growing population. This would be easy to teach from and learn from. It offers a solid historical foundation for further discussion in the classroom, and it belongs on the syllabus."

—Frank H. Wu, president of Queens College, City University of New York

"Huping Ling's *Asian American History* is an important contribution to the growing scholarship that examines the collective experiences of Asian American communities in the U.S. Utilizing the latest source materials, interdisciplinary methodologies, and a wide range of qualitative and quantitative data, this study provides an indispensable account of both historical and current events."

—Rudy P. Guevarra Jr., author of *Becoming Mexipino: Multiethnic Identities and Communities in San Diego* (Rutgers University Press)

"Professor Huping Ling's book is an important read that provides us with a concise understanding of the multiple dimensions of Asian American history. Important key terms, timelines, primary sources, and study questions provide important tools for deepened understanding and application."

—Harvey Dong, coeditor of *Mountain Movers: Student Activism and the Emergence of Asian American Studies*

"*Asian American History* is a well-documented, comprehensive textbook. Major themes of the Asian American historic experience—racism and resistance, work, and family—as well as the rich, ethnic particularities of each group are integrated to offer a full picture of our communities. Further, Ling covers emerging themes, such as new community formations and transnational shifts, to address the pressing issues of Asian Americans."

—Russell Jeung, professor of Asian American studies at San Francisco State University, California, and cofounder of Stop AAPI Hate

"Enchanting, meticulous, and informative, *Asian American History* offers the most updated, all-encompassing portrayal of Asian American history since the 1760s. Its transnational perspective, interdisciplinary approach, incorporation of new scholarship, fascinating stories, and user-friendly features make it one of the finest textbooks on the history of Asian Americans."

—Philip Q. Yang, author of *Asian Immigration to the United States*

"Huping Ling's *Asian American History* offers a nuanced perspective to bridge the past and present over the span of more than 250 years in the making and remaking of Asian America. It shows how generations of Asian immigrants and their native-born offspring strive to become an integral part of the American nation—an invaluable resource for educators, scholars, and anyone interested in understanding multicultural America."

—Min Zhou, distinguished professor of sociology and Asian American studies, UCLA

"*Asian American History* builds on and extends the research of scholars in recent decades, including pioneers like Ronald Takaki, Sucheng Chan, and Roger Daniels. It offers encyclopedic coverage and insightful analyses of both broad historical and cultural backgrounds of Asian immigration and vital issues concerning Asian Americans. Readers will also have ample opportunity to hear personal stories and direct voices from individual Asian Americans. Its clear organization, lucid style, and impeccable research make this volume a welcome resource for scholars and a valuable textbook for high-school and college classes on the history and experiences of Asian Americans."

—Yong Chen, author of *Chop Suey, USA: The Story of Chinese Food in America*

ASIAN AMERICAN HISTORY

ASIAN AMERICAN STUDIES TODAY

This series publishes scholarship on cutting-edge themes and issues, including broadly based histories of both long-standing and more recent immigrant populations; focused investigations of ethnic enclaves and understudied subgroups; and examinations of relationships among various cultural, regional, and socioeconomic communities. Of particular interest are subject areas in need of further critical inquiry, including transnationalism, globalization, homeland polity, and other pertinent topics.

SERIES EDITOR: HUPING LING, TRUMAN STATE UNIVERSITY

Chien-Juh Gu, *The Resilient Self: Gender, Immigration, and Taiwanese Americans*

Stephanie Hinnershitz, *Race, Religion, and Civil Rights: Asian Students on the West Coast, 1900–1968*

Jennifer Ann Ho, *Racial Ambiguity in Asian American Culture*

Helene K. Lee, *Between Foreign and Family: Return Migration and Identity Construction among Korean Americans and Korean Chinese*

Huping Ling, *Asian American History*

Huping Ling, *Chinese Americans in the Heartland: Migration, Work, and Community*

Haiming Liu, *From Canton Restaurant to Panda Express: A History of Chinese Food in the United States*

Jun Okada, *Making Asian American Film and Video: History, Institutions, Movements*

Kim Park Nelson, *Invisible Asians: Korean American Adoptees, Asian American Experiences and Racial Exceptionalism*

Zelideth María Rivas and Debbie Lee-DiStefano, eds., *Imagining Asia in the Americas*

David S. Roh, Betsy Huang, and Greta A. Niu, eds., *Techno-Orientalism: Imagining Asia in Speculative Fiction, History, and Media*

Leslie Kim Wang, *Chasing the American Dream in China: Chinese Americans in the Ancestral Homeland*

Jane H. Yamashiro, *Redefining Japaneseness: Japanese Americans in the Ancestral Homeland*

ASIAN AMERICAN HISTORY

HUPING LING

RUTGERS UNIVERSITY PRESS
New Brunswick, Camden, and Newark, New Jersey
London and Oxford

Rutgers University Press is a department of Rutgers, The State University of New Jersey, one of the leading public research universities in the nation. By publishing worldwide, it furthers the University's mission of dedication to excellence in teaching, scholarship, research, and clinical care.

Library of Congress Cataloging-in-Publication Data
Names: Ling, Huping, 1956- author.
Title: Asian American history / Huping Ling.
Description: New Brunswick: Rutgers University Press, [2023] |
   Series: Asian american studies today | Includes bibliographical references
   and index.
Identifiers: LCCN 2022036671 | ISBN 9781978826236 (paperback) |
   ISBN 9781978826243 (hardback) | ISBN 9781978826250 (epub) |
   ISBN 9781978826274 (pdf)
Subjects: LCSH: Asian Americans—History—Textbooks. | United States—Race
   relations—History—Textbooks.
Classification: LCC E184.A75 L564 2022 | DDC 973/.0495—dc23/eng/20220802
LC record available at https://lccn.loc.gov/2022036671
A British Cataloging-in-Publication record for this book is available from the British Library.
Copyright © 2023 by Huping Ling
All rights reserved

No part of this book may be reproduced or utilized in any form or by any means, electronic or mechanical, or by any information storage and retrieval system, without written permission from the publisher. Please contact Rutgers University Press, 106 Somerset Street, New Brunswick, NJ 08901. The only exception to this prohibition is "fair use" as defined by U.S. copyright law.

References to internet websites (URLs) were accurate at the time of writing. Neither the author nor Rutgers University Press is responsible for URLs that may have expired or changed since the manuscript was prepared.

⊖ The paper used in this publication meets the requirements of the American National Standard for Information Sciences—Permanence of Paper for Printed Library Materials, ANSI Z39.48-1992.

rutgersuniversitypress.org

CONTENTS

PREFACE — ix

PART I Coming to America, 1765–1840s

1 ROOTS OF ASIAN MIGRATION TO AMERICA — 2

Cultural Heritage of Asian Migrants — 3
Global Context for Asian Migration — 10
Asian Context and Patterns of Migration — 14
Roots of Asian Migration to America in Historical Perspective — 25

2 RESTRICTIONS AND RESISTANCES — 28

Racial Prejudice — 31
Economic Sanctions — 32
Physical Violence — 35
Exclusion Laws and Policies — 40
The Enforcement of Exclusion Laws — 42
Protests against Exclusion and Discrimination — 50
Asian Immigration Restrictions and Resistance in Historical Perspective — 56

PART II Asian American Experiences, 1840s–1965

3 LABOR — 60

Sugar Plantations, Mines, and Railroads — 62
Urban Niche Economy — 69
Niche in Agriculture — 85
Labor in Historical Perspective — 88

4 DEFINING HOME AND COMMUNITY — 92

- Domesticity and Innovative Family Formations — 94
- Changing Gender Roles — 110
- The Second-Generation "Dilemma" — 113
- Ethnic Community Building — 116
- Asian Immigrant Home and Community in Historical Perspective — 125

5 WORLD WAR II: A TURNING POINT — 130

- Changing Public Mood — 132
- In Military Services — 134
- Home Front — 137
- End of Exclusion — 139
- Japanese Internment — 140
- Asian Americans and World War II in Historical Perspective — 156

PART III Contemporary Asian Americans, 1965–2020s

6 NEW WAVES OF IMMIGRANTS AND REFUGEES — 162

- A More Gender-Balanced Society — 164
- Effects of the Immigration and Nationality Act of 1965 — 169
- Southeast Asian Americans — 174
- Plights and Potentials of Undocumented Immigrants — 185
- "The Quiet Migration": Transnational Transracial Adoption — 194
- New Waves of Immigrants in Historical Perspective — 200

7 MOVING UPWARD — 206

- Educational Attainments — 207
- New Patterns of Employment and Economic Potentials and Constraints — 213
- Political Incorporation — 222
- Myth and Reality of "Model Minority" — 229
- Asian American Upward Mobility in Historical Perspective — 232

| 8 | NEW FORMATIONS OF ASIAN AMERICAN COMMUNITIES | 236 |

    Urban Enclaves (1850s) — 238

    Transnational Urban and Suburban Communities and Cyber Communities (1990s) — 254

    Asian American Communities in Historical Perspective — 264

PART IV The Future of Asian America, 2020s–

| 9 | THEORIZING ASIAN AMERICA: SIGNIFICANT THEORIES AND ISSUES | 270 |

    Asian American Movement and the Construction of Pan-Asian Ethnicity — 272

    Challenges of Asian American Identities in Recent Decades — 275

    Asian American Panethnicity in Historical Perspective — 293

| 10 | THE FUTURE OF ASIAN AMERICA UNDER GLOBALIZATION | 298 |

    China Rise / Asian Rise versus the U.S. Decline — 298

    Importance of Global Collaboration and Various Prescriptions — 305

    New Trends of Migration and Assimilation under Globalization — 307

    The COVID-19 Pandemic and Asian American Communities — 314

    Asian Americans under Globalization in Historical Perspective — 320

CHRONOLOGY — 323
NOTES — 333
INDEX — 367

PREFACE

ASIAN AMERICAN HISTORY provides the most up-to-date synthesis of Asian American studies. It traces the roots of Asian immigration from the time when the first group of Asians stepped on American soil in the late 1700s. It candidly records the work, family, and community experiences of Asian immigrants and incorporates their new socioeconomic development in the post–World War II era and especially post-1965. It digests recent scholarship on multifaceted Asian America over the past three decades. To be user-friendly, it adopts a number of new features that are designed to help students better understand Asian American history.

APPROACHES AND SCOPES OF THE BOOK

Being keenly aware of Asian American studies as an interdisciplinary and panethnic academic field, *Asian American History* employs research methodologies from various disciplines of the humanities and social sciences and utilizes a broad range of primary and secondary sources from those disciplines. It is both qualitative as well as quantitative in its data collection and analysis. It gleans primary sources not only from such traditional sites as the Immigration and Naturalization Service, the National Archives and its regional branches, museums and historical societies, the U.S. Census Bureau, and private and government agencies, but also from the more recent sources of oral history interviews, visual arts, and online literature. It garners the most recent scholarship from books, dissertations, theses, journal articles, and conference proceedings from all academic fields in the humanities and social sciences. It spans from the late 1700s to the present and covers all major groups of Asian Americans, with a focus on their economic conditions, family structure and gender roles, construction of community and ethnicity, and participation in politics both in the homeland and in the host society. Meanwhile, scholarly discourses on the critical issues of immigration, naturalization, cultural adaptation, the preservation of ethnic traditions, and many more are also carefully incorporated throughout the chapters. The book also adopts an approach that portrays Asian Americans not as merely passive victims of capitalistic exploitation and racial discrimination but active agents who have strived to attain their American dream on their own terms with ingenuity, courage, and perseverance.

This book is organized chronologically in four parts, each corresponding to a historical period marked with characteristics on the nature of immigration and naturalization for Asian Americans. Within each part, the book treats the materials thematically, with each chapter focusing on a given topic. Each chapter covers various ethnic groups individually and collectively.

Part I, "Coming to America, 1765–1840s," covers the period from the first arrival of Asian immigrants in America to the 1840s, when Asian immigrants were completely barred from entering into the United States. In this period, Asian immigrants transformed from indispensable and inexpensive laborers to unwelcome aliens. Within this framework, the part focuses on the hostility and discrimination against Asian immigrants and their resistance and struggle in the face of adversities. Chapter 1, "Roots of Asian Migration to America," traces the cultural, socioeconomic, and geopolitical backgrounds for Asian immigration to America and the immigration patterns for each of the earlier Asian immigrant groups, namely Chinese, Japanese, Koreans, Filipinos, and Asian Indians. Chapter 2, "Restrictions and Resistances," analyzes the principal causes of Asian immigration exclusion and the institutionalized prejudices and discrimination against Asian immigrants in the United States. It also chronicles Asian immigrants' protests and resistance to discrimination and injustice.

Part II, "Asian American Experiences, 1840s–1965" covers the period from when Asian immigrants began to come in large numbers in successive waves (Chinese from 1848, the gold rush in California, to 1882, the passage of the Chinese Exclusion Act; Japanese from the 1880s to 1908, the passage of the Gentlemen's Agreement; Koreans from the 1910s to the 1920s, the passage of Quota Act that banned the coming of Asian immigrants; and Filipinos from the 1920s to 1934, the passage of the Tydings-McDuffie Act that reclassified all Filipinos in the United States as aliens and set a quota of fifty Filipino immigrants per year) to 1965, when American immigration and naturalization laws were revamped. Part II includes three chapters, portraying Asian immigrants' work, family, community, and wartime experiences. Chapter 3, "Labor," examines the working conditions and contributions of Asian immigrants in sugar plantations, mines, and railroads and their survival and success strategy—focusing on a niche economy in both urban and rural communities. Chapter 4, "Defining Home and Community," investigates the various innovative Asian American family structures and community organizations in a difficult time when they were systematically discriminated against and excluded from the larger society. Chapter 5, "World War II: A Turning Point," records Asian Americans' participation in war efforts, with special attention to the injustice against the 120,000 residents and citizens of Japanese ancestry who were interned in ten camps during World War II.

Part III, "Contemporary Asian Americans, 1965–2020s," portrays Asian Americans' socioeconomic conditions and contributions since 1965, when American society had become more tolerant and receptive of Asian Americans and other racial minorities. Part III also includes three chapters. Chapter 6, "New Waves of Immigrants and Refugees," analyzes the 1965 Immigration and Nationality Act and its amendments and their impact on the new immigrants and examines various groups of post-1965 newcomers—war refugees, undocumented immigrants, and the "quiet migrants" of Asian adoptees to American families. Chapter 7, "Moving Upward," examines Asian Americans' educational, occupational, and political accomplishments and obstacles. Chapter 8, "New Formations of Asian American Communities," examines diverse Asian American communities, including traditional inner-city ethnic enclaves, commercial/tourist centers, and suburban cultural communities since the 1960s as well as the transnational urban, suburban, and cyber communities since the 1990s.

Part IV, "The Future of Asian America, 2020s–," contains two chapters. Chapter 9, "Theorizing Asian America: Significant Theories and Issues," traces the historical development of Asian American movement and the construction of pan-Asian ethnicity and delineates the challenges to Asian American identities in recent decades. Chapter 10, "The Future of Asian America under Globalization," analyzes the new socioeconomic conditions of Asian Americans as a result of globalization and pinpoints the new trends of migration and assimilation under globalization.

SPECIAL FEATURES OF THE BOOK

The special features of the book include a *chapter outline* and a list of *significant events* at the beginning of each chapter, which are aimed at helping students grasp the major themes of the chapter and bringing their attention to the key events covered. Throughout each chapter, primary sources pertinent to the content are introduced in *sidebars* for students to learn the skills of analyzing and interpreting primary sources in order to better illustrate and understand historical events. In addition, *maps, charts,* and *illustrations* are also used to enhance the chapter contents. At the end of each chapter, a *historical perspective, key terms, review questions, list of films*, and list of *further reading* are designed to help readers recapitulate the contents of the chapter in critical and historical terms and to help instructors with virtual and textual references on the themes and topics discussed in the chapter. Further, a *chronology* at the end of the book provides a very useful tool for readers to grasp the highlights of Asian American history.

Finally, this book represents a culmination of my forty years of teaching, research, and writing in Asian American studies. It embodies a more complete and fuller understanding and grasping of the essence and extent of the field by a fully trained and hardworking practitioner. It is figuratively my professional life's embodiment and refinement, and it actually took more than two decades for me to write, rewrite, and update the materials and new scholarship numerous times. I hope it will serve as a model textbook for high school and college students, teachers, scholars, and lovers of Asian American history.

I thank all of my students, colleagues, readers of Asian American studies, and Asian American communities across the country. Without their assistance, inspiration, and support, this book would be impossible. I am grateful as well to Rutgers University Press for enthusiastically approving and promoting this project.

HUPING LING

ASIAN AMERICAN HISTORY

PART I

Coming to America, 1765–1840s

1

ROOTS OF ASIAN MIGRATION TO AMERICA

CHAPTER OUTLINE

Cultural Heritage of Asian Migrants
Global Context for Asian Migration
Asian Context and Patterns of Migration
Roots of Asian Migration to America in Historical Perspective

SIGNIFICANT EVENTS

1760s	A small Filipino community is established in Louisiana
1839–1842	Opium War in China
1842	Treaty of Nanjing between China and Great Britain
1846–1848	Mexican-American War
1849	Annexation of Punjab by the British colonial government
1850–1864	Taiping Rebellion in China
1858	Ansei Treaties between Japan and Western powers; American trade open with Japan
1876	Kanghwa Treaty between Korea and Japan; Korean ports open to Japan
1868	Meiji Restoration in Japan
1871	Establishment of the New Army in Japan
1878	United States acquires naval station in Samoa
1892	Tonghak Uprising in Korea
1893	Hawaii coup by white sugar plantation owners
1897	Theodore Roosevelt speaks at Naval War College
1898	Spanish-American War; American annexation of Hawaii
1899	American acquisition of Samoa; Filipino-American War begins
1899–1900	U.S. government declares an "open door" policy with China
1902	Filipino-American War ends; the Philippines becomes American territory

SINCE THE 1840s, waves of Asians have sailed across the Pacific Ocean to the Hawaiian Islands and American mainland in search of better economic opportunities. Instead of being welcomed, Asian immigrants have encountered ridicule, hostility, and discrimination on American soil—partly because of their different physical appearance and cultural values and partly because of the socioeconomic conditions and cultural and racial prejudice in America at the time. What are the Asian cultural backgrounds that differ from those of other Americans? What happened in the world that brought the long-insolated Asian countries into the global economy and capital structure? What happened in their homelands that forced them to leave home and loved ones behind? This chapter answers those questions by tracing the diverse cultural and historical heritage in Asia, by looking at the imperialistic expansions that impacted Asia, and by examining the multifaceted socioeconomic conditions in Asian countries that sent their migrants to America.

CULTURAL HERITAGE OF ASIAN MIGRANTS

Asian Americans can trace their diverse cultural and religious roots to the lands of their ancestors. In the past millennia, the peoples of the land mass of Asia (broadly defined to include East, South, Central, and West Asia, although the U.S. Census Bureau does not include peoples from West Asia as part of the term "Asian Americans") and maritime Southeast Asia have been able to embrace the rich and diverse cultural and religious institutions of Confucianism, Daoism, Hinduism, Buddhism, Sikhism, Islam, Shintoism, and Christianity. A brief review of the ethnocultural and historical background of Asian peoples will help us understand their actions and behaviors, which are inevitably influenced by their Asian traditions and interactions with American society.

Confucian Dominance in East Asia

THE ORIGINS OF CONFUCIANISM IN CHINA. The East Asian countries of China, Japan, Korea, and Vietnam (also defined as part of Southeast Asia geographically, but culturally it adheres to Confucian ideas and gravitates toward China more than its southeastern neighbors) shared a common cultural heritage of Confucianism resulting from China's long-term influence. All these countries derived much of their high culture and writing systems from ancient China.

The great bend of the Yellow River in North China has been known as the cradle of Chinese civilization; here the earliest Chinese dynasty, Xia (2205–1766 BCE), arose. The succeeding Shang dynasty (1766–1122 BCE) has been credited with the invention of the writing system in China, the *jiagu wen*, with characters inscribed on turtle shells and animal bones. The Zhou dynasty (1122–221 BCE) that replaced the Shang contributed

> **CHINESE FOLK SONG ON GOLD MOUNTAIN MEN**
>
> In the second reign year of Haamfung,* I began my perilous journey.
>
> Sailing a boat with bamboo poles across the seas,
> Leaving behind wife and sisters in search of money,
> No longer lingering with the women in the bedroom,
> No longer paying respects to parents at home.
>
> ---
>
> *Source*: Marlon K. Hom, *Songs of Gold Mountain: Cantonese Rhymes from San Francisco Chinatown* (Berkeley: University of California Press, 1987), 39.
>
> * The second reign year of Haamfung (*Xianfeng* in Pinyin) refers to 1852. Xianfeng (r. 1851–1861) was the seventh emperor of the Qing dynasty.

greatly to the contending schools of philosophy in ancient China, of which Confucianism and Daoism have been the most enduring.

Confucianism is named for its originator, Kong Fuzi, or Master Kong (Latinized as Confucius). Confucian ideology has strongly influenced spiritual and political life in East Asia; rulers of successive dynasties found it a most effective governing ideology. Consequently, it became entrenched in Chinese society and was introduced to its neighboring countries of Korea, Japan, and Vietnam. Throughout history, generations of Chinese scholars have interpreted and elaborated on Confucian teachings in numerous volumes; however, the essential ideas of Confucianism are centered on basic concepts of governance and individual behavior. In terms of governance, Confucian ideology stresses the moral ethic of the ruler and the ruler's government. Meanwhile, individuals maintain their proper place in a hierarchical society by obeying central, local, and familial authorities in their roles as subjects, wives, and sons or daughters.

Confucianism is believed to be responsible for the subordinate role of women, a status women were supposed to cherish. For Chinese women, the multilayered hierarchical Confucian structure is encapsulated in the Three Obediences and Four Virtues. Under this scheme, a Chinese woman is expected to obey her father before marriage, her husband after marriage, and her son when widowed. She is also expected to possess the virtues of obedience, reticence, pleasing manners, and domestic skills. These rigid ideological constraints were reinforced by physical torments such as foot binding, a custom that instilled the concept of women as weaker and therefore inferior creatures.[1] The practice of foot binding may have begun with dancers at the imperial court during the Tang dynasty (618–907 CE). By the Song dynasty (960–1279 CE), the custom had been introduced among upper-class women. During the Qing dynasty (1644–1911 CE), it became common throughout Chinese society. At an age of three to five, girls had their feet tightly wrapped and gradually bent until the arch was broken and the toes, except for the big one, turned under. The "lily foot" produced by such practice crippled women to the extent that they could barely walk without support.[2]

CONFUCIANISM IN KOREA. The origins of Koreans are related to the movement of people from the Manchurian area of China into the Korean Peninsula. Tan'gun, supposedly a scion of the Shang royal line of China, founded the Korean state in 2333 BCE. The area came under China's direct rule when Wudi of the Han dynasty (206 BCE–220 CE) conquered Chosŏn (the ancient name of Korea) in 109/8 BCE and established four commanderies on the peninsula. When the Chinese colonies in Korea dwindled in the fourth century, three native Korean kingdoms emerged and divided the peninsula among themselves: Koguryŏ in the north, Paekche in the southwest, and Silla in the southeast. By the late seventh century, the peninsula was unified by Silla. During the Silla period (668–935 CE), Korean society was greatly influenced by the Chinese ideals of the Tang dynasty; the sinicization of the peninsula was so profound that the state was nicknamed Little Tang. Yet it was the Yi dynasty (1392–1910 CE) that was seen as a model Confucian society.[3] The Koreans of the era adopted Confucianism with great enthusiasm and restructured their government, value system, and society strictly along the Chinese lines, revering and observing Confucian principles as dogmatic rituals. Koreans faithfully practiced filial piety and dutifully observed the three-year period of mourning for parents. Women were restricted socially, and the remarriage of widows was severely condemned.

CONFUCIANISM IN VIETNAM. The Vietnamese people can be traced back to Mongoloid groups who, in prehistoric times, migrated from South China into the Southeast Asian peninsula. The Red River delta around Hanoi is the heart of North Vietnam. China extended control over this region by the end of the third century BCE and called it Nam Viet, meaning "South Yue," referring to the southern frontier of Chinese civilization. The Han dynasty annexed the region and established a Chinese government, along with the Chinese writing system, Confucian classical learning, and Chinese officialdom. Chinese domination continued until late in the Tang dynasty (about 939 CE), when disorder in South China encouraged the Vietnamese upper class to develop a sense of national identity. They established the Vietnamese dynasties of Later Li (1010–1225), Tran (1225–1400), Later Le (1428–1789), and Nguyen (1802–1945). Though purely Vietnamese regimes, these dynasties continued the precedent of imitation of Chinese government, high culture, literature, dress, and code of conduct.[4]

CONFUCIANISM IN JAPAN. The Japanese, like their neighbors in Korea and China, are a homogeneous Mongoloid people. But unlike Korea and Vietnam, Japan was never conquered by Chinese armies, despite the two expensive yet unsuccessful invasions of Japan in 1274 and 1281 led by the Mongol ruler Kublai Khan. Chinese culture and ideologies, however, influenced Japanese society and government no less than in Korea and Vietnam. While the oceanic boundary protected Japan from continental invasion, it also made the Japanese more aware of their cultural isolation and more conscious of borrowing from the outside. The Japanese state, which dates back to the first emperor, Jimmu, in the seventh century BCE, had regular contact with the continent, especially Korea. This contact strengthened the Japanese Yamato government culturally and economically. In the sixth century Buddhism reached Japan through Korea.

The introduction of Buddhism ushered in a series of cultural and institutional changes including the establishment of the Chinese type of central government, nationalization of land, taxation, adoption of the Chinese writing system and the Chinese calendar, and regular trade with China. Sinicization came to a halt during the Heian period (794–1185 CE), when China's Tang dynasty began to decline and the Japanese were so immersed in many aspects of Chinese culture that further borrowing became irrelevant. The decline of the central government in Japan resulted in the rise of a feudal system dominated by a ruling class of *samurai* (warriors) that lasted seven centuries. The Confucian ideologies associated with bureaucratic skills were valued again during the Tokugawa Shogunate (1600–1868), when prolonged peace meant the government was more in need of Confucian scholar-bureaucrats than of warriors. Consequently, Confucian codes of conduct were reinstated and a substantial portion of the samurai transformed themselves from roughshod warriors into refined Confucian scholars.

During the Meiji period (1868–1912), the government abandoned feudalism and encouraged economic growth and industrialization to modernize Japan and enable it to meet the challenges coming from the West. The entire country was mobilized to help realize the patriotic dream, with women's role defined as ensuring the smooth operation of a male-centered, authoritarian, traditional family. The Meiji government's slogan, "Good Wife, Wise Mother," promoted Japanese state policy and emphasized a woman's responsibilities in the domestic sphere. The Meiji Civil Code of 1898 established the samurai ideal of the *ie* (house) as the legal unit of society and the national standard for the family. The code legally subordinated women to men in several ways: a wife needed her husband's consent before entering a legal contract; a husband could divorce his wife on the grounds of adultery; and a woman under age twenty-five could not marry without the permission of the household head.[5] These Confucian-centered and authoritarian restrictions placed women in a disadvantageous position socially. They also helped form the perception among outsiders that Asian women were more family-oriented, docile, and submissive.

Other Religious Traditions

Confucianism, though not a religion, has been revered as such by many in East Asian countries. Other religions, including Hinduism, Buddhism, Sikhism, Islam, Shintoism, and Christianity, have also contributed to the cultural traditions of Asian Americans.

HINDUISM. The term "Hindu" is derived from the Sanskrit *Sindhu*, referring to the River Indus. The earliest known Indian civilization is the so-called Indus Valley Civilization dated to about 2500 BCE. The Aryan invaders who arrived in the Indus Valley in the second millennium BCE practiced the Vedic religion, which was based on the worship of deities related to natural phenomena with rituals centered on animal sacrifices and the use of soma to enter a trancelike state. The language of the scripture is Sanskrit, which is derived from the language of the Aryans. Modern Hinduism evolved from the ancient Vedic religion, with the development of philosophical concepts of ethics and duties (*dharma*), the cycle of birth, life, death, and rebirth (*samsara*), action and subsequent reaction (*karma*), and liberation from the cycle samsara (*moksha*). According to the Hindu doctrines, the ideal life for a Hindu man consists of four stages: *brahmacharya*, a period of discipline and education; *garhasthya*, the life of the householder and active worker; *vanaprasthya*, the retirement stage, a time for retreat and for the loosening of bonds to the material world; and *sannyasa*, the ascetic stage, a time of renouncing worldly attachment and preparing to shed the body for the next life. Thus, the Hindu system of values emphasizes the attainment of knowledge, active work, sacrifice and service to others, and renunciation of earthly pleasures.

An important component of Hinduism is its caste system, a product of the multiracial nature of Indian society. The system divides people into social groups depending on descent, marriage, and occupation. There are about three thousand castes, divided into four major groups: Brahmins (priests and religious teachers), Kshatriyas (kings, warriors, and aristocrats), Vaisyas (whose are engaged in commerce and trades), and Sudras (farmers, servants, and laborers). Incidentally, there is a significant population of India that does not belong to any caste, who are now called Harijans; these people outside the caste system are treated as the lowest caste, and their interactions with those in the caste system are severely restricted. Over time, the hereditary caste system has maintained a uniform division of labor, class stratification, and stable social interactions and has therefore been mostly preserved by Indian society. The caste system also prohibits intercaste marriage, although *anuloma* marriage (in which the bridegroom is of a higher caste than the bride) has been acceptable and children of such a marriage belong to the caste of their father.[6] Muslims, Christians, and Sikhs in India also have castes, although they are usually more fluid than Hindu castes. Hindu religious ceremonies generally can be classified into several categories of daily meditations, prayers, and rituals; weekly religious observances such as fasting on a certain day of the week; prayers and penances performed according to the lunar calendar; and annual festivals connected with the worship of particular gods and goddesses of the Hindu pantheon.

BUDDHISM. Buddhism, also originated in India, follows the teaching of Siddhartha Gautama (563-483 BCE), prince of a small kingdom on the southern edge of present-day

Nepal and north of India who renounced his princely life to seek enlightenment. Gautama left his home at the age of twenty-nine, attained enlightenment, and became known as Buddha (enlightened one) when he was thirty-five, after developing a philosophy centered around the Four Noble Truths: (1) life is painful; (2) the origin of pain is desire; (3) the cessation of pain is to be sought by ending desire; and (4) the way to this goal is through his Noble Eightfold Path of right understanding, right motives, right speech, right action, right livelihood, right effort, right mindfulness, and right meditation. After Buddha's death, Buddhism was divided into the separate schools of Mahayana (great vehicle) and Hinayana (lesser vehicle) or Theravada (doctrine of the Elders). While Hinayana seems to be closer to the original Buddhism and is mainly practiced in Sri Lanka, Myanmar (Burma), Thailand, and Cambodia, Mahayana is believed to be more tolerant of different ideas and has spread to China, Korea, Japan, and Vietnam.[7]

SIKHISM. Sikhism originated in the sixteenth century in northern India. The term "Sikh," deriving from Sanskrit, means "disciple," "learner," or "instruction." Sikhism is based on the teachings of Guru Nanak Dev (1469–1538) and his nine successors (Angad Dev, Amar Das, Ram Das, Arjan Dev, Har Gobind, Har Rai, Har Krishan, Teg Bahadur, and Gobind Singh) and a collection of writings called the *Gurū Granth Sāhib*. Sikhism's primary concepts include the belief in one God, disciplined meditation on God, hard work, service to others, and charity. It is the fifth-largest organized religion in the world. The traditions and teachings of Sikhism are closely associated with the history and culture of the Punjab province (province was the administrative structure under the British rule) of India, where most of the world's 23 million Sikhs live.[8] The strong military and political organization of Sikh made it a powerful force in medieval India, and a large number of Sikhs served in the military under British rule or in police forces across the British Empire, which made them more worldly and susceptible to migration. Among the nearly 7,000 Indians who immigrated to the United States between 1899 and 1914, most were farmers from Punjab province, men from martial castes and landowning families.[9]

ISLAM. Emerged from Southwest Asia, Islam, like the other two primary monotheistic religions of the world, Judaism and Christianity, is based on belief in one God as the creator of the universe and humankind and accepts Abraham, Moses, and Jesus as important teachers and prophets. Under the leadership of Muhammad and his successors, Islam rapidly spread by religious conversion and military conquest and has become one of the primary religions also in South and Southeast Asia. Of the estimated 1.4 billion Muslims in the world, 60 percent live in Asia and almost one-third in South Asia.[10] The four nations with the largest Muslim populations—Indonesia (231 million), Pakistan (212 million), India (200 million), and Bangladesh (153 million)—are all in Asia. In addition, China claims 22 million Muslims.

SHINTOISM. Shintoism, the indigenous Japanese religion that originated around the seventh century BCE, combines shamanism, hero and ancestral worship, nature worship, and fertility worship. It does not have a fully organized theology, canon of scripture, or defined set of prayers but is based on a belief that *Kami* (gods or spirits) exist everywhere and that people can mediate their relations with the spirits through certain rituals. According to Shinto mythology, a divine pair of *Kami* named Izanagi and Izanami gave birth to the Japanese islands and their children became the deities of various clans. One of their children, Amaterasu (Sun Goddess), was the ancestor of the Japanese imperial family.

Shinto also emphasizes the notions of pollution and purity. The purification ritual not only is important in spiritual life but also penetrates various aspects of daily life; Japanese people traditionally take baths, wash their hands, and rinse out their mouths often. In Shintoism, death, injury, disease, menstrual blood, and childbirth are considered pollution and should be avoided. Shinto also places a high value on family and tradition; the family is the main mechanism by which traditions are preserved, and morality is based upon what is beneficial to the group.[11]

CHRISTIANITY. Christianity, originated from the ancient Greek *Christianos* and the Latin suffix *itas*, is a monotheistic religion based on the life and teachings of Jesus. It began as a Jewish sect in the first century in the Levant region of the Middle East (currently Israel and Palestine) and quickly spread to Syria, Mesopotamia, Asia Minor, and Egypt. It became the state official church of the Roman Empire in the fourth century. Its canon consists of the Hebrew Bible, or the Old Testament, and the New Testament. Christians believe that Jesus is the son of God, whose ministry, sacrificial death, and resurrection promise salvation and eternal life for all people through divine grace. There are three major groups of Christians: Roman Catholic, Eastern Orthodox, and Protestant.

The Christian influence in Asia in the first millennium, though less known, has also been documented by scholars.[12] After European traders reached Japan in the sixteenth century, Jesuit missionaries followed. Francis Xavier (1506–1552) initiated the Christian missionary movement in Japan in 1549, and Matteo Ricci (1552–1610) was sent to China in 1582. Evangelical missions since then have converted millions of people in East, South, and Southeast Asian countries and impacted Asian immigration to America. Korean immigrants are probably the best example of Christian missions and migration; 40 percent of Korean immigrants to the United States around the beginning of the twentieth century were Christians.

GLOBAL CONTEXT FOR ASIAN MIGRATION

Asian immigration to America is a complex phenomenon. Perhaps the earliest migrants were Filipino sailors aboard Spanish galleons in 1565. They came to America and traded for American silver. They are known to have sent bullion from Acapulco, Mexico, to Manila, Philippines. Large-scale migration occurred in the nineteenth century primarily due to capitalistic and global expansion of the Western powers. To open markets for their manufactured goods, the imperial powers forced Asian countries to open up trade and incorporate their economies into the global capital network, which had a high demand for the cheap resources and labors from these countries. This process took place at a time when the Asian countries also suffered from domestic disturbances and natural disasters. Lured by prospective opportunities and pressured by internal problems, those who were desperate and more daring among the populace sailed across the Pacific Ocean to America and thus began the saga of Asian immigration to America. From the 1840s to the 1930s, nearly a million individuals from China, Japan, Korea, the Philippines, and India immigrated to Hawaii and the United States.

Asian Trade

The early Industrial Revolution in England, beginning in 1760 and spreading to continental Europe and the United States in the early nineteenth century, transformed the relations of Western Europe and North America with the rest of the world. Mechanization and mass production increased productivity for the manufactures but also lowered prices for the mass-produced goods. To maximize profit, the capitalists utilized the cheapest labor force and resources possible and sold the manufactured goods overseas. To meet these needs, the industrialized powers competed for global dominance. In 1750, Britain's empire was mainly based on slave-labor plantations in the Americas, competing with the French, Dutch, Spanish, and Portuguese. A century later, the British had eclipsed their contenders, boasting a global empire on which the "sun never set." The imperialistic global expansion produced new European settlements in southern Africa, Australia, and New Zealand, which attracted mostly European colonists, settlers, and immigrants.

Britain's eastern empire consisted of India, Burma, and the island of Ceylon. In India, British rule was carried out by the East India Company, founded in 1600. The company combated Dutch and French influence and fought challenges from Indians. The British, Dutch, and French companies pushed their profitable trade and persuaded Indian rulers to allow them to establish trading posts at strategic points along the coast. By 1805, the British East India Company controlled the southern and southeastern coastal region and a large area in the north from Calcutta to Delhi. The British colonial government encouraged Indian farmers to grow cotton, opium, and tea for exportation. In return India imported manufactured goods from Britain.

Britain's trade with China, however, was not as profitable as that with India, largely because of Chinese government restrictions. From 1685 to 1759, there were multiple ports in China for trading. In 1760, however, the Qing government limited its international trade to only one port, Canton city in Guangdong province, in a practice known as the Canton system (1760–1842). Under this system, European traders could reside only in designated warehouses called "factories" and trade only with a group of Chinese merchants called *Gonghang*, meaning "security merchants," who were granted a monopoly on foreign trade by the Qing government.

In addition to the Canton monopoly, the British-China trade was a mismatch in terms of demand and supply. The self-sufficient and self-reliant economy in China produced little demand for manufactured goods from Britain. On the contrary, there was a great demand for Chinese tea in Britain. British tea imports reached 15 million pounds in 1785 and doubled by the 1830s. To find a way to pay for the tea and to reverse the trade deficit, the British found a commodity that the Chinese could not resist—opium.

A HUNGER FOR CHINA TRADE

The desire for Chinese goods, especially tea, silk and porcelain, served as a strong driving force for Europeans and the colonial Americans. The possession of Chinese porcelain, rugs, and furniture was regarded as the symbolic of social status and cultural elegance for the American colonial elite, as well illustrated by historian John Kuo Wei Tchen in his study, *New York before Chinatown*.

> When they couldn't get the authentic goods, Europeans and some Americans made copies "after the Chinese taste." The French term *chinoiserie* referred to the seventeen- and eighteenth-century fashion for European-made imitations of Chinese goods. These were the creations of craftsmen who had no firsthand experience of a distant and highly romanticized "Cathay."

Source: John Kuo Wei Tchen, *New York before Chinatown: Orientalism and the Shaping of American Culture, 1776–1882* (Baltimore: Johns Hopkins University Press, 1999), 6.

The United States, as a latecomer to the global competition for resources and markets, also eagerly joined the industrialized European powers in their exploitation of the Asian countries. The direct American-Asian trade started as soon as American independence, as demand for Chinese tea, porcelain, and silk was great. The trade routes between the United States and China were well established by the 1830s, and merchant ships from Philadelphia, New York, Boston, and Salem were most active. Like their British counterparts, American merchants faced a difficulty in finding profitable commodities to sell to Chinese in order to offset their purchases in China. Although American traders sold fur and ginseng in China, bought goods mostly with silver shipped from the Americas.

Opium again became an answer. In 1810, Philadelphia merchants discovered a source of opium in Turkey and began to ship the drug to China.

An American Pacific

The emergence of the United States as a transpacific empire was first made possible through the Mexican-American War from 1846 to 1848. The U.S. annexation of Texas in 1845 caused a territorial dispute about the southern boundary of Texas between Mexico and the United States and the consequential war between the two countries. As expected, the United States emerged victorious. The resulting Treaty of Guadalupe Hidalgo forced Mexico to give up its claim to Texas, to recognize the Rio Grande as the southern border of Texas, and to cede New Mexico and California to the United States. Thus, the United States emerged as a continental and transpacific empire.

Furthermore, the conclusion of the American Civil War and new economic development in the late 1800s boosted western frontier expansion and American dominance of the Pacific Ocean. The successful American acquisitions of Hawaii, Guam, Samoa, and the Philippines prompted American expansionists to view the Pacific Ocean as an "American Lake." Even before the Civil War, American settlers had claimed areas west of the Mississippi and parts of the West Coast. After the war, they continued to move westward, filling lands in the Great Plains, the Pacific Northwest, and the Southwest. Big businesses, frontier families, and daring individuals pushed the westward expansion movement, motivated by such reasons as earning a profit, owning a farm and being one's own boss, and living in a more open and healthier environment, all of which became difficult to obtain on the increasingly crowded East Coast. The California Gold Rush in 1849 further attracted immigrants from all around the world. Farming, mining, and ranching became major sectors of the economy of the American West. Continental American economic development convinced businesses and political leaders that the United States had to secure new markets abroad.

American expansions in the late nineteenth and early twentieth centuries had various motivations. The first was to promote economic growth. By the late 1800s, Americans could not consume all the food and other goods that the nation produced. The overproduction led to financial panics and recessions, resulting in the plight of laborers and farmers. Business leaders as well as politicians agreed that the nation's economic problems could be solved only by expanding its markets overseas.

The second motivation was to protect American security. American naval officers were a strong force behind the expansion. The most representative naval voice came from Admiral Alfred T. Mahan. In his 1890 book titled *The Influence of Sea Power upon History, 1660–1783,* Mahan asserted that a nation's economic future depended on overseas markets and that America needed a strong navy to protect its overseas markets from rivals. The strong naval influence prompted Congress in 1881 to establish a Naval Advisory Board. In 1883, Congress authorized the navy to build three cruisers and two battleships. The Naval Act of 1890 permitted construction of more battleships, gunboats, torpedo boats, and cruisers. By 1900, the American navy emerged as among the most powerful in the world, willing and ready to support American expansion overseas.

The third force was a strong belief that America's destiny was to introduce a Christian and modern civilization to other peoples around the world. Scholars as well as politicians maintained that American vitality depended upon expansion and empire building. Historian Frederick Jackson Turner emphasized the significance of the American western frontier in promoting economic development and preserving democracy. When the frontier was closed in the 1880s, Theodore Roosevelt, then a rising young politician from New York, argued that a quest for empire might restore the nation's pioneer spirit. The prevalent social Darwinism of the time encouraged American leaders to believe that superior peoples and nations had the responsibility to save the rest of the world from primitive and backward culture.

America's imperialist expansionism in the late nineteenth century targeted three main areas: Latin America, the Pacific islands, and China. Through interventions and wars, America had penetrated all these areas, raising its status in international politics and impacting Asian immigration to America.

U.S. victory in the Spanish-American War in 1898 forced Spain to recognize Cuba's independence and to surrender the Philippines, Puerto Rico, and Guam to the United States. Filipino rebels who had fought with American troops in the Spanish-American War expected that victory would bring independence to the Philippines. But the American government ignored Filipino rebel leader Emilio Aguinaldo's declaration of a Philippines Republic in January 1899. Tensions between Filipino rebel forces and American troops resulted in a three-year war and subsequent American dominance of the Philippines.

At the time of Spanish-American and Filipino-American wars, the U.S. government also intervened elsewhere in the Pacific. These interventions brought Hawaii, Samoa, and China into the sphere of American Pacific influence.

Annexation of Hawaii

In the late nineteenth century, Hawaii became increasingly important to U.S. commercial interests. Hawaii and the United States renewed a trade treaty in 1887 allowing Hawaiian sugar exports to the United States free of duty. Hawaii also leased Pearl Harbor to the U.S. Navy for fueling and vessel repairing. White, Hawaiian-born planters also forced the Hawaiian king, Kalakaua, to accept a new constitution that allowed them to control the government. When the king died in 1891, his sister, Liliuokalani, succeed him as queen. Queen Liliuokalani opposed American dominance of the island. Two years later, the U.S. Marines helped white planter Sanford B. Dole oust Queen Liliuokalani. Dole then proclaimed Hawaii a republic and requested that it be annexed by the United States, which Congress approved in 1898.

Acquisition of Samoa

The U.S. expansion in the Polynesian islands of Samoa encountered competition from the European powers of Great Britain and Germany. In 1878, the three powers signed a treaty for the protection of Samoa, which by 1889 resulted in a three-way protectorate. In 1899, Great Britain withdrew from Samoa, and Germany and the United States then divided the islands. After the annexation of Hawaii, the United States acquired Samoa's fine harbor at Pago Pago, further strengthening the American position in the Pacific.

Open Door to China

When American influence reached China in the late nineteenth century, the Asian nation was already divided into "spheres of influence," or areas of economic and political control, by Britain, France, Germany, Japan, and Russia, the other industrial powers of the time. Eager to share benefits with other powers as a latecomer, the U.S. government declared an "open door" policy with China in 1899. Coined by John Hay, the secretary of state under President McKinley, the policy urged other powers to allow equal access to China's huge population and vast markets. Although mostly ignored by European powers, the open-door policy helped U.S. economic and political interests to penetrate into China. It also helped the United States earn the trust of the weak and helpless Qing government at a time when China was being devoured by merciless and diverse imperialist powers. The Chinese government naïvely believed that the United States was a fairer and friendlier "barbarian" country.[13]

ASIAN CONTEXT AND PATTERNS OF MIGRATION

China

The mid-nineteenth century was especially tumultuous for China, as it faced both foreign imperialistic invasions and domestic upheavals and natural disasters. These external and internal troubles, largely described as "pushing" forces in the theoretical paradigm of "push and pull" in scholarship on American immigration, prompted many Chinese to immigrate to America.[14]

The first imperialist war against China was the Opium War (1839–1842), referring to the Chinese government's prohibition of the British opium trade. When China, with its

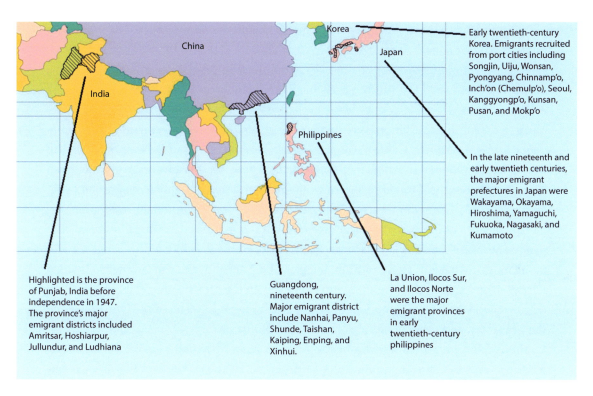

FIGURE 1.1 Map of sending places for emigration from five Asian countries during the late nineteenth and early twentieth centuries. Huping Ling Collection.

army largely equipped with bows and arrows and its navy nonexistent, was defeated by the British army, equipped with cannons and gunboats, it was forced to sign a series of unequal treaties with a number of Western powers, namely Britain, France, and America. The Treaty of Nanjing, signed in 1842 between China and Britain, demanded that the Chinese government pay a $21 million indemnity; abolish the government-chartered Gonghang monopolistic system of trade; open five ports (Canton, Xiamen, Fuzhou, Ningbo, and Shanghai) to foreign trade and for the residence of British consuls and merchants and their families; cede Hong Kong to Great Britain; and have a fixed tariff at a very moderate rate of 5 percent. China also signed treaties with France and the United States respectively regarding their rights to proselytize in China. These treaties were imposed by the victors upon the vanquished at gunpoint, without the careful deliberation normally practiced in international agreements in Europe and America. Ironically, though the war was triggered by the conflict over the opium trade in China, opium was not even mentioned in the treaties as its future status was cautiously avoided by both sides. As a result, opium traffic practically became unrestrained after the war, with devastating consequences for the Chinese for decades.

The importation of opium deepened the social and economic crisis. The volume of imports rose from 33,000 chests in 1842 to 46,000 in 1848 and to 52,929 in 1850, with each chest containing 140 pounds (64 kg) of opium. The year 1848 alone witnessed the outflow of more than ten million taels of silver, which exacerbated the already grave economic dislocation and copper-silver exchange rate.[15] The disruptive economic consequences of opium importation were further compounded by the general influx of foreign goods in the open ports. Canton was particularly hard hit, as it had the longest history of international trade and the most foreign contacts; it now lost this advantage to other open ports. Local household industries were swept away, and the self-sufficient agrarian economy collapsed. Those who were adversely affected thus became potential emigrants.

The decades of the 1840s and the 1850s were full of natural calamities in China. The major ones were the severe draught in Henan in 1847, the flooding of the Yangtze River in the four provinces of Hubei, Anhui, Jiangsu, and Zhejiang, and the famine in Guangxi in 1849. Flood and famine in Guangdong gave way to the catastrophic Taiping Rebellion (1850–1864), which almost toppled the Qing government, devastated the land, uprooted the peasantry, and dislocated the economy and polity.

The foreign invasions and domestic turmoil have provided general explanations for the causes of Chinese immigration to America. However, the fact that it was concentrated in a limited region surrounding Canton city—Sanyi and Siyi—has its special reasons. Canton and its three adjacent counties or Sanyi (Sam Yap in Cantonese) of Nanhai (Namhoi), Panyu (Panyi), and Shunde (Shuntak), together with four other counties or Siyi (Sze Yap) of Taishan (Toishan), Kaiping (Hoiping), Enping (Yanping), and Xinhui (Sunwei), are internationally known as hubs for overseas Chinese in North America, Australia, and Western Europe, while the neighboring province, Fujian, has been a sending place for Chinese emigrants to Southeast Asian countries. The Overseas Chinese Affairs Office of the Nationalist government published statistics in 1945, indicating that among the 8,546,374 overseas Chinese at the time, 5,992,066, or 70 percent, were from Guangdong, mainly from Canton and the Sanyi and Siyi districts.

The Chinese in Guangdong have a long tradition of migration. The first group of migrants was the more than one hundred thousand Han, or mainstream Chinese, dispatched by the authoritarian government of the Qin dynasty (221–206 BCE) to expand the influence of Han culture and to develop the region. In migrating, the Han Chinese moved from a temperate environment into a debilitatingly hot, humid subtropical climate and gradually became accustomed to that habitat in South China. As a coastal province, Guangdong provided easy access to Southeast and South Asia, where many Chinese merchants had opened commercial routes by the first century CE. As early as the third century CE, Canton had positioned itself as an excellent port, attracting Arab merchants from West and South Asia and becoming a great hub for international trade and overseas emigration. By the end of the Tang dynasty (618–906 CE), to escape the frequent social upheavals and civil wars, some Chinese emigrated to Southeast Asian countries, where they were called *Tangren* (people of the Tang dynasty) by the locals. This was the first large-scale Chinese emigration from Guangdong.

The Song dynasty (960–1279) saw the rapid development of Chinese maritime commerce. Residents from Fujian and Guangdong frequently traveled between the two provinces and trading ports in Southeast Asia. Merchants stranded by typhoons, illness, or debts became accidental settlers in those foreign lands. They were later joined by political refugees escaping persecutions by the Chinese authorities and others seeking their fortunes overseas. By the thirteenth and fourteenth centuries, Chinese emigration to Southeast Asia reached its peak, as a result of Mongol military expeditions and Ming government-sponsored maritime expeditions to the region, which left behind many Chinese soldiers and civilians in localities they came in contact with.

Quanzhou and Zhangzhou in Fujian together with Canton in Guangdong were well-developed Chinese ports for international trade as early as the Song dynasty. Canton, however, was selected as the only official port for international trade by the Qing government (1644–1911) in 1760. Writers have pointed out a number of reasons why the Qing court chose Canton as the only open port. First, the rampant piracy in the coastal provinces of Fujian and Guangdong forced the Qing government to close the coastal areas for self-defense. Second, the Manchu rulers were convinced that the "foreign devils" would corrupt the Chinese populace and therefore should be contained in the most distant port possible. Third, the Qing rulers believed it more practical to delegate international trade to the experienced merchants in Canton, who were called Gonghang (Cohong), or security merchants, than for it to be handled by the court.[16] The Canton monopoly in international trade allowed Western influence to penetrate the port city and nearby regions, making Canton and its adjacent counties premier locations for sending Chinese laborers overseas.

Guangdong was also the region where Hakka (or "guest people") lived in compact communities. The Hakka were originally residents of central China who migrated to Guangdong and Guangxi during the Southern Song (1127–1278 CE), when the dynasty moved south under the barbarian threat. They were the social "out-group," and their different dialects, habits, and lifestyles made it difficult for them to mix or assimilate with the locals. Collision between the two groups was bound to occur. As people without deep social roots, the Hakka were more independent, daring, and prone to action than were the natives. The Hakka provided a large proportion of Chinese immigrants in the nineteenth century, especially to Hawaii.

The Chinese emigrants, referred to by their compatriots as Gam San Haak ("travelers to Gold Mountain" or "Gold Mountain guests"), were mostly male, either single men or married men who left their wives behind. They largely could not afford their $50 passage from Hong Kong to San Francisco by steamboat and had to rely on the credit-ticket system. Under this system, they obtained passage from Chinese merchants who recruited them.

The Chinese merchants were then reimbursed by relatives of the travelers or by future employers. In return, the emigrants worked for whoever extended the credit until the debt was paid.

In January 1848, flakes of gold were discovered at Sutter's Mill, California. The news of the discovery spread like wildfire to every corner of the world, with thousands of gold seekers attracted to California. Of these gold seekers, 325 came from Tangshan, a term for China proper used by overseas Chinese. In the early 1850s, the number of Chinese in America increased dramatically—2,716 in 1851 and 20,026 in 1852.[17] By 1882, when the passage of the Chinese Exclusion Act ended large-scale Chinese immigration, there were about 300,000 Chinese living in the continental United States.[18]

The importation of Chinese laborers at this time was entangled with the slavery issue in antebellum America. Both slave owners and abolitionists passionately opposed the Chinese coolie trade. Humphrey Marshall, the U.S. commissioner to China and a Kentucky planter, argued that coolies "threatened both American imperial ambitions and American slavery." New England abolitionists also called for the prohibition of coolie laborers from abroad, as the coolie trade would taint the reputation of the country.[19] U.S. officials quickly moved to prevent American citizens from importing Chinese coolies.

Both contemporary observers (see sidebar) and present researchers (see note 19) have frequently compared the Chinese coolie trade and the African slave trade. Yet significant differences existed. First, while many Chinese coolies were kidnapped and forced into servitude, not all coolies were coerced; many were voluntary laborers driven from their native homes due to natural calamities, wars, social disturbances, or a lack of economic opportunities. Second, coolies received wages, though much lower than those paid to local laborers, and many survived their eight-year contracts to become free. And finally, both the Chinese central and local governments protested the mistreatment of Chinese coolies by middlemen and owners and punished the Chinese individuals involved in the "sale of pigs," as the trade was commonly known. But the most obvious and important fact is that the Chinese coolie trade was primarily prevalent in Cuba and that the Chinese laborers brought to the United States were mostly free agents. Nonetheless, interest groups conflated the Chinese coolie trade with the African slave trade and exploited the free labor issue to guide the formation of the nation's immigration policy, eventually leading to the complete exclusion of Chinese.

Japan

Japan in the mid-nineteenth century also faced threats from the vigorous and expansionistic Western powers backed by their gunboats and cannons, very similar to what happened to its neighbor China. However, unlike China, Japan had a different response to the Western threats and instead chose the path to modernization.

THE COOLIE AND SLAVE TRADE: HORRORS OF THE COOLIE-TRADE A LEGALIZED SYSTEM OF FREE CHINESE EMIGRATION IMPORTANT DISPATCH FROM LORD JOHN RUSSELL.

Some official "Correspondence respecting Emigration from Canton" has been laid before Parliament, which shows the abominable character of the coolie-trade, carried on at Canton and Whampoa. Foreign vessels arriving there to engage and embark emigrant laborers, have sought the assistance of native brokers, who, in their turn, have employed crimps (also Chinese) to collect coolies for them. Thirty dollars a-head or more were being paid last year for coolies delivered on board; arrived at Havana, the "contracts" could be sold at $400 a-head. An iniquitous system was thus created, which grew until not only men were inveigled on board receiving ships on false pretexts, such as promises of work, but force also was used, and no man could leave his house in open day without danger of being hustled, under false pretences of debt or delinquency, and carried off by the crimps to be put on board ship and taken to sea, never again to be heard of. Chinese women have been employed. For instance—a woman with a child on her back caused the child's bonnet to fall as she passed two men; on their picking it up she expressed her thanks and offered them some cakes for their civility; these were eaten, and, being drugged, the men sat down stupefied; the woman's confederates then came up, offered to carry the two men home, but lodged them in a receiving ship instead. A few months ago, in consequence of exposure, above 100 coolies were rescued from receiving-vessels, and described the way in which they were kidnapped, and got into boats, where they were intimidated or tortured, in order to wring from them, when taken on board the receiving-ship, a nominal consent to an eight years' engagement in Cuba, deception being also practiced to make them believe that their shipment had the sanction of the authorities. "I was very unwilling to go," said one, "but still more unwilling to be punished," and he added that a mandarin told him he had better say he was willing, or he would certainly be killed. The torture consists in tying a man up by the thumbs and toes, and in other painful positions, and beating him; applying a lighted stick to the feet, binding the hands together, and then driving a wedge in between them, ducking him in the water, and keeping him half drowned; and it is alleged that some who attempted to escape by swimming were harpooned by their countrymen like fish. If in the receiving ship they would not give their consent to go, they were taken back into the Chinese boat for a renewal of the torture. The system became so terrible last year that a popular rising was apprehended. Then the Governor of Canton tried severe measures. Convicted crimps were beheaded (eighteen on one day,) and one woman who had been the instrument of kidnappers was subjected by the authorities to mutilations which it would be shocking to describe. Several kidnappers, also, were killed by the mob, with a vindictive cruelty to which there was too much provocation. In these circumstances LAOU, acting Governor General of the Two Kwang, "decorated with a button of the first rank," consented, notwithstanding the old law forbidding Chinese to leave their country, to endeavor to put an end to this "sale of pigs," as it is called, by substituting for it a legalized system of free emigration.

Source: London Times, August 16, 1860, http://www.nytimes.com/1860/08/16/news/coolie-slave-trade-horrors-coolie-trade-legalized-system-free-chinese-emigration.html?pagewanted=all.

While the opening of China was a result of the Opium War and the subsequent unequal treaties imposed on China by the Western powers, the opening of Japan was spearheaded by the United States without warfare. In 1853, an armed mission led by U.S. Commodore Matthew C. Perry and the treaties that followed the mission ended the seclusion policy of the Tokugawa Shogunate (1600–1868), a military government that ruled feudal Japan, in which the emperor was revered but sidelined.

The Japanese military government opted to accept the almost identical unequal treaties forced upon it by the big powers as the Treaty of Nanjing upon China. There were at least two probable reasons for the Japanese reaction to the Western intrusions. First, as a small island nation neighboring the giant and continental China, Japan had become accustomed to accepting foreign elements for its own benefits in cultural, economic, and political developments throughout its history. Therefore, Japanese leaders were less resistant to the "barbarian" influences than their counterparts in China. Second, China being brutalized by the Western military invasions had served as an immediate and effective reminder that military resistance was not a viable or wise option.

A series of treaties, known as the Ansei Treaties, were signed in 1858 between Japan and the Americans, Dutch, Russians, British, and French. They permitted the residence of foreign diplomats in Edo (Tokyo); the opening of the ports of Shimoda and Hakodate on Hokkaido Island for ships seeking provisions; trade free from Japanese governmental intervention; fixed tariffs for foreign goods at a low rate of 5 percent; benefits of extraterritoriality for Western traders; and "most favored nation" treatment for all participating powers.

The Ansei Treaties exacerbated the internal instability that already appeared late in the Tokugawa era. The rebellious samurai from Satsuma on Kyūshū Island and Chōshū in Southwest Honshū Island, who had long been mistrusted by the *bakufu* ("tent government," referring to the Tokugawa government), challenged the latter in January 1868. This civil war overthrew the Tokugawa Shogun and restored the power of the Japanese emperor in the "Meiji Restoration," when the sixteen-year-old Meiji emperor (1852–1912) was moved to Tokyo, the new capital.

The Meiji Restoration dismantled the feudalism and ushered in a rapid Westernization of Japan. It is believed that among the renovations and reforms, two changes in particular contributed significantly to the Japanese emigration to Hawaii and the continental United States. One is the abolition, in 1871, of the samurai privileges as professional military men with annual stipends and the right to wear swords. A fundamental change that cut right to the heart of the feudal system, the subsequent establishment of a new army demanded all adult males to serve in the military. Since the 1870s, Japanese farmers had resisted conscription by mass protests or feigned illness. The second change was the new land tax. While the old tax was payable by the village to the *daimyo*, or local lord, based on the yields of the crops, the new tax was collected by the government in money according to the assessed land value. This change resulted in an increase of tenancy rate from about 25 percent before the Meiji Restoration to about 40 percent twenty years later.[20]

Japanese farmers who were hard hit by these changes found going overseas a viable alternative. Many Japanese emigrants saw themselves as only *dekasegi*, temporary workers away from home to earn money to pay off their debts. The monthly wage of ten to fifteen dollars in Hawaii was twice as much as the earnings of a skilled artisan in Japan and six times a Japanese farmer's income.[21] Thus going to Hawaii became somewhat of a craze among indebted farmers in the late nineteenth century.

As in the case of China, geographical clustering also became a prominent feature of Japanese emigration to Hawaii. Most Japanese emigrants originated from southwestern Japan, including Yamaguchi, Hiroshima, Okayama, and Wakayama prefectures on western Honshū Island, and Fukuoka, Nagasaki, and Kumamoto prefectures on Kyūshū Island. Scholars have attributed such geographical concentration to one American individual, Robert Walker Irwin, who had cultivated friendship with the Japanese foreign minister and businessmen.[22] Such a connection facilitated Japanese emigration.

Hawaii consul Robert Walker Irwin had served as an advisor to a prominent Japanese trading company, Mitsui Bussan. The company's president, Masuda Takashi, was from Yamaguchi prefecture. He was concerned about his fellow countrymen there and advised Irwin to recruit laborers from the southwestern prefectures; he even dispatched employees from his company to assist the recruiting efforts by Irwin's men from village to village. Under the agreement between Irwin and the Japanese government, from 1885 to 1894, about 29,000 Japanese went to Hawaii as contract laborers; fewer than a quarter of them were women. The contract term was usually three years; it stipulated that plantation owners would provide the Japanese emigrants' "passage to Hawaii, lodging, fuel, medical care, and interpreter service." The plantation owners, however, often passed these expenses onto the emigrants.[23]

After an almost decade-long operation, the Japanese government turned the emigration business over to private companies in 1894 because of its lack of interest in continuing the enterprise. These companies operated under more strict regulations and charged the prospective emigrants various fees for application process, passport, ticket booking, medical examinations, and temporary lodging before departure. Between 1895 and 1908, these companies sent more than 130,000 Japanese mostly from southwestern Japan to Hawaii and the continental United States, about 15 percent of whom were women.[24]

Korea

When China and Japan were pressured by the Western countries, the "hermit country" Korea also felt the outside threats from industrialized powers. The difference in the case of Korea is that Japan, the nearby and aggressive neighbor, became Korea's immediate threat.

After the Japanese expeditions in 1592 and 1597, led by Toyotomi Hideyoshi, the forerunner of Japanese expansionism, and the Qing invasions of the 1630s, Korea practiced seclusion for over two centuries. The opening of China and Japan also led outside powers to Korean waters. American minister Frederick Low led five ships and 1,200 men on a punitive expedition in May 1871 and attacked the city of Kanghwa and forts on the island. The Koreans fought to the death and defeated the American invasion. However, the post-Meiji Japanese military force posed more of a threat to Korea. In 1875, the Japanese warship *Unyō* invaded Pusan, and a second ship joined the operation two weeks later. The Korean shore batteries fired on the Japanese gunboats but were silenced by the superior Japanese firepower. In the following year, the Japanese government forced Korea to sign the Kanghwa Treaty, which was nearly identical to the Treaty of Nanjing and the Ansei Treaties; the only difference was that Japan was the victor, as the Western powers had been in the latter. The treaty requested Korea to recognize the authority of Meiji government, agree to open Pusan and two other ports to Japan, permit the Japanese to survey Korean waters, and allow Japanese to reside in treaty ports with the right of extraterritoriality.

In 1882, the United States also signed a treaty with Korea, soon followed by treaties with Great Britain, Germany, Russia, Italy, and France. Korea now entered a decisively different stage; it not only had to deal with its two traditional East Asian neighbors—China, which was determined to maintain control over its periphery, and Japan, a rapidly modernizing and expansionistic country—but also had to handle the Western "barbarian" nations of Britain, France, the United States, and Russia. The foreign intrusion intensified the internal factional conflicts within the Korean court and among the *yangban*, the civil servants and military officials. Attempting to manage the complex situation, the court initiated reforms. In 1881, King Kojong set up the Office for the Management of State Affairs, established a special Skills Force of eighty cadets under a Japanese army adviser to learn modern military science, and sent a Gentlemen's Observation Mission of twelve officials to Japan to study the modern institutions and technologies there.

Meanwhile, Korean peasants suffered the burden from the tax increase to support the reforms. A new religious movement known as Tonghak (East Learning), founded in 1860 and advocating Confucian learning, triggered the peasant uprising in 1892. Several thousand followers gathered and demanded tax cuts, the elimination of the *yangban* ruling class, the punishment of corrupt officials, and the end of grain exports to Japan. The situation turned violent in the country's southeast. The panicky Korean government requested assistance from China, and the Chinese government quickly dispatched naval and land forces to Korea. Reacting to China's action, Japan also sent troops to Korea, precipitating the First Sino-Japanese War in 1894. The war ended with China's defeat and the signing of the Treaty of Shimonoseki. In that treaty, China relinquished Korea as its tribute state, recognized Korea as an independent state, ceded Taiwan and the Liaodong Peninsula to Japan, and agreed to pay a war indemnity to Japan.[25]

As in the case of Japanese immigration, individual Americans more than any government policy played a significant role in bringing Koreans to Hawaii and America. In 1884, Horace N. Allen, a medical missionary, arrived in Korea and gained the trust of King Kojong by saving the life of a relative of the queen. His close connection with the royal family helped other American Protestant missionaries proselytize in Korea. In 1890 Allen was named secretary of the American legation in Seoul, and seven years later he was appointed as the American minister to Korea, remaining in that post until 1905. During his career in Korea, Allen had served as a liaison between the two governments and between American individuals and Korean authorities. In that capacity, he was instrumental in the immigration of Koreans to Hawaii and America.[26] In 1902, he convinced King Kojong to allow his subjects to immigrate to Hawaii, as the sugar planters there had trouble with the growing militancy of the Japanese plantation workers and wanted to replace them with Korean laborers. With the help of missionaries who persuaded members of their congregations to go to Hawaii, 7,000 Koreans, about 40 percent of whom were Christian converts, came between 1902 and 1905. Unlike Chinese and Japanese immigrants who originated from specific agricultural areas, Koreans came from various places and were more diverse, consisting of laborers, former soldiers, and artisans.[27]

The Philippines

Filipinos possess a unique position in American immigration history. At the conclusion of the Spanish-American War, the United States acquired the former Spanish colony and governed it as an American territory until its independence in 1946. The Filipinos were thus U.S. "nationals," not foreigners. This special legal status made Filipino workers ideal for Hawaiian sugar planters who desperately needed more stable supplies of laborers since the Gentlemen's Agreement of 1908 stopped Japanese immigration, Korean immigration ended in 1905, and other Asians were banned by other restrictive immigration laws in place at the time.

The coastal provinces of Ilocos Norte, Ilocos Sur, La Union, Abra, and Pangasinan on Luzon Island were specially targeted by the recruiters of the Hawaiian sugar planters. These areas were the country's most densely populated but also had limited economic opportunities, as the narrow coastal lands were not suitable for large-scale cultivation of profitable crops. Migrating out for better opportunities had become a means of survival for the locals. By the end of 1910, more than 4,000 Filipinos had arrived in Hawaii. The number reached 28,500 between 1907 and 1919, 29,200 between 1920 and 1924, 44,400 between 1925 and 1929, and nearly 20,000 between 1930 and 1935. In addition to

> ### SIKHS ALLOWED TO LAND
>
> The four Sikhs who arrived on the Nippon Maru the other day were permitted yesterday to land by the immigration officials. The quartet formed the most picturesque group that has been seen on the Pacific Mail dock for many a day. One of them, Bakkshlied Singh, speaks English with fluency, the other just a little. They are all fine-looking men, Bakkshlied Singh in particular being a marvel of physical beauty. He stands 6 feet and 2 inches and is built in proportion. His companies—Bood Singh, Variam Singh, and Sehava Singh—are not quite so big. All of them have been soldiers and policemen in China. They were in the Royal Artillery, and the tall one with the unpronounceable name was a police sergeant in Hong Kong prior to coming to this country. They hope to make their fortunes here and return to their home in the Lahore District, which they left some twenty years ago.
>
> Source: *San Francisco Chronicle*, April 6, 1899.

Hawaii, Filipinos also came to the U.S. mainland. More than 50,000 landed at ports of entry on the West Coast in the 1920s and 1930s.[28]

It is worth noting that although the majority of Filipino workers came to Hawaii and America in the early twentieth century, a small Filipino community was established in Louisiana as early as the 1760s when a group of Filipino sailors jumped ship to build a settlement in St. Bernard Parish within the Spanish colony.[29] This was one of the oldest Asian American communities in North America.

South Asia

Although the present South Asian or Indian American population consists of diverse groups from all geographical areas, the bulk of Indian immigrants to North America came from the Punjab region of northwestern India (presently in Pakistan), an area known as India's breadbasket. Despite the region's rich agricultural resources, the 1849 annexation of Punjab by the British colonial government produced circumstances conducive to emigration. The colonial administration decided to collect land taxes in cash instead of in kind, the system previously practiced. This new policy wounded farmers, and many had to mortgage their lots to ensure cash for tax payments. Many eventually lost their land and became migrant workers or joined the British colonial army or police force, thus becoming world travelers when dispatched to various parts of the vast British Empire. The overseas experiences made Punjabi Sikhs daring fortune seekers.[30]

Generally, the passage from Punjab to North America was much longer and more difficult and expensive than the passages from ports in China, Japan, and Korea to San Francisco for immigrants from East Asia. The Punjabi emigrants had to board a train first to New Delhi, then to Calcutta, where they could board steamers to Hong Kong and then to many major ports of the world, including San Francisco. The early Sikh migrants to California numbered around 5,000, mostly employed by lumber and railroad companies. However, the Sikh migrants later turned to agriculture, mainly concentrating in two areas: the Imperial Valley in the south and the Sacramento Valley in the north. In agriculture, Sikhs were initially laborers, but many later became proprietors and tenants. They suffered legal and extralegal discrimination similar to that other Asians faced, including the alien land laws.

A small number of women came with their husbands. According to immigration records, from 1871 through 1899, 491 Indians entered the United States with no females recorded, and among the 5,800 East Indian immigrants entering between 1901 and 1911, there were only 109 women.[31] The shortage of Asian Indian women and the prevalence of anti-miscegenation laws in all thirty-eight U.S. states of the time, which outlawed interracial marriage between a white and a colored person, resulted in many interracial marriages between Sikhs and Mexican women.[32] Imperial Valley Sikhs established a family life by marrying Mexican women, and the Sikh husband and Mexican wife was a persistent marital pattern for at least a generation.[33]

Smaller Asian Indian communities were also developed in New York and other eastern and midwestern cities. Most members of these communities were merchants and middle-class professionals from Hindu backgrounds.

ROOTS OF ASIAN MIGRATION TO AMERICA IN HISTORICAL PERSPECTIVE

The millennia of civilizations in Asia had produced rich and diverse thoughts and values. Among the myriad philosophies and religions in Asia, Confucianism had secured its dominance in China and its neighbors Korea, Japan, and Vietnam since the first century. While the hierarchical system helped the governments of these countries manage their land and large populations, conservative and male-centered Confucianism also restricted the minds, actions, and behaviors of East Asian peoples. In other parts of Asia, Hinduism, Buddhism, Sikhism, and Islam have played significant roles in shaping the culture and society. Shintoism has been influential in Japan, and Christianity has also impacted the histories of Asian countries in the age of imperialism.

The Industrial Revolution in England and on the European continent and the consequential capitalistic overproduction prompted the European powers to search for markets abroad and to exploit the natural and human resources of the unindustrialized countries in other parts of the world, especially the populous countries of Asia. In their quest for empires, Great Britain, the United States, and Japan actively persuaded, pressured, intervened in, and invaded Asian countries and forced their threatened or defeated governments to accept unequal treaties and provisions. The influx of foreign manufactured goods disrupted the domestic economy and intensified already tense social confrontations. The presence of foreign diplomats, merchants, and missionaries and Christian proselytizing further divided the elite and masses of the Asian countries. When compounded by natural calamities and disasters, the socioeconomic disturbances drove the most desperate population from the economically depressed regions out of their homelands in search of a better life overseas.

The penetration of imperialist powers in Asia also propelled and facilitated the Asian emigration to America and other parts of the world. In addition to the large forces of imperialist expansions and exploitations, individual efforts from American diplomats, businessmen, and missionaries were responsible for the Asian exodus. At the same time the local geographical conditions and historical traditions of the Asian countries also played parts in the Asian emigration. All of these factors contributed to the different migration patterns. While many Chinese laborers sailed to America under the credit-ticket system, Japanese, Koreans, and Filipinos came as contract laborers through the recruitment efforts of Hawaiian sugar plantation owners, and Punjabi Indians traveled to America as free agents. The regional concentration of the emigration origins, in the cases of Chinese, Japanese, Filipinos, and Asian Indians, manifests the theory of "chain migration." Despite these variations in emigration patterns, Asian emigration was overall a product of global imperialistic expansion and the subsequent worldwide movement of labor, capital, and modern technologies since the seventeenth century.

KEY TERMS

Confucianism
Daoism
Buddhism
Shintoism
Hinduism
Islam
Sikhism
Opium Wars in China
Treaty of Nanjing
Taiping Rebellion
Ansei Treaties

Kanghwa Treaty
Meiji Restoration
Spanish-American War
American annexation of Hawaii
"open-door" policy to China
credit-ticket system
Filipino-American War
Robert Walker Irwin
Horace N. Allen
Punjab

REVIEW QUESTIONS

1. How can learning of the diverse Asian heritage help you understand Asian Americans better?
2. How did global imperialistic expansions in the past few centuries impact Asian countries and the Pacific region? How did the changes in Asian countries resulting from imperialism influence Asian emigration to Hawaii and the American mainland?
3. Compare and contrast the similarities and differences of the socioeconomic conditions of the Asian countries discussed in this chapter.
4. Compare and contrast the various means and patterns of emigration among the five groups of Asians in this chapter.

FILMS

Ding, Loni. *Ancestors in the Americas*, pts. 1 and 2. Documentary (60 minutes each). Pt. 1 tells the story of how Filipinos, Chinese, Asian Indians first arrived in the Americas. Pt. 2 relates the history of Chinese immigrants in California, ca. 1997–1998.

Tajima-Peña, Renee (producer/writer/director). *My America; or, Honk if You Love Buddha*. 87-minute documentary. A humorous and good introduction to Asian American studies. 1996.

FURTHER READING

Chan, Sucheng. *Asian Americans: An Interpretive History*. Boston: Twayne, 1991.

Daniels, Roger. *Asian America: Chinese and Japanese in the United States since 1850*. Seattle: University of Washington, 1988.

Ling, Huping. *Voices of the Heart: Asian American Women on Immigration, Work, and Family*. Kirksville, MO: Truman State University Press, 2007.

Low, Lisa. *Immigrant Acts*. Durham, NC: Duke University Press, 1996.

Okihiro, Gary Y. *Island World: A History of Hawaii and the United States*. Berkeley: University of California Press, 2008.

Takaki, Ronald. *Strangers from a Different Shore: A History of Asian Americans*. Boston: Little, Brown, 1989.

RESTRICTIONS AND RESISTANCES

CHAPTER OUTLINE

Racial Prejudice
Economic Sanctions
Physical Violence
Exclusion Laws and Policies
The Enforcement of Exclusion Laws
Protests against Exclusion and Discrimination
Asian Immigration Restrictions and Resistance in Historical Perspective

SIGNIFICANT EVENTS

1852	The Foreign Miners' License Tax is passed; capitation tax in California requires the masters of vessels to pay between five and ten dollars per alien passenger, which is increased to fifty dollars in 1855; white miners hold the second Columbia Miners Convention and declare that "no Asiatic or South Sea Islander shall be permitted to mine in this district"
1855	Chinese miners in Tuolumne and Mariposa counties attack the tax collectors and are killed
1857	Chinese residents in Columbia are blamed for a fire that destroys many buildings and are forced to move outside of the town limits
1858	Mayor of Mariposa orders that no one may rent to the Chinese
1860	Fishing license law is passed
1870	San Francisco legislature demands that laundries without a wagon for delivery pay fifteen dollars every three months
1871	Brutal violence erupts in Los Angeles on the night of October 24; seventeen Chinese are lynched and two are knifed to death

1875	Page Law forbids the entry of Chinese, Japanese, and "Mongolian" contract laborers, and women for the purpose of prostitution
1877	In Chico, California, arsons and violence consume the lives of four Chinese and wound two
1880	Riots against Chinese in Denver cause the death of one Chinese, injuries to many, and the destruction of more than $20,000 worth of property
1882	The Chinese Exclusion Act bars the entry of Chinese laborers for ten years
1883	In St. Louis, police officers arrest six Chinese men from Hop Alley as suspects in a murder
1885	Violence against Chinese in Rock Springs, Wyoming, leaves twenty-eight Chinese dead and fifteen wounded and $147,000 worth of property damaged; anti-Chinese movements in Tacoma and Seattle, Washington, drive many Chinese out of town; Chinese stores and homes are burned, their shops are looted, and 350 federal troops are sent to Seattle to patrol for weeks
1887	The Snake River Massacre leads to thirty-one Chinese miners being robbed, murdered, and mutilated by a group of white miners in Hells Canyon in Oregon
1888	Congress passes the Scott Act, which declares all return certificates "void and of no effect," preventing the reentry of some 20,000 Chinese with return certificates
1892	The renewal of the Chinese Exclusion Act, known as the Geary Act, propels a new round of anti-Chinese persecution and sentiment in the United States; Chinese in Chicago are forced by immigration officers to take photographs
1893	Chinese journalist Wong Chin Foo criticizes the Geary Act
1903	Police and the Immigration Bureau jointly search Boston Chinatown for the tong murderers
1905–1906	Anti-American Boycott Movement in China
1906	A group of Japanese scientists in San Francisco are stoned by white boys; nineteen Japanese immigrants are physically attacked; white mobs smash the windows of several Japanese restaurants in San Francisco
1907	Under the Gentlemen's Agreement, the Japanese government agrees not to issue passports valid for the continental United States to laborers; a series of "anti-Hindu" riots break out in Bellingham, Washington
1908	A mob drives about one hundred Asian Indian farm workers out of their camp in Live Oak, California, then burns down the camp
1910–1940	Immigration station on Angel Island in operation to process Asian immigrants

1913	California alien land law prohibits "aliens ineligible to citizenship" from owning land; in Hemet, Riverside County, California, fifteen Korean laborers are surrounded and asked under threat to leave by several hundred unemployed Euro-Americans
1914	Chinese minister Wu Ting Fang publishes book to criticize the Chinese Exclusion Acts
1917	The Immigration Act of 1917 (also known as the Asiatic Barred Zone Act) bars most immigrants of East Asia and the Pacific Islands from entering the United States
1921	The Alien Land Law is passed in Washington; fifty-eight Japanese farm workers in Turlock are awoken from sleep by mobs and driven out of town
1922	*Takao Ozawa v. U.S.* denies Japanese immigrant Ozawa naturalized citizenship
1923	*U.S. v. Bhagat Singh Thind* denies Asian Indians naturalized citizenship
1930	A mob of four hundred raids the Northern Monterey Filipino Club, beating up scores of Filipino farm workers and killing one
1934	The Tydings-McDuffie Act reclassifies all Filipinos in the United States as aliens and sets a quota of fifty Filipino immigrants per year

IN THIS CHAPTER, we will examine the multifaceted forces that have contributed to the hostility toward, discrimination against, and exclusion of Asian immigrants. Racial prejudice and misconceptions of Asians and their cultures have been blamed as causes of the early hostility and conflicts between the natives and the aliens. However, the flare-ups and outbreaks of violence against Asian immigrants often coincided with economic recessions. Under depressed economic conditions, white laborers, farmers, and nativists found the Asian immigrants easy targets to blame for the problems they were facing at the time. Pressured by these forces, the U.S. Congress passed a series of discriminatory exclusion laws to drive the Asian immigrants out. The enforcement and administration of these exclusion laws caused injustice toward and mistreatment of many Asian immigrants, who were unwelcome and were considered inassimilable to American culture.

We will also look at the responses of Asian immigrants to the exclusion laws and their enforcement. Asian immigrants were not always passive victims. They protested the unfair treatment and discrimination. Protests from the governments of the Asian countries often fell on deaf ears and yielded limited results. White American lawyers hired by Asian immigrant community organizations succeeded in some cases. A few pioneer Asian civil rights activists defended their rights and openly debated politicians and white union leaders. Courageous individual immigrants also protested their mistreatment through legal battles, through boycotts, and in the extreme but not uncommon act of suicide. The poignant story of Angel Island best illustrates the biases, defects, and problems of the enforcement and administration of the exclusion laws.

RACIAL PREJUDICE

As the first group of large-scale Asian immigrants, Chinese immigrants endured the first and most hostility and prejudice. What led to these racial prejudices? There are two primary ways to understand the genesis of racial prejudice against Asian immigrants: one is based from white Americans coming in contact with Asian people, and the other is through the racial problem in America.

Prejudice from Contact with Asia

It has been believed that three groups of Americans who had close contact with China were responsible for spreading the negative image of China and the Chinese among the American public: American merchants, American diplomats, and Protestant missionaries. The first group consisted of American merchants who were involved in the early American China trade from 1785 to 1840. These Yankee traders, frustrated with the Qing government's restrictive practice over international trade (or Canton trade, discussed in the previous chapter), had developed a dominant perception that the Chinese were a very "peculiar" people. The Chinese peculiarity included bizarre habits and tastes ranging from making medicines from the horn of a rhinoceros or soup from a bird's nest to their fondness for eating dogs, cats, and rats.

The second group consisted of American diplomats, who had seen substantial parts of the interior of China from 1785 to 1840, an experience not available to traders and missionaries prior to the Opium War. They claimed their views of China were more authoritative. In their publications, they complained about the Chinese scientific and technological crudity, the lack of cleanliness, the practice of infanticide, and the official arrogance.

The third group consisted of the Protestant missionaries who had preached in China since 1870 and enjoyed the widest audience in America through their missionary publications such as the *Missionary Herald* and the *Chinese Repository*. The Protestant pioneers described China as a "Satan's empire" where the government deployed action against Christian missionaries and their converts.[1]

The unflattering accounts of China from these three groups contributed to the public prejudice against Chinese in the late nineteenth and early twentieth centuries. As early as 1840, American children's textbooks had associated Chinese with rats and other

> Chinkie, Chinkie, Chinaman,
> Sitting on the fence;
> Trying to make a dollar
> Out of fifteen cents
> Chinkie, Chinkie, Chinaman,
> Eats dead rats;
> Eats them up
> Like fingersnaps.
>
> Source: Arthur Bonner, *Alas! What Brought Thee Hither? The Chinese in New York, 1800–1950* (Madison, NJ: Farleigh Dickinson University Press, 1997), 16.

animals. By the 1870s and 1880s, the association of Chinese and rats had become a dominant popular image across the country, as illustrated in the sidebar, and cartoons portraying Chinese as rat eaters were ubiquitous.

Prejudice in the Context of Existing Racial Problems

In the wake of the abolition of the slave trade and slavery, the importation of Asian laborers was important to the plantations in the American South and the Caribbean. The opening of China following the Opium Wars promised not only Chinese goods but also cheap Chinese laborers. To proslavery Americans, the Chinese laborers were a needed replacement for the African slaves; and to abolitionists, they were an improvement over the enslaved labor.[2] Meanwhile, as the older and earlier European immigrant groups from Northern and Western Europe were gradually assimilated into the white Anglo-Saxon Protestant culture, the rapid economic expansion in antebellum America demanded new immigrants to maintain the pool of cheap and unskilled labor. These demands were satisfied by those from Asia and Southern and Eastern Europe.

Similarly, the coming of Japanese, Korean, and Filipino laborers was also perceived as a response to the emancipation of African slaves and the ascendance of other European immigrants into American notions of whiteness. These Asian immigrants were viewed by the American public as a "yellow peril" threatening to displace white or European American laborers.

The racialization of Asians as physically and culturally different from or "inferior" to "whites" at the time of domestic economic crisis propelled the immigration exclusion acts and laws against the naturalization of Asians in 1882 (Chinese), 1917 (Asian Indian), 1924 (Japanese and Korean), and 1934 (Filipino) (see discussion in the "Exclusion Laws and Policies" section).[3]

ECONOMIC SANCTIONS

Parallel with the anti-Chinese prejudice, a series of legislation was passed to curb the earnings of Asian immigrants. In the mining industry, as more Chinese poured into mines in the 1850s, the California legislature passed laws to tax them. The Foreign Miners' License Tax, passed in 1850 and renewed in 1852, demanded $2.50 per month. Orig-

WONG CHI FOO FIGHTS THE ANTI-CHINESE PREJUDICE

Some Chinese stood out to fight the public prejudice against Chinese. Wong Chi Foo was one of the earliest Chinese civil rights activists and one of the most colorful Chinese intellectuals in America during the late-nineteenth-century. He was born in China in 1851, and came to the United States in 1864 at the age of fourteen, landing in New York. Utterly different from his counterparts in America, he removed his queue as soon as he arrived in America, wore western suits, and cultivated a cosmopolitan demeanor. He was educated at Yale in journalism, but returned to China after his graduation in the early 1870s. Scion of a Chinese "aristocratic" family, Wong inherited a strong sense of duty for the fate of his homeland and openly expressed his intense anti-Manchu sentiments, a hallmark characteristic among Chinese intellectuals during the Qing dynasty. He called for the overthrow of the Manchu dynasty and the establishment of a Republic. His anti-Qing speeches and activities agitated the Qing court, which put him on the most-wanted list with a $1,500 award for his head, and consequently he had to flee China in 1872. He first went to Japan, where he was continuously pursued by the Qing government. He barely escaped the pursuit and sailed back to America with the help of Charles O. Shephard, the U.S. Consul in Tokyo, to whom Wong was forever grateful and eventually presented him a rare chair shipped from China, supposedly used by Confucius, as a gift.[1] Wong soon realized that he had to become an American citizen to exercise his civil rights and to continue his cause. On April 3, 1874, he applied for naturalization to the court in Grand Rapids, Michigan, one of the stops of his lecture tour across the country, and was granted citizenship immediately.

He was known as "one of the best educated Chinese," and "famed" as a writer and journalist contributing frequently to several leading journals in English, and an itinerant lecturer traveling around the country to deliver speeches. In his writings and lectures he was vehement in promoting Chinese civilization, advocating for his compatriots to assimilate, and defending the Chinese as valuable immigrants and potential American citizens. He engaged in debates with American politicians and commentators on issues pertinent to China and the Chinese. On the negative portrayal of the Chinese as rat-eaters, he declared, "Chinese don't eat rats. I would pay someone $500 if they can prove that the Chinese eat rats." He rebutted the notion of Chinese being inassimilatable, as he told his audience once, "Assimilation? You try it. Anyone here wants to become a Chinese?" He publicly and repeatedly challenged the most prominent anti-Chinese political leader of the era—Irish working-class demagogue Dennis Kearney—to a duel in an open debate when the latter was touring the East Coast in 1883. His unconventional attitude and his sharp tongue earned him fame as a popular speaker, and the places of his lectures were often packed with large audiences.

Source: Huping Ling, *Chinese Chicago: Race, Transnational Migration, and Community since 1870* (Stanford, CA: Stanford University Press, 2012), 38–39.

inally, the law was intended to exclude Spanish Americans, French, and other foreigners from mining. However, in practice, it became directed specifically against Chinese and the levies became economically beneficial to the state and local governments; state officials found that the taxation brought significant income and many counties could not exist without it. Between 1850 and 1870, the state collected five billion dollars, with nearly 95 percent paid by the Chinese. In the same time period, Nevada County collected $103,250 in Foreign Miners' License Tax, almost exclusively from the 3,396 Chinese miners in the county.[4] It was believed that at some points as much as 96 percent of the Chinese miners' income went to tax.

The success of the Foreign Miners' License Tax encouraged legislators to tax other occupations primarily undertaken by the Chinese. In 1853, an attempt was made to tax the Chinese in certain kinds of fishing, particularly the catching of abalone, a shellfish highly prized by the Chinese for consumption and for export to China. In 1860 a fishing license law was passed. It required all Chinese engaged in fishing to pay four dollars per month or face the seizure of fish, boats, and other property. Under the pressure of Italians, Greeks, and Dalmatians, who composed the majority of fishermen in San Francisco, another law was passed in 1876 targeting the small-mesh shrimp nets, which were mainly used by the Chinese.[5]

As laundry had become a major occupation of the Chinese in San Francisco since the 1860s, laws restricting the Chinese laundry industry were also passed. The legislature in San Francisco in 1870 demanded that laundries without a wagon for delivery pay fifteen dollars for every three months. Since most Chinese did not use horses, the law was in fact directed against the Chinese.

In addition to taxation against the Chinese in certain occupations, governments also passed capitation (head) taxes on the Chinese. In 1852 California legislature passed a bill requiring the masters of vessels to pay between five and ten dollars per alien passenger. In 1855, the capitation tax levied on foreign passenger was increased to fifty dollars.

In the rural areas, Asian immigrants were subjected to the alien land laws. During the last two decades of the nineteenth century, American farmers organized to protect their interests. Frustrated midwestern and western farmers found the prohibition on landownership by aliens to be an easy solution to their economic difficulties and consequently launched an alien land law movement. Between 1885 and 1895, twelve states in the Midwest and West passed alien land laws. Indiana first instituted a comprehensive alien land law in 1885. Illinois, Colorado, Wisconsin, Nebraska, and Minnesota followed Indiana's example in 1887. The Iowa legislature passed a similar law in 1888. Two years later, Washington joined the movement. In 1891, Kansas, Texas, and Idaho also adopted alien land laws. In 1895, Missouri became the last state to participate in the alien land movement of the nineteenth century.[6] Although this nineteenth-century movement was aimed primarily at large absentee land owners from Europe and most of the related laws were repealed by the legislatures of these states by the end of the century, it set an example for the later alien land laws in California and Washington that primarily targeted Asian laborers and especially Japanese farmers who were the major competitors to white farmers in these states.

Beginning in 1913, the California alien land law forbade "aliens ineligible to citizenship," namely Chinese, Japanese, Koreans, and Asian Indians, from owning land. The law barred aliens from owning or leasing land for more than three years. In Washington, a similar law was enacted in 1921. Scholars have pointed out a number of impacts of these alien land laws on Asian farmers. First and most significant, to circumvent the law, Asian farmers had to till land by vesting the title in the names of their American-born children. Those who did not have citizen children had to form a corporation under the trusteeship of white attorneys. The corporation bought land and then redistributed it to farmers. Despite such practice, the alien land law is believed to have contributed to the population shift of Japanese to urban areas by 1920. However, one should note that compared to the Chinese, 90 percent of whom were city dwellers in 1940, the Japanese urban population increased much less, to only a little more than half during the same period. In addition to banning Asian farmers from owning land, the laws produced a psychological effect that was more disturbing to Asian farmers; it reinforced the notion that Asians were aliens and encouraged other unpleasant and discriminatory laws and actions in the future.[7]

PHYSICAL VIOLENCE

The taxation and other economic sanctions were tickets to violent expulsion by whites. Some cruelty toward Asian immigrants was spontaneous, but much of it represented an organized effort to drive Asians out of certain areas and cities.

Anti-Chinese Violence

Anti-Asian violence from white mobs first emerged in mining towns. The motivations behind the violence resulted mainly from the economic difficulties of white miners, as gold mining was becoming less profitable after the 1850s, when large number of Chinese laborers arrived in the mining areas and were perceived as cheap "coolies," or indentured laborers, at a time when the abolitionist calls for "free labor" were embraced by white laborers. Economically frustrated white miners blamed Chinese for their unemployment and other problems. They vented their anger at the Chinese, who had little protection from the Chinese or the U.S. government, as illustrated in *People v. Hall* (1854; although the Chinese government protested the mistreatment of the Chinese laborer in the United States, their protests were ignored, as discussed in a later section). On

August 9, 1853, a white miner named George Hall shot and killed Chinese miner Ling Sing. The California Supreme Court ruled that "Asiatics" could not testify against a "white man."[8] *People v. Hall* thus incentivized a rush of roundups of Chinese by tax collectors as well as white miners.

One common sport of the attacks was to tie the queues of the Chinese miners together or tie their long braids to trees, while the tax collectors looted their tools, boots, and other belongings. The Chinese miners tried all they could to protect themselves. Some bribed the collectors or paid the tax, others hid in the forest, refused to pay, or fought back. In 1855, a group of Chinese miners in Tuolumne and Mariposa counties attacked the tax collectors and were later killed by a white mob. In the first five years of the gold rush, there were reportedly 4,200 murders in California, including hundreds of Chinese victims. On May 8, 1852, white miners held the second Columbia Miners Convention, which declared that "no Asiatic or South Sea Islander shall be permitted to mine in this district."

The anti-Asian expulsion then spread to cities. In 1857, Chinese residents in Columbia were blamed for a fire that destroyed many buildings and were subsequently forced to move outside of the town limits. In 1858, the mayor of Mariposa ordered no one to rent to the Chinese, as they cooked over open fires, lit firecrackers on holidays, and burned joss sticks before their gods. He declared Chinatown a fire hazard and that it should be demolished.[9]

Brutal violence erupted in Los Angeles on the night of October 24, 1871. The conflict started two days earlier when the leaders of two rival Chinese factions clashed over a runaway prostitute, Ya Hit. Earlier that evening, the leaders of the two groups fired upon each other. The police chief arrived and ordered a large group of white men to shoot any Chinese on sight. Rumors spread throughout Los Angeles that the Chinese had stores of hidden gold and were "killing the white man by wholesale." An angry mob soon gathered, and the lynching, looting, and killing spree began. The mob beat and kicked the Chinese victims before hanging them and ransacking Chinese houses for gold and valuables. A Chinese man's finger was severed from his left hand as the impatient mobsters tried to take the rings he wore. By the time the massacre was over, seventeen Chinese had been lynched and two knifed to death.[10]

Another outbreak of anti-Chinese violence occurred in Chico, a small town in Butte County located in the Sacramento River Valley. In 1876 when the anti-Chinese zealots unsuccessfully demanded that farmers and ranchers of Butte County dismiss their Chinese employees, they decided to resort to violence, arson, and murder. Early the next year they torched the soap factory owned by John Bidwell, a land baron in Butte County who was the largest employer of Chinese in the state, and then burned the barn of a widow who hired the Chinese. In the following weeks, they set fire to a building in Chinatown and a Chinese camp near the railroad tracks, and then burned a Chinese laundry at Chico Creek. This series of arsons and violence consumed the lives of four Chinese and wounded two. The Chinese responded by purchasing shotguns and pistols. They also marched through Chico in protest, banging cymbals and playing music.[11]

The decade of 1880s was also marked by violent outbreaks against the Chinese. Two major shifts occurred in the violence in this decade. While the earlier violence broke out mostly in California, the violence in the 1880s spread to the Pacific Northwest. In addition, this unrest was often organized by labor unions, such as the Knights of Labors, the largest and one of the most important labor organizations in the 1880s that strongly supported the Chinese Exclusion Act of 1882. Although the ultimate cause of this discord was the depressed economic conditions in the region, the passage of the Chinese Exclusion Law in 1882 was believed to be chiefly responsible for these changing patterns of violence against the Chinese in the 1880s, as the legislation encouraged and virtually legitimized such violence.

The 1880 riots against Chinese in Denver occurred without any provocation and caused the death of one Chinese, the injuries of many, and the destruction of property worth more than $20,000. In 1885 violence against Chinese erupted in Rock Springs, Wyoming, a mining town where the Union Pacific Railroad had hired 331 Chinese and 150 white workers. On September 2, 1885, a dispute over assignment to a more desirable area of the mine led to exchanges between the Chinese and white miners. Two Chinese were beaten by white miners who were mostly members of the Knights of Labor. That evening, the armed white miners attacked the Chinese quarters. The mob shot fleeing Chinese and torched their shelters. The official tally counted twenty-eight Chinese dead, fifteen wounded, and $147,000 worth of property damaged. The Incident drove out the entire Chinese population of Rock Springs, about six to seven hundred.

The Rock Springs massacre led to more persistent anti-Chinese movements in Tacoma and Seattle, in the Territory of Washington. The Knights of Labor was again the major driving force. On September 21, 1885, a representative of the Knights ordered the Chinese to move from Tacoma and Seattle and warned they would face "riot and bloodshed [and a] proceeding similar to that which lately happened in Wyoming territory." Consequently, many Chinese were driven out of the towns, Chinese stores and homes were burned, and shops were looted. To control the disorder, 350 federal troops were dispatched to Seattle to patrol for weeks.

The Snake River Massacre of 1887 was the last major bloody incident of the decade in the Pacific Northwest region. Thirty-four Chinese miners were robbed, murdered, and mutilated by a group of white miners in Hells Canyon Oregon.[12]

In California, violence against Chinese continued in the 1880s. New developments ranged from new ordinances and regulations to the burning of Chinese quarters and the expulsion of Chinese. According to Elmer Clarence Sandmeyer, disturbances occurred in Pasadena, Santa Barbara, Santa Cruz, San Jose, Oakland, Cloverdale, Healdsburg, Red Bluff, Hollister, Merced, Yuba City, Petaluma, Redding, Anderson, Truckee, Lincoln, Sacramento,

San Buenaventura, Napa, Gold Run, Sonoma, Vallejo, Placerville, Santa Rosa, Chico, Wheatland, Carson, Auburn, Nevada City, Dixon, and Los Angeles. In San Francisco the Knights of Labor and the Cigar-makers Union held public meetings and processions and boycotted Chinese-made products.[13]

Violence against Other Asians

Other Asian immigrants also suffered from violence, although not with the same magnitude that the Chinese endured. An anti-Japanese movement developed on the West Coast, born of similar characteristics as those in anti-Chinese movement. It started with negative and racist portrayals of the Japanese as another group of "Mongoloids" who would corrupt white civilization and evolved into campaigns supported by labor organizations to restrict Japanese immigration.

Most anti-Japanese incidents took place in San Francisco, where the most important Nihonmachi, or Japantown, developed and the Japanese consul general was located. While derogatory and racist comments about Japanese occurred from the 1860s onward, the overt anti-Japanese movement did not appear until the 1890s. In 1890, the first recorded anti-Japanese violence was directed at Japanese shoemakers in the city. Between 1891 and 1893, a significant anti-Japanese flurry was triggered by deteriorating economic conditions compounded by the arrival of several hundred poor and illiterate Japanese immigrants from southwestern Japan. In 1891, a San Francisco newspaper commented on the "filthy state" of the Japanese immigrants and mocked the imitative Japanese who dressed "in an American necktie tied around a Japanese skin free of any shirt" and "an old vest several sizes too large for him."[14] The *Bulletin*, a pro-labor newspaper in San Francisco, warned the city's residents that the Japanese were as "undesirable" as the Chinese, with headlines such as "Undesirables," "Another Phase in the Immigration from Asia," "Japanese Taking the Place of the Chinese," and "Importation of Contract Laborers and Women" in its May 4, 1891, issue.[15] The old anti-Chinese politician Dennis Kearney modified his slogan of "The Chinese Must Go" to "The Japs Must Go."[16]

However, anti-Japanese agitation did not evolve into a violent movement like that which affected the Chinese, likely due to a number of factors. The first and probably decisive reason was that the number of Japanese was very small. The 1890 census counted only 1,147 Japanese in California and fewer than 1,000 in the rest of the country, compared to 107,488 Chinese across the country. Second, Japanese government officials were more conscious about the appearances of their country fellows. Sutemi Chinda, the Japanese consul general in the early 1890s, suggested that Japanese government demand Japanese migrants carry at least fifteen dollars with them or they would be rejected.[17]

Physical violence against the Japanese occurred a decade later. In 1906 four Japanese scientists, including Dr. F. Omori, a prominent Japanese seismologist of the Imperial University in Tokyo, arrived in San Francisco to inspect the ruins of the devastating San Francisco earthquake and subsequent fire. There they were stoned and molested by groups of white boys. When Dr. Omori continued his investigation in Eureka, California, he was again assaulted. The mayor of the city blamed "labor troubles," not racial prejudice, as the cause of the assault.[18]

In summer of the same year, nineteen Japanese immigrants filed complaints with a federal investigator stating that they had been physically attacked. In October white nativists in San Francisco boycotted Japanese restaurants, demanding prospective white customers to "patronize your own race." They smashed the windows of several Japanese restaurants and beat their owners. The local police ignored the incidents until the Japanese consul protested. The boycott lasted about three weeks and finally ended when Japanese restaurant owners agreed to pay $350 for their "protection."[19]

Japanese agricultural workers seemed to have borne more physical assaults than their urban counterparts. On a summer night in 1921, eighteen Japanese farm laborers in Turlock, a small town in the San Joaquin Valley, were awoken by an armed mob of fifty to sixty local white business owners and laborers. These Japanese were herded into trucks and driven to the railroad tracks, where they were dumped in the dark of the night. The mob warned them not to return to the town or they would be lynched. The same mob then raided a bunkhouse and three Japanese-operated farms, forcing forty more Japanese laborers to leave the town.[20]

The most severe violence against Japanese Americans was their internment during World War II. This terrible episode will be discussed in chapter 5, as this federal government–directed violation of the civil rights of Japanese Americans represents the worst and largest scale of violence against an ethnic group of Americans in the history of the United States and merits separate coverage.

Asian Indians were also subjected to physical violence. In 1907, a series of "anti-Hindu" riots broke out on the West Coast. The first flared up in Bellingham, Washington, a canning and lumber mill town about twenty miles south of the Canadian border. About 250 Asian Indians, mostly Sikh men from the Doaba region of the Punjab in northern India, lived in the town, among them 153 employed by five different lumber mills. Locals' anger toward the Asian Indians, fanned by the claim that whites had been replaced by the lower-paid "Hindus" at the lumber mills, escalated to a succession of incidents. On September 2, Labor Day, several Indian immigrants were beaten on the streets. The following night, five separate assaults on Asian Indian workers took place, and young men and boys smashed the windows of two houses where the Indian immigrants lived. On the night of September 4, 1907, over four hundred locals formed a mob and attacked the Indian quarters, with the intention of "scar[ing] them so badly that they will not crowd white labor out of the mills."[21] In 1908, a mob drove about one hundred Asian Indian farm workers out of their camp in Live Oak, about thirty miles south of Chico, California, and burned the camp.[22]

Even the very small group of Korean farm laborers could not escape hostility. In 1913, an orchard owner in Hemet, Riverside County, California, hired fifteen Korean fruit pickers. When the laborers arrived, they were surrounded by several hundred unemployed white Americans who threatened them and told them to leave immediately or face physical harm. The frightened Koreans took the next train out of town.[23]

Filipino immigrants also encountered xenophobic violence in the 1920s and 1930s when their population on the mainland United States rapidly increased from approximately 4,000 in 1920 to 45,000 in 1930. Competitions for jobs and women triggered the violence. The effort to drive out Filipino workers first began in the state of Washington. On September 19, 1928, white farmworkers in Yakima Valley forced all Filipino workers to leave the area. Two days later, about two hundred white farm laborers formed mobs and chased twenty Filipinos out of Wenatchee. The large-scale anti-Filipino violence, however, happened in California in 1930. On January 19, a white mob attacked a dance hall in Palm Beach, near Watsonville, where a large number of Filipino laborers were hired as seasonal farmhands. There the Filipino workers would dance with white women. One Filipino was killed and the Filipino camp burned. Nine days later, a Filipino clubhouse in Stockton was bombed, injuring many. It was the Tydings-McDuffie Act of 1934 that restricted Filipino immigration that finally ended the anti-Filipino violence.[24]

EXCLUSION LAWS AND POLICIES

The violent outbursts against Asians were aimed at not only driving them out but banning them from entering the country. During the late nineteenth and early twentieth centuries, a series of federal laws were passed to exclude Asian immigrants from entering the United States. These laws effectively barred their entry until 1965, when they were finally repealed.

Exclusion Laws against Chinese

The first national exclusion legislation was the Page Law of 1875. It forbade the entry of Chinese, Japanese, and "Mongolian" contract laborers and of women for the purpose of prostitution. Since the Page Law was more effective in restricting the entry of Chinese women than of Chinese men, Congress passed the 1882 Chinese Exclusion Act. This was the first law banning a specific ethnic group from entering the United States. It barred the entry of Chinese laborers for ten years but exempted merchants, diplomats, students, teachers, and travelers. It also required Chinese laborers to obtain certifications for reentry and excluded Chinese immigrants from U.S. citizenship.

White workers, particularly those in California, who had succeeded in gaining approval of the 1882 Exclusion Act, were dissatisfied with its effectiveness. In September 1888, Congress passed an act that allowed Chinese laborers who left the country to return only if they owned at least $1,000 in property or had a wife in the United States. To tighten the law further, on October 1, 1888, Congress passed the Scott Act. It declared all return certificates "void and of no effect" and thus prevented the reentry of some 20,000 Chinese who had return certificates. When the 1882 Chinese Exclusion Act was about to expire ten years later, it was renewed in 1892 and again in 1902. Finally in 1904 it was renewed indefinitely.

Exclusion Laws against Other Asians

The laws to exclude other Asians were less blatant than the 1882 act, as none of them bore the word "exclusion" in their titles. In addition, the circumstances concerning other Asians were more complex, and exclusion efforts thus required more creativity from the lawmakers.

In the case of Japanese, the United States was more cautious in dealing with the subjects of the rising military power in Asia. Unlike the 1882 Chinese Exclusion Act, which was unilaterally handled by the United States, an effort to bar Japanese laborers from entering America required a year and a half of negotiations and six notes exchanged between the two governments. Finally, in 1908 the Japanese government accepted the so-called Gentlemen's Agreement, which declared that the United States would not impose restrictions on Japanese immigration and Japan would not issue passports valid for the continental United States to Japanese laborers unless such laborers were coming to occupy a formerly acquired home, to join a parent, spouse, or child, or to assume active control of a previously acquired farming enterprise. Although the Gentlemen's Agreement stopped the influx of Japanese immigrants, under the terms of the agreement thousands of male Japanese residents of the United States would marry and bring their wives to America under the practice of "picture bride," in which a Japanese woman would marry her future husband in Japan by proxy and then join him later in the United States. In 1920 the Japanese government again agreed to not issue passports to picture brides.[25]

The U.S. government did not have to exclude Koreans, since Korea had been a Japanese colony since 1905 when defeat in the Russo-Japanese War forced Russia to surrender its interest in Korea. In 1910 Japan formally annexed Korea. The Japanese colonial government had already restricted Korean emigration. However, a small number of Koreans who first emigrated to Russia, Manchuria, and Europe also managed to land on American shores after 1910.[26]

To exclude Asian Indians, whose racial status was unclear, U.S. lawmakers had to adopt a geographic criterion. The Aryan (a group of Caucasians from the Caucasus region who migrated to South Asia) arrival in India between 1500 and 1300 BCE caused Aryanization (the spread of Aryan culture to non-Aryan peoples) and the racial integration between the Aryans and the Dravidians, the earlier inhabitants of India. Anthropologists have consequently classified Asian Indians as Aryans. Yet it is uncertain if Aryans were the same as whites since the skin complexion of inhabitants of the Indian subcontinent varies, ranging from very fair to very dark, and Indians have been called "Black Caucasians." The murky racial and ethnographic situation forced American politicians to depend on a geographical criterion. On February 4, 1917, the U.S. Congress passed the Immigration Act of 1917 (also known as the Asiatic Barred Zone Act). This legislation added "idiots," "feeble-minded persons," "criminals," "epileptics," "insane persons," alcoholics, "professional beggars," all persons "mentally or physically defective," polygamists, and anarchists to the list of undesirables barred from entering the United States. A clause of the law designated an Asiatic Barred Zone, a region east of an imaginary line drawn from the Red Sea to the Mediterranean, Aegean, and Black seas, through the Caucasus and the Ural Mountains, covering most of East Asia and the Pacific Islands from which people could not immigrate. Asian Indians of course fell within the barred boundaries.

Filipinos also had a special legal status. The acquisition of the Philippines in 1898 made the archipelago American territory, thus Filipinos were "nationals." These nationals were neither aliens nor citizens. Exclusionists decided to change the status of the Filipinos in order to exclude them. On March 24, 1934, Congress passed the Tydings-McDuffie Act (officially called the Philippines Independence Act), sponsored by Maryland senator Millard E. Tydings and Alabama representative John McDuffie. It provided for self-government of the Philippines and for Filipino independence from the United States after a period of twelve years. It also reclassified all Filipinos in the United States as aliens; Filipinos were no longer permitted to work legally in the United States; and a quota of fifty immigrants per year was established. This act paved the way for the Filipino Repatriation Act of 1935, which offered Filipinos free passage back to the Philippines. Under this act, some 2,190 Filipinos returned to their homeland.

THE ENFORCEMENT OF EXCLUSION LAWS

The enforcement of exclusion laws was initially vested in the office of the Secretary of the Treasury. However, various details of administration remained in the hands of the Collectors of Customs. In 1900, Congress transferred the administration of exclusion to the commissioner-general of immigration. Three years later, the entire immigration service and its officers were transferred to the Bureau of Commerce and Labor, leaving the enforcement of the exclusion laws again in the hands of the commissioner-general of immigration, but subject to the secretary of commerce and labor. Since three-fourths of all Chinese immigrants arrived through the port of San Francisco and half of the remainder came through other Pacific ports, the administration of the law at these ports was vital.[27]

For Asian immigrants who entered the country by fraudulent documentation or through illegal entry, immigration authorities and local police launched raids to arrest and then eventually deport them.

Exclusion at the Entry Ports: Story of Angel Island

Despite the exclusion laws, many Chinese immigrants entered the United States by impersonating family members of classes exempted from the Exclusion Act—merchants and U.S. citizens. Some Chinese laborers, in order to bring their families to America, changed their status from laborer to merchant by faking a partnership in a grocery store. Others were smuggled by train or boat from Canada, Mexico, or the Caribbean.[28]

How Chun Pong's case vividly depicts how the smuggling was conducted. How Chun Pong landed in Vancouver, Canada, in 1899, where he worked as a laundryman for four years, and then was smuggled to the United States by train. Later he moved to St. Louis to run a hand laundry until he was arrested in 1913. In his testimony, he described his illegal entry to Harry C. Allen, the U.S. immigration inspector: "I boarded the train with a white man at Montreal. It was quite dark, and when I got in the car there was no one there except the white man and myself, when the train run about several hours until daylight and then the train stopped, I don't know the name of the station. I was put in a small room on the train first and then I was brought out in the car where there [were] other passengers. And I left the train at New York City. . . . [I paid] $130 to the Chinese smuggler [in Montreal] and he paid the white man."[29]

In 1924, Canada and Mexico also passed their own exclusion laws, which meant a double barrier for smugglers to overcome. Therefore, smuggling was no longer a commonly used method of illegal entry.[30]

Immigration authorities responded by assuming all Chinese immigrants guilty of fraudulent entry until proven otherwise and singled them out for prolonged detention and interrogation at entry points. The immigration station on Angel Island was especially set up to process Asian immigrants. San Francisco commissioner of immigration Hart Hyatt North was in charge of the construction of the station and its operation. From 1910 to 1940 when it was in operation, one million people who arrived or departed the port of San Francisco were processed. They consisted of 341,000 aliens and returning residents and 209,000 U.S. citizens arriving in the United States, and more than 483,000 aliens and 183,000 U.S. citizens departing the country through San Francisco. Among those who arrived, an overwhelming majority (77 percent, or 54,223 of the 70,052 Angel Island arrival case files) were aliens from China (44,585), Japan (8,620), the Philippines (362), Korea (360), and India (296).[31]

Even though some historians have compared Angel Island with Ellis Island and called it the Ellis Island of the West, the two immigration stations were very different. Located in the Hudson River, Ellis Island immigration station opened on January 1, 1892, and processed mostly immigrants from Europe. It was merely a way station; for the vast majority of European immigrants, the processing took only three to five hours. The questioning of new immigrants usually took about two minutes and covered their occupation, marital status, place and date of birth, political orientation, destination, and job situation. After the short interview, 80 percent of the new immigrants were cleared to enter the United States. Most of those detained for medical reasons were eventually released. Only 2 percent were denied entry and deported to their home countries. These unfortunate people usually were unaccompanied women, children, the elderly, trachoma patients, and contract laborers.[32]

FIGURE 2.1 Plaque in front of the immigration station, Angel Island, erected in 1978. The engraved Chinese characters read, "Leaving home behind and being detained in wooden shed, looking for new life by the Golden Gate." Huping Ling Collection.

On the other hand, the immigration station on Angel Island was built more like a detention center than a way station. Immigration officials would board the arriving ship in San Francisco and inspect the documents of each passenger. Only those with satisfactory papers were allowed to go ashore. The remainder were transferred to a small steamer and ferried to the immigration station on Angel Island to await hearings on their application for entry.

Upon arrival on Angel Island, immigrants were first taken to a hospital for a medical examination. Those afflicted with parasitic diseases such as trachoma, hookworm, and liver fluke were excluded and deported. The rest were sent to their dormitories in a two-story wooden building, where men and women were separated. They languished for months in a prison-like conditions waiting for their hearings.[33]

Regardless of the validity of the arrival's legal documents for entry, an immigrant had to go through an extensive cross-interrogation on family, home life, and native village. The ques-

FIGURE 2.2 Room for detained immigrants before they were either admitted or denied to land, immigration station, Angel Island, 1910–1940. Huping Ling Collection.

tions asked in the case of Wong Shee were typical of the cross-interrogation. Wong Shee was the wife of Mark Tau, a native-born Chinese laundryman in San Francisco. In September 1920, she and her two young sons, Mark Woon Koey and Mark Woon Hew, came to America to join her husband and her elder sons, Mark Woon Nging and Mark Woon Noon. As soon as the ship arrived in San Francisco on September 1, Wong Shee and her sons were detained in the immigration station on the Angel Island. During her hearing on October 22, she was asked the following questions shown in the sidebar by immigrant inspector J. P. Butler.

In Wong Shee's case, Butler repeatedly probed Wong Shee on the question of the fish pond because her witnesses Mark Tau, Mark Woon Nging, and Mark Woon Noon had testified that there was a fish pond in their native village. After comparing the testimony of Wong Shee, her husband, and her sons, Butler found that there were no other discrepancies except for that on the fish pond. On this issue, Butler considered Mark Tau's statement that the pond was dry for most of the year. Therefore, he concluded that there was no discrepancy on this point. Consequently, Wong Shee and her two sons were granted the right to land after almost two months detention.

INTERROGATION OF IMMIGRANTS ON ANGEL ISLAND

Q Which way does the village face?
A It faces north.

Q How are the houses arranged in the village?
A Arranged in rows.

Q How many in each row?
A All in one row across the front of the village from head to tail.

Q Which one is your house?
A Counting from the east, mine is the second house.

Q Have you ever lived in any other house in that village?
A No.

Q Is there a wall around your village or any side of it?
A No.

Q Any trees or bamboo on any side?
A Trees and bamboo on both sides and a hill in the rear.

Q Any trees or shrubs of any kind in the rear?
A No.

Q What is in front?
A Nothing in front.

Q Has your village a fish pond?
A No.

Q Was there ever a fish pond in the front of your village?
A No.

Q Is there any ditch of water in the front?
A No.

Q Is there any low land in the front of the village in which the water remains?
A No.

Q Is there a fish pond on any side of your village?
A No.

Q Do you know what a fish pond is?
A Yes, it is a pond that holds fish but we have no pond in our village.

Q Is there any pond near your village which might belong to some other village?
A I don't know of any.

Q What kind of country is your village located on?
A It is farm land, level.

Q State the name of the village in the immediate vicinity of yours, as well as direction and distance.
A Gop Son village, two li east. Hock Bo to the west, two li. Lung Chee Hong, 21 li south. Lung Mee village to the north, two li.

Source: Case 19571/18-5, RG 85, National Archives, Pacific Sierra Region, San Bruno, CA.

In another case, the applicant's testimony disagreed with that of the witnesses, and her entry was denied. Wong Yee Gue was the wife of Yee Home Sue, a native-born Chinese in New York.³⁴ On April 19, 1915, Wong Yee Gue arrived in San Francisco and applied for admission as the wife of a native. Two days after she was detained on Angel Island and faced her hearing (in this case, the wait was brief). Immigrant inspector A. M. Long found Wong Yee Gue's testimony contradictory to that of her witnesses. The issues dealt mainly with the questions of natural feet and the status of the neighbor in Wong Yee Gue's village. Long therefore recommended Wong Yee Gue's admission be denied.

As presented in the above two cases, an applicant's testimony could largely determine the result of their application. Under such practice, a felon could gain entry as long as they and the witnesses were prepared to produce the same testimony, while a bona fide applicant could be denied if they failed to provide expected testimony. Moreover, the different personalities and work styles of immigrant inspectors also played a role in the approval of an application. Some were meticulous but fair. Others were inclined to find discrepancies through frivolous and tedious interrogations. Finally, some of the questions required very specific knowledge of a setting or an event that people normally do not consider, making such questions difficult to answer. The immigration authorities, however, relied heavily on these interrogations to determine an applicant's eligibility for entry. Any lack of answer or inconsistency could lead to rejection.

There was great deal of fear of rejection and deportation among the immigrants before their interrogation. Most complied with officials, but some protested their brutal treatment. One immigrant woman recalled her experience when she was interned on Angel Island: "While I was waiting in the immigration shed, Grandpa sent a box of *dim sum*. I threw the box of *dim sum* out the window. I was still waiting to be released. I would have jumped in the ocean if they decided to deport me."³⁵ Though this act was not much help in improving her situation, this form of resistance served as an emotional outlet for some detained immigrants. The detainees' resistance reflected the cruelty and inhumane nature of the immigration station on Angel Island. To deal with the depressed and irritated detainees, the officials constructed an isolation room, a nine-square-foot tiny room without windows. The agitating inmates were locked in this room for hours until they managed to "calm down."³⁶

Some strong and resourceful immigrants were successful in fighting for their right to entry by applying American immigration regulations to their cases. Gee Quock Shee was one such courageous and capable immigrant. She went to China with her husband, a Chinese merchant in San Mateo, in 1907. Her husband remained in China conducting business. When she returned to the United States in February 1910 and tried to enter as the wife of a merchant, she was denied entry because her husband was not presently in America. Defiantly, she provided evidence that she owned one-half shares in the business and had been actively managing the family enterprise, Yee Hing & Co. Therefore, she was qualified to be a merchant herself. "If the law prevents me from being in this country at the present time," she

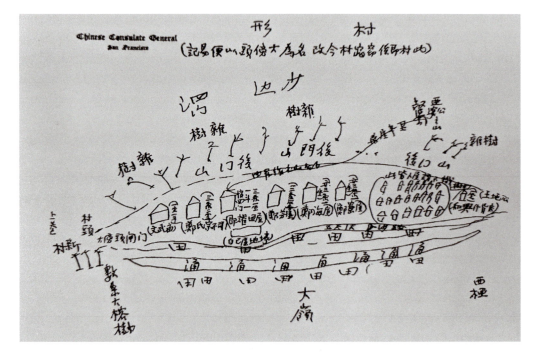

FIGURE 2.3 Map of village in China prepared by Chinese immigrants for interrogation by American immigration officials in Chinese, 1927. Courtesy National Archives–Pacific Sierra Region, San Bruno, California.

challenged J. B. McChesney, the immigration inspector on Angel Island, "I therefore request that my application be withdrawn and renew it, having a status of a merchant myself." After investigation, the officials accepted her status as a merchant and admitted her.[37]

Exclusion at the Local Level

Despite the exclusion laws, large numbers of Chinese, Japanese, and Filipinos and small but visible pockets of Asian Indians and scattered Koreans remained in the country. Anti-Asian social groups thus had to use the institutionalized and systemic ways to further restrict or confine the Asian immigrants who refused or lacked the means to leave.

Chinese immigrants who entered the country during the exclusion period continued to face exclusion and discrimination from immigration authorities and local law enforcement agencies. Between the 1880s and 1920s, many immigrant settlements in gateway cities and hinterland areas faced joint raids by immigration authorities and local police forces, doggedly hunting for "unlawful" Chinese "within the United States."

The renewal of the 1882 Chinese Exclusion Act on May 5, 1892, known as the Geary Act, propelled a new round of anti-Chinese persecution and sentiment in the United

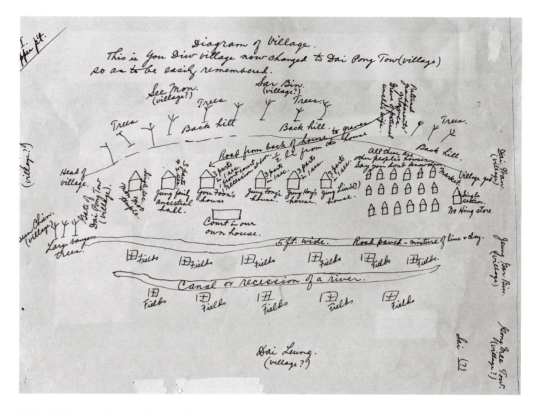

FIGURE 2.4 Map of village in China prepared by Chinese immigrants for interrogation by American immigration officials in English, 1927. Courtesy National Archives–Pacific Sierra Region, San Bruno, California.

States in the following decades. In Chicago, the situation was particularly compounded by preparations for the World's Columbian Exposition of 1893. The Chicago immigration office was especially alarmed by a rumor that scores of Chinese would be smuggled to the fair and then disappear into the crowds. Like their counterparts in other port cities, the Chinese in Chicago were asked to be photographed by immigration authorities for further scrutiny and for distinction from the illegal Chinese smuggled in along with staff members of the Chinese display booths at the fair. The Civil Case Files of the U.S. District Court in the Northern District of Illinois show a number of arrests of Chinese in 1911, allegedly for being unlawful residents in Chicago. Responding to the arrests, On Leong, one of the major early Chinese community organizations, hired white American lawyers to represent the cases. Despite these efforts, most arrested Chinese were ordered for deportation to China by Mark A. Foote, U.S. commissioner for the Northern District of Illinois.[38]

Similar raids targeting Chinese in connection with the Chinese Exclusion Acts of 1882, 1888, 1892, 1902, and 1922 also took place in other major midwestern cities, such as

St. Louis, where in 1883 the so-called Highbinder Murder Case took place in the city's Chinatown. An African American man named Johnson was killed in "an alley between the Seventh and Eighth and Market and Walnut Streets," known as Hop Alley, Chinatown, and later his head was found in a basket of rice. Local police believed that a conflict between the man and a Chinese gambler who was connected with the Highbinders, a Chinese secret society allegedly associated with many murders in large Chinese communities, was the cause of the murder.[39] Without any witnesses, police arrested six Chinese men from Hop Alley as suspects. The Chinese men were vigorously prosecuted, but the court was unable to convict them due to a lack of evidence. Not only were the local police quick and inclined to suspect Chinese as criminals, but the news media even mistakenly regarded all Chinese residents in St. Louis as Highbinders. The *St. Louis Globe-Democrat* estimated in 1892 that there were "about three hundred Highbinders in St. Louis." This number represented practically the entire Chinese population of St. Louis.[40]

Aroused by sensational and exaggerated media reports and guided by Chinese exclusion mentality, St. Louis law enforcement agencies assumed a large number of illegal laborers and criminals among the Chinese in the city and therefore took serious actions targeting the city's entire Chinese population. Police records indicate that 1895 and the period from 1905 to 1911 marked the peaks of police arrests of Chinese. The heightening of police harassment of Chinese unsurprisingly coincided with renewals of the Chinese Exclusion Act in 1892, 1902, and 1904. According to the *Globe-Democrat*, on August 25, 1897, St. Louis police rounded up all 314 Chinese in the city as requested by a government agent who was investigating reports that illegal Chinese immigrants had been smuggled into the city. Thirteen Chinese men were found without proper legal documents and were arrested to await deportation. In the first two decades of the twentieth century, St. Louis police repeatedly raided Hop Alley and apprehended scores of Chinese individuals, charging them with the smuggling, manufacture, and sale of opium.[41]

PROTESTS AGAINST EXCLUSION AND DISCRIMINATION

Asian immigrants and their governments protested the unfair treatment and exclusion laws. The protests ranged from official complaints by diplomats of the Asian countries involved to boycotts of American goods by the masses in Asian countries and by Asian immigrants, legal battles between district courts and the Asian immigrants who hired white American lawyers to represent them, public debates and responses to racial and prejudiced comments and acts by pioneering Asian American civil rights activists, and suicides committed by desperate and distraught individuals who were victimized by the exclusion laws and their enforcement.

Official Protests by Asian Governments

Asian governments did protest to the American government regarding the mistreatment of their subjects in the United States. Yet in most cases their complaints were dismissed out of hand since at the time the agrarian Asian countries were too weak to challenge the industrialized Western powers in any meaningful way.

China's Qing government faced tremendous disadvantages after the Opium War. Historically, various Chinese governments had handled international relations with their neighboring states and those far away using the tributary system, under which other states recognized Chinese superiority and were subjected to Chinese suzerainty, and in return China aided the vasal states in times of trouble. During their contacts and conflicts with the Western powers since the sixteenth century, the Chinese government had applied to European powers the same principles, which were tolerated by the seafaring "barbarians" who were eager to trade with China until the brink of Opium War. The Treaty of Nanjing and the successive unequal treaties enabled the Western powers to institute diplomatic relations with China along the lines of European diplomatic practices and norms, which however were by no means fair to China. Suddenly thrown into the international political arena, the Qing government was inadequately equipped in modern diplomacy and had very few officials with knowledge of the international affairs of the time.

The appointment of Anson Burlingame, the retiring American minister to China, as China's envoy to negotiate with European and American governments in 1867 was a case in point, and it has been repeatedly quoted as a notorious and consummate example of the inadequacy of Chinese diplomacy at the time. Although Burlingame marginally defended China's interests in his negotiations with the European powers, in dealing with the U.S. government he signed on his own authority, without the prior consultation and approval of the Chinese government, the Burlingame Treaty with Secretary of State Seward on July 28, 1868. Along with other provisions, the treaty permitted the sending of Chinese consuls and laborers to the United States.[42] Under such circumstances, it is not difficult to understand the ineffectiveness of the protests from the Chinese government on the mistreatment and exclusion of the Chinese in the United States.

Liang Cheng, the Chinese minister in Washington from 1903 to 1907, demonstrated the diplomatic efforts of the Chinese government. Having studied in the United States as a young student and worked as an embassy employee, Liang had firsthand experience of the hostility against Chinese immigrants in America. In his memorial to the emperor upon his 1903 arrival in Washington as the Chinese minister, Liang pledged he would "alleviate the hardship of the Immigrants, and to glorify the nation's dignity on the basis of justice." After learning the news about a Chinese diplomat who committed suicide following his humiliation before San Francisco police, Liang urged the Chinese consul general and Chinese in San Francisco to "fight hard" for justice.[43]

Wu Ting Fang, the Chinese minister to the United States, represented probably the strongest voice from the Chinese government. A Hong Kong–born Chinese, Wu earned his law degree in London and served as China's minister to the United States, Spain, and Peru from 1896 to 1902 and again from 1907 to 1909. In this capacity, Wu presented a trenchant voice in the diplomatic remonstrations. He delivered official complaints to the State Department, but the latter courteously and repeatedly evaded them. Wu protested the hardships of Chinese immigrants directly caused by the excessively strict regulations and firmly argued his case based on the terms of treaties between the two governments.[44]

During his terms, Wu also lectured widely on Chinese culture and history to promote American public appreciation of the Chinese heritage in order to counter the Chinese exclusion. To that end, he published a book titled *America, through the Spectacles of an Oriental Diplomat* in English in 1914. In this book, Wu discretely criticized the Chinese Exclusion Acts as policies tarnishing the American reputation and blemishing its relations with China.[45]

Local government officials in southern China also pleaded for help protecting the overseas Chinese. In 1866, the governor of Guangdong suggested that China follow the examples set by Western countries by dispatching state officials to protect their commercial interests abroad. In the early 1870s the governor of Fujian and the treasurer of Jiangsu further recommended that the Qing government send officials to overseas port cities with large concentrations of overseas Chinese.[46]

The Japanese government took different actions to deal with the racial exclusion in America by reforming its immigrant masses. As Eiichiro Azuma documented, the Japanese diplomats and immigrant elite ironically agreed with the exclusionists concerning the "inferior" quality of Japanese laborers and prostitutes compared with their Chinese counterparts. The elite Japanese in San Francisco concurred with the notions that Chinese living quarters were "filthy" and that Chinese men were tong criminals and Chinese women prostitutes. Similarly, the Japanese diplomats and elite also distinguished themselves from their compatriots from rural Japan, whom they scorned as "degenerated class," "dirt peasants," and "ignorant fools." In 1900, with the support of Japanese consular officials, Issei leaders in San Francisco formed the first coalition against sinicization, in order to separate themselves from their Chinese neighbors. The Japanese Association of America in San Francisco, Los Angeles, Portland, and Seattle also launched moral reforms on the West Coast in the 1910s, with the support of the Japanese government, which provided funds, personnel, and guidelines. The chief objectives of these reforms included a campaign against Chinese gambling and cultural assimilation with the goal of becoming "100 Per Cent American." Both Japanese diplomats and the immigrant elite believed that racial discrimination would disappear once Americans realized who the "real" Japanese were. Japanese immigrant women, especially educated Christians, also assisted the reform movement within their communities.[47]

Boycotts of American Goods

To protest the Chinese exclusion laws and the harsh treatment of their compatriots in the United States, Chinese in China spearheaded the nationwide Anti-American Boycott in 1905, and this "tidal wave" of sentiment soon spread to Chinese immigrant communities across America. The movement started in Shanghai, the premier industrial and commercial center of China, when the Shanghai General Chamber of Merchants announced a nationwide boycott of American goods to protest Chinese exclusion laws on May 10, 1905. Millions of Chinese in China and abroad responded to the call. The 1905–1906 Anti-American Boycott Movement has been regarded as the beginning of mass politics and modern nationalism in China and a landmark event signifying Chinese Americans' national consciousness.[48]

The once solitary voice of Chinese immigrants over anti-Chinese hostility and exclusion now became a deafening outcry throughout China and beyond. As historian Yong Chen noted, the magnitude of support from China was unprecedented. The boycott spread geographically from north to south, from coastal regions to the hinterland. In Guangdong province, where most Chinese immigrants to the Americas originated, the movement penetrated to rural areas. In Xinning county, one of the prime sending places of Chinese immigrants to America, the leaders of the boycott displayed American imports to demonstrate to citizens what to boycott. In major Chinese port cities such as Beijing, Tianjin, Qingdao, Nanjing, Suzhou, and Hankou, the protests were most vigorous. The leaders of the movement consisted of merchants and intellectuals. While the Chinese merchant class was most active in the movement through financing and organizing boycotts, intellectuals acted as catalysts by organizing rallies and writing editorials, plays, novels, and folk songs to depict the plight of Chinese immigrants. The Chinese populace responded enthusiastically. The far-flung movement also aroused protests among Chinese overseas communities in Japan, Vietnam, Thailand, Singapore, the Philippines, Australia, Canada, and Panama.[49]

Although the economic impact of the 1905 boycott was considered miniscule by scholars, its long-term impact in connecting Chinese immigrants and their compatriots in China has been recognized by writers.[50] The Chinese Consolidated Benevolent Association (CCBA or Zhonghua Huiguan), the influential and chief community organization among Chinese immigrants in America, formed the General Boycott Committee to coordinate the movement in America. The committee collected funds from various cities across America. Its monthly statement indicates a rapid increase in donations from Chinese immigrants, from $6,347 in the period from June 9 to July 19 to $9,611 between July 20 and August 17.[51]

Legal Battles

Chinese consulates and Chinese immigrant community organizations such as CCBA also employed white American lawyers to defend the Chinese. Frederick A. Bee, who represented Chinese miners in El Dorado County, California, in 1855, was hired as the vice consul by the Chinese consulate in San Francisco. He appeared at the 1876 congressional hearing as the attorney for the CCBA. In the last decades of the nineteenth century, Bee frequently appeared at court on behalf of Chinese immigrants. The Chinese consulate in Boston also hired a white American lawyer, Stephen W. Nickerson, in the beginning of the 1900s.[52] In Chicago, Chinese community leaders also hired a number of white American lawyers defending Chinese immigrants in the late nineteenth and early twentieth centuries.[53]

Two legal cases, *Takao Ozawa v. U.S.* (1922) and *U.S. v. Bhagat Singh Thind* (1923), highlight the racial bias against Asian immigrants in the legal redefinition of whiteness. Takao Ozawa was born in Japan, but he had lived almost all his life in the United States. He graduated from Berkeley High School and attended the University of California. He was a Christian and spoke English at home. In 1922, he filed for U.S. citizenship under the 1906 Naturalization Law that permitted white persons or persons of African origin to naturalize. Supreme Court justice George Sutherland ruled that white meant "Caucasian" and that Ozawa was not Caucasian, therefore ineligible for citizenship.[54]

Three months later, Justice Sutherland made a similar unfavorable ruling in *U.S. v. Bhagat Singh Thind*, concerning an Asian alien. Bhagat Singh Thind was a Sikh immigrant from Punjab, India, who applied for citizenship on the grounds that Indians were considered Caucasians or Aryan by anthropologists. Justice Sutherland interpreted that although all whites were Caucasians, Caucasians were not necessarily considered white.

It is worth noting that many sympathetic white Americans allied with Asian immigrants during the exclusion era. Asian immigrants and organizations were able to depend on the assistance of white attorneys in their legal battle against the discriminatory treatment against them, as documented in numerous immigration records.

Public Protests and Debates

The discriminatory actions against Chinese under the context of the Geary Act of 1892 infuriated Chinese communities throughout the country. On September 22, 1892, nearly two hundred English-speaking Chinese from the East Coast rallied at the Cooper Union in the East Village in Lower Manhattan to form the Chinese Equal Rights League to contest the legality of the Geary Act, which had been passed four months previously. Sam Ping Lee, a Philadelphia merchant, was elected president and Wong Chin Foo secretary of the league. The organization published an appeal, declaring "as residents of the United States we claim a common manhood with all other nationalities, and believe we should have that manhood recognized according to the principles of common humanity and American freedom."[55]

Wong Chin Foo, arguably the first Asian American civil rights activist from New York, enthusiastically participated in the protest movement. He started a handwritten, bilingual, bimonthly newspaper, *Meihua Xinbao* (Chinese American Newspaper), as a revival of his failed newspaper in New York a decade before. In its inaugural issue of June 24, 1893, Wong Chin Foo criticized the Geary Act for discriminating against the Chinese and expressed his disappointment with the Chinese Six Companies for failing to oppose it successfully.[56]

In Chicago, Moy Dong Chow and Moy Dong Hoy, two of the three Moy brothers and early Chinese community leaders, led a protest. When a reporter from the *Chicago Tribune* visited the South Clark district on August 9, 1892, Moy Dong Chow angrily refused to talk to the reporter—the opposite of his usual easygoing and accommodating manner—and Moy Dong Hoy declined to be included in the group photograph of Chinese outside the Hip Lung store. Chow Tar, whose excellent command of English apparently made him the spokesperson for Chinatown, articulated to the reporter the anger of the Chinese community toward the exclusion acts and related measures:

> If that law means that all my countrymen, residents in America are to be measured as criminals and labeled as so many packages of tea it will never be enforced. The ridiculousness of its provisions will kill it. Are we not residents here? Do we not pay taxes as all other property holders? It would be more nearly justice for them to drive us out. So long as we are accepted as residents we are entitled to some rights. We are not law breakers. There certainly would be a great deal of trouble should an attempt be made, such as you have indicated to place all Chinese residents on a par with professional criminals. For the record of such measurements and pictures would be classed as a "rogues" gallery. Would this Chinese "rogues" gallery be put on exhibition in the World's Fair to show the advancement in civilization that this nation has attained? No, no, I think that a telegram stating that such measurements and photographs are now being taken of Chinese in the cities which are ports must be a hoax.[57]

Contrary to the public perception of the "Mongolian" or "Chinamen" as racially debased, politically naïve, and culturally ignorant, Chow Tar was poignant, logical, and piercingly convincing. The Chinese in Chicago protested the Geary Act for singling them out and imposing unjust treatment on them and demanded rights as law-abiding and tax-paying residents.

Suicides by Individuals

Some Chinese immigrants, unable to cope with stress and desperation during their detention in immigration facilities, committed suicide. The chopsticks-slaying case provides one such example. On October 24, 1941, Wong Shee, the wife of a New York businessman, arrived in San Francisco with her nine-year-old son, Hom Lee Min, to join her husband, Hom Hin Shew. Upon arrival, she and her son were separately held at the immigration station at 801 Silver Avenue in San Francisco.[58] As days passed, Wong Shee's worry grew deeper. On November 18, 1941, she became extremely upset when she heard a rumor about the denial of her application. In the early morning of November 19, she was found dead in the women's bathroom. A chopstick had been thrust into her right auditory canal.[59]

ASIAN IMMIGRATION RESTRICTIONS AND RESISTANCE IN HISTORICAL PERSPECTIVE

All groups of immigrants to America have suffered various degrees of prejudice and discrimination against them. Yet Asian immigrants endured the longest and harshest hostility and exclusion during their pursuit of the American dream. What elements made the Asian immigrants different from other ethnic groups in America? Why was the hostility toward Asian immigrants more intense than that toward European immigrants? Were they racially debased, physically unattractive, and culturally peculiar or strange? Were they stealing jobs away from European Americans? These were the central questions and perceptions that the nation was debating and pondering in the late nineteenth and early twentieth centuries. These are the questions that students of American history should logically ask when reading this chapter.

This chapter has answered these questions through narratives of myriad evidence gleaned from archives, museums, media coverage, private collections, and oral history interviews. It has also presented different scholarly interpretations for these questions. Generally speaking, four reasons have been listed as causes of Asian—and especially Chinese—exclusions: (1) cultural and racial prejudice against Chinese and other Asians promoted through publications by American diplomats, merchants, and missionaries; (2) the weakness, backwardness, and victimization of Asian countries in the age of imperialistic global expansion; (3) the periodical economic depressions and difficulties that Americans were facing in the late nineteenth and early twentieth centuries; and (4) the political disfranchisement of Asian immigrants that put them in a disadvantageous position.

KEY TERMS

Foreign Miners' License Tax
fishing license law
anti-Chinese violence in Los Angeles (1871)
Page Law (1875)
anti-Chinese violence in Chico (1877)
anti-Chinese riots in Denver (1880)
Chinese Exclusion Act (1882)
anti-Chinese violence in Rock Springs, Wyoming, and Tacoma and Seattle, Washington (1885)
Snake River Massacre (1887)
Scott Act (1888)
Geary Act (1892)

Anti-American Boycott Movement (1905)
Gentlemen's Agreement (1907)
anti-Asian Indian farm workers riot in Live Oak, California (1908)
immigration station on Angel Island (1910–1940)
Alien Land Laws
Immigration Act of 1917
Takao Ozawa v. U.S. (1922)
Bhagat Singh Thind v. U.S. (1923)
anti-Filipino violence in Palm Beach, California (1930)
Tydings-McDuffie Act (1934)

REVIEW QUESTIONS

1. Provide four reasons for the hostility, discrimination, and exclusion of Asian immigrants in the United States during the late nineteenth and early twentieth centuries.
2. What are the similarities and differences of Ellis Island and Angel Island?
3. What lesson(s) have you learned from this chapter?
4. Would new immigrants take jobs away from Americans? Do they strengthen or harm American society and its values? Should we accept or exclude new immigrants?

FILMS

Angel Island: Story of Chinese Immigration. 12-minute documentary of the history of the Angel Island immigration station where Asian (mainly Chinese) immigrants were processed from 1910 until 1943. MacNeil/Lehrer Productions, 2000.

Lowe, Felicia (producer/director). *Carved in Silence: Chinese Immigration during Exclusion.* 45-minute documentary with dramatic re-creations of the Angel Island immigration station. 1988.

FURTHER READING

Azuma, Eiichiro. *Between Two Empires: Race, History, and Transnationalism in Japanese America.* New York: Oxford University Press, 2005.

Chan, Sucheng. *Asian Americans: An Interpretive History.* Boston: Twayne, 1991.

Chen, Yong. *Chinese San Francisco, 1850–1943: A Trans-Pacific Community.* Stanford, CA: Stanford University Press, 2000.

Daniels, Roger. *Asian America: Chinese and Japanese in the United States since 1850.* Seattle: University of Washington, 1988.

———. *The Politics of Prejudice: The Anti-Japanese Movement in California and the Struggle for Japanese Exclusion.* 2nd ed. Berkeley: University of California Press, 1978.

Espiritu, Yen Le. *Home Bound: Filipino American Lives across Cultures, Communities, and Countries.* Berkeley: University of California Press, 2003.

Helweg, Arthur W. *Strangers in a Not-So-Strange Land: Indian-American Immigrants in the Global Age.* Belmont, CA: Wadsworth/Thomson, 2004.

Lee, Erika. *At America's Gate: Chinese Immigration during the Exclusion Era, 1882–1943.* Chapel Hill: University of North Carolina Press, 2002.

Lee, Erika, and Judy Yung. *Angel Island: Immigrant Gateway to America.* New York: Oxford University Press, 2010.

Leonard, Karen Isaksen. *The South Asian Americans.* Westport, CT: Greenwood, 1997.

Ling, Huping. *Chinese Chicago: Race, Transnational Migration, and Community since 1870.* Stanford, CA: Stanford University Press, 2012.

———. *Surviving on the Gold Mountain: A History of Chinese American Women and Their Lives.* Albany: State University of New York Press, 1989.

Low, Lisa. *Immigrant Acts.* Durham, NC: Duke University Press, 1996.

Posadas, Barbara M. *The Filipino Americans.* Westport, CT: Greenwood, 1999.

Salyer, Lucy E. *Laws Harsh as Tigers: Chinese Immigrants and the Shaping of Modern Immigration Law.* Chapel Hill: University of North Carolina Press, 1995.

Zesch, Scott. *The Chinatown War: Chinese Los Angeles and the Massacre of 1871.* New York: Oxford University Press, 2012.

PART II

Asian American Experiences, 1840s–1965

3

LABOR

CHAPTER OUTLINE

Sugar Plantations, Mines, and Railroads
Urban Niche Economy
Niche in Agriculture
Labor in Historical Perspective

SIGNIFICANT EVENTS

1850–1920	Over 300,000 Asians enter the Hawaiian Islands
1852	25,000 Chinese in California
1863	Peak of Chinese gold mining—80 to 85 percent of the Chinese population in California is engaged in mining
1865–1869	Central Pacific Railroad Company hires 12,000 Chinese, representing 90 percent of its entire workforce
1890s	Chinese restaurants sprout across the United States
1900	The Organic Act establishes Hawaii as a territory of the United States and thus abolishes the contract labor system in Hawaii; more than twenty strikes involving 8,000 workers spread through the plantations in Hawaii
1903–1905	More than 7,000 Koreans arrive in Hawaii to replace the Japanese workers
1906	San Francisco earthquake and the subsequent fire cause devastation for Chinese residents and induce many to move to other states
1910	12,000 to 15,000 Japanese in domestic service in the U.S. West
1913	Alien land law in California prohibits "aliens ineligible to citizenship"—namely, Chinese, Japanese, Koreans, and Asian Indians—from owning land
1920	The Hawaii Laborers' Association is established, embracing the working class of all racial and ethnic backgrounds

1921	Alien land law in Washington prohibits Asians from owning land
1930s	Over 88 percent of working Japanese are employed in three economic sectors—agriculture, wholesale and retail trade, and domestic service
1920–1930	Filipino population increases from fewer than 3,000 to more than 30,000 in California
1934	The Tydings-McDuffie Act grants the Philippines independence from the United States and strips Filipinos of their status as "nationals"
1938	Chinese Ladies Garment Workers Union strike in San Francisco's National Dollar Stores
1940	Nearly 30 percent, or 36,866, of the total Japanese population in the United States reside in Los Angeles County; more than 6,000 farms are operated by Japanese in the three Pacific Coast states

IT IS WELL RECOGNIZED that Asian immigrant workers contributed significantly to the socioeconomic development of Hawaii and the American West. As demonstrated in this chapter, Chinese, Japanese, Korean, and Filipino immigrant workers constituted more than half of the population in Hawaii, and their labor was indispensable to the territory's economy. In the western mining region—from California to the Pacific Northwest, the Rocky Mountains, Idaho, Colorado, and the Southwest—Chinese miners helped extend the period of gold production by working in claims abandoned by the original white miners, contributing to national and regional economic development. The construction of the western portion of the transcontinental railroad would not have been possible without the employment of more than 10,000 Chinese laborers, who braved the Sierra Nevada snow, dangerous explosives, and other harsh working and living conditions.

In urban settings, Asian immigrants established ethnic neighborhoods, conventionally known as ghettos or enclaves, where they sustained themselves and even thrived by carving out "niche" occupations. Chinese laundries, wholesale and retail grocery businesses, restaurants, and garment factories were and remain the primary economic niches of ethnic Chinese enclave communities. Japanese immigrants on the West Coast likewise found their own niche in small businesses selling fresh vegetables and fruit. Many Japanese immigrants also worked as domestic servants. The ethnic enclave economy was not only significant in sustaining the ethnic community but also important to local, regional, and national economic development. The formation of urban ethnic neighborhoods further enriched the sociopolitical and geopolitical landscapes of American metropolises and cities.

In agriculture, Asian farmers focused on growing niche specialty crops that met certain market demands and therefore were more profitable. The cultivation of these crops formed the basis for population growth among Japanese farmers in the first half of the twentieth century and provided them with upward mobility. Although much fewer in numbers, Korean and Asian Indian farmers shared a similar pattern as the Japanese. Filipinos, most numerous among the Asian farming population on the Pacific Coast in the 1920s, were largely migrant farm laborers. Asian farmers not only fed local residents but also contributed to national economic development, as the Pacific Coast played a significant role in the U.S. economy as a whole.

It is worth noting that in the development of the American West and in the economic progress of the country during the century from the 1840s to the 1940s, Asian American laborers occupied a unique position in the complex matrix created by the intersections of class, race, ethnicity, and gender. On the one hand, they were recruited as cheap laborers to fill the pool of labor needed for capitalistic exploitation. They were used as "strikebreakers" by capitalists bent on frustrating the white union movement, and as such they were resented and discriminated against by white laborers. On the other hand, when subjected to capitalistic exploitation and exposed to the white union movement, Asian workers also obtained class consciousness and participated in independent and later interethnic labor or union movements to improve their living and working conditions. In this sense, Asian Americans' experience as laborers has offered yet another dimension to the multiethnic nature of the American union movement.

SUGAR PLANTATIONS, MINES, AND RAILROADS

Asian Laborers in Hawaiian Sugar Plantations

Concurrent with Chinese immigration to California, laborers from China, Japan, Korea, and the Philippines were also recruited to Hawaiian sugar plantations. In the final decade of the nineteenth century, sugar production rapidly increased in Hawaii. A more efficient, large-scale system enabled the yield per acre to increase from less than 6,500 pounds in 1895 to nearly 8,600 pounds in 1900.[1] The growth in sugar production demanded more laborers—and cheap workers from Asia stepped in to make sugar the king of Hawaiian industry. Over 300,000 Asians entered the islands between 1850 and 1920. According to the *Hawaiian Gazette*, in 1853 Hawaiians and part-Hawaiians accounted for 97 percent of the Hawaiian population of 73,137, while Caucasians represented 2 percent and Chinese 0.5 percent; in 1923, Hawaiians and part-Hawaiians constituted only 16.3 percent of the population, while Japanese represented 42.7 percent, Portuguese 10.6 percent, Chinese 9.2 percent, Filipinos 8.2 percent, Caucasians 7.7 percent, Puerto Ricans 2.2 percent, and Koreans 1.9 percent.[2]

This significant demographic shift happened for a number of reasons. It was first caused by the rapid population decline of Hawaiians, who had no immunity to the diseases carried to the islands by Europeans and Americans. More than 80 percent of the native Hawaiian population was wiped out between 1778, when Captain Cook arrived, and the 1850s. Furthermore, after the Hawaiian king allowed Westerners to purchase land for sugar plantations from the 1840s onward, the commercialized and labor-intensive nature of sugar production prompted white planters to form the Royal Hawaiian Agricultural Society in 1850—which evolved into the Planters' Society in 1864—for the purpose of recruiting the laborers they needed.[3]

Life on the sugar plantations in Hawaii was accompanied by some drastic changes for these Asian laborers. While in their homelands they resided in kinship-based villages and worked mostly as individual farmers, on sugar plantations they lived in camps segregated by national origins and worked in gangs watched by *lunas* (foremen) who were white Americans or Portuguese. Living conditions were harsh and primitive. While single men slept on wooden shelves in bunkhouses, families were crammed into rooms created by partitions in bunkhouses and that lacked soundproofing. At night, mothers of crying babies were asked to sleep in the cane fields so as not to disturb the other bunkhouse occupants. In most camps, cooking and recreational facilities were not built until after frequent laborer stoppages and strikes succeeded in forcing planters to acquiesce to workers' demands for improved conditions.[4]

The work in the cane field was regimented and harsh. The loud screams of a siren would wake the workers at five o'clock in the morning. After a brief breakfast, they were rushed to the cane fields, where they worked in gangs of a couple of hundred. All of their movements were closely monitored by lunas and field bosses on horseback. Lunas swung whips to discipline the workers and speed up their pace. The tasks in the fields revolved around the growth cycle of the canes, including plowing and cultivating the fields, planting, watering, hoeing weeds, harvesting sugar canes, and bundling and loading them onto railway cars to be transported to mills. Most of the

A PLANTATION WORK SONG

"Awake! Stir your bones! Rouse up!
Shrieks the Five o'Clock Whistle.
"Don't dream you can nestle
For one more sweet nap.
Or your ear-drums I'll rap
With my steam-hammer tap
Till they burst.
Br-r-row-aw-i-e-ur-ur-rup!
Wake up! wake up! wake up!
　w-a-k-e-u-u-u-up!

Filipino and Japanese;
Porto Rican and Portugee;
Korean, Kanaka and Chinese;
Everybody whoever you be
On the whole plantation—
Wake up! wake up! wake up!
　w-a-k-e-u-u-u-up!
Br-r-row-aw-i-e-ur-ur-rup!

Source: Ronald Takaki, *Strangers form Different Shore: A History of Asian Americans* (Boston: Little, Brown, 1989), 133–134.

FIGURE 3.1 Chinese contract laborers on a sugar plantation in nineteenth-century Hawaii. Courtesy Hawaii State Archives.

work was tedious and backbreaking, but cutting the ripe cane was the dirtiest and most exhausting. Enclosed in the twelve-feet-tall cane "forest," Asian workers endured the pain of blisters on their hands and scratches on their arms from the leaves of canes, the heat of the sun, the humidity of the air, and the dust from the field.[5]

Work in the sugar mills, also owned by the white planters, was not much easier. Within the mill, engines, presses, furnaces, boilers, vacuum pans, centrifugal drums, and other machines crushed the cane and boiled juices into molasses and sugar. The constant and deafening noise of the machines and the stifling heat often drove the workers to the brink of mental and physical exhaustion.

To maximize profits, white planters paid plantation laborers the lowest possible wages. The Chinese—who were the first group of Asian laborers and mostly came from South China as contract laborers with free passage—received three dollars a month in the 1850s and eight dollars in the 1860s when sugar output increased fifteen-fold. Japanese laborers, who outnumbered Hawaiians and the Chinese after the 1870s, were paid a monthly wage of ten to fifteen dollars. These wages should be compared to the wage of fifty dollars per month of a common laborer on the U.S. mainland during the same time period.

Plantation workers not only received low wages but also were subject to fines. To "discipline" workers for violating the rules, planters devised an elaborate system of fines for almost every type of "violation": $5.00 for breaking a wagon through negligence, drunken brawling, and gambling; $2.00 for cutting a harness; $1.00 for insubordination; $0.50 for trespassing, neglecting duty, and drunkenness; and $0.25 for refusal to work as ordered. When fines failed to work, planters resorted to harsher punishments, such as beating, kicking, and whipping workers.[6]

To control their workers, planters also consciously maintained a racial and class hierarchy in the management of plantation. At the top of the food chain were white plantation managers and foremen, who supervised the Asian workers who lived in camps and worked in gangs segregated by ethnicity and nationality. In addition, planters applied a multilayered wage system to divide their workers. They paid different wage rates to different nationalities for the same work; for instance, Japanese cane cutters received 99 cents a day, while Filipino cane cutters got 69 cents. This divide-and-rule strategy succeeded in causing interethnic tensions and conflicts. In 1899, a riot broke out between Chinese and Japanese workers on the Kahuka Plantation on Oahu and resulted in the deaths of four Chinese and many wounded on both sides.

Asian workers nevertheless directed their discontent more toward the plantation owners and the abusive system. As the largest labor force in the industry, Japanese workers' resistance was most noticeable. They engaged in various forms of resistance to the harsh working conditions and cruel treatment. Some pretended to be sick, hoping to be released from work. Others tried to minimize the amount of work assigned to them. Many more deserted the plantation before finishing the term of their contract. However, most resorted to collective action in the form of strikes, demanding better pay and working conditions. The Lahaina Plantation workers' strike of 1900 forced the manager to institute a nine-hour workday and make a $500 payment to the relatives of each victim who died from a work-related accident. The Organic Act of 1900 established Hawaii as a territory of the United States and thus abolished the contract-labor system in the islands. The Spreckelsville Plantation strike led to the termination of all labor contracts. In 1900, more than twenty strikes involving 8,000 workers spread throughout the plantations. While most strikes were initiated mainly by Japanese workers, a few involved interethnic or interracial collaboration. On June 22, Chinese and Japanese workers on the Puehuehu Plantation jointly struck against the practice of wage retention, a vestige of their original labor contracts. In November, forty-three Japanese and Portuguese female field workers on the Kilauea Plantation demanded a wage increase from eight to ten dollars a month and succeeded. Labor-management conflict was further intensified after 1900.[7]

Korean immigrants were brought into Hawaiian sugar plantations to offset the more numerous and rebellious Japanese laborers. Between January 1903 and July 1905, more than 7,000 Koreans arrived in Hawaii on sixty-five separate ships. On many occasions they were used as strikebreakers when Japanese workers walked out. Koreans' willingness to participate in the labor actions was determined not only by the financial rewards offered to them but also by their animosity toward the Japanese, whose government had colonized Korea in 1905.[8] To replace the Japanese, Filipino workers were also brought to Hawaii. In 1909, they constituted only 1 percent of the plantation labor force. By the late 1920s, Filipino workers had become the largest ethnic group in the plantation labor force, followed by the Japanese. Their common experience as working-class laborers enabled Japanese and Filipino workers to look beyond ethnic differences and be united in their fight against the plantation owners. The interethnic union movement for the Japanese Federation of Labor and the Filipino Federation of Labor in the 1920 strike resulted in the formation of a new interracial union, the Hawaii Laborers' Association, embracing the working class of all racial and ethnic backgrounds.

Women were also part of the workforce in plantations. They represented 7 percent of all plantation workers in 1894 and 14 percent in 1920. Over 80 percent of them were Japanese. They were assigned to work in fields like the male laborers but were paid less. For example, in 1915 Japanese female workers were paid 55 cents per day, while Japanese male workers earned 78. Women also worked in camps washing laundry and operating boardinghouses.[9]

The difficult working conditions discouraged laborers from renewing their contracts. Chinese laborers left sugar cane plantations and became peddlers and merchants or went into rice farming either as owner-operators or as tenants. Many Japanese workers at the end of their contracts left the islands for Pacific port cities. Almost 34,000 Japanese went to California and the Pacific Northwest between 1902 and 1906. More than 30,000 Filipino also re-emigrated from Hawaii to the mainland in the 1920s and 1930s.[10]

Asian Immigrants as Miners and Railroad Workers

On the mainland United States, mining and railroad construction were the two occupations that were available to and sustained the early Asian immigrants (those who arrived in the United States between the mid-nineteenth century and early twentieth, especially the Chinese). As miners and railroad workers, Asian immigrants participated in the development of America's western frontier.

Reflecting the popular expectation of the Chinese, gold played a significant role in the lives of the early immigrants from China, and the majority of *gam san haak* (gold mountain guests) worked in the mining areas of California. On February 1, 1849, 44 Chinese resided in California. A year later the number had reached 791, and by the end of 1850 it had surpassed 4,000. In 1851, 2,400 to 2,700 Chinese arrived, and in 1852, the peak period of Chinese immigration, about 18,000 Chinese arrived in the Golden State, bringing the total Chinese population to 25,000. Within two years of the first wave of Chinese immigration peaking, the Chinese had penetrated every

FIGURE 3.2 Chinese gold miners during the California gold rush, ca. 1850. Courtesy National Archives and Records Administration.

mining district in California. Census statistics indicate that almost 100 percent of the Chinese in the continental United States lived in California in 1860, and 24,282 out of the total Chinese population of 34,935 worked as miners. In 1863, the peak of Chinese gold mining, 80 to 85 percent of the Chinese population in California was engaged in the practice.

Chinese gold mining activities generally followed a common pattern. The Chinese normally worked in claims abandoned by white miners: as the surface deposits were skimmed off and the white miners moved onto richer deposits elsewhere, the Chinese came to the foothills and reworked the gravel heaps of the old placer mines. Most Chinese mined placer claims, the cheapest of the three mining methods—placer, hydraulic, and quartz—in terms of operation costs due to its labor-intensive and low-technology orientation. They washed the gold-bearing dirt in a pan or rocker to let the heavier particles of gold settle at the bottom.

Chinese miners worked either for themselves or for Chinese companies. Especially during the early years, most worked as independent miners, but in groups of three or four for their own protection. However, by the late 1880s about one-third of Chinese miners worked as hired labor for white miners, who paid them $1.00 to $1.50 a day in the 1860s and $1.75 to $2.00 by the 1870s.¹¹ They often worked together in groups of a dozen or more, for the sake of self-protection. Their tools included shovels, picks, pans, and cradles. They built dams, ditches, and flumes to divert streams from their natural beds and then worked the streambeds. From California, Chinese miners followed the advance of the mining frontier into the Northwest, the Rocky Mountains, Idaho, Colorado, and the Southwest.

Studies on late nineteenth-century gold mining have recognized the contributions Chinese miners made to the development of the frontier West. First, Chinese mining complemented rather than competed with the work of white miners: the Chinese worked in the surface placer mines left by the white miners when the productivity of those mines had declined. Second, they paid their share of taxes—in the form of miner, property, and poll taxes and other assessments—yet received none of the services their tax dollars provided. Studies have found that the taxes levied on Chinese miners funded the education of the entire Golden State. Third, they contributed to national and local economies by purchasing mining equipment and claims and by being consumers of local produce.¹²

In addition to mining, the construction of the transcontinental railroad absorbed a large number of Chinese laborers, many of whom were former miners. After the end of the Civil War, the federal government could once again devote its attention to the construction of the transcontinental railroad. The eastern part of the railroad was contracted to the Union Pacific Railroad Company to build westward from the Missouri River, and the western part of the railroad, to be built eastward from Sacramento, was awarded to the Central Pacific Railroad Company, nicknamed Big Four as it was formed by four Sacramento merchants—Leland Stanford, Charles Crocker, Mark Hopkins, and C. P. Huntington.

These four young entrepreneurs encountered two big problems: the scarcity of both capital and labor. The U.S. Congress had partially solved the first problem by issuing government bonds and grants of public land along both sides of the projected railroad. The problem of labor seemed more severe. Available laborers in California were scant in the 1860s. Among those who were available for hire, most were white and slightly overage miners and more interested in gold mining.

In 1865, a suggestion was made to hire Chinese labor. In February 1865, fifty Chinese workers were hired by the Central Pacific Railroad as an experiment, largely for the purpose of frightening white laborers who had threatened to strike. The four entrepreneurs were impressed by the Chinese; Stanford described them as "quiet, peaceable, industrious, economical—ready and apt to learn all the different kinds of work required in railroad building."¹³ As the Chinese began to perform a variety of tasks—such as blasting, driving horses, handling rock, and digging with pick and shovel—and proved to be effective and reliable workers, the company began to hire more of them, many of whom had difficulty finding other jobs due to racial prejudice. By the end of 1865, there were

3,000 Chinese in the workforce. During the peak time of construction, the Central Pacific employed 12,000 Chinese, representing 90 percent of its entire workforce.

Few were aware of the dangerous and strenuous conditions the Chinese immigrant laborers had to endure—unreliable explosives, harsh Sierra Nevada winters, and monotonous digging and hauling. At a time when dynamite did not exist, nitroglycerin, recently invented by Swedish chemist Alfred Nobel, was very erratic and frightfully dangerous. Because of its low price and smoke-free properties, it was lavishly used by the Central Pacific. In one terrible explosion on April 17, 1866, six men—three whites and three Chinese—were blown away and killed. Such accidents were almost usual occurrences. When snow fell in December, the Chinese encampments were snowed under. They had to dig chimneys and air shafts and lived by lantern light, while huddling and freezing. They tunneled into the portals of work sites and the work continued, as the construction materials had to be lowered forty feet or more by steam hoist from the surface of the snow, and the waste from the digging was removed in reverse.

In addition to their uncomplaining work ethic, Chinese laborers were cheaper. In 1865, white unskilled laborers were paid thirty-five dollars a month plus board and lodging. The Chinese received the same sum in cash but provided their own food and lodging. Additionally, Chinese labor was also easier to manage. They were hired by groups of fifty to a hundred. In dealing with the company, each group furnished its own cooks, set up its own camp, and was represented by its own agent, usually an English-speaking Chinese. These agents received the wages of the entire gang in monthly lump sums and distributed earnings to the individual men after deducting the costs of food and debt.[14]

The completion of the transcontinental railroad in 1869 forced most Chinese railroad workers to become farm laborers in California, but many others had to migrate south and east, working on southern plantations or in booming industrial towns on the East Coast and in the Midwest.

Asian Indians also worked in railroad construction. Punjabis labored on the Western Pacific Railways in Northern California between 1903 and 1908. Two thousand Punjabis worked on a 700-mile road between Oakland and Salt Lake City, which later became Interstate 80. Most of the Punjabi Sikhs were single men who lived in bunkhouses that could hold forty to fifty people. They earned five cents less per hour than white workers. Like the Chinese, the Punjabi Sikh workers also provided their own food and lodging, cooking for themselves in collective cookhouses and living in bunkhouses.[15]

URBAN NICHE ECONOMY

The economic survival and success of Asian laborers in the late nineteenth and early twentieth centuries largely depended on a number of niche businesses. While the Chinese focused on the "four pillar" urban businesses of laundering, food processing and

FIGURE 3.3 Celebration of completion of the first transcontinental railroad at what is now Golden Spike National Historic Site, Promontory Summit, Utah, May 10, 1869. Courtesy National Park Service.

service, merchandizing, and sewing, the Japanese found their niche in producing and selling fresh vegetables and fruit and providing domestic services. At the same time, Korean, Asian Indian, and Filipino immigrants mostly worked in rural areas as farmhands or seasonal laborers; consequently, their economic lives will be discussed in a separate section. When economically excluded from the larger society, these ethnic enterprises had to rely on transnational ethnic networks in raising capital, procuring supplies, and recruiting employees.

Laundries

During the late nineteenth and early twenties centuries, the laundering business was a predominant occupation of the Chinese in the United States. The Chinese did not "by nature" gravitate into laundry businesses. Their niche began simply because of the shortage of women in the frontier West that rendered laundering a highly demanded service. After the 1870s, prejudice against Chinese immigrants effectively cut them out of the rest of the labor market. Persecuted and harassed, the Chinese could not find jobs and were forced to rely on their own resources. While they were excluded from the literal gold mines, they found an equally lucrative figurative gold mine in the city. They realized that in setting up laundries they did not have to seek out jobs in established industries or incur the risk of heavy capital investment. It is estimated that starting a hand laundry in the late nineteenth century required only about $75. The only needed tools for the business were a scrub board, soap, an iron, and an ironing board. Individuals would canvass a neighborhood, seek out a low-rent location, and open for business.

The first Chinese laundryman was an unsuccessful gold miner named Wah Lee, who hung a sign over his residence at Grant Avenue and Washington Street in San Francisco reading "Wash'ng and Iron'ng" in 1851.[16] With the success of his business, others followed, and the number of Chinese laundries in the city soon increased to 274 (providing 10 percent of the gainful employment among local Chinese) by 1860, 1,333 (12 percent) by 1870, 2,148 (10 percent) by 1880, and 1,924 (13.4 percent) by 1900.[17]

For New York City, there are no statistics available on Chinese laundries in the 1870s. when the Chinese community began to take shape. In 1888, however, according to an article written by Wong Chin Foo (the Chinese activist in New York covered in chapter 2), there were about ten thousand Chinese living in metropolitan New York and "probably a little over two thousand" Chinese "laundries in the city of New York alone, some eight hundred or nine hundred in Brooklyn, and about one hundred and fifth in Jersey City. . . . Each laundry has from one to five men working in it, and they all make money."[18] In the 1910 U.S. census, 3,175 males and 45 females were counted in the categories of "launderers," "laundry operatives," and "laundry owners, officials, and managers" in New York City, and most of them can be assumed to have been Chinese. Most observers of the Chinese community in New York City estimated that from the late 1880s to the 1930s there were seven to eight thousand Chinese laundrymen in the city.[19]

In Chicago, the country's second largest city since 1890, Chinese laundries also grew in number from 37 in 1879 to 199 in 1883, 313 in 1893, 368 in 1913, and 528 in 1918.[20] In St. Louis, another midwestern city, 6 Chinese laundries first appeared in the city's directory in 1873; the number soon climbed to 76 in 1888 and reached its peak of 165 in 1929, on the eve of the Great Depression.[21]

The development of Chinese laundries in American urban centers displays a typical pattern. The laundries were first concentrated in the downtown business district and then were later spread throughout the city. This geographical dispersion was partly a result of the self-governance of the Chinese community, which took measures to prevent unnecessary competition among the laundries. The Chinese *huiguans* (district associations) and the On Leong Merchants and Laborers Association, the de facto Chinese community government in the United States prior to the 1960s (see detailed discussion in the next chapter), established the rule of "one Chinese laundry within the perimeter of a mile." Any Chinese who violated this edict could encounter unexpected catastrophe if not death. More importantly, the Chinese laundrymen followed the fundamental rule of economic supply and demand; they would open a new laundry wherever there was a demand or wherever a Chinese laundry did not yet exist. Since the main clientele of the

> **PORTRAYALS OF CHINESE LAUNDRIES**
>
> Many Chinese laundrymen were illiterate, and they invented a way to keep their books. An interview in Paul C. P. Siu's study revealed how this process worked.
>
> > I don't know how the laundry became a Chinese enterprise in this country. But I think they just learned it from each other. After all, laundry work is not difficult; it requires no high skill. All one has to do is watch how others do it. It would not take long either.
> >
> > In the old days, some of those fellows were really ignorant though. They did not know even how to write down numbers. When a bundle of laundry was done, he had to put down the amount charged for the work. Being so illiterate, he could not write the numbers. He had a way though and what a way! See, he would draw a circle as big as half dollar coin to represent a half dollar, and a circle as big as a dime for a dime, and so on. When the customers came in to call for their laundry, they would catch on to the meaning of the circles and pay accordingly. It is indeed laughable.
>
> *Source*: Paul C. P. Siu, *Chinese Laundryman: A Study of Social Isolation* (New York: New York University Press, 1987), 52.

Chinese laundry were non-Chinese, it was only natural for the Chinese laundries to spread out across the city to meet the demand.[22]

The Chinese laundry shop was a place not merely for work but also for sleeping and cooking. According to Siu, the typical interior arrangement of the Chinese laundry consisted of four parts. First was the front section. It usually occupied one-third of the space of the house, functioning as the office-workshop of the laundryman. In this section, the laundryman ironed and labeled laundry and waited on his customers. Here he kept the necessities for his business: the ironing bed, the abacus, the laundry shelves, the lock counter, and the secret cash drawer. Second, immediately behind the curtained doorway at the center of the house, usually between the laundry shelves, were the living quarters. Third, the drying room was located in the center or rear part of the house. In the center of the room was placed an old-fashioned coal stove, used for drying the wet laundry. About a dozen strong wires were strung across in parallel lines to hang the wet laundry. Finally, there was the rear section, where almost all the laundryman's machines were located, including the washing machine, washing sink, and steam boiler.[23]

This physical arrangement of a Chinese hand laundry in the late nineteenth and early twentieth centuries was not only typical in the major urban Chinese communities of San Francisco, New York, and Chicago but also common in remote small towns where the Chinese population was scarce. In Kirksville, a rural town located in the northeastern corner of Missouri, two Chinese men, Young Kee and Charlie Young, opened a hand laundry in 1913. They worked in the laundry and lived behind their shop.[24] Clearly, to

LABOR

SAM WAH LAUNDRY IN ST. LOUIS

The Sam Wah Laundry is on Laclede Avenue, a few hundred feet east of Newstead and a turn north through a door into St. Louis, a half century ago.

Inside—after passing under a rubber tree plant that grows westward along a system of ceiling hooks and jerry-built supports, a plant that soars out of its pot near the wall and achieves the form of a dragon—is the shop of the brothers Gee Sam Wah and Gee Hong, long out of Canton, China. Wah is 88 years old, Gee is 86.

With its worn wooden washtubs, its drum dryer powered by a noisy and archaic direct current motor, its naked light bulbs and sagging wooden floors, the Sam Wah Laundry seems ready to stand for a spot in the Smithsonian Institution, or at least the Museum of Westward Expansion, this paint-peeling and dusty memorial to a part of the Chinese role in American history.

. . . The Gee brothers live and work in Spartan quarters. They apparently sleep on mats near an old stove. The walls of the laundry are adorned in places by an odd mixture of pictures and photographs—religious art, mostly Jesus Christ at various ages, a newspapers photo of Chairman Mao and former President Gerald R. Ford shaking hands, 1962 calendars from the Canton Market and the Wing Sing Chong Co., Inc., both of San Francisco, and a glossy photo of a standing room hockey crowd at the Checkerdome. There are numerous snapshots of weddings and assembled families.

Gee Sam Wah still uses an antique hand atomizer when he irons shirts. He has had the atomizer since his days in Canton, which probably means at least 80 years or more. Despite the appearance of disorganization, regular customers do not need a ticket, said Wah. The launderers have a system of numbering the bundles and remembering the faces. They do not forget regular customers, and no one, apparently, has had reason to complain. Not-so-regular customers get a ticket. Everything is lettered in Chinese.

Gee Hong and Gee Wah, by western standards, are certifiable workaholics. Even in their 80s, the two are up ironing and washing early in the morning and are at it still late at night, say longtime customers.

They had a television set, presumably for relaxation, but it has been broken and unused for some time. There is also a sickly-looking radio on the premises.

Source: John M. McGuire, "Chinese Laundry Being Pressed," *St. Louis Post-Dispatch*, November 12, 1978, 3G.

---

minimize costs and maximize savings, Chinese laundry operators had to work in crammed quarters and sometimes under humid and unhealthy conditions.

For the wife of a laundryman, life was not easier than that of her husband. Her home was in the back of the laundry, where she slept, cooked, and tended her children. The quarters were humid and dim in all seasons. When she was not busy with her domestic chores, she was expected to help with the laundry work. Her daily life was characterized by long hours, drudgery, and intense loneliness. The only people she saw were customers who brought in their parcels and reclaimed them when they were finished. As depicted in Maxine Hong Kingston's *The Woman Warrior*, Brave Orchid, wife of a New York laundryman, worked at the laundry from six thirty in the morning until midnight. She shifted her baby from an ironing table to a shelf between packages. The dust from socks and handkerchiefs choked her and made her cough every day.[25] The wives of laundrymen were quickly worn out from being overworked, and many suffered physical weariness and emotional stress.

Restaurants

Like laundries, restaurants were one of the most important businesses for the Chinese in the United States. Initially, Chinese restaurants started as a service for the bachelor communities of Chinese immigrants in isolated ranches, logging camps, mining towns, and other areas where Chinese men and women were willing to cook. When the eating places that the Chinese had set up for themselves soon attracted a number of outsiders, the Chinese realized that restaurants were profitable business enterprises.

The earliest Chinese restaurants appeared in San Francisco soon after the first arrival of the Chinese in 1849. The Macao and Woosung Restaurant, arguably the first Chinese restaurant in the United States, was located in San Francisco's Chinatown and was opened by immigrant Norman Asing in 1849. It was followed by the Balcony of Golden Joy and Delight. These early Chinese restaurants offered flavorful fricassees and inexpensive one-dollar meal prices to attract the general population.[26] The popularity of Chinese food was recognized by the local business community as well as by residents. Travel guides encouraged visitors to try the Chinese food nicknamed "Chow Chows," probably deriving from the Cantonese pronunciation of "chow" for "stir fry." A white miner in 1851 commented, "The best eating houses in San Francisco are kept by Celestials and conducted Chinese fashion."[27]

When the economic recession in the 1870s and the anti-Chinese violence on the West Coast chased many Chinese out of the region and dispersed them to the East Coast, the Midwest, and the South, they continued to invest in the niche restaurant business, making it one of the primary trades for the Chinese in the country until today. In the 1890s, Chinese restaurants sprouted across the United States. In New York, six Chinese restaurants appeared in 1885. By 1903, more than one hundred Chinese restaurants were in business in Lower Manhattan.[28] In the Midwest and the South, Chinese eateries appeared in cities and towns where the Chinese population congregated.[29]

The invention of chop suey has been believed to be responsible for the widespread appearance of Chinese restaurants.[30] Generally, two versions of the genesis of chop suey have been circulated. One is associated with the Gold Rush in California. A group of drunken and hungry white miners broke into a Chinese restaurant in a mining town, operated by two Chinese brothers who had just closed the shop for the day. Afraid of the physically much larger white miners, the brothers gathered the leftover rice, meat, and vegetables, fried them together, and presented the food to the hungry miners. When asked about the name of the dish, the brothers wittily referred to it as "chop suey," which in Cantonese means "miscellaneous things." The other version relates to the 1896 visit to the United States of the Chinese viceroy of Zhili (the provinces around Beijing) Li Hongzhang. The degree of excitement among Americans over Li's visit paralleled that of Nixon's China visit in 1972; throngs of media personnel hovered over all of Li's activities during his stay. Reports claim that Li could not eat any Western food other than what his four chefs who accompanied him on the trip prepared and that when he entertained his hosts with Chinese food, one of his favorite dishes was called "chop suey."[31]

Both versions are symbolic and reflect some level of historical truth. The California story indicates the humble origin of chop suey as a dish of cheap ingredients for a working-class clientele. The East Coast version reflects Americans' curiosity about the "exotica" of Chinese food, and the association of chop suey with a high-ranking Chinese official denotes the authenticity of chop suey as a Chinese dish.

The genesis of the Chinese dish is not as crucial to us as the fact that the practical Chinese quickly capitalized on this golden opportunity. Consequently, the Chinese restaurant business witnessed rapid growth from the 1910s onward, and an increasing number of Chinese became restaurant workers and proprietors. The 1920 census revealed that 11,438—or nearly one-fourth—of the 45,614 gainfully employed Chinese in the United States as a whole were cooks, waiters, and/or restaurant operators.[32] In the 1930s, 6 percent of Chinese adult males in California and 20 to 30 percent of them in the East Coast cities worked in the restaurant business. By the late 1940s, around 4,300 Chinese restaurants were found in the continental United States.[33]

The flexibility of chop suey, which varied from region to region based on local tastes and available ingredients, enabled it to become a signature dish of Chinese food in America. There was no fixed recipe. A 1903 *New York Times* article noticed the flexibility of chop suey and commented that "no two cooks make it exactly alike. Everything seems to depend on the mushrooms and the mysterious black or brown sauce that is poured over the stew. . . . That sauce they put on it is a powerful steadier."[34]

More importantly, the modest price of chop suey made it competitive in the food service industry. Bayard Taylor, a young reporter for the *New York Tribune*, was impressed by the one-dollar meals in all three of San Francisco's Chinese restaurants—Kong-Sung's House near the water, Whang-Tong's on Sacramento Street, and Tong-Ling's on Jackson Street—when he visited the city in 1850.[35] In the 1900s, many chop suey shops in New York City served a dish for only 15 cents. The 15-cent chop suey dish was very accessible to a large clientele from a wide range of social and racial backgrounds. It not only

FIGURE 3.4 Chin F. Foin and wife, 1906. Chin F. Foin was arguably the first and most exemplary modernized Chinese restaurateur in Chicago. Courtesy National Archives, Great Lakes Region, Chicago, Illinois.

was served to African Americans in Harlem but also became a meal on Christmas for the Jewish in New York.[36]

While chop suey has been conventionally regarded as the mainstay of Chinese American cuisine, more recent studies have also pointed to the development of upscale Chinese fine dining at the turn of the century. The Chinese in metropolises on the East Coast and Midwest led the trend (although San Francisco had the earliest establishments of fine Chinese food, the rampant anti-Chinese violence in the 1870s and the 1906 earthquake and fire halted this development); Chinese restaurateurs in Chicago in particular were the pioneers of Chinese fine dining, as indicated in the sidebar. The lavishly decorated and furnished upscale Chinese restaurants were established as early as 1903 in New York and 1905 in Chicago, while the first full-service restaurant (as opposed to the traditional chop suey shops) opened outside Chinatown in San Francisco in the late 1920s.[37]

Grocery Stores

The grocery business ranked as a distant third occupation for Chinese immigrants before the 1940s, although it was one of the major enterprises of the Chinese in some southern and western states. Chinese grocery stores provided ingredients for cooking and other

> ### CHIN F. FOIN, A MODERN CHINESE RESTAURATEUR IN CHICAGO
>
> In Chicago, there were about 250 Chinese restaurants throughout the city by the 1920s. Among them quite a few were large, trendy, and upscale ones, characterized with sufficient capital, lavish interior décor, expensive furnishing, large seating capacity, and both Chinese and non-Chinese clients. Their owners were men with vision, a taste of elegance, and a sense of modernity. Chin F. Foin, for example, was arguably the first and most exemplary modernized Chinese restaurateur in Chicago. Born in Xinning county, Guangdong, in China in 1877, Chin F. Foin came to America in 1892 as a fifteen-year-old teenager, and arrived in Chicago in 1895. Young and adaptable, he picked up English and American ways of life quickly. It was believed that he could speak German fluently, and lived a life rivaling that of wealthy and trendy American businessmen. He rode horseback, owned an automobile when they first became available to consumers, joined an exclusive social club, and had connections with both Chinese diplomats and influential Chicagoans. By 1905, in addition to the grocery store Wing Chong Hai Company, he also owned King Yen Lo Restaurant at 277–279 South Clark Street, one of the finest Chinese American restaurants in Chicago at the turn of the century. Located in the original old Chinatown at the corner of Clark and Van Buren Streets, the restaurant was furnished with sumptuous furniture made in China. The wooden tables had mother-of-pearl decorations and were topped with marble, a popular style then. King Yen Lo was patronized by visiting Chinese officials and other prominent Chinese, as well as the upper-class Chicago socialites.
>
> *Source:* Testimony of Ham Sam, September 18, 1905, CCCF, file 374, cited in Huping Ling, *Chinese Chicago: Race, Transnational Migration and Community since 1870* (Stanford, CA: Stanford University Press, 2012), 70–72.

goods for the sustenance of Chinese communities. Unlike Chinese restaurants, grocery stores found their clientele primarily among Chinese and other Asian immigrants, and they were mostly located in Chinatowns and Asian communities.

The operation of Chinese grocery businesses varied according to size. A large Chinese grocery store might have had between ten and twenty partners each investing about $1,000 in the business and sold goods worth from $50,000 to $150,000. The largest shareholder and organizer of the business normally serving as the manager.[38] The larger firms carried not only Chinese groceries but also general merchandise. Sun Fat Company, known as the Chinese Bargain Store, located at 2536 Main Street in San Francisco, was a merchandise house selling Chinese dry goods. It was established at the beginning of the twentieth century and reorganized in 1918. By 1921, the company had nine partners, seven of whom actively participated in the operation of the business. Of the seven active partners, one served as the manager, with a share of $1,500, one as the treasurer, also with a share of $1,500, and the others as the bookkeeper and salesmen, with shares ranging from $500 to $1,000. The manager received a monthly salary of $70, the treasurer

FIGURE 3.5 Employees of Kong Wo Sang Co., a Chinese store selling general merchandise in New Castle, California, 1926. Courtesy National Archives–Pacific Sierra Region, San Bruno, California.

and bookkeeper each $65, and the rest of the members $60. All company members lived on the second floor over the store, where they ate and slept. A cook was paid $60 a month.

Similarly, Tong Sang Company, located at 383–385 Ninth Street, Oakland, was established in the late nineteenth century selling general merchandise. In 1923, it had eighteen partners, each holding a share of $1,000. Among them, eleven were active members, including a manager, a buyer, a broker, and eight salesmen. The company had average annual sales of $150,000, the profit from which allowed the company to pay each member a yearly bonus of $100. Each active member was paid a salary of $50 a month. The company hired a cook at a cost of $45 a month to cook meals for all the members. It also employed a white man to drive the company-owned truck for its delivery service.

Different from the above two firms, the Henry Company of 670 Commercial Street in San Francisco was a wholesale business dealing with imports and exports. As of 1932, it had eighteen partners, six of whom were active. This included a manager with a share of $2,000, a president with a share of $4,000, and four salesmen with shares ranging from $500 to $2,500. The company paid its members salaries from $55 (salesmen) to $75 (president and manager) a month. One member slept on the premises of the firm, and the rest only ate there and shared cooking responsibility.[39]

In addition to retailing and wholesaling, larger businesses often doubled as banks or brokerages to their customers and kinsmen and offered lodging for employees and transitory visitors. Such multiple functions of the Chinese businesses were especially evident in Chicago, a center of distributing merchandise in the heartland of the country, and a hub of land, water, and rail (and later air) transportation.[40]

While the larger firms pooled capital and manpower together—with each member having well-defined responsibilities and receiving a regular salary—many smaller Chinese stores were run as family businesses with unpaid family members supplying the labor needed for keeping the stores in operation. As wives of grocers, the women worked along with their husbands, packing, stocking, and selling goods. As indicated in Connie Young Yu's family history, Chin Shee, Yu's great-grandmother, arrived in San Francisco in 1876 to join her husband, a successful Chinese dry-food store merchant. She lived in the rear of the store, where she bore six children. She not only took care of her children but also helped with her husband's business. All the hard work and responsibilities, Yu has noted, made her face appear "careworn" in middle age.[41]

Most of the small grocers knew very little English, barely enough to tell customers the prices of their goods. As a Hawaiian Chinese girl, Lily Chan, noted, "They [her parents] did not know the English language, but they know enough as to keep a store."[42] Their businesses usually made only a minimal profit, for their clientele, mainly Chinese, were a marginalized minority. Their diligence, frugality, and shrewdness, however, enabled them to survive in the difficult environment.

Chinese women were not always passive and unpaid laborers in family business; some women of energy and ability even had shares in businesses and became the business partners of their husbands. Gee Guock Shee is a good example of a strong and capable early Chinese businesswoman. She was born in San Francisco in 1873 and married Yee Ho Wo in San Mateo, California, when she was eighteen years old. After her son was old enough to be left alone, she joined the family business, Yee Hing & Co., a store selling general merchandise. Being a woman, her name and interest were not mentioned in the business partners list, although she had an equal share of $500 in the company. Jointly having the largest share in Yee Hing & Co. among all the partners, she and her husband were virtually the proprietors of the firm. As a saleswoman and cashier, she played a vital role. Every day, she stood behind the counter looking after the business, took care of the money that came in, and had her husband enter the money into books. Apparently, she served as a manager, and her husband was the bookkeeper in the business. Gee Guock Shee was also responsible for the monetary transactions of the firm. She went to the San Mateo Bank regularly to deposit or withdraw money for the firm, though always accompanied by one of the male members of the company. Without any formal education, she was able to become a successful businesswoman. She earned the respect of many prominent people in San Mateo, including San Mateo Bank cashier Henry W. Hagan and city marshal M. F. Boland.[43]

Garment Shops

Apart from the laundry, restaurant, and grocery businesses, garment making proved to be a vital profession for early Chinese immigrant women. As was the case with Jewish immigrant women, their work began as a sewing business at home. In the late nineteenth and early twentieth centuries, married Chinese immigrant women sewed or mended clothes for Chinese bachelors at home to supplement their family income. The immigration documents from the Office of the Collector of Customs at the San Francisco Port reveal that sewing was a common occupation for Chinese women at this time. Low How See, one of the earliest Chinese women in San Francisco, worked as a seamstress. "I worked in my room," she told the immigration official when she was called to the office of the Collector of Customs as witness for the entry of a Chinese woman on March 26, 1896. "My friends who know me well bring me work to do to my room."[44] Other married Chinese women—Chun Shee, Jow Shee, and Tai See—also indicated that they were seamstresses when asked about their occupation.[45]

Some even ran a tailor's shop in which both husband and wife were involved. The oldest Chinese woman in Butte, Montana, reminisced,

> I made all my pin money sewing dozens upon dozens of [loose-fitting Chinese-style] suits for the merchandise stores. I was always busy. The suits even went to men outside of Butte: they would send in their orders. As soon as I made a dozen, I would start on another. Practically all of the women of the community sewed like I did, or mended. We had all we could do.
>
> I made two kinds of suits; washable ones for every day and woolen ones for special occasions. I never saw the men but my husband took orders at our store. He wrote down the measurements; I made the garments and sent them back through my husband. I saved several thousand dollars doing this until the Revolution [in 1911].[46]

While some women set up a tailoring business at home, more sought employment at a garment shop. Mrs. C's mother went to a sewing factory in Boston to work for ten years after her children grew older.[47] Late nineteenth- and early twentieth-century garment shops varied by size. The smaller ones had only a couple of workers. For instance, Sun Fat Company, a dry goods store in San Francisco (discussed earlier in this section), also hired two women employees, Jow Shee and Wong Shee, to operate its sewing machines. Unlike the male employees of the company who were paid a monthly salary of $60, Jow Shee and Wong Shee were paid by the piece.[48] Apparently, Sun Fat Company not only sold Chinese groceries but also owned a small garment factory. Many of the garment shops consisted of a dozen seamstresses, occupying one floor in a building crowded with sewing machines. The women were paid by the piece at the very low rate of a few cents each garment. Mrs. S reminisced about her mother's experience as a seamstress in San Francisco: "My mother and some other ladies did sewing in a place. They [contractors] rented a store and set up machines. About a dozen women worked there. My mother worked during the day. She came back to cook lunch for us. The hours were very flexible.... They were paid by piece. The pay was low, but it's still something."[49]

This "flexibility" over timekeeping was an important factor in attracting women to work in garment shops despite the low pay and poor working conditions. This remains a common characteristic of today's major garment industry in New York, Los Angeles, and the San Francisco Bay Area, which primarily employs Asian immigrant women.[50] In order to fulfill their household responsibilities while simultaneously supplementing the family income, these women considered the "flexibility" of garment shops as compensation for the low pay. The sewing business, like the restaurant business, originated from practices linked to meeting the basic needs of the bachelors who predominated among Chinese immigrants. Money made from sewing became a necessary part of the family income. Scholars have noted the importance of the economic contributions made by Asian American married women at a time when most married American women did not belong to the paid labor force.[51]

Not only did married Chinese women sew as a business, but Chinese prostitutes were also forced to sew in their free time during the day. Lucie Cheng Hirata's study revealed that prostitutes in nineteenth-century California were assigned to sewing and other forms of work during the day while they had to hawk their bodies at night.[52]

Like other ethnic women in the garment industry, Chinese women garment workers also attempted to unionize to improve their working conditions. Records show that they engaged in strikes in the 1930s. The most publicized strike of Chinese women workers came in early 1938 when the Chinese Ladies Garment Workers Union selected San Francisco's National Dollar Stores as its target. When the strike began, the National Dollar Stores paid its Chinese garment women workers between $4 and $16 per week; union wages for the same work ranged from $19 to $30.[53] In November 1937, the workers presented their demand for better pay to their employers but failed to secure concessions. Disgruntled by the intransigence of the owners, workers organized the International Ladies Garment Workers Union (ILGWU) Local 341, known as the Chinese Ladies Garment Workers Union. This event indicated that at least by 1937 Chinese women garment workers had organized in an independent local union chapter and had taken collective action, as opposed to the conventional view of Chinese women being invisible in the American union movement. When further negotiations produced no compromise, the 108 Chinese women workers walked out on February 26, 1938. With the moral as well as financial support of the ILGWU, the strikers sustained thirteen weeks of picketing and won some concessions from their employer. The agreement signed on June 10 guaranteed a 5 percent increase in weekly wages, a $14 per week minimum wage, and paid holidays.[54]

Japanese Green Businesses

While most Japanese were employed in agriculture (to be discussed in the next section), wholesale and retail trading formed the second major occupation for them and domestic service the third. Over 88 percent of the working Japanese were employed in these three sectors in the 1930s. Los Angeles, San Francisco, and San Diego in California, Seattle in Washington, and Portland in Oregon constituted the major Japanese population centers in the United States between the 1880s and 1940s. In these cities, Japanese small businesses survived and succeeded, largely depending on their engagement in the niche business of market garden produce and reliance on ethnic networks that provided initial capital, procurements, and laborers.

Most Japanese immigrants entered the United States through San Francisco. Consequently, the city became the first large Japanese population center. In 1890, there were 590 Japanese immigrants recorded in San Francisco, 184 in Alameda County, and 51 in Sacramento County. These early arrivals worked for the railroad or in domestic service; many also worked on farms in the Vacaville area of Solano County. By 1900, the Japanese immigrants began to move to other parts of the state, while the above northern counties still held the largest share of the Japanese population. Their numbers had grown to 1,781 in San Francisco, 1,209 in Sacramento County, and 1,149 in Alameda County. In addition, Monterey County had 710, Fresno County 598, San Joaquin County 313, Santa Clara County 284, Contra Costa County 276, and Santa Cruz County 235.

By 1910, the major Japanese population centers had shifted to Southern California. Two factors contributed to the population move southward. One was the rapid development of the Los Angeles area during the Southern California boom era; the other was the San Francisco earthquake in 1906. Los Angeles County alone had more Japanese than did any other state. By 1920, the Japanese population of Los Angeles County more than doubled, increasing to 19,911, more than three times as many as the next most populous county, Sacramento, with 5,800. By 1940, 36,866, or nearly 30 percent of the total Japanese population in the United States, resided in Los Angeles County, and almost two-thirds of these, or 23,321, lived in the city of Los Angeles.[55]

An overwhelming majority of Japanese American retailers and wholesalers hired Japanese employees. In 1941, about 36 percent of all employed Japanese were self-

FIGURE 3.6 A high school girl of Japanese ancestry assisting her family in a strawberry field, Mission San Jose, California, May 5, 1942. Courtesy National Archives and Records Administration.

employed, among whom 47 percent were male.[56] The Japanese American retailers and wholesalers primarily sold Japanese-grown crops. This urban-rural and small entrepreneurial-agricultural alliance has been regarded as the key factor in Japanese American economic success in Los Angeles, as John Modell points out that "agriculture was the foundation of much of the enterprise and prosperity" for the Los Angeles Japanese.[57] This statement is applicable to all the Japanese ethnic economy on the West Coast from San Diego to Seattle.

San Francisco and its adjacent counties formed the second largest Japanese American population center. In 1940, there were over 5,000 Japanese in San Francisco city, over 5,000 in Alameda, and more than 1,000 in San Mateo. Because of San Francisco's cultural primacy, the Nihonmachi, or Japantown, in San Francisco was one of the most colorful and dynamic Japanese ethnic urban centers. It has consistently hosted the headquarters of national organizations such as the Japanese Association and the Japanese American Citizens League.[58] In addition, San Francisco is noted as the city where Issei small businesses were most heavily concentrated prior to World War II.[59]

The real second city for Japanese Americans was Seattle. It had almost 7,000 Japanese residents in 1940, along with 2,700 in surrounding King County and 2,000 more in nearby Pierce County. A 1935 survey on Japanese occupations in Seattle indicated that 45 percent of the 2,867 ethnic Japanese worked in various small businesses and 31 percent in domestic and personal service, most of whom worked in hotels.[60] Japanese entrepreneurship in Seattle exemplifies the survival and success story of the Japanese urban communities. Quintard Taylor's study on Japanese in Seattle from 1890 to 1940 lists 3 banks, 95 hotels, 80 restaurants, 81 fruit and grocery stores, 47 clothing stores, 3 movie theaters, 15 hospitals and clinics, and 7 drugstores in the Nihonmachi were operated by Japanese Americans serving a predominantly white clientele in 1916. By 1935, despite the Great Depression, Japanese Americans still ran 183 hotels, 148 grocery stores, 39 "American" restaurants, and 24 Japanese restaurants. Taylor attributes the Japanese entrepreneurial success to the concentration of Japanese banks in Seattle offering a rotating credit system to provide venture capital, and the Seattle Japanese green grocers' links with nearby Japanese truck farmers, who controlled 16,000 acres in western Washington.[61]

Portland, Oregon, constituted probably the fourth largest urban Japanese community. By 1909, there were 97 Japanese businesses in Oregon, including 14 Western-style restaurants, 13 bathhouses, 12 hotels and boardinghouses, 11 Japanese restaurants, 10 barbershops, and 8 grocery stores, mostly located in Portland. Meanwhile, the Portland Japanese population rapidly increased from 20 in 1890 to 1,189 in 1900 and 1,461 in 1910.[62] In 1920, about one-half of the 4,151 Japanese residing in Oregon lived in Portland and mostly worked as merchants, lodging house proprietors, restaurant owners, tailors, shoemakers, dyers, cleaners, factory workers, or farmhands.[63]

Domestic Services

Domestic service was the third largest occupation of Japanese immigrants. Studies show three kinds of Japanese male domestics, including live-in servants or "schoolboys," day workers, and domestic workers employed in restaurants and Japanese-owned businesses. Many Japanese students entered the United States as "Japanese schoolboys." The term was reportedly coined by a Mrs. Reid, who enrolled some Japanese students in her boarding school in Belmont, California. These students paid for their tuition, room, and board by working in the kitchen and doing other chores.[64] Later on, the term applied to any live-in servants whether they attended school or not. In fact, the work itself was a good education. The new immigrants learned English and American customs. They traded their labor for free room and board, along with a nominal weekly wage of $1.50 a week in 1900. In comparison, professional servants earned $15 to $40 a month. During the peak of Japanese male immigration (1904–1907), more than 4,000 Japanese were employed as schoolboys in San Francisco.[65]

The second type of domestics was day workers who cleaned houses, cooked meals, washed laundry, and tendered yards and gardens for daily pay. They usually came from the same prefectures in Japan and lived in boardinghouses ran by Japanese. By 1910, the U.S. Immigration Commission counted 12,000 to 15,000 Japanese in domestic service in the western part of the country.[66] There were 163 Japanese day work firms listed in the 1913 San Francisco city directory.[67] The third type of domestic workers was those who were employed in restaurants and Japanese-owned businesses.

Japanese women likewise worked as domestic workers. Among the Asian immigrant women, Issei women were probably the pioneers in the trade. They arrived in the United States between 1915 and 1924, mostly as "picture brides" who immigrated to America to join their husbands, whom they knew only by pictures sent home. They found jobs through personal referrals by Japanese churches, businesses, and social organizations. Issei women entered domestic service work by one of two routes. Some began as apprentices, an equivalent of the schoolboys, and were even called "schoolgirl." Typically an Issei woman worked in a schoolgirl job soon after her arrival and before the birth of her first child. Their employers provided training in housekeeping and American cooking, while they received only nominal wages of $5 a month. The second group entered the field of domestic service as part-time day workers after the arrival of children, when family expenses exceeded income. Even Nisei women who were born and grew up in America also entered domestic work because of limited opportunities in the labor market.[68]

NICHE IN AGRICULTURE

While nearly 90 percent of Chinese dwelled in urban America by the 1940s, most Japanese, Korean, Asian Indian, and Filipino immigrants on the Pacific Coast worked in agriculture. Like the Chinese who established an ethnic economy in urban centers by carving out niche businesses, Asian Americans in agriculture also found niche products that enabled them to survive and even thrive. Among the Asian farming population, the Japanese made the most noticeable contributions.

Although Chinese immigrants of the late nineteenth and early twentieth centuries have commonly been perceived as gold miners, railroad builders, laborers, entrepreneurs, laundrymen, and waiters, six to seven thousand of them, about 10 to 15 percent of the Chinese population in California in the late nineteenth century, were tenant farmers and truck gardeners (vegetable growers for market) located mainly in the Sacramento–San Joaquin Valley area. As truck gardening requires relatively little capital and English-speaking ability, it attracted Chinese immigrants; the number of Chinese gardeners kept up with or even surpassed the rate of population increase among Chinese in the state as a whole. Chinese gardeners also became a face-to-face link between the Chinese and the whites and between the urban and rural Chinese populations.[69]

Unlike the Chinese who primarily relied on niche businesses in urban areas, the Japanese immigrant communities established their economic base in agriculture by the 1910s. During the 1910s and 1920s, Japanese farmers grew rice in Northern California. A large number of Japanese were engaged in the farming, distributing, and retailing of rice during this period. Japanese farmers were also very much involved in experimenting with various strains of rice. In the Central Valley and Southern California, they established truck farming where they produced strawberries, grapes, and tree fruits.

By the 1940s, more than one-half of Japanese males were employed in agriculture, forestry, and fishing. Los Angeles County alone had 36,866 Japanese, one-third of the total Japanese American population in 1940–126,947.[70] Eiichiro Azuma's study of Issei Japanese notes that Japanese farmers in California, as well as those in most western states, discovered niche crops that white farmers tended to neglect, such as asparagus, berries, cantaloupes, celery, onions, and potatoes, and the cultivation of niche crops contributed to their population growth and economic success during the first decades of the twentieth century.[71] Leonard Bloom and Ruth Riemer's study indicates a similar pattern: the highest percentage cash crops grown by Japanese American farmers in Los Angeles County in 1941 included celery, peas, spinach, beets, broccoli, radishes, peppers, snap beans, strawberries, turnips, cauliflower, lettuce, green onions, green lima beans, eggplant, romaine, summer, squash, cucumbers, cabbage, and carrots (in order of percentage of total acreage cultivated).[72]

According to John Modell, the Japanese dominated the production and marketing of most of the fresh green vegetables in the Los Angeles area. They organized their produce and flower industries vertically, in which all operations were owned and operated by Japanese, from raising the plants to retail sales. The City Market of Los Angeles, a highly organized central market, hosted most Japanese businesses in the 1930s. It has been estimated that the total annual wholesale produce volume for all Japanese firms was $25 million.[73] Japanese farmers in California produced more than one-half of all artichokes, cauliflower, celery, cucumber, garlic, onion, and snap beans, and more than one-fourth of the asparagus, cabbage, cantaloupe, carrots, lettuce, and lima beans consumed in the state. In addition, they also produced strawberries, apples, peaches, sugar beets, nursery stock, and a major share of the business in cut flowers.[74]

Agriculture provided the Japanese farmers an opportunity to rise economically. They could use their savings to lease land as tenant farmers and eventually buy land as owners.

Many also opened up new lands with their labor-intensive and high-yield style of farming. Although the alien land laws in California in 1913 and in Washington in 1921 prohibited "aliens ineligible for citizenship"—namely, Chinese, Japanese, Koreans, and Asian Indians—from owning land, Japanese farmers, as well as other Asian farmers, managed to own land by vesting the title or lease in the name of their American-born children.[75] By 1940, more than 6,000 farms were operated by Japanese in the three Pacific Coast states.[76]

Like their earlier Chinese counterparts who had formed fishing villages in such places as the Monterey Bay region of California as early as the 1850s and worked in salmon canneries in Oregon, Washington, British Columbia, and Alaska in the summer, many Japanese fishermen fished along the Pacific Coast from Baja California in the south to Alaska in the north. They also worked in the canned salmon industry in Alaska every summer.[77] In Seattle, the second city for Japanese Americans, thousands of Japanese were hired in canneries, earning monthly wages ranging from $71.50 to $80.00.[78]

Compared to the more numerous Japanese farmers, Korean and Asian Indian farmers were much fewer in number. Most Korean tenant farmers worked in the San Joaquin Valley, the Sacramento–San Joaquin Delta, and the Sacramento Valley, where they grew fruit, rice, and other crops. Asian Indian farmers were scattered, except for two concentrations in the Imperial Valley and Coachella Valley in Southern California, where they raised cotton, cantaloupes, and lettuce.[79]

Karen Isaksen Leonard's study on the Punjabi Mexican families in the Imperial Valley in the early twentieth century detailed the agricultural activities of Asian Indians. They normally formed partnerships of two to seven members and contracted to farm together. The partnership could be based on either blood or non-blood relationships. The Punjabis consciously built local business networks that included white landowners, bankers, and lawyers, who were all crucial to success in agriculture.[80] The amicable relationship with powerful whites in local society enabled them to purchase land before 1913. In the early 1900s, Asian Indian communities purchased over 80,000 acres of land in the San Joaquin and Sacramento valleys.[81] They farmed continuously even after the passage of the California Alien Land Laws in 1913.

In the 1920s, Filipinos became the largest group of the Asian farming population on the Pacific Coast. California had the biggest Filipino population in the United States, with census reports noting a more than tenfold increase between 1920 and 1930, from fewer than 3,000 to 40,000. Most of them were migrant farm laborers who moved from one agricultural region to another following harvest season. For example, the Filipino community in Stockton, an agricultural town in California's Central Valley, had a population of more than 6,000 in the summers in the 1920s but only 1,000 in the winters.[82]

LABOR IN HISTORICAL PERSPECTIVE

In the late nineteenth and early twentieth centuries, Asian immigrant workers filled the need for cheap labor in Hawaii and the continental America. They worked on Hawaiian sugarcane plantations, enduring the harsh living and working conditions. They labored in the gold mines abandoned by white miners, collecting the scarce metal through tedious panning. They also constructed the western segment of the transcontinental railroad, braving harsh conditions and explosions. While they significantly contributed to the development of the American West and the multiethnic economy and culture of the United States, their contributions have not yet been acknowledged properly in American history.

In the urban centers, unable to enter the mainstream labor market due in part to their lack of English proficiency and industrial skills, but mostly due to racial discrimination and the prejudices of the larger society, Asian immigrants found their niche businesses in laundries, grocery stores, and the food service industry. In the laundry business, they captured the market through long hours and low prices. In the grocery business, they combined vegetable and fruit growing with grocery retailing. In the restaurant business, they created and modified ethnic cuisines to make them acceptable to the palates of the larger population. These business strategies enabled them to survive and even succeed in an unwelcoming and at times hostile socioeconomic environment.

In rural settings, Japanese, Korean, Indian, and Filipino farm workers also carved out their economic niche. While many Japanese, Korean, and Indian farmers secured land ownership despite the anti-alien land laws prevalent in the country at the time, Filipino immigrants largely worked as seasonal migrant farm workers, a status similar to that of Mexican migrant workers a few decades later.

The significance of the ethnic niche economy in sustaining Asian immigrants and in transforming them into Asian Americans reflects, on the one hand, the ingenuity and adaptability of the Asian immigrants and, on the other, the complex nature of a society that has been shaped by the multifaceted elements of class, ethnicity, gender, and race.

KEY TERMS

Hawaiian sugar plantation
gold panning
transcontinental railroad
niche economy

Japanese schoolboys
Japanese green grocery
Punjabi farmers

REVIEW QUESTIONS

1. Review the harsh working and living conditions on Hawaiian plantations for Asian immigrant workers.
2. How did the Chinese contribute to the development of the American West as gold miners and railroad workers?
3. What are the secrets for Asian immigrants' economic survival and even success?

FILMS

Dong, Arthur (producer/director). *Sewing Woman.* 14-minute documentary on a Chinese immigrant woman's journey from war-torn China to America. 1982.

Dunn, Geoffrey, and Mark Schwartz (producers/directors). *A Dollar a Day, Ten Cents a Dance.* 30-minute documentary providing a historic portrait of Filipino farm workers in America. 1984.

Hart, Jayasri Majumdar (producer/director). *Roots in the Sand.* 57-minute documentary on Punjabi men in Southern California's Imperial Valley. 1998.

Kelly, Nancy, and Kenji Yamamoto (directors). *Thousand Pieces of Gold.* 105-minute fact-based drama depicting a Chinese woman in an Idaho gold-mining town fighting against racism and sexism. 1991.

FURTHER READING

Azuma, Eiichiro. *Between Two Empires: Race, History, and Transnationalism in Japanese America.* New York: Oxford University Press, 2005.

Chan, Sucheng. *Asian Americans: An Interpretive History.* Boston: Twayne, 1991.

———. *This Bitter-Sweet Soil: I Chinese in California Agriculture, 1860–1910.* Berkeley: University of California Press, 1986.

Chang, Gordon H. *Ghosts of Gold Mountain: The Epic Story of the Chinese Who Built the Transcontinental Railroad.* Boston: Houghton Mifflin Harcourt, 2019.

Chung, Sue Fawn. *In Pursuit of Gold: Chinese American Miners and Merchants in the American West.* Urbana: University of Illinois Press, 2011.

Coe, Andrew. *Chop Suey: A Cultural History of Chinese Food in the United States.* New York: Oxford University Press, 2009.

Daniels, Roger. *Asian America: Chinese and Japanese in the United States since 1850.* Seattle: University of Washington Press, 1988.

Espana-Maram, Linda. *Creating Masculinity in Los Angeles's Little Manila: Working Class Filipinos and Popular Culture, 1920s–1950s.* New York: Columbia University Press, 2006.

Glenn, Evelyn Nakano. *Issei, Nisei, War Bride: Three Generations of Japanese American Women in Domestic Service.* Philadelphia: Temple University Press, 1986.

Hong, Grace. *Ruptures of American Capital: Women of Color, Feminism, and the Culture of Immigrant Labor.* Minneapolis: University of Minnesota Press, 2006.

Leonard, Karen Isaksen. *Making Ethnic Choices: California's Punjabi Mexican Americans.* Philadelphia: Temple University Press, 1992.

Ling, Huping. *Chinese Americans in the Heartland: Migration, Work, and Community.* New Brunswick, NJ: Rutgers University Press, 2022.

———. *Chinese Chicago: Race, Transnational Migration, and Community since 1870.* Stanford, CA: Stanford University Press, 2012.

———. *Voices of the Heart: Asian American Women on Immigration, Work, and Family.* Kirksville, MO: Truman State University Press, 2007.

Matsumoto, Valerie J. *Farming the Home Place: A Japanese American Community in California, 1919–1982.* Ithaca, NY: Cornell University Press, 1994.

McKeown, Adam. *Chinese Migrant Networks and Cultural Change, Peru, Chicago, Hawaii, 1900–1936.* Chicago: University of Chicago Press, 2001.

Park, Kyeyoung. *The Korean American Dream: Immigrants and Small Business in New York City.* Ithaca, NY: Cornell University Press, 1997.

Siu, Paul C. P. *Chinese Laundryman: A Study of Social Isolation.* New York: New York University Press, 1987.

Takaki, Ronald. *Strangers from a Different Shore: A History of Asian Americans.* Boston: Little, Brown, 1989.

4

DEFINING HOME AND COMMUNITY

CHAPTER OUTLINE

Domesticity and Innovative Family Formations
Changing Gender Roles
The Second-Generation "Dilemma"
Ethnic Community Building
Asian Immigrant Home and Community in Historical Perspective

SIGNIFICANT EVENTS

1852–1854	Six Chinese *huiguans* (district associations), commonly known as the Chinese Six Companies, are founded on the West Coast
1882	The six *huiguans* form a national umbrella organization, the Chinese Consolidated Benevolent Association (CCBA or Zhonghua Huiguan)
1899	Emperor Protection Society, or Baohuang Hui, is established by Chinese reformer Kang Youwei
1903	The first Korean self-governing community organization, the dong-hoe, or village council, is established on every plantation in the Hawaiian Islands; Sin-Min-Hoi (New People's Society) is founded in Honolulu's Korean immigrant communities
1905	The Korean Episcopal Church is founded in Hawaii; the Korean Methodist Church forms in Los Angeles
1909	The Japanese Association of America is founded; the Korean National Association (KNA) is established, with headquarters in San Francisco, more than 3,200 members, and more than 130 local chapters
1910s	The Central Japanese Agricultural Association of California functions as an umbrella organization for farmers in Northern and Central California,

	and the Southern California Central Agricultural Association for farmers in Southern California
1912	The Khalsa Diwan (Free Divine) Society among the Sikhs is established in Stockton, California, and builds the first Sikh temple in America
1919	The Korean Women's Patriotic League is founded in Dinuba, California
1920	The Great Filipino Lodge is founded in San Francisco in 1920
1921	Caballeros de Dimas-Alang for Filipino immigrants is formed in San Francisco
1924	Legionairios del Trabajo for Filipino immigrants is formed in San Francisco
1920s–1930s	Nihonmachi, or Japantowns, grow rapidly throughout California due to increased economic opportunities and population growth

DURING THE LATE NINETEENTH- AND early twentieth centuries, every ethnic group of Asian immigrants had an uneven or lopsided male-to-female sex ratio, ranging from three to one (Koreans and Japanese) to twenty to one (Chinese, Filipinos, and Asian Indians). Consequently, each of the early Asian immigrant communities has been described as a "bachelor society," and the family lives of Asian immigrants had been mostly missing from scholarly works until the 1960s. Thanks to earlier literary works, such as novels and biographies, and a steadily growing body of scholarship on Asian American studies since the 1970s, it is now possible for us to re-create the family lives of early Asian immigrants. Studies have found that Asian immigrants have contested the conventionally recognized normative framework of family and domesticity, inventing and reinventing innovative variations of family, marriage, permanent or temporary sexual relationships, and same-sex intimacies, co-ethnically, interethnically, and interracially.

When jointly negotiating the new environment, Asian immigrant men and women found that intergender roles had changed from those of their homelands. Asian immigrant males mostly lived a bachelor existence in the new land, struggling to maintain their traditional male role as supporters of families without the day-to-day support and comfort of a family. The absence of a normative family life was replaced by a variety of substitutions—bigamy, interracial marriage, long-term sexual partners or occasional sexual encounters, and same-sex intimacies. Once in a different milieu and a completely new culture, married Asian female immigrants, though much fewer in number than their male counterparts, found that they were becoming joint heads of their households and coproviders for their families and were sharing decision making with their husbands; these new roles were as refreshing as they were overwhelming.

Compared to their immigrant parents, whose values and outlooks were still largely influenced by those of their homelands, native-born second-generation Asian Americans were conflicted and confused by their Asianness (their physical "foreign" appearances and their Asian cultural heritage) and their Americanness (being native-born, being educated mostly through the American public education system, and practicing Western values in public and in personal daily life) in a classed, gendered, and racialized society. They found themselves marginalized in schools, at work, and in public places.

The necessity of survival required Asian immigrants to construct their communities as soon as they arrived in the new land. A wide array of community organizations played mutual-aid roles and provided social order for the Asian immigrants. In building their communities, Asian immigrants transplanted some social and economic organizations from their homelands, such as district and clan associations among the Chinese, village councils among Koreans, and business guilds among all groups. They also established a community structure emulating that of the larger society. While these community organizations were formed for the purpose of mutual aid and self-governing on American soil, they were also established to promote nationalist movements in their homelands.

DOMESTICITY AND INNOVATIVE FAMILY FORMATIONS

Unlike their European counterparts who mostly came as families, Asian immigrants during the late nineteenth and early twentieth centuries were largely bachelors—single or married men who left their families behind in the homelands. The male-to-female sex ratio for Chinese was 18.6:1 in 1860, 12.8:1 in 1870, 21.1:1 in 1880, 26.8:1 in 1890, 18.9:1 in 1900, 14.3:1 in 1910, 7:1 in 1920, 3.9:1 in 1930, and 2.9:1 in 1940. For Japanese it was 17:1 in California, 34:1 in the other 47 states, and 3.9:1 in Hawaii in 1900; 5.6:1, 9.8:1, and 2.2:1 in 1910; 17:1, 2.3:1, and 1.3:1 in 1920; 1.4:1, 1.6:1, and 1.2:1 in 1930; and 1.3:1, 1.4:1, and 1.1:1 in 1940. The sex ratio for Koreans was roughly 10:1 in Hawaii in 1900 and 3:1 in 1920. For Filipinos, it was 4:1 in Hawaii and 19:1 on the mainland in 1920. Only a handful of Asian Indian women came to America prior to World War II, and several hundred Asian Indian men married Mexican women in Southern California's Imperial Valley.[1] Scholars have found that the factors contributing to the shortage of women in Asian immigration included Confucian restrictions from the traditional Asian societies of China, Korea, and Japan; the alienating and sometimes hostile environment in America; institutionalized exclusion from federal and local governments; and vigorous police raids of immigrant neighborhoods.[2]

The shortage of women resulted in diverse and creative forms of marriage and interpersonal intimacies within heterosexual or same-sex couples. The shortage of women also rendered prostitution a profitable business, serving the physical needs of "bachelors."

Chinese Marriage Patterns

Historical records reveal a few distinctive marriage patterns among the early Chinese immigrant families in America. They can be classified into three categories: (1) the transnational split marriage—Taishanese "widows" and American "concubines"; (2) traditional marriage; and (3) modern American urban marriages, such as love unions and interracial marriages. Like their male counterparts, the early Chinese immigrant women, those arriving during the last decades of the nineteenth century, were predominantly from a geographically confined area—Taishan, Guangdong—and many were concubines. The traditional patriarchal polygamous marriage, however, became variegated when it was transplanted to the new land; the husband did not live with multiple wives simultaneously but left the first wife (in most cases) in China to carry out duties of filial piety and brought a concubine to America or married a woman in America to carry on a family life. In the early decades of the twentieth century, traditional marriage, in which the Chinese male returned to China, got married, and brought his bride with him when returning to America, remained a dominant pattern. Meanwhile, the American urban marriage was gaining in popularity, especially among the American-born Chinese or the younger immigrants, who were more likely to find mates in their socioeconomic circles in America. In addition, interracial marriages or unions also emerged in the last category.

TRANSNATIONAL SPLIT MARRIAGE: TAISHANESE "WIDOW" AND AMERICAN "CONCUBINE." Chinese immigrants' attempts to establish family life in America encountered a series of obstacles, including ideological, socioeconomical, and physical restrictions in China and the alienating and frequently hostile environment in America.[3] To overcome these obstacles, Chinese immigrants devised a mechanism to negotiate their immigrant reality. It has been characterized as the "transnational split marriage: Taishanese 'widow' and American 'concubine,'" a marital arrangement in which the husband left his wife behind in Taishan or other sending places in China due to the aforementioned difficulties, but on one of his returning trips brought a concubine with him to America or married (or lived with) a woman in America without divorcing his wife in China in order to ease his immigrant life. This pattern is evident among early Chinese immigrants.[4]

Taishan, as one of the traditional emigrant-sending places in southern China and dubbed the "first county of overseas Chinese," has dispatched so many emigrants to North America that Taishanese (Taishan dialect) had been regarded as the standard Chinese language among early immigrants. The immigration records indicate that a majority of early Chinese immigrants came from Taishan. Although we are unable to tally the actual percentage of Chinese concubines among the married Chinese in the United States, as polygamy was an illegitimate practice, case studies in Chicago showed that, among the dozen Chinese families resident there during the 1880s and 1890s, most women were concubines, "probably not a single one among the early Chinese families in Chicago was the first wife."[5] Oral history interviews from other places across the country also display a similar pattern.[6]

Ample Chinese gazetteers, overseas Chinese magazines, and folk songs further demonstrate that the Taishanese widow and American concubine arrangement was a widespread practice. A folk song popular among the villages in the main Chinese sending regions starts with the lyric "dang nian a gong xia nan yang, jia li a po ku duan chang" (When a man lives overseas, his wife weeps until her death), depicting the plight of wives who were left behind by their emigrant husbands. Villages with substantial number of Chinese overseas were called "widow villages." Such folk songs and sobriquets describe well the split social and economic life a transnational family had to endure. Numerous literary works also reflect this reality, with Louis Chu's 1979 novel *Eat a Bowl of Tea* and its motion-picture adaption as one of the best-known examples. Chu's story vividly and lightheartedly portrays the life of a split immigrant family. The wife laments that her absent husband periodically sends her modern household gadgets from America while he is the one that she wants most.[7]

The plight of the virtual widow of an immigrant Chinese shows only a part of the transpacific saga; a complete picture of the transnational stories of Chinese migrants and their families is unraveled by close scrutiny of the transnational split marriage. This marriage was a social arrangement and a practical compromise invented by migrants and their families to cope with the marital separation caused by migration. In many cases, a concubine was arranged by parents or the first wife of an emigrant, with a specific purpose of taking care of his physical needs while abroad; at the same time, the first wife remained in the home village to fulfill the duties of filial piety. Through such an arrangement, a concubine and a wife jointly completed the biological, socioeconomic, and emotional responsibilities expected of a wife by the traditional society. Despite the inferior status of a concubine in family and society, concubinage was recognized as a workable alternative for girls from impoverished families and in desolate and desperate situations. Many concubines were illiterate slave-maids from the same or nearby villages, sold into servitude at a young age by impoverished parents. A slave-maid's destination in life was dictated by her master; she could be married to a male servant or become a concubine of the master at the master and mistress's will. The latter choice was considered a better alternative for many slave-maids, since as a concubine she was no longer a slave but a member of the masters, offering an upward social move. Concubines among the earlier merchant families in Chinatowns were often slave-maids prior to their emigration.[8]

Although concubinage had been practiced in China for centuries, polygynous conditions among Chinese immigrants in the United States existed more as ramifications of immigration than Chinese cultural habits. In America, it was not only well-to-do Chinese merchants who had concubines; even common laborers acquired them. Before the repeal of the Chinese exclusion laws in 1943, most Chinese immigrant men had left their families in China due to their financial inability to transport their families to America, U.S. immigration restrictions preventing family unification, and Chinese patriarchal rules dictating that the woman should stay in China to take care of her children and parents-in-law while securing remittances from the man living abroad.[9] A few fortunate ones were eventually able to arrange for their families to come to America.[10] Many others managed to return to their native villages in China to see their families periodically.[11] However, the latter practice was deemed impossible by the passage of the Scott Act in 1888, which barred Chinese laborers from reentry to America even if they only temporarily left the country. Unable to bring wives to America or go to China to see them, some successful Chinese laborers, such as farmers, employed laborers, service workers, and even gamblers, purchased women from brothels or married those who successfully escaped servitude, while still being legally married to their first wives in China.

It is important to note that bigamy was practiced among Chinese immigrants in America more for practical reasons—physical sustenance of the men and survival of Chinese immigrant communities—than for psychological ones—display of one's wealth through possession of concubines, as was the case for many wealthy Chinese in China. An ordinary Chinese migrant needed to meet his basic physical needs (food, shelter, and sex) in order to function normally to work for his American dream. With the absence of his wife, he had to find an alternative, either a marriage, a common-law coinhabitance, or a long-term or short-term relationship with a prostitute.

TRADITIONAL MARRIAGE. The transnational split marriage pattern, of course, does not encompass all early Chinese immigrant families, and not all the wives of the earlier Chinese immigrants were concubines. A majority of the marriages among the early Chinese immigrants were traditional ones; many wives managed to come to America to join their husbands. In most cases, the Chinese man migrated to America first. He worked and saved until he had enough money to travel back to China to bring his wife and children. Kwong Long, a Chinese merchant in New York City, went back to China in 1886 and returned with his wife and daughter after he worked in the United States for several years.[12] Gue Lim, another Chinese merchant also in San Francisco, petitioned for and was granted the admission of his wife and children in 1900.[13]

Oral history interviews have underscored the traditional marriage pattern for Chinese immigrants. Mrs. C's father, a Chinese tea merchant from Guangdong, came to the United States around the turn of the twentieth century. He first arrived in San Francisco and later moved to Boston. There he worked as a bookkeeper. When he had saved enough

FIGURE 4.1 Young Ng She and Young Sum Wood, wife and child of Chinese merchant Young Kwong Hoy of Hawaii, 1918. Note Young Ng She's bound feet. Courtesy National Archives–Pacific Sierra Region, San Bruno, California.

FIGURE 4.2 Low Joe, a Chinese merchant in San Francis and his wife, Chan Shee, 1916. The 1882 Chinese Exclusion Act prohibited the entry of Chinese laborers but exempted Chinese merchants and U.S. citizens. All Chinese immigrants had to provide documentation indicating their status as merchants or family members of merchants or U.S. citizens. As indicated here, when the couple entered the United States, Low Joe had to present to the immigration authorities a certificate to prove his merchant status in order to apply for the admission of his wife to America. Courtesy National Archives–Pacific Sierra Region, San Bruno, California.

money to support a family, he went to Guangdong to marry his bride and brought her to America. He then started his own business and bought a house in Boston.[14] Most traditional marriage couples resided in Chinatown, and the majority of these men were restaurateurs, grocers, and lottery housekeepers, merchants who were exempted from the Chinese Exclusion Acts.

AMERICAN MARRIAGE: LOVE UNION AND INTERRACIAL MARRIAGE. Along with the transnational split marriage and the traditional marriage, there were also matrimonies resulting from romances rather than parental or familial arrangements. The love union was more likely to occur among the American-born second-generation Chinese or the more Americanized Chinese immigrants who came to the country at a younger age. They were mostly better-educated professionals, and their marital partners shared similar cultural and educational backgrounds with them. They lived outside Chinatown in more affluent neighborhoods, and their contacts with Chinatown were limited mostly to business ones.

Despite anti-miscegenation laws, a small number of interracial marriages existed among Chinese immigrants. For those Chinese men who married non-Chinese women, the intermarriage usually occurred among small entrepreneurs or laborers. The racial and ethnic background of their wives varied from region to region.[15]

In the South, most Chinese men were laborers from California or Cuba recruited to the South by railroad companies or sugar plantations. They found wives among Black women or Irish or French immigrant women. The 1880 census for Louisiana indicated that among the 489 Chinese in the state, 35 were married, widowed, or divorced. Of the married Chinese men, only 4 had a Chinese wife. The remaining Chinese men married non-Chinese women, among whom 4 had married mulatto women, 12 Black women, and 8 white women, including 6 of Irish or French immigrant background.[16]

In New York City, census reports and contemporary newspapers reveal an interracial marriage pattern of Chinese men and Irish women consistent through the last decades of the nineteenth century. *Harper's Weekly* and other magazines and newspapers frequently featured stories of "Chinamen" and "Hibernian" women, in which Irish women praised their Chinese husbands.[17]

In the Midwest, interracial marriages occurred among Chinese entrepreneurs and laborers. Significant numbers of interracial marriages occurred among the Chicago Chinese. In the 1930s, there were at least 27 such marriages, representing 20 percent of the 137 total families investigated. Twenty-six of the interracial marriages involved Chinese men and white women, mostly Polish, and one between a Chinese man and a Black woman. The white women who married Chinese men generally fell into three social backgrounds: Polish dishwashers at Chinese restaurants, chop suey house waitresses or cashiers, and veteran prostitutes. Twelve of the interracially married couples lived in Chinatown, while fifteen resided outside.[18] The profile of Chinese interracial marriage in other midwestern cities, such as St. Louis and Minneapolis–Saint Paul, was similar to that of Chicago.[19]

A few cases of interracial marriages in Chicago in the 1930s are revealing as regard to social acceptance, cultural assimilation, and ethnic identity of the individuals involved. T. Chan met his future wife in a Chinese chop suey house where she worked as a waitress. Despite the seemingly physical incompatibility—Chan was short and slim, and she tall and stocky—they fell in love. After the marriage, they lived on the South Side for three years, when T. Chan was employed by a large company as a treasurer. He later quit his job and opened a small chop suey shop. Unfortunately, the business was so slow that he could not even pay the rent. The landlord evicted him, and he lost thousands of dollars on the venture. When the Great Depression came, the couple had to move to Chinatown to ease their situation. Living in a small apartment on Twenty-Fifth Street in the Italian community and at the edge of Chinatown, T. Chan found a job as a waiter at the Pagoda Inn restaurant in Chinatown. Occasionally, Mrs. Chan would take their son to the Pagoda Inn to see her husband and to have dinner. Some fellow workers there would tease the little boy and bribe him with small change to make him speak Chinese.[20]

H. Chan, a cook at a Chinese chop suey house, married a Polish woman, a dishwasher at the same restaurant. H. Chan was always kind to her and often cooked special dinners for her. The romance that developed in the kitchen eventually led to marriage. In the first twenty years of their union, H. Chan prospered, as the chop suey business was bustling in Chicago. He was able to buy a house on the South Side where Chinatown was located, and his wife quit her job and stayed home to take care of their three children, two girls and a boy. The first daughter graduated from a normal school on the South Side and worked as a bookkeeper in a Chinese restaurant. In her teen years, she wanted to be a nun and was in denial of her Chinese heritage, unwilling to associate with any Chinese. As she matured, she changed her entire attitude toward Chinese. She became actively involved in the Chinese community, attending Chinese social meetings and going to dancing parties held by the Chinese student association at the University of Chicago, while her younger sister, a seventeen-year-old high school student, tagged along. Both girls ended up finding boyfriends among the Chinese students. When their father was at work in a Chinese restaurant where he was a manager, they would have parties with their boyfriends at home.[21]

Compared to Chinese men, few Chinese women of this period married men outside of their racial group, largely due to the unbalanced sex ratio among Chinese immigrants. The male to female sex ratio among the Chinese in America was roughly twenty to one in the last decades of the nineteenth century and improved to fourteen to one in the early twentieth century.[22] The great gender disparity consequently forced Chinese men to look where possible for partners in other ethnic groups, whereas Chinese women had a large pool of mates to choose from within Chinese communities, and therefore intermarriage made little sense to them.

The rarity of interracial marriages among early Chinese women was also due to racial and cultural prejudice from white American society as well as cultural concerns within Chinese immigrant communities. During the late nineteenth and early twentieth centuries, Chinese in America were generally perceived negatively as ignorant "coolies" and "strike breakers," or evil and seductive prostitutes. They were barred from the mainstream labor market and excluded from mainstream social and cultural life by legal restrictions and popular practices. Meanwhile, as a discriminated small minority, the Chinese immigrant society also objected to interracial marriages between Chinese women and non-Chinese men in order to preserve its population, since Chinese generally regarded married women as members of their husbands' clan, or race in this case.

Japanese Picture Brides

The marriage pattern among Japanese immigrants was dominated by the so-called picture bride, emerging after the Gentlemen's Agreement, signed between the U.S. and Japanese governments in 1907, which ended the immigration of Japanese laborers to the United States but permitted the entry of the wives and children of Japanese immigrants already residing in America. The military strength of post-Meiji Japan was a major reason why the Gentlemen's Agreement rather than exclusion became law. This arrangement prompted the practice of the "picture bride," in which a Japanese woman would marry a Japanese migrant after both parties had exchanged pictures and accepted the marriage proposal and then register in her husband's household to qualify as the wife of the Japanese migrant. According to historian Yuji Ichioka, the Japanese government set up strict economic standards to regulate the flow of the Japanese female exodus in order to prevent the entry of prostitutes: only men with sufficient means to support families were allowed to summon wives. No laborers were permitted to summon wives until 1915, when only those with savings of $800 were allowed to bring wives. Farmers and merchants were eligible to summon wives, but the former had to earn $400 to $500 in annual income and the latter $1,200, and both had to possess savings of $1,000. Meanwhile, the picture brides had to have their names entered into their husbands' family registries for six months before they were eligible for passport applications.[23]

By 1908, more than 20,000 Japanese picture brides had entered the country, and many of them soon discovered the bitterness of these marriages. Upon arrival in America, many picture brides were disappointed that their husbands were fifteen to twenty or more years older than they appeared in the pictures. Most of them had to work in low-paying domestic service jobs or help with their family farms.[24] Kazue Aoki's story portrays the typical life of a Japanese picture bride.

Kazue Aoki was born in 1892 and grew up on a rice farm in Honshu, Japan. She had eight years of education and was trained as a nurse. Her first marriage was childless and ended when she was sent back to her parents. In 1912, she came to America as a picture bride at the age of twenty to join her husband, a farmer in Fresno, California. After a monthlong and rough voyage, she was detained in the "prison-like" Angel Island immigration station. She was released a few weeks later because she had all proper papers. When she met her husband for the first time, she was shocked to discover that he looked at least fifteen years older than shown in his picture.

Despite her disappointment, she devoted her life to her family. She raised their five children and worked alongside her husband on their family farm. Even when she gave birth to a new baby, she would return to the field only a few days after, with the baby on her back. While working on the farm, she dreamed of the future when her daughters could obtain an education. When the 1913 California Alien Land Law restricted land leases to three years and the 1920 Alien Land Law deemed it illegal for immigrants to lease land, Kazue Aiko wisely transferred the family farm to her eldest daughter, so that the family could continue to own the property. Like other Issei women, she maintained traditional values, spoke Japanese at home, and emphasized the importance of education to her children.[25]

The practice of picture brides helped counterbalance the lopsided sex ratio among Japanese immigrants and helped sustain the Japanese immigrant community. While the U.S. census counted only 410 married women among the total Japanese population of 24,326 in 1900, by 1910 the number had increased tenfold to 5,581 out of the total Japanese population of 72,157; the number of married women further increased to 22,192 out of the total Japanese population of 111,010 in 1920 and 23,930 out of 138,834 in 1930.[26] During the 1920s and 1930s, most Japanese communities throughout California experienced rapid growth.

Korean Picture Brides

Among the seven thousand Koreans in Hawaii, about 80 percent were bachelors. Many of the bachelors were in their thirties or older, but there were virtually no Korean women available for them to marry and interracial marriage was unthinkable at the time. The shortage of women resulted in social problems, such as gambling and fighting within the labor camps, which worried the Korean immigrant community as well as the plantation owners, who were also interested in the productivity and reproductivity of their Korean laborers.

When the idea of picture brides was brought up, both plantation owners and the American government cooperated. Many plantation owners approved the plan, and U.S. immigration authorities allowed Korean women to enter with Japanese passports and granted them permanent residence. Such practices were possible because Koreans were regarded as Japanese subjects after Japan's annexation of Korea in 1910; Korean women followed the same practice as the Japanese under the Gentlemen's Agreement. Between 1910 and 1924, more than eight hundred Korean picture brides arrived in Hawaii, and more than one hundred went to the mainland, mostly to San Francisco, Los Angeles, Sacramento, and Portland, Oregon. Sara Choe was reportedly the first Korean picture bride when she arrived in Honolulu on November 28, 1919.

A majority of the picture brides were young girls and were shocked when they found out their husbands were much older than they had expected. It has been reported that when a ship carrying picture brides arrived in Honolulu, the bridegrooms would dress in their best suits to greet their brides at the dock. Some of the brides passed out upon seeing their husbands, who were much older and uglier than they imagined. Some threw their hands up and cried *Aigo omani* ("O dear me, what shall I do?"). The bridegrooms were as confused and embarrassed as their brides were disappointed. Eventually, however, most of the brides had to adjust to their new situation. Many of the married couples moved to Honolulu, where they ran family-operated small businesses, such as laundries, restaurants, shoe-repair shops, and used furniture stores.

Jung-soon's story illuminates the life of a picture bride. Jung-soon was born in 1895 in Pusan, the largest port city in Korea. When she was nineteen, she was engaged to Roh Shin-tae, a Korean immigrant in Sacramento, because she was fascinated by the idea of moving overseas. Roh left Korea in 1905, seeking better economic opportunities in Hawaii. He worked on a sugar plantation but left after a year because of the hardship of plantation work. He arrived in San Francisco right after the great earthquake of 1906 but could not find employment. He then moved to Sacramento to work on a farm and remained there for seventeen years before returning to Korea to marry his bride.

After the marriage, the Rohs left Korea on March 3, 1923. First they went to Japan, where they underwent a physical examination that took a week. When they finally arrived in San Francisco on May 15, 1923, they were quarantined for three days before they could go to Sacramento. Mrs. Roh found her life in America was miserable. She stayed with her aunt while her husband worked on the farm for five dollars a day. Mrs. Roh encouraged her husband to learn a skill, and two years later Roh decided to become a barber. He borrowed $125 from a friend to attend school to learn the trade. Three months later, Roh finished his training and the family moved to Oakland, where Roh's friend had a barbershop. Roh worked there for two months and then opened his own barbershop. However, the money he earned as a barber was not enough to feed the family, so they had to rely on welfare for a while. After three to four years, the barbershop finally started paying off. By 1941, Roh was making $35 to $45 a day. The same year Mrs. Roh started her own business, a public shower and bath facility, earning $30 a day. By 1942, the Rohs were finally able to save some money to buy a small hotel. By 1945, the family income had increased to about $2,000 a month, finally delivering economical security.

This story reveals that a picture bride was instrumental in her family's survival and financial success in America. It was Mrs. Roh who encouraged her husband to switch from farming to a skilled job and who ran her own business to supplement the family income, in addition to raising six children.[27]

While many similarities existed between the practices of Japanese and Korean picture brides, a key difference stands out. The operation of the Japanese picture bride migration was closely monitored and strictly regulated by the Japanese government, indicating a stronger nation-state identity and a sense of self-image. On the contrary, the practice of Korean picture brides was initiated and promoted by white Hawaiian planters and the American government, reflecting the weakness of the Korean government under Japanese colonization. Meanwhile, Koreans residing within and outside of the Korean Peninsula regarded themselves as a stateless people. Clearly, the socioeconomic and political imperatives of labor and capital, migration and restriction, colonialism and imperialism all intertwined at once in the regulation of the picture bride migrations.

Some comparative study can also help us better understand the practice of picture brides. They were also common among European Americans on the western frontier in the late nineteenth and early twentieth centuries. Having braved the frontier hardship and achieved personal financial success, many bachelors desired to settle down and start a family. A common practice thus emerged, under which the men wrote letters to churches and advertised personal information in magazines and newspapers. The interested spinsters, often women who longed for financial security or a different life, would write back and send along their photographs. Courtship would follow via correspondence until the woman agreed to marry a man whom she had never met.[28] Obviously, the picture bride and present-day mail-order bride are products of human migration that transcend cultural, geographical, socioeconomic, and racial boundaries.

Punjabi-Mexican Families and Stanger Intimacies

As discussed in chapter 1, the extreme gender imbalance among the early Asian Indian immigrants (109 females among 5,800 males who entered the United States between 1901 and 1911) and anti-miscegenation laws resulted in a distinctive matrimonial pattern among Punjabi farmers in California: the Punjabi-Mexican marriage. Utilizing county records and interviews, Karen Isaksen Leonard compiled statistics on 378 spouses of Asian Indians residing in California between 1913 and 1949. Her study shows that marriage between Punjabis in California and Mexican or Mexican American women made up 80 percent of all marriages under investigation, and almost two-thirds of the couples lived in the Imperial Valley. Generally, the average age at marriage for the men was thirty-five and for the women twenty-three. Many marriages resulted from arrangements through female relatives who had already married Punjabis. Other brides were daughters of poor Mexican families who came into contact with Punjabis through agricultural field work. The grooms included Hindu, Sikh, and Muslim Indians who had no intention of returning to India and married Mexican women in order to establish a family in America.[29]

Recent research indicates that interracial homosocial relationships and homosexual intimacies also transpired among Asian Indian migrant workers during the first decades of the twentieth century. In lumber camps, canneries, and agriculture communities across the North American West, some Asian Indian migrant workers developed intimate friendships or erotic ties with native-born European coworkers or with local youths, usually newspaper boys, as revealed in numerous legal records of sexual crimes, domestic disputes, and social disorder in locales along the Pacific Rim from Canada to the United States and Mexico. On the night of February 10, 1918, two policemen patrolling downtown Sacramento spotted Stanley Kurnick, a nineteen-year-old boy of Austrian descendant, accompanied by Jamil Singh, a forty-year-old "Hindu." Both men were ranch hands and found temporary work in the Sacramento Valley. After Kurnick complained of his hunger and living on the streets to Singh, the latter offered him some money for dinner and invited him to share his room at a boardinghouse. Later that night, the police followed a lead from a local resident and looked through the keyhole, observing sexual intercourse between the men. The police broke into the room and arrested both men.[30]

> ### EXAMPLES OF PUNJABI-MEXICAN MARRIAGES
>
> The Alvarez family, consisting of Mrs. Alvarez, three of her daughters (Antonia, Anna Anita, and Ester), and a son (Jesus), had come from Mexico in 1916 via El Paso. The family lived on the Edwards ranch near Holtville and picked cotton for the Punjabi partners who leased the ranch, Sher Singh and Gopal Singh. At the time of the weddings, the men were thirty-six and thirty-seven and the sisters were twenty-one and eighteen. A fourth sister, Valentina, soon came from El Paso to join her mother and sisters. Valentina was older; she had been married already and had four daughters, whom she brought with her. She married Rullia Singh in October 1917, and a month later her fourteen-year-old daughter, Alejandrina, married a Sikh friend of his, a man who had taken the American name of Albert Joe. The youngest Alvarez sister, Ester, married another Sikh, Harnam Singh Sidhu, in 1919.
>
> Source: Karen Isaksen Leonard, *Making Ethnic Choices: California's Punjabi Mexican Americans* (Philadelphia: Temple University Press, 1992), 64.

Legal reports of sexual crimes involving "Hindus" peaked in the 1910s and 1920s but drastically declined in the decades after World War II, when all Asian exclusion laws were repealed one after another and the Asian immigrant "bachelor" societies were replaced by more gender-balanced families. Although perceived as "immoral," "deviant," and "perverse" offenses against the normative conception of family, marriage, and domesticity, these "stranger intimacies" helped sustain the survival, mobility, autonomy, and protection of the transient Asian migrant workers during the exclusion era.[31]

Filipino Family Lives

Although the Filipino laborers who arrived in Hawaii and the mainland were predominantly single males, a few Filipino women were recruited to Hawaii, so family lives also existed among the Filipino immigrants. On sugar plantations, some Filipinas worked in the field while others worked as cooks. On the mainland, the tightly knit ethnic community helped sustain the "bachelor" Filipino migrant workers. Connie Tirona's family history typifies the experience of the Filipino laborers, manifesting the issues of global capitalism and exploitation, labor solidarity, and ethnic cohesion. But most of all it illuminates the family lives of Filipino immigrants, which were filled with bittersweetness.

Connie Tirona's parents were recruited to Hawaii as laborers in the 1920s. Her mother came with four or five other Filipinas, and she suffered a miscarriage in the steerage class on one of the American President liners. Upon arriving in Hawaii, her parents were sent to the Wailua Sugar and Pineapple Plantation. They lived in labor camps and were mistreated by the crew bosses. The common working experience prompted Filipino and Japanese workers to become united against the cruel Portuguese foremen. While some women would go to the fields to work along with their men, Connie's mother worked as a cook. From her Japanese coworkers, she learned to cook many traditional Japanese dishes.

Five years later, her parents left the plantation and went to the mainland to join their friends who had found employment there. Her parents worked in Northern California, first in Selma and later in Oakland, as migrant farm workers following the seasonal crops. Connie was born in 1929 in Selma and grew up in the Filipino community of migrant workers. While most of the men were single and lived in the barracks, the married couples dwelled in cottages that were dilapidated shacks but allowed the families to prepare their own food. Connie recalls that during cockfights, one of their favorite pastimes, the women would cook special Filipino delicacies.

Several Filipino families would pitch in to buy a car so that they could travel from camp to camp. Sometimes there was not enough work for everyone, and the one who got work would buy groceries for all the families. When Connie was four or five years old, her father got a job at a shipyard in Oakland, where he worked for twenty years. Though away from the agricultural job, every other week Connie's family visited the *manongs*, the

Filipino men without families, in the labor camp in the Sacramento–San Joaquin area. Prior to their visits, the manongs would fix up and clean their rooms to prepare for the "families." Connie's mother would bake Filipino delicacies all week long in anticipation of such visits. The children would perform for the men, singing and dancing, bringing tears to the faces of these men who dearly missed their own families in the Philippines.[32]

Connie Tirona's family history illustrates some important features of Filipino family life. The low pay and transient nature of agricultural migrant work prevented most Filipino migrant workers from having their own families; instead, they lived a communal life, where they slept on bunk beds in barracks, ate meals prepared by camp cooks, and were entertained by the children of the state's few Filipino families. This collective life provided them with day-to-day sustenance and protection. The few families present among the overwhelmingly bachelor Filipino population helped glue the community together, by making ethnic delicacies during holidays and special occasions and more importantly by providing living examples of a family life to give encouragement to the bachelors to work hard to establish their own families in the United States in the near future. Here, the meaning of family and domesticity has expanded beyond the "normative" individual and private family life, becoming more collective and public.

Prostitution

The absence of family inevitably invited prostitution, the millennia-old profession, to the Asian immigrant life. During the California Gold Rush era, prostitution thrived in the predominantly male society. At first, the majority of prostitutes were of Mexican, Spanish, or French descent and came from Mexico, Brazil, or Peru. Later, most were white prostitutes from the East Coast. Chinese women, most under coercion, also joined this trade. According to Lucie Cheng Hirata's research, Chinese prostitutes composed 85 percent of the Chinese women in San Francisco in 1860, 71 percent in 1870, and 21 percent in 1880.[33] Other writers, however, disputed Hirata's estimate, maintaining that the number of Chinese prostitutes was exaggerated and the number of Chinese wives underestimated, because census enumerators concealed the identities of individuals not engaged in prostitution, suggesting instead that non-prostitutes may have composed 50 percent of the adult females in San Francisco's Chinese population in 1870.[34] Even if we consider the latter's argument, there was one prostitute for every two Chinese women in San Francisco during the 1870s. Therefore, it is important to examine these women's lives closely.

As part of the global movement of laborers, most of the Chinese prostitutes in the late nineteenth century were young girls from Hong Kong, Canton, and neighboring areas who were kidnapped, purchased, or stolen by procurers and then smuggled to America.[35] After their arrival in San Francisco, these young women were transported to Chinatown and housed in temporary quarters known as the barracoons, where they were displayed for bids. Generally, the "fortunate" ones were sold to well-to-do Chinese as concubines or mistresses; some merchants considered experienced prostitutes to be ideal wives because they were attractive, sociable, and adept at entertaining guests. A small number were recruited to high-class establishments; they lived in upstairs apartments in Chinatown and had a more or less long-term regular customer or customers. While they seemed to be treated well, they could be sold at their master's will.[36]

Except for those "fortunate" women, most Chinese girls ended up in brothels of various grades, according to their attractiveness. During the typical four years of servitude, slave girls had to work for their owners without wages. And they could take off only a total of one month for their menstrual period during the four years and had to work for an extra year if they got pregnant.[37] These lower-grade prostitutes tended to attract working-class white and Chinese customers due to their comparatively low fees of twenty-five to fifty cents. The living conditions of these young women were miserable. Most of them lived in street-level basement apartments. Their daily activities were restricted to these tiny rooms, usually four by six feet, with a door that held the barred window facing a dim alley.[38] They were often mistreated by their owners and customers. Some owners occasionally beat them to death or otherwise injured them, and sometimes clients forced them to engage in aberrant sexual acts.

Since virtually all of these women were illiterate, there is no direct account of their lives. However, a great deal of literature from crusading Protestant missionaries, many of them in San Francisco, has survived. The literature decries the horribly degrading conditions to which Chinese "slave girls" were subjected. The writers also praised the valiant efforts of such individuals as Donaldina Cameron of the Protestant Home Mission at 920 Sacramento Street to rescue these girls from further exploitation. Besides these early records of Chinese prostitution, scholarly work since the 1960s has also revealed the miserable lives these Chinese prostitutes led.[39] Some scholars have further argued that Chinese prostitutes were victims of not only class and gender oppression but also economic exploitation.[40] Others have asserted that Chinese prostitutes were not mere victims but defiant individuals who resisted their fate as well.[41]

Under the harsh living and working conditions, these slave girls had short life expectancies. Many of them suffered from chronic ailments such as tuberculosis and venereal diseases and died in their teens and twenties. According to the Chinese Mortuary Record of the City and County of San Francisco, among the over six hundred women listed between 1870 and 1878, most died in their teens, twenties, or thirties of tuberculosis, venereal diseases, or unknown causes. Since none of the women had their occupation listed in the record, a large number of them probably were prostitutes.[42]

In the mining camps, prostitutes faced a worst fate because conditions were more primitive and alienating than in urban brothels. In 1875, there were eighty-four Chinese women on the Comstock Lode in Nevada, only nine of whom were not prostitutes.[43]

These women worked in public establishments and served a racially mixed clientele of miners and laborers. They were often called "Chiney ladies," "moon-eyed pinch foots," or "she-heathens" by their white customers.[44] Some catered to whites by dressing in exotic silks and jewels. By and large, however, the lower-rank Chinese prostitutes dressed in plain cotton and worked for fees ranging from twenty-five to fifty cents per customer. In the isolated mining areas, Chinese prostitutes were also prone to ethnic crimes. In the 1870s, for instance, four Chinese prostitutes in Comstock Lode were kidnapped by rival tongs. Only one of the victims was later found alive on the railroad, nailed inside a crate being shipped from San Francisco to Reno.[45]

Some Chinese prostitutes escaped by running away or committing suicide. One prostitute in Nevada escaped from her owner and hid in the hills. When she was found, "both her feet had frozen and had to be amputated"; she finally "courted death by refusing to take medicine or food." In Virginia City, Nevada, six Chinese prostitutes ended their miserable lives by suicide.[46]

A few fortunate prostitutes succeeded in escaping enslavement by taking court action and later enjoyed a normal family life. Annie Lee was one. A beautiful young Cantonese woman, Annie Lee was owned by a member of the Yeong Wo Company in Idaho City around 1875. After her escape to Boise to marry her lover, a young Chinese man named Ah Guan, her owner charged her with grand larceny for leaving town. When she was arrested and taken to court, she won the sympathy of the judge. At a hearing, she clearly expressed her desire to end the enslavement and marry the man she loved.[47] Her case dismissed, she returned to her husband.

It is instructive to compare Chinese and Japanese prostitutes in the late nineteenth and early twentieth centuries. Like Chinese prostitutes who were forced to be in this business, Japanese prostitutes in Hawaii, in most cases, were coerced into hawking their bodies. They were sold to be prostitutes, however, not only by procurers but also by their own husbands. Some Japanese men sold their wives to other men for profits of $100 or $200. The amount collected by the husbands rose from $50 to $100 or even to $1,000 when some wives were bought to be resold to brothels. Profits such as these resulted in more wives being brought to Hawaii to sell. Not all wives sold or prostituted, however, were victims or economic commodities; some ran off with other, more attractive or richer men or left for the city where money could be earned more easily than by working in the fields for thirty-five cents a day. A prostitute earned fifty cents to a dollar per customer, and at least $4 to $5 in an evening. A popular one with a pretty face could make $20 per night. Even after subtracting the cost of renting the shop and buying clothes and food, a busy woman could have about $200 left at the end of the month. The working conditions of Japanese prostitutes also resembled those of Chinese prostitutes. Japanese prostitutes worked daily from seven o'clock in the evening to midnight. Their shops were usually shed-like buildings standing in rows along the street. Each building had a frontage of six feet and a depth of twelve feet, which held a low, small glass window. Through the window a guest could examine the women who sat inside, dimly lit by hand lamps. If he chose a woman, he would enter the sleeping area behind a partition of wood.[48]

In contrast to Chinese and Japanese prostitutes, many Caucasians worked as independent professionals. They did very well, especially during the boom days, when competition was limited and prices were high. One madam on the mining frontier made $100,000 within less than a year.[49] These women were high-class prostitutes and considered their occupation a business. Obviously, Asian prostitutes did not enjoy such a fate. Yet regardless of racial and rank differences in the prostitution business, all of them regarded their trade as a form of work: an obvious means of economic survival that occasionally offered even some small degree of upward mobility.[50]

In summary, the "problem" of prostitution in Asian communities was a product of immigrant life in America due to institutionalized exclusions and socioeconomic sanctions against them, rather than "natural" and "cultural defects" of the Asian peoples. In the gaping void of family life, prostitution readily and easily took over the spare time of the Asian "bachelors," substituting for the absent family life, and providing temporary relief to Asian immigrants' otherwise diligent and dull daily existence. In addition, along with gambling and alcoholism, prostitution has been the classic urban vice since the dawn of history, indiscriminately plaguing all racial and cultural groups.

CHANGING GENDER ROLES

As Joint Heads of Households

Immigration to America changed women's role in their families.[51] First, Asian women became joint heads of their households, a clear promotion from their previous position in Asia. A traditional and predominant Asian family was an extended family in which several generations lived together under the same roof and was ruled by the patriarchal familial authority. Once married, a woman—the daughter-in-law of her husband's family—had to serve and please every family member, especially the parents-in-law, in order to conform to the social norms of filial daughter-in-law, submissive wife, and nurturing mother.

This predominant family pattern of three or more generations in one household, however, was not transplanted into America, and Asian immigrant families in America were mostly nuclear ones. Having suffered the pain of leaving familiar surroundings, enduring seasickness for months, and suffering prolonged interrogations and detention at the immigration station on Angel Island or other federal facilities, Asian immigrant women, and young wives especially, found that they were no longer subjected to the authority of their mothers-in-law and for the first time were female heads of their families. "It's better to be a woman in America," said Helen Hong Wong of San Francisco. "At least you can work here and rule the family along with your husband. In China it's considered a disgrace for a woman to work and it's the mother-in-law who rules."[52]

As Providers for Their Families

Asian immigrant women also found that they had become providers for their families. Although most Asian immigrant women had woven at home and tilled the fields to supplement family income prior to immigration, Asian immigrant women's participation in family economic activities and wage-earning work were more essential and indispensable for the survival of their families in the United States.

In urban communities, as wives of laundrymen, restaurant owners, grocers, cooks, and laborers, the majority of married Asian immigrant women had to work side by side with their husbands, in addition to their daily household duties. During the late nineteenth and early twentieth centuries, the laundering business was a predominant occupation of the Chinese, and Koreans to a degree, in the United States. The laundry shop was not merely a place of work but also a residence. For the wife of a laundryman, her life was not easier than that of her husband. Her home was in the back of the laundry, where she slept, cooked, and tended her children. The living quarters were humid and dim in all seasons. When she was not busy with domestic chores, she was expected to help with the laundry work. Her daily life was characterized by long hours, drudgery, and intense loneliness. The only people she saw were customers who brought in their parcels and reclaimed them when they were finished. The wives of laundrymen were easily worn out from hard work and suffered physical weariness and emotional stress.[53]

Like laundries, restaurants constituted another important type of business for Asian immigrants in the United States and sprouted across the country in the 1890s.[54] Most small Chinese restaurants were run as husband-and-wife businesses; the husband served as cook and dishwasher in the kitchen, while the wife worked as waitress and cashier in the front. Some Asian women even became successful proprietors despite the harsh environment. Gue Gim Wah, a pioneer Chinese woman in Prince, Nevada, for instance, helped her husband run a boardinghouse for Chinese miners in the area in 1930. After accumulating enough capital and experience, she opened her own restaurant in 1942, which became a big success.[55]

The grocery business ranked as a distant third occupation for Asian immigrants before the 1940s. While the larger firms seemed to have pooled capital and manpower together, with each member having well-defined responsibilities and receiving a regular salary of between $45 and $75, many smaller Asian stores were run as family businesses with unpaid family members meeting the labor demands.[56] As wives of grocers, the women worked along with their husbands, packing, stocking, and selling goods.

While the Asian immigrant women in urban communities engaged in the above work, their counterparts in rural areas shared farming and other productive activities with their husbands in addition to their domestic chores. They gardened and tended livestock. Some of the Asian farmers' wives took part in farm work. This expansion of women's labor was more common and noticeable in Hawaii. Unlike immigrant laborers on the mainland, Asian laborers in Hawaii were encouraged to bring their wives, who were paid to work on sugar or rice plantations.

In this sense, Asian immigrant women's new role could be seen as that of coprovider for their families, though they were not necessarily making 50 percent of the family income. To most Asian immigrant women, the focus of their lives was survival through hard work. The labor conducted by Asian immigrant women was vital for their family economy, as illustrated in the case of Mrs. Roh discussed earlier. Their wage-earning and non-wage-earning work made survival possible for their families in a strange land. As commented by historian Roger Daniels, the fact that many married Asian women worked "illustrate[s] an important and often unnoticed factor in Asian American economic success: that is, the contribution made by Asian American married women at a time [when] most married women in this country were not in the labor force."[57] Therefore, Asian immigrant women were not only producers of children but also providers of a bowl of rice.

As Co–Decision Makers

These new roles reinforced Asian immigrant women's position in families, and they began to share decision making with their husbands. When working jointly with their spouses, immigrant women generally had more input in family affairs and decision making, as was the case with Irish immigrant women. Historians have found that Irish immigrant men generally experienced a decline in status and power within their families as a result of migration, which pushed women into more authoritative roles than they had experienced in Ireland. The comparatively open range of economic options for many young Irish women made them more influential in the family and community.[58] Similar changes were also evident among Asian immigrant women. For most Asian immigrants, the family was a basic productive unit, in which husband and wife formed a team and were indispensable to each other. The equal or cosharing of responsibilities enabled the wife to have a higher voice in family decision making.

When Asian immigrants came to the New World, they faced a strange and hostile environment in which they were discriminated against and excluded from the mainstream labor market. They consequently had to work in trades that white laborers were unwilling to embrace, such as hand laundries, restaurants, and grocery stores, or work as common laborers and farm laborers. The necessity of survival required all Asian immigrant family members, especially the wives, to participate in productive activities. The majority of early Asian immigrant women, as discussed earlier, whether living in urban communities or rural areas, had to raise their families and help with their husbands' businesses or work in the fields and tend gardens and livestock. Therefore, Asian immigrant women's labor was indispensable to their families' survival. Moreover, Asian immigrant families in urban areas often lived in the back of their family businesses. The overlapping of family life and work life made a wife's involvement in the family business inevitable. The expansion of the female sphere enhanced Asian immigrant women's sense of self-esteem and self-confidence. They consequently became more comfortable in sharing family decision making with their husbands.

During the late nineteenth and early twentieth centuries most Asian immigrant women, however, were still careful to pay homage to ideas of male authority. Although immigration elevated a woman's position in her family as she became joint family head and coprovider for the family, moving from Asia to America did not shake her belief in the idea that family solidarity could be achieved and maintained only when a wife was subordinate and compromising. As one Chinese girl in Hawaii noted, her father "was the dominating head of the family," even though her mother played an important role in her family life.[59] This conservative attitude toward family order was not uncommon among many immigrant groups in the United States.

THE SECOND-GENERATION "DILEMMA"

In the 1920s and 1930s more American-born or second-generation Asian Americans had come of age. Educated in American public schools and raised with Asian values at home, most second-generation Asian Americans had to deal with issues of cultural affinity and identity. Meanwhile, they also encountered racism as they interacted with the larger society.

Generational and Cultural Conflicts

Generally, Asian parents valued education highly as they believed that education would be the ticket for their children to have a better future in America. As indicated in table 4.1, in 1920 the school attendance rate for both Asian males and females was comparable to that of the native white population but higher than those for the foreign-born white and Black population; beginning from 1930, it was higher than the rates of all the other groups.

Although attending American public schools, many second-generation Asian Americans were brought up according to strict Asian values at home. Similar to other immigrant children, most second-generation Asian Americans growing up in the early twentieth century followed Asian traditions at home in their daily lives. One Hawaiian-born Japanese boy wrote in the 1920s, "My parents were born in Hiroshima prefecture in Japan.

TABLE 4.1 SCHOOL ATTENDANCE (5 TO 20 YEARS), BY RACE AND SEX FOR THE UNITED STATES, 1910–1940 (PERCENTAGE)

Census year	Native white		Foreign-born white		Black		Other race[a]	
	Male	Female	Male	Female	Male	Female	Male	Female
1940	76.3	73.1	59.7	53.4	70.2	68.1	82.6	80.4
1930	74.9	72.3	58.9	51.8	65.3	63.0	75.1	79.6
1920	67.5	66.7	47.7	42.8	57.9	58.8	63.6	67.0
1910	62.5	62.0	40.4	38.4	48.5	50.4	48.3	59.7

Source: U.S. Census Bureau, "Census of the United States 1940, Population Vol. 2, Characteristics of the Population" (2021), 37–39, https://www.census.gov/library/publications/1943/dec/population-vol-2.html.

[a] Asians were counted under "other race."

They have lived in Hawaii for nearly thirty years so they understand English quite well, but they cannot speak English very freely. We speak the Japanese and English language[s] at home." Another Hawaiian-born Chinese of the same time period also noted, "The food [we eat] . . . are rice, meat and fresh vegetables. In my family, my mother and I was dressed in Chinese costume, it was high collar and long sleeve." Many second-generation Chinese girls also sewed at home, one of the domestic duties considered necessary to be passed to daughters by Chinese mothers. Mrs. S, a San Francisco–born second-generation Chinese woman, "learned sewing from mother" and made all her own clothes.[60]

The second generation's exposure to Western culture in public and preservation of Asian culture at home inevitably caused generational and cultural conflicts with their parents. Numerous oral history interviews with second-generation Asian Americans provide ample evidence of such conflicts.[61] Asian American children universally had heavier burdens after school. They had to attend Asian language schools to learn reading and writing, along with cultural traditions. In urban areas, many second-generation Asian Americans had to work in family laundries, restaurants, and grocery stores or in garment factories. In rural communities, they had to tend livestock or work in fields. In large families, Asian American youth, especially females, were expected to help their mother with cooking, cleaning, taking care of younger siblings, and other household chores. While many regarded these activities as their responsibilities, others resented these duties and challenged parental authority by breaking curfews or running away from home when their parents had arranged for their marriage without their consent.

Many children from Punjabi-Mexican families married by their own will. In many cases, the second-generation Punjabi-Mexican girls married across religious boundaries, which was an important attribute of Punjabi culture, to Muslim Asian Indians against their parents' wishes. Younger girls growing up in Arizona and isolated from the large

Punjabi-Mexican community were often fascinated with Indian men and became engaged to non-Punjabi Indians against their fathers' advice.[62]

Racism and Limited Opportunities

While having generational tensions at home, second-generation Asian Americans had to confront racism in public. At schools, Asian American students sometimes were called "Chink," "Jap," or "Hindu" by fellow students. After graduation from high school or even university, second-generation Asian Americans found that they had limited occupational opportunities because of their race. As a result, they remained in the niche occupations created by their fathers or grandfathers. Many Chinese American college graduates worked in restaurants; Nisei entered agriculture and the sale and distribution of crops. Filipino American youth also found their occupational choices limited, despite their qualifications,

GROWING UP IN THE 1930s AND 1940s

My mother took care over some of our chores if we had a lot of homework to finish. I think she regretted the fact that she was not able to finish school. But I told her not to feel that way, as we, her children, have learned a lot from her. I think she envied women who worked in offices, who were able to be out with people and carry out conversations with them. She was not ashamed of herself, but she felt that her life could have been more fulfilling. She really encouraged me to do more, and I did more. Even in her last years she was always proud of what I have done.

When I was a teenager, in the later 1940s, I was Miss Philippines of this particular fraternal organization in northern California. We were chosen for our intelligence and personality, and also on the number of tickets we could sell. Since I had made many friends among the *manongs* and I was their adopted daughter, I had little trouble selling tickets. The *manongs* usually bought them by the fistful.

Through the years, at birthday and baptism parties, I would listen to my parents' friends talk about discrimination and prejudice. They knew that they could only go so far in their jobs and that they would never be promoted, no matter how hard they worked. There was just so much prejudice back then.

I still remember that time that we went to Santa Maria, Pismo Beach. My father was hungry, so we stopped at this restaurant. But the owners told us that we could not be served in the restaurant but we could get food in the back. As far as obtaining part-time work while in high school, there were a lot of jobs that I couldn't have even though I was well qualified, much more qualified [than the whites]. The only jobs they would offer me were as a stock girl, where they put you in the back.

Source: Excerpt from Connie Tirona, "Sometimes, I Am Not Sure What It Means to Be an American," in Yen Le Espiritu, *Filipino American Lives* (Philadelphia: Temple University Press, 1995), 72–73.

as illustrated by the story in sidebar. Few second-generation Asian American college graduates practiced their professional trainings.

ETHNIC COMMUNITY BUILDING

Need for survival in a foreign and unwelcoming land was the primary motivation for Asian immigrants to construct their communities in America. They did so through a variety of social structures, including district or family associations, religious institutions, and political associations. Two features stand out across ethnic lines among Asian immigrant community organizations: most groups were fraternal in nature, and leadership positions were dominated almost without exception by merchants or the professional elite.

Organizations for Mutual Aid and Self-Governing

Most early Asian immigrant community organizations were self-governing bodies that provided mutual aid. This is most pronounced in the case of the Chinese, whose early community organizations, including district associations, clan associations, secret societies, and guilds, were mainly founded for the purpose of mutual aid and self-governance. The district associations first emerged to assist new immigrants. The first two district associations, or *huiguan*, were established by 1851 in San Francisco. They were Sanyi Huiguan, consisting of people from Nanhai, Panyu, and Shunde, three districts surrounding the city of Guangzhou (Canton), and Siyi Huiguan, comprising people from four districts of Xinhui, Taishan, Kaiping, and Enping. By 1854, there were six such huiguans on the West Coast, which were commonly known as the Chinese Six Companies. In 1882, in response to the harsh treatment of Chinese immigrants from the public and lawmakers as a result of the Chinese Exclusion Act, the six huiguans formed a national umbrella organization, the Chinese Consolidated Benevolent Association (CCBA or Zhonghua Huiguan).[63] As the district associations grew, clan associations were formed to provide services to those who lacked support from the district associations.

After the passage of the Chinese Exclusion Act in 1882, a third type of organization, the secret society, became very active and widespread. Many of the secret societies bore the name *tong* (*tang* in Pinyin, meaning a hall) and were allegedly associated with criminal activities, such as gambling, smuggling, and tong fighting; scholars have recognized both the benevolent and criminal activities of the tongs.[64] Chih Kung (Zhigong), On Leong (Anliang), and Hip Sing (Xiesheng) were the most influential tongs. On Leong in particular is comparable with the CCBA in the services it provided and dominated Chinese immigrant communities in the Midwest and on the East Coast.[65]

The above organizations offered a variety of mutual aid services. They dispatched representatives to steamers or trains to meet new immigrants. They provided temporary

FIGURE 4.3 Officers of the Six Companies, San Francisco, ca. 1900. Courtesy Roy Daniel Graves, Wikipedia.

lodging and food at their headquarters and properties they owned. They organized rotating credit associations, settled disputes, cared for the sick and disabled, built altars and temples, purchased graveyards, and sent exhumed bones to ancestral villages in China for final burial.[66] They also sponsored Chinese language schools to help preserve Chinese culture.

Chinese immigrants also formed guilds to protect their economic interests. Guilds for laundrymen, shoemakers, and cigar makers had been founded by the late 1860s. The laundrymen's guild, Tung Hing Tong, for example, set up uniform prices for different items, divided up different neighborhoods among its members, and collected funds to hire lawyers to defend their interests.[67]

Like the Chinese, Japanese immigrants also formed self-governing organizations between the turn of the twentieth century and the eve of World War II. In each Japanese community in North America, there was a local Japanese association, Nihonjinkai. These associations were established by either government officials or business leaders. In August 1891, the Japanese consulate in San Francisco helped the local community to form a Greater Japanese Association. The association was dissolved a decade later but was revamped and expanded in 1909 in response to increasing anti-Japanese sentiment and activities on the West Coast. In February of that year, the Japanese consulate general in San Francisco prompted the founding of the Japanese Association of America.

In addition to Nihonjin-kai, Japanese immigrants also formed *kenjinkai*, or prefectural organizations. In Japan, each *ken*, or prefecture, has its own distinctive foods, customs, and habits. Japanese immigrants from the same prefecture tended to settle in the same area in America and consequently established a prefectural organization to help ease their adjustment and survival in the strange land. Like Nihonjin-kai, kenjinkai also sponsored various social activities.

The leaders of the reorganized associations were almost exclusively economically successful individuals. Businessmen, editors of Japanese newspapers, and agricultural entrepreneurs were the typical leaders of the national and local associations. The first president of the national Japanese Association of America was George Shima (born Kinji Ushijima), an extremely successful agricultural entrepreneur who was dubbed the "Potato King" by the media and was arguably the first Issei millionaire. Many of the association leaders were selected from the local business class.

Organizationally, each local association reported to a regional body corresponding to Japanese consular districts. The regional bodies included the United Northwestern Japanese Association, headquartered in Seattle and with fifteen chapters in Washington and Montana; the Japanese Association of Oregon, based in Portland and overseeing residents in Oregon and Idaho; the Japanese national headquarters in San Francisco, which had forty chapters in Northern California, Nevada, Utah, and Colorado; and the Central Japanese Association of Southern California, which was based in Los Angeles and in charge of residents across Southern California, New Mexico, and Arizona.

The annual membership dues of three to six dollars were collected and used to secure endorsements for Japanese consular documents. The Japanese consulates allowed half of these fees to go to the associations to support community activities. The Gentlemen's Agreement of 1907–1908 stipulated that the Japanese government collect information on Japanese nationals living in the United States. The U.S. government and Japanese consulates authorized the local Japanese associations to issue return certificates for the Japanese immigrants who visited Japan. In addition, local Japanese associations dealt with family registration and passport applications, which allowed the Issei to bring their wives and children to America. Most Japanese belonged to local associations until 1924, when it was no longer possible to secure passports for immigrants' family members.[68]

Japanese immigrants also formed trade associations. The first trade association was the Japanese Shoemakers' League, organized in 1893 in San Francisco. In 1903, the Art Goods and Nations Commercial Association was established to minimize the keen competition among many Japanese import-export merchants. In 1908, the business owners of dye shops started the San Francisco Japanese Cloth Dye Trade Association. In 1915, the American Magazines and Books Association was organized for sellers of Japanese books and magazines. In addition, almost all the different trades had their own associations, eventually enabling the formation of a Japanese Chamber of Commerce in 1915.

As agriculture provided the foundation of the Japanese ethnic economy, the trade associations involving the production, processing, distribution, and marketing of farm products were most relevant to the majority of Japanese immigrants. In the 1910s, the Central Japanese Agricultural Association of California functioned as an umbrella organization for farmers in Northern and Central California, and the Southern California Central Agricultural Association for farmers in Southern California. Additionally, growers of various vegetables and fruits also founded their own associations. Normally, successful farmers served as officers of these associations and enjoyed an elite status similar to that of the urban merchants.[69]

One significant form of mutual aid among Asian immigrants is the *rotating credit association* that existed among early Chinese, Japanese, and Korean immigrants. The generic term for the Chinese rotating credit association is *hui*, meaning "association" or "club." Such associations are believed to have been around for over 800 years in China. Chinese immigrants in the United States employed the hui as a means acquiring capital for initiating a business. A typical hui may consist of a dozen people, each member promising to pay a certain amount on a specific day of each month for a given length of time. At each meeting, the highest bidder gets the entire payment of the month from all members; at the last meeting each member receives the total payment of each month. The earliest recorded hui was found among the Chinese in New York City in the 1890s.[70] *Ko*, *tanomoshi*, or *mujin*, the Japanese forms of the rotating credit association, were likely adapted from the Chinese institution in the thirteenth century. Japanese immigrants brought the institution with them when immigrating to the United States. Like the Chinese, Japanese also used a bidding and lottery system. In Hawaii, the Pacific Northwest, and California, Japanese immigrants established these rotating credit associations.[71] The rotating credit associations appearing in Korea as early as the 1660s, known as *kye*, also existed among Korean immigrants, but little research has been conducted on the topic. A 1990 study suggests using the surveys conducted by the Japanese American Research Project on 18,000 Issei who had migrated to the United States before 1924 as a basis for comparison with Korean immigrants of the same time period.[72]

At a time when white-owned banks in California discriminated against Asian businessmen and farmers, the rotating credit associations enabled Asian immigrants to capitalize business enterprises on their own. The associations differed depending on nationality. While the Japanese ones tended to be open to all Japanese, as the Japanese had developed a strong national identity after the Meiji Restoration, their Chinese counterparts were mostly confined within kinship networks of district associations, clan associations, secret societies, and guilds.

The first Korean self-governing community organization was the *dong-hoe*, or village council, established on every plantation in the Hawaiian Islands in 1903. Different from their Chinese and Japanese counterparts, the Korean immigrant community organizations bore two distinctive features. First, most of the early Korean community organizations were influenced by Korean Christian churches in their principles, functions, and structures. Second, most Korean immigrant social, political, and cultural organizations were formed for the purpose of protesting against Japanese interference in Korean affairs and later dominance of Korea after 1910 when the country was annexed by Japan.[73] For these reasons, Korean community organizations will be discussed more extensively in the sections below on political parties and religious organizations.

Sikhs in North America also organized their own self-governing bodies, as represented by the Khalsa Diwan (Free Divine) Society. It was first organized by Sikhs in Vancouver, British Columbia, Canada, in 1906. The society called for the preservation of Indian culture and promoted the cohesiveness of Sikh communities in North America. As a mutual aid community organization, it opened the first Sikh temple in Vancouver in 1908. The temple housed a copy of Sikh sacred writings and had a hall for worship and meetings. It also ran a kitchen to provide free meals and a school as well. A few years later, the Khalsa Diwan Society spread to the United States. A chapter of Khalsa Diwan was established in Stockton in 1912. Its chief goal was to look after the welfare of Asian Indian immigrants. The organization was soon incorporated and acquired land to build its own temple (discussed in the next section).

In 1903, Filipino students known as *pensionados* came to the continental United States under government scholarships to study at American universities and colleges. They were part of the U.S. government's effort to assimilate their "brown brothers" into American culture. In contrast, sugar planters recruited *sakadas* (recruits) to labor in Hawaii beginning in 1909. As a result of America's influence, many American-style fraternal organizations emerged among the Filipinos.

The earliest Filipino mutual aid organization was the Great Filipino Lodge, founded in San Francisco in 1920. Affiliated with the Freemasons, the lodge intended to provide mutual aid to its members and to support social activities. The next oldest organization was the Caballeros de Dimas-Alang, formed in San Francisco in 1921. The organization was named to honor the Filipino nationalist leader Jose Rizal, who wrote under the pen name of Dimas-Alang and was executed on December 30, 1896. Each year on the anniversary of Rizal's martyrdom, the organization held parades, speeches, and dinners. In the 1930s, it had more than two thousand members and one hundred lodges. The third organization was Legionairios del Trabajo, formed in 1924 also in San Francisco. It expanded to eighty-six chapters in forty-six states as well as the territories of Hawaii and Alaska. The three organizations became known as the Big Three and remain greatly influential in Filipino American communities.[74]

Political Parties

In 1903, the first political Korean organization in U.S. territory, Sin-Min-Hoi (New People's Society), was founded in Honolulu. The primary goals of the organization were to protest Japanese aggression and to rebuild Korea through rejuvenating its national spirit at home and abroad. Between 1903 and 1907, more than twenty other political organizations were established in Hawaii. In 1908, community leaders sought to form a unified organization in order to more effectively fight Japanese aggression.

The consolidated organization, the Korean National Association (KNA), was established on February 1, 1909. With its headquarters in San Francisco, it had more than 3,200 members and developed more than 130 local chapters in California, Hawaii, Mexico, Siberia, and Manchuria. The membership primarily came from among political refugees, students, and professionals. KNA worked on two fronts: fighting for the independence of Korea and protecting Koreans in America. It lobbied for the U.S. government to differentiate between Korean and Japanese immigrants and to consult KNA on matters concerning Korean immigrants. It also sponsored student refugees to come to America, helped Korean immigrants find jobs, and arbitrated disputes between employers and employees.

While KNA remained as the most influential political organization among Korean immigrants, it was plagued by factionalism. Within the organization, the three most notable Korean leaders in America were Park Yong-man, Rhee Syngman, and Ahn Chang-ho, and each had his own political ambition and preference. Park started the League of Korean Independence in 1919 with 350 members, while Rhee established the Dong-Ji Hoi (Comrade Society) in Honolulu in 1921, which focused solely on supporting the provisional government in Korea. Ahn established the Hung Sa Dan (Young Korean Academy) in San Francisco in 1913 to train young Koreans by developing their minds, bodies, and virtues. These competing organizations divided the Korean Immigrant community, resulting in the emergence of yet smaller organizations. With the liberation of Korea in 1945, the nationalist movement lost its purpose and ceased operations.

Korean women also formed their own nationalistic organizations. The first such organization, the Korean Women's Society, formed in San Francisco in 1908 to provide educational and social services to Korean immigrants and their children. In March 1919, a group of Korean women in Sacramento formed the Korean Women's Association, and a group of Korean women in Los Angeles founded the Women's Friendship Association. Two months later, the three women's organizations merged into a single body, the Korean Women's Patriotic League, based in Dinuba, California.[75]

Like the Korean groups, the Chinese immigrant society in America was also connected to and impacted by political developments in their homeland. The Emperor Protection Society, or Baohuang Hui, established in 1899 by prominent reformer Kang Youwei while in exile immediately following his failed 1898 reform movement in China, attracted supporters from among the Chinese communities in America. At the turn of the twentieth century, branches of the society were established in San Francisco, New York, and Chicago.

Similarly, revolutionaries developed close associations with Chinese communities in America. The rise of Sun Yat-sen, hailed as the founding father of the Republic of China, can be traced to his intimate ties with the Chinese community in Hawaii, where he spent his teenage years. In the 1900s, he traveled among Chinese communities throughout the continental United States to raise funds for his cause. After the 1911 Revolution that overthrew the Manchu imperial court and founded the Chinese Republic, major Chinese immigrant communities in America formed branches of the Nationalist Party, or Guomindang.

Nationalist fervor was equally high among Asian Indians. In New York, Asian Indians founded the Pan Aryan Association and the Indo-American Association in 1906. They spread their anti-British sentiment back to the homeland by sending revolutionary literature to India. Their activities alarmed the British authorities in India who noticed that the United States had been a breeding ground for Indian nationalist movements.[76]

Religious Organizations

Confucianism, Daoism, Buddhism, and various folk traditions have played important roles in Chinese people's spiritual lives, and they were transplanted to the New World by Chinese immigrants. Most of the early Chinese immigrants, however, were more likely to practice one or another of these traditions privately at home, around the family altar with a shrine dedicated to a god, such as Dudi gong, the Earth God, or Guan gong, General Guanyu, a war hero from the popular historical novel *The Three Kingdoms* who is believed to bring prosperity to family, or to ancestors. This practice makes it difficult to estimate the number of religious organizations. Christian churches, on the other hand, have been recorded relatively better.

The first Chinese Christian church was established in San Francisco in 1853, connected with the Presbyterian Board of Foreign Missions. Four Chinese who had been converted in China were the charter members of the church. Other denominations also followed to expand their missions to Chinese laborers: Methodists in 1868 and Baptists, Congregationalists, and Episcopalians in 1870. By 1892 there were ten Chinese churches established by eleven denominations. Together they provided 271 Chinese Sunday schools and missions in thirty-one states. They all followed a similar pattern: the pastors of the churches were Caucasian, and Chinese Christians could serve only as assistants to white missionaries. During the Chinese exclusion era (1882–1943), the goal of these churches was to bring the "heathen" Chinese to Christianity and send them to China to help with the missionaries there.[77]

Among the Asian immigrants, Koreans were the most influenced by Christian organizations. This distinction can be traced to their conversion to Christianity in Korea and the Christian sponsorship of Korean immigration to the United States, as discussed in chapter 1. Korean Christian churches were almost as old as the Korean immigration. On July 4, 1903, only half a year after their arrival in Hawaii, the territory's Korean immigrants held their first worship service at the plantation camp in Molokai. On November 10 of that year, they formed the Korean Evangelical Society in Honolulu. In December 1905, the Hawaiian Mission of the Methodist Episcopal Church held its first service for three language groups: English, Japanese, and Korean. By the early 1910s, Methodist churches had increased to twenty-five with seventy-five mission stations on the island. On the mainland, Koreans in Los Angeles held their first church service in 1904 and founded the Korean Methodist Church the following year. During the 1910s and 1920s, there were around a thousand Korean immigrants along the Pacific Coast who had founded more than a dozen churches.[78]

For the Japanese, both Buddhist and Christian churches played significant part in their American life. The first Buddhist church was established in Hawaii in the 1890s. In 1899, the first official Buddhist priests, trained and authorized by the religious authorities in Japan, arrived in San Francisco and opened the first American Buddhist temple. Soon other Buddhist temples were founded in places where sizeable Japanese immigrants had settled, including other cities in the Bay Area, the agricultural Central Valley, and Southern California, as well as other cities and agricultural areas in Washington State. Buddhist temples were usually sites for weddings, funerals, and other ceremonial rituals. At the same time, most Japanese immigrants, like their Chinese counterparts, practiced Buddhism at home. They built home shrines called *butsudan* and lit incense, contemplated Buddhist teaching, and recited prayers.[79]

Although Buddhism enjoyed dominance among the Japanese immigrants, Christianity competed with it from the beginning. It has been noted that wherever the Buddhists started a successful language school, Christians launched a competing facility.[80] Japanese adoption of Christianity was closely associated with the pragmatist attitudes among many new immigrants from Asian countries. As Christian churches focused their work on charitable activities such as free English language classes, food, and fashion, many early Japanese immigrants found employment through churches, especially as houseboys who were often referred as "mission boys." In addition, Christianity was less complicated and expensive compared to Shin Buddhism, a branch of Buddhism popular in both Japan and America, whose wedding and funeral services were costly.

The evolution of Christian churches among the Japanese normally follows a pattern that was also common for Christian churches among other Asian immigrants. Initially, Japanese Christians attended the services presided over by Caucasian ministers and mixed congregations. But they formed all-Japanese congregations as soon as they accumulated enough followers and funds. Both Buddhist and Christian churches held Sunday schools and Sunday services and offered social services and women and youth programs.[81]

Religious organizations were equally important among Asian Indians. Erroneously called Hindus in America, Asian Indian immigrants were overwhelmingly Sikhs from Punjab, and only one-third were Muslim, with a small fraction Hindu. The Sikhs in Stockton built their first temple in America in 1912. The first Hindu priest in the United States was Swami Vivekananda. He lectured on Hinduism at the World's Columbian Exposition in Chicago in 1893 and around the country.[82]

The Philippines is the only majority-Catholic country in Asia, with 80 percent of Filipinos Catholic, about 10 percent Muslim, and 5 percent Protestant, with the remaining 5 percent including Buddhists and followers of indigenized Christian sects and indigenous religions. When migrating to the United States, Filipinos realized that religion helped them sustain their traditional customs and values. Probably due to their seasonal migrant pattern, there were few established Catholic churches among the Filipino laborers.[83]

In addition, religious practices and spirituality outside of formal organizations also provided important emotional support for Asian immigrants. Asians have been known for their religious synchronization of different religions and a more informal approach to religion. Among the Asian immigrants in the United States, many built home shrines or alcoves to worship gods and icons from Confucianism, Buddhism, Daoism, Shintoism, Hinduism, Islam, Sikhism, Christianity, and indigenous traditions. These spiritual homes provided them comfort and strength and eased the drudgeries and difficulties of their daily lives.[84]

ASIAN IMMIGRANT HOME AND COMMUNITY IN HISTORICAL PERSPECTIVE

As Asian immigrants of varied races and classes encountered, interacted with, and integrated with American society in various urban and rural communities, they contested and redefined the normative meaning of family and domesticity. The severely uneven sex ratio among all groups of Asian immigrants propelled them to invent and practice diverse forms of family building—marriage, sexual partnerships, interdependent relationships, both heterosexual and homosexual, coethnic, interethnic, and interracial.

The split marriage—the Taishanese "widow" and American "concubine" pattern—among Chinese immigrants, picture brides among Japanese and Korean immigrants, and Punjabi-Mexican marriage among Asian Indian immigrants were all creative attempts to normalize the "abnormal" and incomplete existence of Asian immigrants caused by the destructiveness of the human migration movement and unfavorable immigration regulations and restrictions. Both "normative" and "non-normative" marriages and intimacies helped Asian immigrants maintain some level of autonomy, mobility, and protection in an alienating environment. This more flexible and expanded domesticity was pivotal for Asian immigrants in negotiating migration and global capitalism.

Family life for Asian immigrants on American soil also meant changing gender roles for both Asian immigrant men and women. While in Asia most families lived in extended, multigenerational households where in-laws ruled, in America most Asian immigrant wives found themselves as joint family heads and coproviders for their families. Reinforced by their economic power within the family, they could share decision making with their husbands.

Unlike their immigrant parents who were more anchored with the traditional values they brought with them to the new land, second-generation Asian Americans had to deal with their "dilemma." Born in America and educated in American public schools, they expected to be treated as citizens and to enjoy the rights and freedoms legitimated by their citizenship. On the contrary, they confronted racism and discrimination and found limited job opportunities in the larger society. They could find comfort in neither American nor Asian culture.

In addition to family building, the construction of community through various types of geographical, lineal, occupational, political, and religious organizations effectively provided social services crucial for the survival of Asian immigrants. The goals of these organizations mostly focused on mutual aid, providing social services intended to ease the difficulties faced by immigrants. At the same time, the missions and agendas of these organizations often linked with the socioeconomic conditions and political trends of their homelands.

KEY TERMS

- Taishanese "widow" and American "concubine" pattern
- Japanese picture brides
- Korean picture brides
- Punjabi-Mexican families
- second-generation dilemma
- Chinese Six Companies
- rotating credit associations
- Baohuang Hui (Emperor Protection Society)
- *dong-hoe* (village council)
- Korean churches
- Japanese Association of America
- Korean National Association (KNA)
- Central Japanese Agricultural Association of California
- Southern California Central Agricultural Association
- Khalsa Diwan (Free Divine) Society
- Korean Women's Patriotic League
- Great Filipino Lodge
- Caballeros de Dimas-Alang
- Legionairios del Trabajo

REVIEW QUESTIONS

1. Discuss the various types of marriages and interdependent intimacies among Asian immigrants prior to World War II. What factors contributed to the formation of these innovative marriages or domestic relationships? How was "domesticity" transformed and redefined under the social context of Asian immigration?
2. How did changing gender roles take place among Asian immigrant families? How different or similar were Asian immigrant women's lives in America compared to those in their homelands?
3. List the major functions of Asian immigrant community organizations and explain why they were crucial to the survival and success of Asian immigrants.

FILMS

Adolfson, Nathan (producer/director). *Passing Through*. 37-minute document on a Korean adoptee who grew up in Coon Rapids, MN. 1998.

Law, Lindsay, and John K. Chan (producers). 102-minute drama adopted from Louis Chu's novel *Eat a Bowl of Tea*. In New York's Chinatown of the late 1940s, young Ben Loy, fresh out of the service, has his whole life spread out before him—including a job, an apartment, and a marriage arranged by his father. 2003.

Nair, Mira (producer/director). *The Namesake*. 122-minute drama about the American-born son of Indian immigrants who feels pulled between his ethnic heritage and his desire to assimilate, especially after becoming involved with two very different women. 2007.

Sarin, Ritu, and Tenzing Sonam (producers/directors). *The New Puritans: The Sikhs of Yuba City*. 27-minute documentary of generational conflict between traditional value systems and customs and the American ideas and ways in the Sikh community. 1985.

Wang, Wayne (producer/director), and Amy Tan (producer/writer). *Joy Luck Club*. 139-minute drama of four lifelong friends, whose lives are filled with joy and heartbreak, showing how their experiences have affected the hopes and dreams they hold for each of their children. 1994.

FURTHER READING

Azuma, Eiichiro. *Between Two Empires: Race, History, and Transnationalism in Japanese America*. New York: Oxford University Press, 2005.

Choy, Bong-Youn. *Koreans in America*. Chicago: Nelson-Hall, 1979.

Espiritu, Yen Le. *Asian American Women and Men: Labor, Laws, and Love*. 2nd ed. Lanham, MD: Rowman & Littlefield, 2007.

Fujita, Stephen S., and David J. O'Brien. *Japanese American Ethnicity: The Persistence of Community*. Seattle: University of Washington Press, 1991.

Ichioka, Yuji. "Amerika Nadeshiko: Japanese Immigrant Women in the United States, 1900–1924." *Pacific History Review* 49, no. 2 (May 1980): 339–357.

Kim, Richard S. *The Quest for Statehood: Korean Immigrant Nationalism and U.S. Sovereignty, 1905–1945*. New York: Oxford University Press, 2011.

Leonard, Karen Isaksen. *Making Ethnic Choices: California's Punjabi Mexican Americans*. Philadelphia: Temple University Press, 1992.

Lim, Shirley Jennifer. *A Feeling of Belonging: Asian American Women's Public Culture, 1930–1960*. New York: New York University Press, 2006.

Ling, Huping. *Chinese Americans in the Heartland: Migration, Work, and Community*. New Brunswick, NJ: Rutgers University Press, 2022.

———. *Chinese Chicago: Race, Transnational Migration, and Community since 1870*. Stanford, CA: Stanford University Press, 2012.

———. *Chinese St. Louis: From Enclave to Cultural Community*. Philadelphia: Temple University Press, 2004.

———. *Surviving on the Gold Mountain: A History of Chinese American Women and Their Lives*. Albany: State University of New York Press, 1989.

———. *Voices of the Heart: Asian American Women on Immigration, Work, and Family*. Kirksville, MO: Truman State University Press, 2007.

Matsumoto, Valerie J. *Farming the Home Place: A Japanese American Community in California, 1919–1982*. Ithaca, NY: Cornell University Press, 1993.

Okihiro, Gary. *Common Ground: Reimagining American History*. Princeton, NJ: Princeton University Press, 2001.

Shah, Nayan. *Stranger Intimacy: Contesting Race, Sexuality and the Law in the North American West*. Berkeley: University of California Press, 2011.

Yang, Fenggang. *Chinese Christians in America: Conversion, Assimilation, and Adhesive Identities*. University Park: Pennsylvania State University Press, 1999.

Yoo, David K. *Contentious Spirits: Religion in Korean American History, 1903–1945*. Stanford, CA: Stanford University Press, 2010.

Yung, Judy. *Unbound Feet: A Social History of Chinese Women in San Francisco*. Berkeley: University of California Press, 1995.

5

WORLD WAR II
A Turning Point

CHAPTER OUTLINE

Changing Public Mood
In Military Services
Home Front
End of Exclusion
Japanese Internment
Asian Americans and World War II in Historical Perspective

SIGNIFICANT EVENTS

1931	Japanese Imperial Army invades the Manchuria region of China
1937	Japan begins a full-fledged invasion of China
1940	Congress passes the Alien Registration Act, requiring enemy aliens to register annually at post offices
1941	On December 7, Japan attacks the American naval base at Pearl Harbor on the Hawaiian island of Oahu; the next day President Roosevelt asks Congress to declare war on Japan
1941–1945	Asian Americans participate in American war efforts by enrolling in the armed forces, working in defense industries, and raising funds and donating blood
1942	The First and Second Filipino Infantry Regiments are formed; thousands of Filipinos fight beside American soldiers in defending Bataan and Corregidor in the Philippines; in Los Angeles, 109 Koreans, one-fifth of the city's Korean population, join the California National Guard; President Roosevelt signs Executive Order 9066 on February 19, authorizing the mass removal of Japanese citizens and residents from the West Coast

1942–1944	More than 110,000 individuals of Japanese ancestry are interned in ten camps; more than 27,500 Japanese Nisei serve in the armed forces, of whom 18,000 enroll in the all-Nisei 442nd Regimental Combat Team; 15,000 to 20,000 Chinese serve in the armed forces
1943	The Army's Military Intelligence Service Language School (MISLS) is established in San Francisco in November; the Chinese Exclusion Acts are repealed on December 13; the Supreme Court upholds the constitutionality of the Japanese curfew law in *Minoru Yasui v. United States* and *Hirabayashi v. United States*
1944	The federal government revokes the mass evacuation order on December 17; on December 18, the Supreme Court declares the constitutionality of the mass removal of Japanese in *Korematsu v. United States*; the same day, the Supreme Court orders Mitsuye Endo's release from the internment camp
1945	World War II ends
1946	57,251 Japanese internees return to the Pacific West; the Luce-Celler Act allows Asian Indians (including present-day Pakistanis and Bangladeshis) and Filipinos to enter the country on an annual quota of 100 and to become naturalized
1970s–1980s	The redress movement seeks an official apology and reparations from the federal government for interning Japanese American citizens and residents during World War II
1976	The Japanese American Citizens League (JACL) forms the National Committee for Redress (NCR)
1979	The JACL establishes the National Council for Japanese American Redress (NCJAR) to seek a legislative sponsor to introduce a redress bill in Congress
1980	The Commission on Wartime Relocation and Internment of Civilians (CWRIC) is formed by Congress to study the mass removal and internment of Japanese Americans
1988	The Civil Liberties Act of 1988 is signed by President Ronald Reagan, providing a one-time payment of $20,000 and a formal apology to each surviving Japanese American who had been interned during the war

WORLD WAR II proved to be a turning point for Asian immigrants and their American-born children. Scholars have pointed out four positive changes to four of the early five groups of Asian immigrants—Chinese, Filipinos, Koreans, and Asian Indians—as the governments of their homelands allied with the

United States. The general public perception of Asians had turned more positive. This more favorable social attitude enabled some members of these groups to enter into professions that once were closed to them, allowed Asians to enlist in the American Armed Forces, and finally led to the repeal of the exclusion laws that discriminated against individuals of Asian ancestry for over a half century. When evaluating the impact of the war on American society, historians have also noted three types of positive changes: "changes in the rules by which Asian American communities were governed by the larger society; changes in the way that these communities regarded themselves; and finally, changes in the racial ideology of the larger society." The war, on the other hand, also produced "one of the grossest violations of the constitutional rights" of 70,000 American citizens of Japanese ancestry. Along with their immigrant parents, they were ordered to move from their homes on the Pacific Coast and be confined within ten internment camps across the country.[1]

CHANGING PUBLIC MOOD

Although both Chinese and Japanese, along with other Asian immigrants, had been discriminated against in the United States, their respective perceptions by the American public changed during the war—Chinese now were viewed as brave, heroic, honest, and hardworking allies, whereas Japanese were scorned as cowardly, conniving, and despicable enemies. What caused such a drastic change of attitude toward the two groups of Asians in America?

Two factors may explain the changing American public mood toward Chinese and Japanese. The first is the heroic resistance of Chinese armies to the Japanese invasion of China. In 1931, the Japanese Imperial Army invaded the Manchuria region of China; the operation expanded to a full-fledged invasion of the entire country in 1937. Chinese armies and civilians bravely fought the brutal Japanese invasion and occupation through traditional as well as guerrilla warfare. Meanwhile, the Chinese American community's participation in the war effort in China helped enhance the U.S. public's awareness of Japanese imperialism and aggression and Chinese heroic resistance. The frequent media coverage in America and the increased tension between the governments of Japan and the United States helped turn American public sentiment around.

The second factor is the Japanese attack on the American naval base at Pearl Harbor on the Hawaiian island of Oahu. The surprise assault in the early morning of December 7, 1941, by 180 Japanese airplanes killed more than 2,400 and wounded nearly 1,200 Americans, damaged or destroyed nearly 300 American warplanes, and sunk 18 American warships. The entire country was outraged by the sudden attack. The next day, President Roosevelt asked Congress to declare war on Japan.

To understand why and how an aesthetic and peace-loving people had changed into imperialistic and militaristic aggressors to their neighboring countries, the British and Dutch colonies in southeast Asian, and the American sphere in the Pacific Rim since the Meiji Restoration in 1868, it is important to note that a series of American actions and treatments of Japan had turned around to haunt the United States. They began with the arrival of Commodore Matthew Perry's "black boats" at Edo in 1853 to pressure the Tokugawa government to open the country to American interests and the unequal treaties that followed in 1858, which actually ended the Tokugawa seclusion, continued with the 1924 Immigration Act that purposefully and unnecessarily singled out Japanese as particularly unwelcome, and concluded with Woodrow Wilson's refusal to recognize Japan's argument that the League of Nations should declare all races equal. These humiliating experiences prompted the Meiji government and its successors to industrialize and militarize, believing that only by practicing a "rich country and strong military" policy could the Japanese be treated properly in the international political arena. The invasions of China, Vietnam, the Philippines, and the British and Dutch colonies in Southeast Asia and the inevitable confrontation with the United States across the Pacific were all necessary steps toward Japanese pan-Asian empire building.[2]

The imperialistic struggle between the industrial powers was now further entangled by race-motivated sentiments. The racial sentiments toward Chinese and Japanese, the two large Asian populations, however, were completely opposite. Gallup polls taken in 1942, right after the Pearl Harbor attack, when the Chinese became the heroic allies of the United States and Japanese the sneaky attacking foes, showed the contrasting images of the two groups. While the Chinese were regarded as "hardworking, honest, brave, religious, intelligent, practical" (the top six highest rated qualities), the Japanese were viewed as "treacherous, sly, warlike."[3] Although anti-Japanese sentiment had appeared in the United States since the late nineteenth century when Japanese, along with Chinese, were viewed as a "yellow peril" taking jobs away from natives, it reached hysterical levels in the wake of the Pearl Harbor attack. Government propaganda and nongovernmental media joined hands to launch a "Jap hunt." The Office of War Information (OWI) was established in June 1942 to work with magazine publishers, advertising agencies, and radio stations. *Life* magazine published an article on how to distinguish a Japanese from a Chinese person by the shape of their nose and the stature of their body (see sidebar). Many nongovernmental "Jap hunting licenses" were circulated around the country. These "licenses" often characterized Japanese people as subhuman, in the form of rodents or serpents.

Similarly, when thousands of Filipinos fought beside American soldiers in defending Bataan and Corregidor in the Philippines in the spring of 1942, the Filipinos in the United States were perceived more positively. Individual Filipinos, who felt "something

> **HOW TO TELL YOUR FRIENDS FROM THE JAPS**
>
> Virtually all Japanese are short. Japanese are seldom fat; they often dry up as they age. Most Chinese avoid horn-rimmed spectacles. Japanese walk stiffly erect, hard heeled. Chinese, more relaxed, have an easy gait. The Chinese expression is likely to be more kindly, placid, open; the Japanese more positive, dogmatic, arrogant. Japanese are hesitant, nervous in conversation, laugh loudly at the wrong time.
>
> Source: "How to Tell Your Friends from the Japs," *Time*, December 22, 1941.

intangible in the air" that said America had learned to respect them, were pleased by the abrupt changes to the attitudes of the American public.[4]

IN MILITARY SERVICES

Individuals of Asian ancestry responded to the war enthusiastically, as they viewed it as a chance to prove their loyalty to the United States as well as to get rid of the Japanese aggressors of their homelands. Sizeable numbers of Chinese and Filipinos were enlisted into the U.S. military. For them, obtaining citizenship also provided a major incentive to join the American Armed Forces. As servicemen were desperately needed, the government was able to amend the requirement of citizenship for service. Mass naturalization ceremonies were often held before induction. About 40 percent of Chinese enlistees were foreign-born and became naturalized upon signing up. It has been estimated that between 15,000 and 20,000 Chinese men and women served in the military forces, 70 percent in the Army and 25 percent in the Army Air Force.[5] Young Chinese were found within the long lines of enlistees outside recruiting offices across the country.

Richard Ho's experiences during the war provide some insight into Chinese participation in the war effort. Ho started out as a defense worker at Curtiss-Wright United in St. Louis. He then was drafted into the Army Air Force and stationed in Texas. When the war ended, he was honorably discharged back to St. Louis. Because of his military service, Ho was able to become a naturalized citizen. He then went to Hawaii by steamer and was immediately recruited as a serviceman at Hickam Field, a U.S. Air Force base. In September 1946 he was reassigned to the Fifth Air Force and stationed in Nagoya, Japan. In 1948, he returned to Hickam Field.[6]

Some Chinese enlistees were able to utilize their college education and Chinese language ability to serve America, as exemplified in the wartime experience of Hong Sit, a graduate who joined the Army in 1943 from Hop Alley (nickname of Chinatown in St. Louis) (see sidebar).

Like their male counterparts, young Chinese American women also served in the armed forces during the war. Although no statistics exist on how many Chinese women actually served, individual monographs reveal Chinese women served in the Army Nurse

> ### THE WARTIME EXPERIENCE OF HONG SIT
>
> It [the military training] was strenuous. . . . Before being inducted, I was expecting terrible ordeals ahead. Both Sam [Sit's brother] and cousin Wayne had entered the service earlier, and both reported it was "hell on earth." . . .
>
> There were the usual obstacle course and endurance races, plus crawling on our belly under barbed wires with a pack and rifle while a machine gun fired just over our heads. Our barracks had to be immaculate, clothes hung pressed and pleated, shoes shined, and beds made with blankets so tight that the inspection officer could bounce a coin on it.
>
> . . . Before long I was back in Camp Crowder, Missouri, as a Second Lieutenant, training a new Signal Center Team. We soon received orders to ship out by train to the West Coast. . . . We finally boarded a troop ship at Long Beach. It took a month to reach our destination in Bombay, India. . . . After an arduous and mosquito-infested train ride on hard benches, we arrived in Calcutta, then flew over the hump, from Camp Kamchaparan to Kunming, China. Then it was another back-breaking, liver-shaking truck ride along the eastern terminus of the Burma Road to Kweiyang [Guiyang], our home for the next half year. We set up a communication center and soon were preparing for the big push to throw the Japanese invaders out of China. . . . When the war was over and our Signal unit was disbanded, I received orders to accompany Chinese troops to take over Taiwan from the Japanese. . . . After Taiwan, I found myself assigned to Beijing, as translation officer of the interpreters section.
>
> Source: Hong Sit, *My View from a Bridge* (Houston, TX: Blessing Books, 1999), 41–47, cited in Huping Ling, *Chinese St. Louis: From Enclave to Cultural Community* (Philadelphia: Temple University Press, 2004), 120.

Corps, the WAVES (Women Accepted for Volunteer Emergency Service, the women's corps in the Navy), the WAC (Women's Army Corps), and the WASP (Women Airforce Service Pilots). Helen Pon Onyett of San Francisco was among the first Chinese American women to volunteer for the Army Nurse Corps. With four years of nursing experience, she felt she could do better in the military than in civilian life. She nursed numerous wounded soldiers on ships off North Africa and at a military hospital in the United States. During her thirty-five years of service, she was awarded eight major decorations for distinguished military service.[7]

Two Chinese American women stood out for their service in the elite WASP. Hazel Ah Ying Lee (usually referred to as Ah Ying in the literature on WASP) was the daughter of a Chinese immigrant family in Portland, Oregon. She and her older brother were interested in flying and completed flight instructions with the support of the local Chinese community in 1932. She joined the first class of the WASP in 1943 and was known for her "handy, hearty laugh" among her fellow pilots. She graduated and went on active duty.

Unfortunately, in November 1944 when she was carrying out a mission, her plane experienced a malfunction and crashed in Great Falls, Montana. She was severely injured and died in a local hospital a few days later.[8] Maggie Gee of San Francisco became the second Chinese American woman to join the WASP. Among her class of 107 young women, she was the only Chinese. She and her fellow students went through training just as strenuous as the male pilots. Maggie graduated and flew with WASP. After the war, she returned to school and later became a physicist.[9]

Filipinos made important contributions to the war effort in the Pacific. When they rushed to recruiting offices to volunteer their services, they were turned down because of their "nationals" status, which rendered them ineligible for service. They immediately protested. President Roosevelt responded by changing the draft law to include Filipinos. In February 1942 the First Filipino Infantry Regiment was formed, followed later that year by the Second Filipino Infantry Regiment. Filipinos eagerly responded to the call to arms. Together, the two regiments had 7,000 Filipinos enrolled. In California, 16,000 Filipinos—or 40 percent of the state's Filipino population—registered for the draft. Filipino soldiers were shipped to the Philippines, where they operated behind the enemy lines, destroying Japanese communications. Their service was recognized as significant to the recapture of the Philippine islands.[10]

Like the Filipinos, Korean immigrants also eagerly participated in the American war effort against Japan. In Los Angeles, 109 Koreans, one-fifth of the city's Korean population, joined the California National Guard. Older Korean men who passed the age of military duty nevertheless participated in military drills to show their patriotism or volunteered as emergency fire wardens. Elderly Korean women also served in the Red Cross. Koreans' skills in the Japanese language made them especially valuable, and many were hired as Japanese language teachers to train military personnel, as translators of secret Japanese documents, as propaganda broadcasters, and as agents for underground work in Japanese-occupied territory.

Bong-youn Choy's wartime experiences are most exemplary. In 1942, Choy, a Korean college student in America, was employed by the U.S. government as an interpreter of Japanese. He delivered lectures on Korean and Japanese politics to the OWI in San Francisco and broadcasted to Korea on Saturdays and Sundays. He was also hired as an instructor in Oriental language at the University of California, Berkeley. In addition to his full-time teaching on campus, he taught Japanese language extension courses two nights a week in Oakland and San Francisco. He was also asked to teach Japanese for special Army Training Program (located in San Francisco) classes. In addition, Choy was often called by the federal court to translate documents in connection with Japanese property.[11]

Although Indian participation in Allied campaign was strong, especially in the China-Burma-India theater by providing the base for American operations in support of China, Asian Indian immigrants' participation in the American home front has drawn little notice from both the general public and academia. This absence of historical record perhaps is largely attributed to the group's relatively small and aging population. By 1940, according to the U.S. Census Bureau, there were only 2,405 Asian Indians in the country, mostly old males (56 percent were forty or older and 32 percent fifty or older) residing in California's agricultural communities.

While their families were interned, numerous Japanese Nisei (second-generation) served in the U.S. Armed Forces. One of the most noted efforts from Japanese Americans was a small army language school, which later became the Defense Language Institute. It was established in San Francisco to teach Japanese to military personnel. The school hired a number of Asian nationals and Americans of Asian ancestry as instructors. As the war progressed, many more Japanese Americans were hired. In addition, young Japanese Americans also served directly in the armed forces. According to selective service records, 3,188 Americans of Japanese ancestry had been enlisted into the armed forces by November 1941. However, after Pearl Harbor, many recently inducted Nisei were removed from active duty into the enlisted reserve, were made permanent kitchen police, were given other menial assignments, or were placed in special labor battalions, treatments identical to those received by African American soldiers.[12]

HOME FRONT

The wartime shortage of labor helped lower racial barriers for Asian immigrants and their American-born children. For the first time, the Chinese had a chance to work outside Chinatown. Many labored in defense industries, especially in shipbuilding, as the San Francisco Bay Area was one of the major U.S. shipbuilding sites. During the war, there were six major shipyards in the area: the Kaiser yards in Richmond, Mare Island Navy Yard in Vallejo, Naval Drydocks in San Francisco, Marinship in Sausalito, Moore Dry Dock Company in Oakland, and Bethlehem Steel in Alameda and South San Francisco.[13]

Labor shortages and federal regulations against discrimination made these shipyards eager to recruit minorities. In May 1942 they began advertising jobs in local Chinese newspapers. The Kaiser yards announced that they would hire Chinese regardless of their citizenship status or English skills. In a recruitment speech, the owner of the shipyards, Henry J. Kaiser, urged the local Chinese to work in his shipyards to show their patriotism. The Moore Dry Dock Company in Oakland went even further. It hired Chinese-speaking instructors in its welding school and provided its Chinese trainees a shuttle bus service between the shipyard and Oakland's Chinatown.

The Chinese responded to the call enthusiastically for a number of reasons. These jobs would allow them to demonstrate their patriotism. They paid well and could be used for draft deferment for men. The defense employees could apply for government-subsidized housing, which would afford the Chinese the rare opportunity to live outside of Chinatown. By 1943 around five thousand Chinese Americans worked in defense jobs in the San Francisco Bay Area, and between five and six hundred of them were females. These Chinese "Rosie the Riveters" were mostly young women who grew up in America, and some were college students. Chinese in other parts of California and around the nation also worked in the defense industry, especially in port cities such as Los Angeles, Portland, Seattle, Chicago, New York, and Boston.[14]

In St. Louis, similarly, young Chinese women worked in a St. Louis ammunition plant, along with their white counterparts. Most of the women were hired as gaugers, earning $30 a week—better pay than that offered by most jobs available to women at the time. The factory also employed women as cartridge inspectors; those positions required at least two years of college education. Among the cartridge inspectors were a few Chinese women. Rose Lee, for example, a "small and pretty" young Chinese woman, was one of the inspectors.[15]

An improvement similar to that of the Chinese also occurred among other non-Japanese Asian communities, and the opportunities to serve beyond ethnic confines continued even after the war was over. Korean immigrants and young Korean Americans enjoyed the opportunities to work outside of their ethnic circle. Approximately 250 Japanese-speaking Koreans were recruited by the U.S. government to work as interpreters, translators, and intelligence workers with various wartime agencies, including the OWI and the armed forces. After the war, many Koreans returned to South Korea working as civilian employees of the American military government there.[16] The U.S. military also needed services from Filipinos. A. B. Santos was drafted into the U.S. Army in 1943 when he was a college student at the University of California, Berkeley. Once inducted, he was sworn in as a U.S. citizen, and after basic training at Camp Cooke, California, was dispatched to Oro Bay, New Guinea, with the Filipino Infantry. In 1944 when the United States was preparing to invade the Philippines, he was called to conduct counterintelligence in the Philippines. When Japan surrendered, Santos was ready to go back to the United States to finish his education, but the army kept him and assigned him to work for the U.S. Veterans Administration as a contract representative.[17]

However, these improvements appeared temporary. As millions of American GIs returned home when the war was over, many Asian immigrants and Americans of Asian ancestry had to surrender the positions they obtained during the war to returning war veterans, as did many women, African Americans, and Latinos. Nevertheless, Asian Americans' wartime participation had left irreplaceable marks on their individual and collective memories. These memories could be readily rekindled and turned into political activism in support of equal rights for Asian Americans when opportunity knocked at the door again.

END OF EXCLUSION

The Chinese exclusion laws prevailing since 1882 seemed up to this point to have been "an untouchable cornerstone of American immigration and naturalization policy," as historian Roger Daniels commented.[18] However, the changing public mood was now able to reverse the government policy. The key organization in the campaign was the Citizens Committee to Repeal Chinese Exclusion and Place Immigration on a Quota Basis. The committee consisted of more than 150 individuals from a wide spectrum of the American upper class and intelligentsia.

Pressures for repealing the Chinese exclusion laws also came from China and Chinese Americans. In the spring of 1943, Madame Chiang Kai-shek toured the United States and delivered an eloquent speech on the war in Asia to a joint session of Congress. She told the congressmen that repeal of the Chinese exclusion laws would boost Chinese morale and China's war effort. Meanwhile, Chinese American community organizations such as the CCBA asked Congress to repeal the exclusion acts. Chinese in Hawaii and major cities on the mainland raised funds to finance the campaign for repeal.

Other Asian communities also supported repeal of the Chinese exclusion laws. Kilsoo K. Haan of the Korean National Front Federation expressed Asians' desire for political and economic equality when speaking at a congressional hearing on the repeal bill. Taraknath Das, an Indian immigrant and professor at the City College of New York, challenged the contradiction between American racist practice at home and promotion of principles abroad.[19] Facing pressures from the public and other interest groups, along with fear that China might defect to the Japanese side, Congress repealed a number of exclusion laws. On December 13, 1943, President Roosevelt signed the Act to Repeal the Chinese Exclusion Acts, to Establish Quotas, and for Other Purposes.

The act consisted of three parts: (1) it repealed all past acts relating to exclusion and deportation of Chinese aliens; (2) it permitted Chinese aliens in the United States to apply for naturalization; and (3) it provided for the admission of 105 Chinese per year, with preference of up to 75 percent of the quota given to those born and raised in China. The first two parts were long overdue and corrected past injustices done to the Chinese in immigration and naturalization law. However, some restrictions adhering to the 105 quota made the statute racist and particularly restrictive to Chinese. The law stipulated that a Chinese person was defined as one who had "as much as one half Chinese blood" and that all such immigrants must be charged to the Chinese quota of 105, irrespective of their country of birth. The law also regulated that Chinese wives and children of American citizens were chargeable to the Chinese quota of 105, while European wives and children of American citizens were admitted on a nonquota basis.[20]

In July 1946, Congress extended the quotas and the right of naturalization to other Asian allies. The imminent independence of India from Britain and the Philippines from the United States was an important factor that prompted American policy makers to reconsider the rights of these people. Proposed by Republican congresswoman Clare Boothe Luce from Connecticut and Democratic congressman Emanuel Celler from New York in 1943, the Luce-Celler Act of 1946 was signed into law by President Truman on July 2, 1946. Based on the model of the 1943 act repealing Chinese exclusion, it allowed Asian Indians (which included present-day Pakistanis and Bangladeshis) and Filipinos to enter the country on an annual quota of 100 and to become naturalized.

JAPANESE INTERNMENT

While World War II brought favorable changes to other groups of Asian Americans, it caused trauma, chaos, and violations of civil liberty for Japanese immigrants and American citizens of Japanese ancestry. Two months following the Pearl Harbor attack by the Japanese Imperial Navy, more than 40,000 Japanese living along the Pacific Coast and 70,000 of their American-born children were forced to evacuate from their homes, taking with them only what possessions they could carry on their backs, and relocated to ten internment camps mostly in mountainous and desert areas. The United States had thus entered one of the darkest moments in its history.

Reasons behind Japanese Internment

A number of reasons have been attributed to Japanese internment. Military leaders demanded the evacuation of Japanese aliens and their American-born children from the West Coast because of "military necessity," a myth challenged by legal experts due to the discovery of documents proving otherwise. News media fanned the hysteria on the potential Japanese "Fifth Column." Politicians launched the movement for Japanese removal. White farmers in California viewed Japanese farmers as competitors. Finally, Japanese were singled out because they were a small ethnic minority. "The report of the Commission on Wartime Relocation and Internment of Civilians titled *Personal Justice Denied*" concluded that "race prejudice, war hysteria and a failure of political leadership" (not "military necessity") were the major causes of the internment.

Military leaders first raised the issue of the military necessity for Japanese removal. General John L. DeWitt, head of the Western Defense Command, at a meeting of federal and state officials in his San Francisco headquarters on January 4, 1942, argued that military necessity justified the mass evacuation of Japanese: "We are at war and this area—eight states—has been designated as a theater of operations.... [There are] approximately 288,000 enemy aliens... which we have to watch.... I have little confidence that the enemy aliens are law-abiding in any sense of the world. Some of them yes; many, no. Particularly the Japanese. I have no confidence in their loyalty whatsoever. I am speaking now of the native-born Japanese—117,000—and 42,000 in California alone."[21] Ironically, Japanese on the Hawaiian Islands, the mostly Hawaiian-born 160,000 who would have a major influence at the ballot box in the future, were allowed to stay. It also appeared that every argument made to justify the evacuation of Japanese, almost without exception, was identical to the earlier campaigns to rid the West Coast of the Chinese, who were regarded as "honorary Caucasians" during World War II.

However, the evidence of a deliberate campaign by the War Department and the Justice Department to present tainted records to the Supreme Court for a mass evacuation of Japanese was not found until four decades later. In 1983, the civil rights lawyer Peter Irons discovered documents that revealed "a legal scandal without precedent in the history of American law," in which War Department officials had destroyed documents by Justice Department lawyers charging a key military report on Japanese evacuation with "intentional falsehood," and the Justice Department had deliberately misled the Supreme Court by presenting altered records.[22]

Although the officially stated reason for the Japanese evacuation was military necessity, the military leaders' position was in fact reflective of public and political pressure for Japanese removal. West Coast newspapers reported the Pearl Harbor attack with headlines such as "Fifth Column Treachery Told" and "Secretary of Navy Blames 5th Column for Raid." A month later, more articles reported Japanese fifth column activities on the West Coast and called for mass removal. Patriotic organizations also joined the campaign for Japanese removal. In January 1942 the California Department for the American Legion demanded that all Japanese with dual citizenship be placed in a "concentration camp." The Native Sons and Daughters of the Gold West echoed with the same demand. At the same time, Californian politicians were leading a movement for Japanese removal. The boards of supervisors of sixteen California counties passed resolutions urging removal.[23] In addition, many white farmers in California viewed the removal as an opportunity to rid themselves of competition from Japanese farmers.

Demography and race also played out as factors behind the Japanese removal. No removal happened to the 160,000 Japanese in Hawaii, as they constituted 34 percent of the population in the islands and their removal would have paralyzed the economy of Hawaii, while the Japanese on the West Coast represented only a small minority. In 1940, Congress passed the Alien Registration Act that required enemy aliens to register annually at post offices and keep the government apprised of any change of address. After the United States went to war, there were over a million unnaturalized natives of the Axis powers resident in the United States—696,363 Italians, 314,715 Germans, and 91,858 Japanese—all of whom were potential internees.[24] However, Japanese, two-thirds of them native-born citizens, were the only ones singled out for mass internment because of their smaller population and racial background.

> **FEDERAL GOVERNMENT SEARCHES TERRORIZE JAPANESE AMERICAN COMMUNITY**
>
> One day I came home to find two F.B.I. men at our front door. They asked permission to search the house. One man looked through the front rooms, while the other searched the back rooms. Trembling with fright, I followed and watched each of the men look around. The investigators examined the mattresses and the dressers and looked under the beds. The gas range, piano and sofa were thoroughly inspected. Since I was the only one at home, the F.B.I. questioned me, but did not produce sufficient evidence of Fifth Columnist in our family. This made me very happy, even if they did mess up the house.
>
> Source: War Relocation Authority Mss., collection of letters from Poston, 1942–1945, Bancroft Library, Berkeley, CA.

Even before the mass evacuation, Japanese American communities on the West Coast had been terrorized by such government measures as searches of Japanese residences and confiscation of personal belongings that allegedly could be used to facilitate espionage activities. On December 29, 1941, the Justice Department ordered all enemy aliens in seven western states to surrender their radios, shortwave sets, binoculars, and any weapon they possessed. Following the order, FBI agents searched the homes of many residents of Japanese ancestry. A teenaged Nisei girl from San Jose described the search at her house when she returned home from school (see sidebar).

Executive Order 9066 and Mass Evacuation

Agitated by the report of a committee headed by Supreme Court justice Owen J. Roberts that investigated the destruction of Pearl Harbor and concluded that the attack had been assisted by an alleged espionage network of American citizens of Japanese ancestry, DeWitt drafted a statement, known as his "Final Recommendation," calling for the removal of all persons of Japanese ancestry on racial grounds.

The army chief of staff and civilian heads of the War Department immediately approved the "Final Recommendation" and drafted an executive order for the president's signature. President Roosevelt signed it as Executive Order 9066 on February 19, 1942, the same day it was presented to him. The order authorized the secretary of war to designate military areas and remove Japanese aliens and citizens from these areas. The secretary of war then appointed DeWitt to carry out the order with full authority.

In early March, General DeWitt declared the western halves of Washington, Oregon, and California, and the southern half of Arizona as military areas 1 and 2. He ordered enemy aliens of German, Italian, and Japanese ancestries and all persons of Japanese ancestry to move from these areas. However, the Italians and most Germans were never

FIGURE 5.1 A Japanese grocery store in California, 1942. It was sold hurriedly before the owner was evacuated to the internment camps. Note the sign "I am an American." Courtesy National Archives, Washington, D.C.

FIGURE 5.2 The Japanese quarter of San Francisco on the first day of evacuation from this area. About 660 merchants, shopkeepers, tradespeople, and professional people left their homes on this morning for the Civil Control Station, from which they were dispatched by bus to the Tanforan Assembly Center. This photograph shows a family about to get on a bus. The little boy in the new cowboy hat is having his identification tag checked by an official before boarding, April 29, 1942. Courtesy National Archives and Records Administration.

actually ordered to move. The Wartime Civil Control Authority (a unit created within the Western Defense Command) took over the forced evacuation of more than 100,000 persons of Japanese ancestry, while 8,000 people had already left Washington, Oregon, and California voluntarily.

There was virtually no resistance to the mass evacuation. After the Pearl Harbor attack, many male Japanese leaders were arrested and imprisoned, so that not only families but entire ethnic communities were socially decapitated. Many Japanese also had their liquid assets frozen, as they kept their money in American branches of Japanese banks and the Treasury Department seized and closed all enemy-owned banks. The evacuees had only a week (from July 22 to 28, 1942) to sell or store their property. They were instructed to carry only their bedding, clothing, toilet articles, and cooking utensils.[25] Feelings of numbness, shock, anxiety, anger, shame, confusion, and resignation were overwhelming to most of the evacuees. Sucheng Chan well describes the poignant moment: "People quietly stood in long lines, wore tags around their necks showing the numbers assigned their families, tried to keep their children from crying, allowed themselves to be examined by the medical personnel and searched by soldiers, and traveled on buses and trains (often with the blinds drawn down the window) to unknown destinations."[26]

TEMPORARY DETENTION CAMPS IN CALIFORNIA, 1942

Name	Location	County	Previous Use
1. Fresno	Fresno	Fresno	Fairgrounds
2. Arboga	Marysville	Yuba	Labor camp
3. Merced	Merced	Merced	Fairgrounds
4. Pinedale	Pinedale	Fresno	Labor camp
5. Pomona	Pomona	Los Angeles	Fairgrounds
6. Walerga	Sacramento	Sacramento	Labor camp
7. Salinas	Salinas	Monterey	Rodeo grounds
8. Santa Anita	Arcadia	Los Angeles	Horse racetrack
9. Stockton	Stockton	San Joaquin	Fairgrounds
10. Tanforan	San Bruno	San Mateo	Horse racetrack
11. Tulare	Tulare	Tulare	Fairgrounds
12. Turlock	Turlock	Stanislaus	Fairgrounds
13. Manzanar	Owens Valley	Inyo	Aqueduct land

Source: National Park Service, "A History of Japanese Americans in California," http://www.nps.gov/history/history/online_books/5views/5views4b.htm.

The evacuees were first relocated in sixteen assembly centers set up at fairgrounds, race tracks, and other facilities large enough to hold more than five thousand located in Washington, Oregon, California, and Arizona. Assembly centers were sometimes pigpens and horse stalls where a horse or cow had been kept, as indicated in the sidebar. Meanwhile the ten permanent "relocation centers" were under construction by the Army Corps of Engineers on federal lands: Tule Lake and Manzanar, California; Minidoka, Idaho; Heart Mountain, Wyoming; Topaz, Utah; Poston and Gila River, Arizona; Amache, Colorado; and Rohwer and Jerome, Arkansas. All the sites were harshly inhospitable: eight were located in unirrigated deserts known for debilitating dust storms, harsh summers, and frigid winters; the two Arkansas sites sat in heavily wooded and undrained swampland. Each of the camps could house about ten thousand people on average.

Life in the Internment Camps

Life in the internment camps was regimental and harsh. The camps were enclosed by barbed-wire fences and guard towers equipped with machine guns and searchlights. The military police patrolling had orders to shoot anyone attempting to escape (see sidebar).

Inside the camps, the civilian-staffed War Relocation Authority (WRA), established on March 18, 1942, through a second executive order, 9106, administered the internees. Milton Eisenhower served as the first director for three months and was replaced by Dillon S. Myer. WRA administrators and staff lived in spacious and well-furnished residential houses, while the rest of the living quarters in the camps were crude and austere black tarpaper barracks designed to house single male army recruits.

Communal life was the dominant feature of the internment experience that resulted in the erosion and disintegration of the internees' traditional family structure. Each barrack housed

> The life here cannot be expressed. Sometimes, we are resigned to it, but when we see the barbed wire fences and the sentry tower with floodlights, it gives us a feeling of being prisoners in a "concentration camp." We try to be happy and yet often times a gloominess does creep in. When I see the "I'm an American" editorial and write-ups, the "equality of race etc."—it seems to be mocking us in our faces. I just wonder if all the sacrifices and hard labor on [the] part of our parents has gone up to leave nothing to show for it?
>
> —LETTER FROM SHIZUKO HORIUCHI, POMONA ASSEMBLY CENTER, MAY 24, 1942
>
> *Source*: Valerie Matsumoto, "Japanese American Women during World War II," *Frontiers* 8 (1984): 6–14.

FIGURE 5.3 Housing in a Japanese relocation camp, 1942. Courtesy National Archives and Records Administration.

five families, with each person assigned a single military cot. The noise, discomfort, and lack of privacy made the barracks merely a place to sleep. Internees ate and bathed in communal facilities (see "The Legend of Miss Sasagawara" in sidebar). The Issei, who used to be independent and self-employed, now lost their source of income and had to depend on their American-born children in garnering income and dealing with the camp authorities. During mealtimes in mess hall, internees were seated not by family but by generations, as teenage Nisei preferred to sit with their friends. Consequently, Issei gradually lost their parental authority. The camp schools that were generally staffed by white teachers reinforced Americanization of the Nisei children. The generational conflict between Issei and Kibei (American-born but largely educated in Japan), who were proud of their Japanese heritage and resentful of the incarceration, and Nisei, who were eager to be accepted as Americans and recommended cooperation with camp administration, became one of the major emotional scars of the Japanese internment experience.

Internees could find jobs in the camps but were paid lower than standard wages, ranging from $19 a month for doctors and teachers to $12 for unskilled jobs. Many internees, including those whose children served in the U.S. Army, lost property as they failed to pay mortgages due to the meager earnings from the camps, while a property protection was applied to other American servicemen. As agricultural tasks posed little competition to

FIGURE 5.4 Japanese youth in an internment camp dancing in their spare time, 1942. Courtesy National Archives and Records Administration.

private industry, about 10,000 incarcerees were permitted to work as seasonal farm workers. While outside the camps, the workers had to carry identification cards indicating the location and duration of their authorized assignments.

There were cases in which camp guards shot and killed unarmed internees. In April 1943, a sixty-three-year-old Issei internee named James Hatsuki Wakasa was shot to death by a guard in the camp at Topaz, Utah. The uproar over Wakasa's killing forced an investigation that revealed lies and cover-ups by the U.S. Army. Army personnel first lied that the internee was killed because he was trying to escape the camp by crawling

THE LEGEND OF MISS SASAGAWARA

Even in that unlikely place of wind, sand, and heat, it was easy to imagine Miss Sasagawara a decorative ingredient of some ballet. . . . I imitated the young men of the Block (No. 33), and gasped, "Wow! How much does *she* weigh?"

"Oh, haven't you heard?" said my friend Elsie Kubo, knowing very well I had not. "That's Miss Sasagawara."

It turned out Elsie knew all about Miss Sasagawara, who with her father was new to Block 33. Where had she accumulated all her items? Probably a morsel here and a morsel there, and, anyway, I forgot to ask her sources, because the picture she painted was so distracting: Miss Sasagawara's father was a Buddhist minister, and the two had gotten permission to come to this Japanese evacuation camp in Arizona from one farther north, after the death there of Mrs. Sasagawara. They had come here to join the Rev. Sasagawara's brother's family, who lived in a neighboring Block, but there had been some trouble between them, and just this week the immigrant pair had gotten leave to move over to Block 33. They were occupying one end of the Block's lone empty barracks, which had not been chopped up yet into the customary four apartments. The other end had been taken over by a young couple, also newcomers to the Block, who had moved in the same day.

"And do you know what, Kiku?" Elsie continued. "Ooooh, that gal is really temperamental. I guess it's because she was a ballet dancer before she got stuck in camp, I hear people like that are temperamental. Anyway, the Sasakis, the new couple at the other end of the barracks, think she's crazy. The day they all moved in, the barracks was really dirty, all covered with dust from the dust storms and everything, so Mr. Sasaki was going to wash the whole barracks down with a hose, and he thought he'd be nice and do the Sasagawaras' side first. You know, do them a favor. But do you know what? Mr. Sasaki got the hose attached to the faucet outside, and started to go in the door, and he said all the Sasagawaras' suitcases and things were on top of the army cots and Miss Sasagawara was trying to clean the place out with a pail of water and a broom. He said, 'Here let me flush the place out with a hose for you; it'll be faster.' And she turned right around and screamed at him, 'What are you trying to do? Spy on me? Get out of here or I'll throw this water on you!' He said he was so surprised he couldn't move for a minute, and before he knew it. Miss Sasagawara just up and threw that water at him, pail and all. Oh, he said he got out of that place fast, but fast. Madwoman, he called her."

Source: Hisaye Yamamoto, *Seventeen Syllables and Other Stories* (New Brunswick, NJ: Rutgers University Press, 2001), 20–21.

through the barbed-wire fence and then conducted cover-ups to hide the lie. A year later, on May 24, 1944, another internee named Shoichi James Okamoto was shot to death by guards at Tule Lake.[27]

The resentment toward internment and internal divisions soon erupted into mass protests in camps. The first large-scale protest occurred at Poston, Arizona, in November 1942 when the camp military police detained two Kibei accused of beating another Kibei, and it was discovered that the prisoners would be tried outside the camp. One thousand internees gathered and demanded the release of the prisoners. When the camp administration ignored their demands, an emergency committee made up of seventy-two internees called for a general strike. As most jobs in the camp were performed by the internees, the camp became dysfunctional. The strike lasted ten days and ended only after the camp administration released one Kibei and tried the other within the camp.

The most violent mass protest broke out at Manzanar, California. On December 6, 1942, more than three thousand internees gathered to protest the arrests of several Kibei for assaulting Fred Tayama, a Nisei JACL leader who had turned in the names of Pro-Japan Issei and Kibei to the FBI. The angry protesters rushed to the hospital where Tayama was staying in an attempt to kill him and stormed the jail in hopes of freeing Harry Y. Ueno, a Kibei who was arrested for having tried to organize kitchen workers for better working conditions and accusing camp officials of misusing rationed sugar and meat intended for internees. When the protesters at the jail refused to disperse, soldiers on guard threw tear gas and fired into the crowd of unarmed men. Two internees were killed, and ten more were injured. Angry protesters beat up several persons suspected as "informers." On the following day, the camp police arrested the leaders of the protesters and moved them to an isolation camp at Moab, Utah. The camp administration also moved sixty-five JACL members to an abandoned Civilian Conservation Corps camp for their safety. The army was deployed and martial law was in effect in the camp for more than a month.

While the outbreaks at Poston and Manzanar reflect the internal tensions between the Nisei and Kibei factions regarding internment in particular and Americanization in general, the internee reaction to the U.S. Army's decision in January 1943 to induct Nisei into an all-Japanese combat unit reveals Japanese Americans' open protest of the violation of their liberty. In an attempt to separate the "loyal" from the "disloyal," the Army devised a questionnaire to be filled out by males over seventeen: Selective Service Form 304A, "Statement of United States Citizen of Japanese Ancestry." It contained twenty-eight questions, of which the final two concerned the issue of loyalty. Question 27 asked male Nisei, "Are you willing to serve in the armed forces of the United States on combat duty, wherever ordered?" Question 28 inquired, "Will you swear unqualified allegiance to the United States of America and faithfully defend the United States from any or all attack by foreign or domestic forces, and forswear any form of allegiance or obedience to the Japanese emperor, or any other foreign government, power, or organization?" In February, the WRA modified the army's questionnaire and distributed it to all internees. Under the title "Application for Leave Clearance," the WRA questionnaire was vague and confusing. The most troubling were questions 27 and 28. Question 27 asked female citizens and aliens, "If the opportunity presents itself and you are found qualified, would you be willing to volunteer for the Army Nurse Corps or the WAAC (Women's Army Auxiliary Corps)?" Many female Issei and Nisei women answered in the negative.

Question 28 violated the Geneva Convention regarding the treatment of enemy aliens by calling upon Issei to voluntarily become stateless: "Will you swear unqualified allegiance to the United States of America and forswear any form of allegiance or obedience to the Japanese emperor, or any other foreign government, power or organization?" When WRA officials realized this problem, they hastily changed the question to read, "Will you swear to abide by the laws of the United States and to take no actions which would in any way interfere in the war effort of the United States?" However, the confusion remained: would answering yes imply that the internee had an allegiance to Japan? Among the 21,000 male Nisei eligible for the draft, 4,600, or 22 percent, answered no or gave qualified answers to the loyalty questions. Many of them said they were not expressing disloyalty but were protesting the internment (see story in sidebar).[28]

Nisei Soldiers

The original intent of the loyalty questionnaire was to attract 3,500 volunteers for an all-Japanese combat unit. Only 1,200 male Nisei volunteered. This presented an embarrassment for the government publicity machine. At the beginning of 1944, the Army Selective Service reintroduced the draft for Japanese Americans. While more than 80 Nisei defied their draft orders, many responded to the call for service to prove their loyalty to the country of their birth. More than 25,700 Nisei, including several hundred women, served in the armed forces during the war.

The first and least-publicized Nisei soldiers were those trained at the Army's Military Intelligence Service Language School (MISLS). It was established in November 1943, first headquartered in San Francisco and later moved to Fort Snelling, Montana. Six thousand Japanese Americans were recruited; perhaps five thousand of the MISLS graduates were sent overseas to various parts of the Pacific theater. They served with the U.S. Army, Navy, Marine Corps, and Air Force, and for the Allied forces of Britain, Australia, New Zealand, Canada, China, and India. They followed Allied troops into areas retaken from Japanese forces to interrogate prisoners, translate Japanese documents, and monitor radio traffic.[29]

> ### NO-NO BOY
>
> What had happened to him and the others who faced the judge and said: You can't make me go in the army because I'm not an American or you wouldn't have plucked me and mine from a life that was good and real and meaningful and fenced me in the desert like they do the Jew in Germany and it is a puzzle why you haven't started to liquidate us though you might as well since everything else has been destroyed.
>
> And some said: You, Mr. Judge, who supposedly represent justice, was it a just thing to ruin a hundred thousand lives and homes and farms and businesses and dreams and hopes because the hundred thousand were a hundred thousand Japanese and you couldn't have loyal Japanese when Japan is the country you're fighting and, if so, how about the Germans and Italians that must be just as questionable as the Japanese or we wouldn't be fighting Germany and Italy? Round them up. Take away their homes and cars and beer and spaghetti and throw them in a camp and what do you think they'll say when you try to draft them into your army of the country that is for life, liberty, and the pursuit of happiness? If you think we're the same kind of rotten Japanese that dropped the bombs on Pearl Harbor, and it's plain that you do or I wouldn't be here having to explain to you why it is that I won't go and protect sons-of—bitches like you, I say you're right and *banzai* three times and we'll sit the war out in a nice cell, thank you. . . .
>
> Please, judge, said the next one. I want to go in your army because this is my country and I've always lived here and I was all-city guard and one time I wrote an essay for composition about what it means to me to be an American and the teacher sent it into a contest and they gave me twenty-five dollars, which proves that I'm a good American. Maybe I look Japanese and my father and mother and brothers and sisters look Japanese, but we're better Americans than the regular ones because that's the way it has to be when one looks Japanese but is really a good American. We're not like the other Japanese who aren't good American like us. We're more like you and the other, regular Americans. All you have to do is give us back our home and grocery store and let my kid brother be all-city like me. Nobody has to know. We can be Chinese. We'll call ourselves Chin or Yang or something like that and it'll be the best thing you've ever done, sir. That's all, a little thing. Will you do that for one good, loyal American family? We'll forget the two years in camp because anybody can see it was all a mistake and you didn't really mean to do it and I'm all yours.
>
> Source: John Okada, *No-No Boy* (Seattle: University of Washington Press, 1979).

The 100th Battalion, a Hawaiian National Guard unit composed of Nisei, was another group of Japanese American soldiers who fought bravely during the war. The battalion was trained at Camp Shelby, Mississippi, in April 1943 and departed in September for North Africa and then Italy. By the fall of 1943 the 100th Battalion was heavily engaged in Italy. The exemplary combat record of the battalion convinced the War Department to form a larger unit of Japanese American soldiers.[30]

To recruit sufficient numbers of Nisei volunteers from the mainland internment camps, Army personnel resorted to creating a large, all-Nisei combat unit in January 1944. That February the military announced that even Japanese aliens would be allowed to volunteer for military service. Eighteen thousand Nisei served in the unit—the 442nd Regimental Combat Team. They were trained at Camp Shelby and arrived in Italy in June 1944 when the 100th Battalion merged with it. The unit engaged in the bloodiest military action when it was sent to save a "lost" battalion of Texans near Bruyeres, France. By the end of the campaign, the 442nd suffered 2,000 casualties, with 140 dead.[31]

The 442nd was known as "the most heavily decorated unit in the history of the U.S. Army" according to Army and WRA public relations experts. It received seven Presidential Distinguished Unit Citations. Its members earned 18,000 individual medals, including a Congressional Medal of Honor, 47 Distinguished Service Crosses, 350 Silver Stars, and more than 3,600 Purple Hearts.[32] However, such honor was paid with lives. In seven major European campaigns, the 442nd suffered 9,486 casualties (or 300 percent of the unit's original strength), including 600 killed.

Supreme Court Cases

While the mass protests broke out in internment camps, four young Japanese Americans separately challenged the government policies of evacuation and internment and pressed their cases all the way to the U.S. Supreme Court. Minoru Yasui, Gordon Hirabayashi, and Fred Korematsu defied the curfew and evacuation orders, and Mitsuye Endo challenged the government's right to detain her in an internment camp.

The first Japanese American to challenge the curfew law was Minoru Yasui. Yasui was born in 1916 to a Japanese immigrant family in Hood River, Oregon. His father was the owner of an apple orchard who was accepted into the white growers' circle and acted as the leader of the six hundred Japanese Americans in the valley. All seven children of the family were raised as Methodists and sent to college. Yasui entered the University of Oregon in 1933, volunteered for military training, and was commissioned as a secondary lieutenant in the U.S. Army Infantry Reserve. After his graduation from the University of Oregon Law School in 1939, he worked as a clerk at the Japanese consulate in Chicago. As an American citizen, he duly registered with the State Department as a foreign agent. The day after the Pearl Harbor attack, he resigned from his job with the Japanese consulate and reported for duty at Fort Vancouver, where he was turned down eight times. Meanwhile his father was arrested as a community leader and interned at Fort Missoula, Montana.

On March 28, 1942, General DeWitt imposed a curfew on all persons of Japanese ancestry; Yasui felt it was discriminatory and decided to challenge its constitutionality. He first walked around the streets in Portland hoping to be arrested, and then walked to a police station asking to be arrested on the grounds of violating the curfew. In a federal district court, the judge found him guilty of a curfew violation based on the rationale that he had become an enemy alien by working for the Japanese consulate and registering as a foreign agent. He was sentenced to one year of imprisonment. When his case finally reached the Supreme Court, the justices decided to set it aside, waiting for the case of *Hirabayashi v. United States*.

Like Yasui, Gordon Hirabayashi also turned himself in for violating the curfew. A senior at the University of Washington, Hirabayashi decided to offer himself as a test case. On May 16, 1942, he was arrested and later convicted by a grand jury in Seattle for violating the curfew and for failing to report for the mass evacuation. On June 21, 1943, in *Hirabayashi v. United States*, the Supreme Court unanimously upheld the curfew policy without dealing with the constitutionality of the mass removal. On the same day, the justices ruled that the federal district court judge had erred in classifying Yasui as an enemy alien on the ground of his employment at the Japanese consulate but sustained the conviction that Yasui violated the curfew, thus upholding the constitutionality of the curfew and evacuation.

Unlike Yasui and Hirabayashi, Fred Korematsu defied the curfew for personal reasons. A twenty-three-year-old welder in San Leandro, California, Korematsu evaded the evacuation order in order to stay with his white girlfriend. He underwent minor plastic surgery to conceal his true identity. On May 30, 1942, he was arrested but released on bail. He was then arrested by military police and sent to await trial at Tanforan assembly center, where he decided to become a test case plaintiff. On December 18, 1944, in *Korematsu v. United States*, in a six-to-three decision, the Court ruled the evacuation order constitutional and upheld Korematsu's conviction.

Different from the other three cases, Mitsuye Endo's case was carefully selected by the JACL as an ideal one with which to challenge the internment. Twenty-two-year-old Endo was a Methodist, had never visited Japan, and could not speak or write Japanese, and her brother had served in the U.S. Army. She was a clerical worker with the California Department of Motor Vehicles in Sacramento. Along with other employees of Japanese ancestry, she was dismissed by the California State Personnel Board. When detained at the internment camp at Topaz, Utah, she filed for a writ of habeas corpus in July 1942, challenging the right of the government to incarcerate her. She turned down the WRA offer of releasing her if she withdrew her legal challenge and remained in the camp for more than two years until the Supreme Court made a unanimous decision to order her release on December 18, 1944.

Japanese American communities and civil rights activists were disappointed at the Supreme Court decisions. Yale University professor Eugene Rostow criticized the Supreme Court for ruling based on General DeWitt's racism rather than factual evidence. Peter Irons many years later discovered that the WRA lawyers concealed from the Supreme

Court the FBI analysis based on its agents' investigation that General DeWitt's claims of Japanese American espionage and sabotage activities were unfounded. Meanwhile it was believed that the lawyers of the plaintiff and the national board of the American Civil Liberties Union (ACLU) made a deliberate decision not to attack the constitutionality of the internment out of their respect for and loyalty to President Roosevelt.[33]

Release and Resettlement

The release of internees occurred even before the evacuation from the temporary assembly centers to the ten permanent camps. There were five types of avenues for internees to leave the camps: colleges, temporary agricultural employment, military service, permanent employment, and segregation camp or federal penitentiaries for those who were deemed "disloyal." The resettlement policy was primarily motivated to ameliorate the labor shortages created by the war. The labor of the highly skilled and hardworking Nikkei was desirable to white agriculturalists. The procedure for resettlement was slow and lengthy. The prospective resettlers had to obtain an "application for leave clearance" for an FBI security check and then apply for an individual leave permit, which could take as long as a month, though after 1943 this was reduced to a few weeks. The pace of resettlement accelerated after the registration crisis in mid-1943. By the end of 1944, 35,000 Japanese Americans left camps through the resettlement policy. The jobs offered to the evacuees varied but mainly were in agriculture, mining, railroads, fruit and vegetable picking and canning, hotels and cafes, and domestic work.[34]

As many young internees left the camps to do farm work, attend college, or serve in the armed forces, the camps were mostly populated by young children and the elderly. On December 17, 1944, the day before the *Endo* ruling, the federal government revoked the mass evacuation order. The WRA announced that the internment camps would be closed within six months or a year. At the end of the war, in August 1945, 44,000 internees remained in the camps. While the young Nisei between the ages of seventeen and thirty-five welcomed the opportunity of resettlement as it offered more money, freedom, and adventure, Issei and Kibei were afraid of returning to the hostile outside world; some even committed suicide. When the camps were finally closed, the remaining internees were forced to reenter a society that was not ready to accept them.

The majority of the Internees returned to the Pacific West. According to WRA statistics, by 1946, 57,251 Nikkei (of Japanese descent) lived in the West Coast states, more than half of the 112,353 who had resided there in 1940. However, the ex-internees encountered concerted efforts to keep them out, especially in California. The Native Sons of the Golden West, headquartered in San Francisco, opposed the return of Japanese to the state and even wanted to revoke the citizenship of American-born Nisei. The returnees found their household possessions stolen and farms and businesses seized by their neighbors. In Los Angeles and other cities, returnees discovered that their neighborhood in the inner city had been occupied by poor African Americans. They also faced verbal abuse and harassment in their everyday life. Many were turned away at markets and real estate offices, denied business licenses by local bureaucrats, and forced to forfeit their original policies and start anew at higher rates by insurance companies. Physical violence also threatened the returnees in cities, suburbs, and rural areas. There were reportedly gun shots from cars at returnee residences at night. Anonymous phone calls warned Japanese American merchants that their shops would be dynamited, and many of the threats were actually carried out.

Many resettled in the Intermountain West, Midwest, and East Coast. Of the original 100,000 internees, about 43,000 scattered to Illinois (15,000), Colorado (6,000), Utah (5,000), Ohio (3,900), Idaho (3,500), Michigan (2,800), New York (2,500), New Jersey (2,200), and Minnesota (1,700).[35] Chicago, the site of the first WRA field office, was the most favored resettlement designation, owing to the city's diverse ethnic population and tolerance of Asian Americans. Most resettlers ended up living in ethnic enclaves of the city. Other midwestern cities including Cleveland and Des Moines also welcomed Japanese American resettlers. This eastward Nikkei migration resulted in significantly larger Nikkei communities in Illinois, New York, Ohio, Minnesota, and Michigan. For those who chose the Intermountain West states, Salt Lake City was a preferred location for resettlement because of the tolerance of Mormons. A Nisei girl in Salt Lake City recorded that people were "openly sympathetic" in the city's "very friendly atmosphere." However, when many seasonal beet pickers entered the city, residents became alarmed and their tolerance dissipated. Of the city's business owners, 80 percent indicated that they would not hire Japanese Americans.[36]

Redress Movement

The redress movement was a long-term struggle by the Japanese American community and sympathetic European Americans to obtain an apology and compensation from the U.S. government for incarcerating Japanese American citizens and residents during World War II. Its origins can be traced to two circumstances. First, some white American leaders with a strong sense of justice apologized for Japanese internment and helped young Japanese Americans enroll at universities, which helped plant the seed for a later redress movement. During World War II, Colorado governor Ralph Lawrence Carr publicly apologized for the internment of American citizens. He was the only elected official to make such an apology. Although his actions cost him reelection, he gained the gratitude of the Japanese American community, which erected a statue of him in

Sakura Square, Denver's Japantown. William Dennis, the president of Earlham College in Richmond, Indiana, instituted a program in 1942 to enroll several dozen Japanese American students, which helped strengthen the college's ties to the Japanese American community.

Second, the younger generation of Japanese Americans were inspired by the civil rights movement in the 1960s and initiated the redress movement, seeking an official apology and reparations from the federal government. The movement focused on the broader injustice of internment rather than on documented property losses.

The campaign for redress was launched by the Japanese American community in the 1970s. At the 1970 convention of the Japanese American Citizens League (JACL), former internee and educator Edison Uno called upon the organization to pursue compensation from the U.S. government for the internment of more than 112,000 Japanese Americans during the war. In 1976, the JACL formed the National Committee for Redress (NCR) with its own recommendations. In 1979, the JACL established the National Council for Japanese American Redress (NCJAR) to seek a legislative sponsor to introduce a redress bill in Congress. In July 1980, the Commission on Wartime Relocation and Internment of Civilians (CWRIC) was formed by an act of Congress to study the mass removal and internment of Japanese Americans during the war and recommend appropriate remedies.

The CWRIC published its findings in December 1982 and issued its formal recommendations in June 1983: $20,000 in individual compensation to surviving internees, a formal apology, and presidential pardons for Fred Korematsu, Gordon Hirabayashi, and Minoru Yasui. The CWRIC recommendations formed the basis for new congressional redress bills. Finally, a redress bill, H.R. 442, passed the House on September 19, 1987, and followed by S. 1009 in the Senate in April 1988; on August 10 the legislation was signed into law by President Ronald Reagan as the Civil Liberty Act of 1988. The act provided a one-time payment of $20,000 to each surviving Japanese American who had been interned during the war and a formal apology.[37]

ASIAN AMERICANS AND WORLD WAR II IN HISTORICAL PERSPECTIVE

World War II had a profound impact on different groups of Asian immigrants and their American-born children. For Chinese, Filipinos, Indians, and Koreans, assistance to the war efforts in their homelands and participation in home-front war efforts gave them a strong sense of pride. More importantly, these activities changed Americans' perception of Asian immigrants, and the changing public mood eventually helped lift the Asian exclusion acts that had long restricted the entry of Asian immigrants. The incarceration of Japanese and Americans of Japanese ancestry during World War II separated their

FIGURE 5.5 President Ronald Reagan signs the Civil Liberties Act of 1988 in an official ceremony, August 10, 1988. Courtesy National Archives and Records Administration.

wartime experience from that of other Asian ethnic groups. It was and remains a controversial issue in the American history.

KEY TERMS

changing public mood toward Chinese and Japanese during World War II
Helen Pon Onyett
Hazel Ah Ying Lee
Maggie Gee
Bong-youn Choy
Pearl Harbor attack
Executive Order 9066
Japanese internment

442nd Regimental Combat Team
Minoru Yasui
Gordon Hirabayashi
Fred Korematsu
Mitsuye Endo
First and Second Filipino Infantry Regiments
repeal of the Chinese Exclusion Acts
Luce-Celler Act (1946)
redress movement

REVIEW QUESTIONS

1. What factors contributed to the changes in American public opinion of Chinese and Japanese during World War II?
2. List the new opportunities open to Asian Americans as a result of World War II.
3. Analyze the reasons behind Japanese internment. Were they justifiable or not? Was Japanese internment an avoidable episode in American history?

FILMS

Ding, Loni (producer/director). *Nisei Soldier: Standard Bearer for an Exiled People.* 29-minute documentary of Japanese American soldiers of the 442nd Regimental Combat's Team during World War II. 1984.

Dong, Arthur (producer/director). *Forbidden City, USA.* 56-minute documentary on a San Francisco nightclub during World War II. 1989.

Ind, Satsuki (producer). *Children of the Camps.* 57-minute documentary on the journey to healing of six Japanese Americans confined in internment camps during World War II. 1999.

Kim-Gibson, Dai Sil (producer/director). *Silence Broken: Korean Comfort Women.* 57-minute documentary on Korean women who were forced into sexual servitude by the Japanese Imperial Army during World War II. 1999.

Korty, John (director). *Farewell to Manzanar.* 120-minute fact-based drama about one of the internment camps used during World War II to detain 120,000 Japanese Americans. 1976.

Young, Don (producer/director/editor) *Resettlement to Redress.* 55-minute documentary on Japanese Americans' readjustment to society upon their release from the internment camps. 2005.

FURTHER READING

Austin, Allen W. *From Concentration Camp to Campus: Japanese American Students and World War II.* Urbana: University of Illinois Press, 2004.

Chan, Sucheng. *Asian Americans: An Interpretive History.* Boston: Twayne, 1991.

Ch'oe, Yŏng-ho. *From the Land of Hibiscus: Koreans in Hawaii, 1903–1950.* Honolulu: University of Hawai'iI Press, 2007.

Daniels, Roger. *Asian America: Chinese and Japanese in the United States since 1850.* Seattle: University of Washington Press, 1988.

———. *Concentration Camps USA: Japanese Americans and World War II*. New York: Holt, Rinehart and Winston, 1972.

———. "Incarceration of the Japanese Americans: A Sixty Year Perspective." *History Teacher* 35 (2002): 297–310.

———. *The Japanese American Cases: The Rule of Law in Time of War*. Lawrence: University Press of Kansas, 2013.

———. *Prisoners without Trial: Japanese Americans in World War II*. Rev. ed. New York: Hill & Wang, 2004.

Houston, Jeanne, and James D. Houston. *Farewell to Manzanar*. Bel Air, CA: Ember, 2012.

Irons, Peter H. *Justice at War*. Berkeley: University of California Press, 1983.

Kim, Lili M. "The Limits of Americanism and Democracy: Korean Americans, Transnational Allegiance, and the Question of Loyalty on the Homefront during World War II." *Amerasia Journal* 29, no. 3 (2003–2004): 79–96.

Lyon, Cherstin M. *Prisons and Patriots: Japanese American Wartime Citizenship, Civil Disobedience, and Historical Memory*. Philadelphia: Temple University Press, 2012.

Ng, Wendy. *Japanese American Internment during World War II: A History and Reference Guide*. Westport, CT: Greenwood, 2002.

Norman, Michael, and Elizabeth M. Norman. *Tears in the Darkness: The Story of the Bataan Death March and Its Aftermath*. New York: Picador, 2010.

Odo, Franklin. *No Sword to Bury: Japanese Americans in Hawai'i during World War II*. Philadelphia: Temple University Press, 2004.

Okada, John. *No-No Boy*. Seattle: University of Washington Press, 1979.

Okihiro, Gary Y. *Cane Fires: The Anti-Japanese Movement in Hawaii, 1865–1945*. Philadelphia: Temple University Press, 1991.

Robinson, Greg. *A Tragedy of Democracy: Japanese Confinement in North America*. New York: Columbia University Press, 2009.

Takaki, Ronald. *Strangers from a Different Shore: A History of Asian Americans*. Boston: Little, Brown, 1989.

Wong, K. Scott. *Americans First: Chinese Americans and the Second World War*. Cambridge, MA: Harvard University Press, 2005.

Yamamoto, Hisaye. *Seventeen Syllables and Other Stories*. New Brunswick, NJ: Rutgers University Press, 2001.

Zhao, Xiaojian. *Remaking Chinese America: Immigration, Family, and Community, 1940–1965*. New Brunswick, NJ: Rutgers University Press, 2002.

PART III

Contemporary Asian Americans, 1965–2020s

6

NEW WAVES OF IMMIGRANTS AND REFUGEES

CHAPTER OUTLINE

A More Gender-Balanced Society
Effects of the Immigration and Nationality Act of 1965
Southeast Asian Americans
Plights and Potentials of Undocumented Immigrants
"The Quiet Migration": Transnational Transracial Adoption
New Waves of Immigrants in Historical Perspective

SIGNIFICANT EVENTS

1945	War Brides Act of December 28 enables alien wives of veterans to enter America as nonquota immigrants
1946	G.I. Fiancées Act of June 29 enables alien wives and children of veterans and American citizens to enter America as nonquota immigrants
1948	Displaced Persons Act grants "displaced" Chinese students, visitors, and others who already had a temporary status in the United States to adjust their status to that of permanent residents
1950–1953	War in the Korean Peninsula between North Korea and South Korea, also involving China (on the North's side) and the United States (on the South's side)
1953	Refugee Relief Act allots 3,000 visas to refugees from Asia and 2,000 visas to Chinese whose passports had been issued by the Chinese Nationalist government, which lost control of mainland China in 1949; the beginning of transnational transracial adoption from Korea
1961	Exchange Visitor Program (EVP) designed to solve the shortage of nurses in the United States enables a large number of Filipino nurses to come to America

1965	The Immigration and Nationality Act of 1965 abolishes the 1924 quota system and sets up three immigration principles of family reunification, the need for skilled workers, and the admission of refugees
1975	The end of the Vietnam War brings about 130,000 refugees to the United States; "Operation Babylift" airlifts about 3,300 Amerasian children from Vietnam
1976	The first major revision of the 1965 Immigration Act extends the seven preferences and allotted each country a quota of 20,000 regardless of which hemisphere the country is located in
1978	Amendment to the 1965 Immigration Act merges the two hemisphere ceilings into a single worldwide ceiling of 290,000 a year for all nationalities
1980	Refugee Act increases the annual number of refugees to 50,000 and reduces annual quota numbers to 270,000
1986	The Immigration Reform and Control Act (IRCA) imposes penalties on employers who knowingly hired undocumented immigrants and offers amnesty and the right for permanent residency after two years for all undocumented aliens in the country on or before January 1, 1982
1990	The Immigration Act of 1990 expands the post-1965 immigration system and categorizes immigrants into three groups of family-sponsored immigrants, employment-based immigrants, and diversity immigrants (individuals who are chosen through a lottery from countries with low rates of immigration to the United States)
1991	Chinese adoption law is promulgated, spurring transnational adoption to the United States
1992	Total Southeast Asian arrivals reach 1,223,699
1988–1993	Peak of undocumented immigrants from Fujian, China
2002	The U.S. and Cambodian governments reach a repatriation agreement, under which about 2,000 Cambodian Americans are threatened with deportation (around 300 have been forcefully deported to Cambodia since 2010)
2006	20,679 children from overseas are adopted by American families, including 5,454 Chinese adoptees, the largest group
2009	An estimated 12 million undocumented individuals are living in America
2013	On June 28, the Senate passes the Border Security, Economic Opportunity, and Immigration Modernization Act, a comprehensive immigration overhaul bill that provides a pathway to citizenship for undocumented immigrants, increases the number of visas available for employers to hire foreign workers, and increases security at the U.S.-Mexico border

THE REPEAL OF THE CHINESE EXCLUSION ACTS, combined with the War Brides Act, G.I. Fiancées Act, Displaced Persons Act, and Refugee Relief Act, had brought a more gender-balanced society to Asian Americans in the postwar years. The Immigration and Nationality Act of 1965 helped further increase the Asian American population, attracting more highly educated professionals to the country. The fall of Saigon and the successive wars and persecutions in the Southeast Asian peninsula drove millions of refugees to the United States; they constitute the Asian American subgroups with the highest rates of people living below the federal poverty line. The experiences of undocumented new arrivals from Asia manifest the plights and potentials of these new immigrants in America. The coming-of-age of Asian American adoptees and their relationships to Asia, Asian America, as well as the United States further contribute to the diversity and complexity of Asian American history.

A MORE GENDER-BALANCED SOCIETY

War Brides

In spite of the repeal of the Chinese Exclusion Acts, the Chinese immigrant quota designated by the American government was only 105 per year. This figure was calculated as one-sixth of one percent of the number of the Chinese in the United States in 1920, as determined by the census of that year. Nevertheless, additional nonquota immigrants were also allowed to immigrate. More Chinese scholars came to teach in the United States, with an annual average of about 137, in comparison with only 10 per year during the previous decade. More importantly, under the War Brides Act of December 28, 1945, and the G.I. Fiancées Act of June 29, 1946, alien wives and children of veterans and American citizens were also permitted to enter America as nonquota immigrants. During the three-year operation of the War Brides Act, approximately 6,000 Chinese war brides entered the country.[1]

Many Chinese women also came under other laws. The Displaced Persons Act of 1948 and the Refugee Relief Act of 1953 allowed several thousand Chinese women to immigrate to America. The 1948 act granted "displaced" Chinese students, visitors, and others who already had a temporary status in the United States to adjust their status to that of permanent residents. The 1953 act allotted 3,000 visas to refugees from Asia and 2,000 visas to Chinese whose passports had been issued by the Chinese Nationalist government, which lost control of mainland China in 1949.[2] Although it appears at first glance that they were passed for humanitarian reasons, these two laws were in fact designed under the influence of the "China Lobbies"—former U.S. diplomats, businessmen, and other sympathizers of the defeated Nationalist regime—to prevent U.S.-trained Chinese scholars and students from returning to their homeland and helping in the construction of the new communist China. On September 22, 1959, Congress passed an act under which even more Chinese on the quota waiting list were able to obtain nonquota status.

Under these favorable immigration laws, more Chinese women entered the United States. In 1948 alone, 3,317 women immigrated, whereas only 60 Chinese women entered the country on average each year during the 1930s. During the period from 1944 to 1953, women composed 82 percent of Chinese immigrants to America. For the first time, the number of Chinese women and families in the United States noticeably increased, and the male/female ratio dropped from 2.9:1 in 1940 to 1.8:1 in 1950 and 1.3:1 in 1960. According to the 1960 census, the number of Chinese in the United States had reached 237,292. This included 135,549 males and 101,743 females.[3]

While many of the Chinese women came under the War Brides Act and married their coethnics, most other Asian wives of American servicemen married non-Asians and entered the United States as "nonquota immigrants," spouses of U.S. citizens thanks to the terms of McCarran-Walter Act of 1952, which granted entry to America to immigrants with special skills and relatives of U.S. citizens.[4] This act also abolished the racial restrictions found in the U.S. immigration and naturalization statutes dating back to the Naturalization Act of 1790. A dark side of the act is that it allowed the government to deport immigrants or naturalized citizens engaged in subversive activities and also allowed the barring of suspected subversives from entering the country. These Asian war brides included Japanese, Korean, and Filipino women, composing 85 percent of all war brides during the period from 1955 to 1975. Approximately 85 percent of the Asian brides' non-Asian husbands were white.[5] Asian war brides became the single largest group of Asian women to have ever entered the United States. Between 1947 and 1964, about 72,700 Asian women immigrated to America as war brides, including 45,853 Japanese, 14,435 Filipinas, 6,423 Koreans, and approximately 6,000 Chinese.[6]

Two factors seem to have contributed to the interracial marriages between American servicemen and Asian women. One is the American military presence in the Asian Pacific area, and the other is the socioeconomic conditions of these Asian countries in the post–World War II era. Japanese women who entered the country as spouses of American servicemen were the largest group among all war brides until the 1970s. After World War II, American occupation forces controlled Japan until 1952. The Japan-U.S. Security Treaty of 1951 allowed a continued American military presence in Japan for its defense. During both the Korean War and the Vietnam War, American servicemen also came to Japan for vacation and recreation. Meanwhile, the destruction of Japan at the end of World War II resulted in a shortage of Japanese males of marriageable age and dislocation and hardship for adolescent Japanese females, many of whom worked on American military bases. The loneliness of American servicemen and difficult socioeconomic conditions of many Japanese women thus made the interracial marriage a viable choice.[7]

Korean women who entered the United States as war brides came from similar circumstances. Since the end of World War II, American troops had been stationed in South Korea. American troops fought during the Korean War from 1950 to 1953 and continued to be stationed in thirteen army and air military bases throughout South Korea, with about 40,000 servicemen still based there today. Between 1948 and 1965, a total of 16,271 Koreans entered the United States, among whom 40 percent were war brides and 30 percent were orphans of the Korean War.[8] Young Korean women working at or near American military bases were attracted to American servicemen, hoping that the latter would help them in realizing their "dreams to go to America and become rich."[9] The Korean War orphans were often children of mixed parentage; about 46 percent of these Amerasian children had mixed blood of Korean and European Americans and 13 percent of Korean and African Americans (see more discussion on Korean and other Asian American adoptees in the "The Quiet Migration": Transnational Transracial Adoption section).[10]

Filipino women also came to the United States in significant numbers during the postwar era. The majority of them entered as dependents of U.S. citizens. Many of them married U.S. servicemen in the Philippines, including a sizeable number of Filipino Americans serving in the U.S. Navy. Almost half of the 16,000 Filipino immigrants who came between 1946 and 1954 were the wives of U.S. servicemen.[11] Others came to join their Filipino husbands who already lived in the United States.

Filipino Nurses

In addition to war brides, Filipino nurses were the second most important source of Filipino female immigration to the United States. The influx of Filipino nurses was a result of the combination of nursing shortages in the United States and the abundant supply of Filipino nurses who were trained by the Americanized nursing system in the Philippines. A reoccurring and endemic shortage of nurse was the primary economic force that attracted Filipino nurses to the United States. Statistics show that between 1965 (when the Medicare and Medicaid programs were established) and 1990, medical expenditures increased by 220 percent, while both private and public medical expenditures on health care as a portion of the total national expenditure increased only from 7.4 percent to 11.2 percent.[12]

Meanwhile, the Americanized training hospital system in the Philippines, a legacy of American colonial rule, afforded the United States a ready supply of well-trained Filipino nurses. Under Spanish colonial rule, before the U.S. annexation of the Philippines at the turn of the twentieth century, midwifery was the only career in health care open to Filipino women. American colonial rule introduced new professions, such as nursing, and educational and travel opportunities in the United States. An Americanized nursing curriculum in the Philippines was one of the most significant preconditions for the mass migration of Filipino nurses. From 1907 to 1910, Filipino nursing students were first trained for a year in the classroom at the Philippine Normal School. They then carried out their practical nursing work at three different hospital schools of nursing: St. Paul's Hospital, the Civil Hospital (later known as Philippine General Hospital), and University Hospital (later known as St. Luke's Hospital). From 1910 onward, Filipino nursing students completed both their classroom and practical nursing work in their designated hospitals, a system identical to nurse training in the United States. The curriculum of their nursing study resembled that of their counterparts in the United States: material medical, massage, and bacteriology. Use of the English language was also an integral part of their training. The nursing schools consciously recruited young women from "respectable" families.[13]

> Nursing in the Philippines has a history on which we may look back with satisfaction, for, while carried on almost entirely by Americans in the early days of the occupation, its speedy adoption into the life and education of the Filipinos themselves and its wonderfully rapid development have probably not been surpassed elsewhere.
> —LAVINIA DOCK, SECRETARY OF THE INTERNATIONAL COUNCIL OF NURSING, *A HISTORY OF NURSING*, 1912.
>
> Source: Catherine Cenaza Choy, *Empire of Care: Nursing and Migration in Filipino American History* (Durham, NC: Duke University Press, 2003), 15.

However, a number of factors turned the relatively small migration of the Filipino nursing elite in the early twentieth century into a mass migration in the post-1965 era. First, the rapid expansion of nursing schools in the Philippines created a large pool of labor in the nursing profession. From 1950 to 1970, the number of nursing schools in the Philippines rose from 17 to 140. The proliferation of nursing schools also extended their presence beyond greater Manila to the provinces. This resulted in a high number of health care providers.[14]

Second, the U.S. government opened the door for foreign-trained health practitioners through a number of immigration regulations. The creation of the U.S. Exchange Visitor Program (EVP) in 1961 to solve the shortage of nurses in the United States enabled a large number of Filipino nurses to come to the United States. As the EVP stipulates that the Filipino nurses would have to return to the Philippines after staying in the United States for two years and would then have to remain in the Philippines for at least two years, many returned to the Philippines, waited for the required two years, and then applied for immigration visas. The EVP thus acted as a vehicle for transforming nursing into an international profession.[15]

More importantly, the Immigration and Nationality Act of 1965 was a watershed in the migration of Filipino nurses. It opened new opportunities for Filipino nurses to work in the United States. Under the rulings of this act, the Immigration and Naturalization

A FILIPINO AMERICAN NURSE: MARIE BORNALES

Marie Bornales was born into a family of educators in Ilocos Norte, Philippines in 1931. She came to the United States in 1954 as a nurse under an exchange visitor program and then returned to the Philippines. She immigrated to America in 1961 with a green card and has since lived in St. Louis, Missouri. She was a seventy-two-year-old retired nurse at the time of the interview in 1999.

My name is Marie Bornales. I was born in Ilocos Norte, in the northern part of the Philippines, in 1931. My parents completed only a grade school education, which was basically the only thing that existed in the Philippines at the time, but both became English teachers later in life. Most people in the Philippines were like my mother and father in terms of education. I have eight siblings, five sisters and three brothers. Two of my brothers didn't finish college, and the other died early, when he was forty. Two of my sisters finished their college education (one is a nurse, one is a teacher), but my older brother and sisters got married early. Since we had so many children, I was sent to live with my grandparents at a young age, which is common in the Philippines.

I came to the United States for the first time in April 1954, when I was twenty-three. I had read in the paper that registered nurses were being recruited for an exchange program with the United States. I entered on a visa especially for this exchange visitor program. Under this program, we could only stay in the United States for two years and then we had to return to the Philippines to teach what we had learned in the United States. I ended up coming back to the United States a few years later because it is a beautiful country and I really liked it here. Everything is available and the quality of education is much higher these days than when we lived in the Philippines and it is more progressive. The number of opportunities and the ability to advance is what I like most about living in America. It is still the best country I have ever known.

Most of the time, speaking the language in America was not especially difficult; when I was in the Philippines, we learned to speak English. Sometimes, though, I had difficulty understanding my teachers, especially their pronunciation. My classmates were very nice to me; they helped me a lot, taking me out to dinner or the movies or opera house because we lived around St. John's Hospital near Kingshighway Blvd. They were mostly American; I was the only Filipino at St. John's and I became homesick. After a year, I moved to a city hospital and took a post-graduate course in operating room techniques, and then I moved to St. Anthony's Hospital, where there were more Filipinos.

Source: Huping Ling, *Voices of the Heart: Asian American Women on Immigration, Work, and Family* (Kirksville, MO: Truman State University Press, 2007), 88–89.

Service (INS) and the Department of Labor could alternatively limit and expand the supply of foreign-trained nurses. The U.S. secretary of labor could issue automatic labor certification to nurses without the prior sponsorship of an employer, thus allowing foreign-trained nurses to enter the United States as immigrants under the occupational preference quotas (see the next section for more details on the Immigration and Nationality Act of 1965).[16]

The influx of these childbearing-age women led to a more gender-balanced Asian American society and an increased number of Amerasian children. The more gender-balanced composition of the Asian American population is pivotal to its postwar socioeconomic transformation.

EFFECTS OF THE IMMIGRATION AND NATIONALITY ACT OF 1965

Two factors primarily contributed to the successful passage of the Immigration and Nationality Act of 1965—the broad socioeconomic reforms of the 1960s and the support of the Lyndon B. Johnson administration. Twentieth-century American liberalism reached its climax in the 1960s. The Kennedy and Johnson administrations both responded to the civil rights movement, but it was Johnson who succeeded in passing a raft of civil rights laws intended to help underprivileged Americans achieve their American dreams.

Civil rights reform was Johnson's top legislative priority and an integral part of his Great Society program. The centerpiece of his administration's antipoverty campaign was the Economic Opportunity Act of 1964, which provided education and training for unskilled youth who were trapped in the poverty cycle. The provision of health care to the aged, through Medicare, and those on welfare and or unable to afford private medical insurance, through Medicaid, was the most important expansion of federal welfare programs since the Social Security Act of 1935.

The Great Society also included Immigration reform. The existing U.S. immigration policies, which severely restricted the admission of Asians and Africans, and preferred Northern and Western Europeans over Southern and Eastern ones, were an embarrassment to Johnson. A politician with an expansive vision of the possibilities of reform and known for his ability to get things done, Johnson took on the task of reforming immigration policy and pushed for the passage of a law that would accomplish this. On October 3, 1965, with overwhelming support from both the House (326–70) and Senate (76–18), Johnson signed the legislation into law at the foot of the Statue of Liberty as a symbolic gesture and remarked, "This [old] system violates the basic principle of American democracy, the principle that values and rewards each man on the basis of his merit as a man. It has been un-American in the highest sense, because it has been untrue to the faith that brought thousands to these shores even before we were a country."[17]

FIGURE 6.1 President Lyndon B. Johnson signs the Immigration Act as Vice President Hubert Humphrey, Lady Bird Johnson, Muriel Humphrey, Senator Edward (Ted) Kennedy, Senator Robert F. Kennedy, and others look on, Liberty Island, New York, New York, October 3, 1965. Courtesy Lyndon Baines Johnson Presidential Library & Museum.

The Immigration and Nationality Act of 1965 and the consequent influx of new Asian immigrants contributed to the transformation of Asian American society. The law abolished the National Origins Quota System of 1924 and set up three immigration principles of family reunification, the need for skilled workers, and the admission of refugees. According to these principles, the visas were allocated among quota immigrants from the Eastern Hemisphere according to the following percentages:

1. 20 percent of total annual visas to unmarried children of citizens of the United States
2. 20 percent to spouses and unmarried children of permanent residents
3. 10 percent to professionals, scientists, and artists with "exceptional ability"
4. 10 percent to married children of citizens of the United States
5. 24 percent to siblings of citizens of the United States
6. 10 percent to skilled and unskilled workers in occupations "for which a shortage of employable and willing persons exists in the United States"
7. 6 percent to refugees.[18]

The architects of the 1965 Immigration Act intended to make the immigration policies appear more humanitarian and impartial to applicants on the one hand, and more beneficial to the United States on the other. The new law allowed 20,000 quota immigrants from every country in the Eastern Hemisphere to be admitted to the United States each year, regardless of the size of the country. It reserved 74 percent (including 20 percent in preference 1, another 20 percent in preference 2, 10 percent in preference 4, and 24 percent in preference 5) of the total 170,000 visas annually allotted for the Eastern Hemisphere for family reunification (120,000 visas annually were allotted to immigrants from every country in the Western Hemisphere). Although the 1965 Immigration Act was the first nonracist U.S. immigration law, the lawmakers anticipated that European immigrants would continue to be the largest cohort of new immigrants since there was a very small percentage (0.5 percent of the total U.S. population in the 1960s) of Asian Americans in the country. Two occupational preferences (preference 3 and 6) allowed the Immigration and Naturalization Service and the Department of Labor to carefully select only applicants with special training and skills who would fill a vacuum in the American job market. In the years following this act, the Asian American population increased dramatically. In addition to immigrants of the laboring class, a large number of professionals (the better-educated and the wealthier from China, Taiwan, Hong Kong, and Southeast Asia) also arrived in the period since 1965. These new immigrants benefitted from the 1965 Immigrant Act, which gave priority to those who had close family members in the United States, to applicants who had skills, education, and capital, and to refugees.

Since its passage, the 1965 Immigration Act has undergone several major revisions. In 1976, the first major revision extended the seven preferences and allotted each country a 20,000 quota regardless of which hemisphere the country was located in. This amendment thus reaffirmed the principle that all immigrants should be treated equally. Two years later, the 1978 amendment merged the two hemisphere ceilings into a single worldwide ceiling of 290,000 per year for all nationalities.

The Refugee Act of 1980 attempted to solve the refugee problem. Although the 1965 Immigration Act set up 6 percent of the annual immigration quota under the seventh preference for annual admission (6 percent of the projected 290,000, or 17,400 a year), this number clearly grew insufficiently following the end of the Vietnam War in 1975. Between 1975 and 1979, under the Ford and Carter administrations the parole programs had brought 400,000 Vietnamese and other Southeast Asians to the United States. This experience with Southeast Asian refugees largely shaped the Refugee Act of 1980. It increased the annual number of refugees to 50,000 and reduced the annual quota to 270,000.

The Immigration Reform and Control Act of 1986 (IRCA) was intended to handle undocumented immigrants. Signed on November 6 of the year by the 99th Congress, the law imposed penalties on employers who knowingly hired undocumented immigrants and offered amnesty and the right to permanent residency after two years for all undocumented aliens who had arrived in the country on or before January 1, 1982.[19]

The Immigration Act of 1990 expanded the post-1965 immigration system and categorized immigrants into three groups—family-sponsored immigrants, employment-based immigrants, and diversity immigrants (individuals who are chosen through a lottery from countries with low rates of immigration to the United States). It increased the worldwide level of family-sponsored immigrants to 480,000, employment-based immigrants to 140,000, and diversity immigrants to 55,000 for the fiscal year 1992 and onward.[20]

The 1965 Immigration Act and its amendments contributed to a continuous increase in the volume of immigration from Asia. From 1966 to 2009, the number of Asian immigrants totaled 9,552,207; Asia and Latin America have become the main sources of immigration. As indicated by sociologist Philip Q. Yang, several patterns emerging among the post-1965 immigration from Asia graphically demonstrate the relationship between Asian immigration and American immigration laws as well as the socioeconomic conditions of the sending countries. First, immigration from China, the Philippines, and India has increased at high levels and the three countries have been the major suppliers of Asian immigrants. While the Philippines remained in the leading position in sending immigrants between 1968 and 1992, it yielded the position to either China or India after 1993. The closure of the last two large military bases in the Philippines in 1992, which ended the possibility of international marriages between American servicemen and Filipinas, may have contributed to the decline of Filipino immigration.

The number of immigrants coming from China has been increasing since 1965. Prior to 1979, nearly half of all Chinese immigrants were from Taiwan. However, after Sino--U.S. diplomatic relations were renormalized in 1979, the proportion of Chinese immigrants coming from mainland China (PRC) increased rapidly. Despite some fluctuation in the early 2000s, China has from 1998 onward been the largest sending country in Asia. Indian immigrants have consisted of mostly highly educated professionals—physicians, engineers, scientists, and computer specialists, many of whom were students-turned-professionals who completed postgraduate programs at American universities, found employment, and became permanent residents. Since 1991, Indian immigration accelerated thanks to the Immigration Act of 1990, which permitted many Indians to enter the United States under employment-based immigrant quotas. India has surpassed all Asian countries as the leading immigrant-sending country in Asia since 2001, and the trend will likely remain.

Similarly, the Immigration Act of 1990 also contributed to a substantial increase of immigration from Pakistan and Bangladesh since the 1990s, which was relatively low before the 1990s. The Diversity Immigrants program, commonly known as the Green

Card Lottery program and introduced by the Immigration Act of 1990, has clearly benefitted Pakistani and Bangladeshi immigrants. Between 1992 and 2009, 34,040 Bangladeshis and 12,836 Pakistanis were admitted as diversity immigrants. Together with India, Nepal, and Sri Lanka, they have paralleled or surpassed Chinese immigration.

While the trend of immigration from China and South Asia has been upward since the 1990s, immigration from Korea, Japan, Hong Kong, and Taiwan, the more affluent countries and regions in Asia, has declined or fluctuated during the same period. The number of Korean immigrants increased from 1965 to 1977, remained at much the same level in the late 1970s and throughout the 1980s, and declined in the 1990s as a result of South Korea's rising living standard, democratization, and improved security following the relaxation of tensions with its neighbor North Korea. Immigration from Korea rebounded in the early 2000s because of a major economic crisis in Korea.

Immigration from Japan had been stable at a low level up to the 1980s, but has significantly increased since the 1990s. Although devastated by World War II, Japan rose as an economic power within a generation in the late 1960s and surpassed the United States in per capita income between 1987 and 2000. Affluent Japanese society discouraged emigration, and most of those who migrated to the United States were women who were pushed out by severe gender inequalities in Japan and married American men. Other Japanese immigrants were mostly males, working on a three- to five-year rotational basis in American subsidiaries of the Japanese corporations they represented. Although a large proportion of them had permanent resident status, many returned to Japan after their term of service. However, the burst of the bubble economy in 1990 and the subsequent prolonged economic recession produced increasing levels of Japanese immigration.

Immigration from Hong Kong and Taiwan had also been stable but has decreased in more recent years. Immigration from Hong Kong jumped from 3,000 to 7,000 annually from 1966 to 1987. The IRCA of 1986 increased the annual quota for Hong Kong immigrants from 600 to 5,000, and the Immigration Act of 1990 raised the quota again—to 10,000 beginning in the fiscal year 1992 and then to 20,000 beginning in the fiscal year 1995—in response to the increased uncertainty among the people of Hong Kong over the British colony's return to China in 1997. The increased quota facilitated a significant rise in immigration from Hong Kong between 1988 and 1996. However, as Hong Kong largely remained unchanged after the Chinese takeover, the "emigration fever" cooled down and immigration from Hong Kong has seen a declining trend since 1997. Taiwan shared an annual quota of 20,000 with China before 1982 but had its own quota of 20,000 per year since 1982. Immigration from Taiwan fluctuated between 1982 and 1996, but fell below 10,000 after 1996. The decline of immigration from Taiwan was a result of rising living standards, improved graduate programs at its universities, and a high degree of globalization and IT development in Taiwan.[21]

SOUTHEAST ASIAN AMERICANS

Among Asian Americans, Southeast Asian Americans constitute the most recently formed ethnic group. Unlike earlier Asian American groups, Vietnamese, Laotian, Hmong/Mong, and Cambodian Americans are refugees and their American-born children. Their immigration patterns and their lives in America are thus inevitably intertwined with the refugee experience.

Causes of Southeast Asian Exodus

Since the end of the Vietnam War in 1975, over two million refugees and immigrants from Vietnam, Cambodia, and Laos have arrived in the United States. The Vietnam War was a tragedy that not only affected millions of Americans but also devastated many more Vietnamese, Cambodians, Laotians, and Hmong/Mong (two groups of mountain people from Laos with distinctively different dialects, customs, and habits, but collectively called Hmong by the U.S. government and the public).[22]

The massive U.S. involvement in Vietnam was a logical culmination of the anticommunist containment policy. It began under Harry Truman in the late 1940s and was continued by the successive administrations of Eisenhower, Kennedy, Johnson, and Nixon, none of whom questioned the assumption that the U.S. national interest required American involvement in Vietnam. Having witnessed communist control established in China, North Korea, and North Vietnam following the end of World War II, the U.S. government felt urged to fill the vacuum created by the withdrawal of French colonial rule in order to counter the potential threat of communism spreading from Vietnam to Laos, Cambodian, Burma (now Myanmar) and other Southeast Asian countries. The U.S. involvement in Vietnam escalated from a limited military advisory role to large-scale direct participation in the fight against communist North Vietnam. The Vietnam War became the single most divisive event in U.S. history since the Civil War. The war cost the country 58,000 lives and $150 billion. Over 300,000 Americans were wounded, and more than 2,000 remain missing in action.

The war not only divided America but also devastated Vietnam, Laos, and Cambodia. During the period of U.S. involvement, starting from the French withdrawal from Vietnam after their defeat at Dien Bien Phu in 1954 and ending in 1975 when the last U.S. troops retreated, an estimated four million Vietnamese soldiers and civilians on both sides were killed or wounded. In South Vietnam, a third of the total population was displaced during the war and over half of the total forestation and 10 percent of all agricultural land was partially destroyed by aerial bombardment, tractor cleaning, and chemical defoliation from "agent orange." In Laos, the Hmong, an ethnic minority of the mountainous highlands who originally migrated from southwest China, fought on the U.S. side against the Pathet Lao and bore the brunt of war casualties. By 1975, about a third of the Hmong population had been uprooted by war. In Cambodia, to which the war expanded in 1970, a quarter of the population died in the horror of the late 1970s.[23]

Waves of Southeast Asian Refugees

The Southeast Asian refugee exodus has been shaped by complex political and socioeconomic factors. The 1.2 million refugees from Vietnam, Laos, and Cambodia who entered the United States after 1975 came in several waves of multitudes escaping the terror. The first wave of Vietnamese refugees was primarily composed of an elite class who left Vietnam due to the communist takeover, during the period from the eve of the fall of Saigon to 1978. They included army officers and their families, government bureaucrats, teachers, doctors, engineers, lawyers, students, businessmen, and Catholic priests and nuns. In 1975, about 130,000 refugees arrived in the United States.

The later waves of Southeast Asian refugees consisted of individuals from more modest backgrounds, including farmers and fishermen escaping continuing regional military conflicts and deteriorating economic conditions between 1978 and 1992.[24] About 450,000 Southeast Asian refugees arrived between 1979 and 1982. Since 1982, Southeast Asian refugees have oscillated between 40,000 and 80,000 annually. Between 1975 and 1992, 650,000 Vietnamese refugees were admitted. The number of Vietnamese arrivals was further swelled by a flow of over 170,000 nonrefugee Vietnamese immigrants. By 1992, total Southeast Asian arrivals reached 1,223,699: 845,464 Vietnamese (69 percent), 230,385 Laotians (19 percent), and 147,850 Cambodians (12 percent). Of them, 86 percent entered the United States as refugees, the rest as immigrants; four out of five arrived since 1980. In addition, children born in the United States by Southeast Asian refugees, estimated at nearly 200,000 by 1985, helped increase the Southeast Asian American population to over 1.4 million in the early 1990s.[25] While Vietnamese elites and professionals were joined and outnumbered by the masses of refugees who were relocated to American bases in Guam and Philippines under emergency conditions after the fall of Saigon, elites from Laos and Cambodia were more likely to be settled in France.

The Southeast Asian refugees fled their home countries by planes, by boats, or on foot. They experienced the terror of pirates on the high seas, the brutality of refugee camps in Thailand, and the anxious waiting in refugee camps in Guam and Wake Island before being sent to their sponsors in the United States. The intense emotional trauma haunted many refugees for a prolonged period of time after they settled in America. The elderly refugees especially, having difficulty in learning English and being reluctant to reach out for federal assistance, suffered a high level of mental stress.[26]

FIGURE 6.2 Guam tent city in the early stages of the emergency parole program for Vietnamese refugees, 1975. Courtesy Immigration and Nationalization Service.

FIGURE 6.3 Vietnamese refugees wait in tent shelters outside a processing center, Fort Indiantown Gap, Pennsylvania, 1975. Courtesy Immigration and Nationalization Service.

FIGURE 6.4 Ha, former Vietnamese refugee and case management coordinator at International Institute of Metro St. Louis, interviewed by Huping Ling, 1999. Huping Ling Collection.

Government Refugee Policies and Settlement Patterns

According to Rubén G. Rumbaut's study, Southeast Asian refugees were processed in four reception centers: Camp Pendleton, California; Fort Indiantown Gap, Pennsylvania; Fort Chaffee, Arkansas; and Eglin Air Force Base, Florida. The typical procedure for handling these refugees was an initial interview at one of these centers followed by their placement with their sponsors, which comprised ordinary citizens and religious and civic groups. The U.S. government policy was to avoid the concentration of refugees at any one particular area, and the government made efforts to populate those areas that had fewer refugees. For instance, the 130,000 Southeast Asian refugees arriving in 1975 were placed in 813 separate zip codes in all fifty states, with two-thirds ending up in zip codes that had fewer than 500 refugees.

Despite the efforts to disperse the refugees throughout the United States, the secondary migration of these refugees in subsequent years led to the formation of large Southeast Asian population concentrations, mostly in California, perhaps due to the milder climate, family ties, and better economic opportunities. In ten years, the Southeast Asian population in California increased from 20 to 40 percent, mostly around Los Angeles, San Diego, and San Jose.

DUNG NGUYEN'S REFUGEE EXPERIENCE

Dung Nguyen was a Vietnamese refugee who fled the country with her brother by boat in 1975 when she was fourteen, while the rest of her family remained in Vietnam. She and her husband and their children lived in a midwestern city at the time of the interview in 2003.

On April 29, 1975 . . . my four cousins and I went to a small Chinese merchant ship in Saigon. It only held a couple hundred people. Most were getting ready to move their families back to China or Hong Kong, out of the war. We jumped on. I thought we were going to one of the islands of Vietnam to get out of harm's way because there was fighting everywhere. I never thought we were going to America. If I did I never would have gone. I would have been too afraid to do that. That was the day before we found out we had lost the war.

The Chinese weren't really helping us, they were trying to get themselves out; everybody was trying to get away from the North Vietnamese. We just happened to jump on the ship and there was space for us. We were all packed on very tight. I slept standing up. A couple days later, after we gave them all of our Vietnamese money, the Chinese dropped us off on a pontoon, like the ones the American army travels in from their big ships to land. The Chinese ship couldn't dock with an American ship because the American ships were so huge and would smash it. The Chinese didn't want to take us to Hong Kong, and we didn't want to go with them either. We were left there and waited until an American ship came and transferred half of the people; women, the elderly, and the sick went first. Later, during the night, another ship came, a merchant ship, which took the rest of us. We hadn't had water for over twenty-four hours. We scrounged for rice on the floor of the pontoon because we were so hungry.

We had to walk on a gangplank up onto the American ship. It was really high and scary. As soon as we got on they gave us water, because we hadn't had any, and a c-ration, what the American armies eat, I think. I think that the American government might have prepared them because they were carrying all kinds of c-rations so we all got a box. We went down two or three levels to stay wherever we could find a little space to lay our blankets out.

This ship went to the Philippines. It was such a long trip that some of the elderly, women and children got sick. They had to restock their supplies because there were so many of us. They left the sick people in the Philippines. Then we went to Guam or Wake Island; I stopped at Guam Island. We got off and the Red Cross helped us register. We didn't speak English, so there was no way to communicate with the Americans. The army gave us hot food—rice, spam, and fruit cocktail. I remember because I didn't know how to eat those things yet. We don't usually eat sweet and salty on the same plate. We would run after they gave us the spam and rice before they could scoop out the fruit cocktail. They thought it was funny.

They put each family in tents where we slept. They brought our things to us in shopping carts. We wanted to carry our own things but a soldier would not let us. He carried them and put them in the tent we chose. The next morning we had breakfast and then they put us on airplanes and we flew to Wake Islands where we got to stay in a little house. It was also a barracks for the American Army. That night we got a cot and

> a sheet, a white sheet. We took it and made pajamas out of it. We had a bucket with soap, shampoo, and personal items in it. We had to register again. We were checked for tuberculosis and lice. Then we got shots.
>
> When we first came to America we were flown to Fort Chaffee in Arkansas, another army base. There we were matched up with sponsors who had signed up in their churches or with the Red Cross, and then we got to go wherever they were. We didn't need proof of residency because we all came in as refugees. When I registered myself I also registered my family, my parents and my brothers and sisters so they could contact me if they came.
>
> Source: Huping Ling, *Voices of the Heart: Asian American Women on Immigration, Work, and Family* (Kirksville, MO: Truman State University Press, 2007), 319–322.

The ethnic social network impacted the Southeast Asian refugee settlement more in a later time when the much larger waves of Southeast Asian refugees arrived in the United States in the late 1970s and during the 1980s. By the early 1980s, "about a third of arriving refugees already had close relatives in the United States who could serve as sponsors, and another third had more distant relatives, leaving only the remaining third without kinship ties subject to the dispersal policy," observed Rumbaut.

The ethnic networks of different groups led to different localities of concentration for each ethnic group. The largest Cambodian population center formed in the Long Beach area of Los Angeles County, the largest Lao population in San Diego, the largest Hmong population in Fresno, and the largest Vietnamese population in Orange County.

Aside from the population centers of the Southeast Asian refugees in California, there are significant population centers of Vietnamese, Cambodian, and Lao in some other states. For instance, Vietnamese are the largest Asian American minority group in Texas, Louisiana, Mississippi, Arkansas, Kansas, and Oklahoma, with a strong presence in Houston and Dallas; Cambodians form a significant presence in Minnesota and Wisconsin, and Hmong/Mong are the largest Asian American group in the same states. Laotians are the most dispersed among the Southeast Asian refugees.[27]

More recent data reveal that the Hmong/Mong are migrating in greater numbers into the Midwest. In the 2000 U.S. Census, California had the largest population of Hmong, with 65,095, and Minnesota had 41,800. In the 2005 American Community Survey, California held steady with 65,345, but Minnesota rose to 46,352. In the same survey, Wisconsin had 38,814, Michigan had 7,769, and Colorado had 4,285. The Pacific Coast state of Washington had 1,380, while Alaska had 1,285 and Oregon had 1,091. In the South, in the 2000 census, North Carolina had 7,093 and Georgia had 1,468, but in the 2005 American Community Survey, North Carolina had 4,172, while Georgia had 3,324.[28] A

FIGURE 6.5 Hmong community members at a recognition celebration in Saint Paul, Minnesota, April 4, 2011. Hmong immigrants have formed a major population center in the Twin Cities area, Minnesota. Courtesy Ramsey County, Minnesota.

recent study also finds that Minneapolis–Saint Paul has replaced Fresno, California, as the metropolitan area with the largest Hmong/Mong population by 2005, as a result of the Hmong's re-migration within the United States.[29]

Social and Economic Characteristics

Rubén G. Rumbaut has noted that some social and economic characteristics of Southeast Asian Americans are quite different from those of the general Asian American population, based on his analysis of the 1990 U.S. census and annual government surveys of nationwide samples in the 1990s. Rumbaut pointed out the following characteristics. First, all groups of the Southeast Asian population were much younger than other Asians or the total American population. Clearly, much higher levels of fertility among the Southeast Asians contributed to the younger age of the population. While American and Asian American women on average had fewer than 2 children born per woman between the ages of 35 and 44, Vietnamese women had 2.5, Lao and Cambodians 3.5, and Hmong 6.1. The high proportion of dependent children among Southeast Asian families was a key social context shaping the adaptation of these groups, especially over changing gender roles and intergenerational conflicts.

Second, there were fewer single-parent female-headed households among the Southeast Asian Americans than the U.S. general population. However, there were a few exceptions. Cambodian refugees had higher rate (25 percent) of single-parent female-headed households, attributed to widows whose husbands were killed during the Pol Pot regime (a dictatorship led by the communist revolutionary, whose policy of evacuating urban dwellers to the countryside resulted in the deaths of more than a million people) from 1976 to 1979. In addition, Vietnamese had a lower percentage (73 percent) of children under eighteen living at home with both parents than that of Asian Americans generally (85 percent) because a large number of unaccompanied Vietnamese refugee children fled their homeland with other relatives or adult guardians.

Third, the vast majority of the Vietnamese, Cambodians, and Laotians did not speak English very well. All of the Southeast Asian groups were on average much less educated than other Asian Americans, with only about a third of the refugees from Laos and Cambodia being high school graduates, while 38 percent of all Asian American adults had college degrees and 14 percent also had postgraduate degrees.

Fourth, while Asian Americans generally had higher rates of labor force participation, lower rates of unemployment, and a higher percentage of professionals and managers, on the contrary each of the Southeast Asian groups exhibit the opposite on each of these attributes. Southeast Asian Americans were twice as likely to work as menial laborers, and their levels of self-employment, family and per capita income, and rates of home ownership were much lower than those for Asian Americans and the general U.S. population.

Finally, poverty rates for the Southeast Asian groups were two to five times higher than for the U.S. population. About a quarter of the Vietnamese, one-third of the Lao, half of the Cambodians, and two-thirds of the Hmong/Mong fell below the federal poverty line and received public assistance income, whereas the poverty rates for the U.S. and Asian American general populations remained more or less the same (13 to 14 percent), with fewer than 10 percent of households receiving public assistance.[30]

The more recent census data and research indicate that these characteristics remain largely unchanged, albeit displaying signs of progress in all of the above categories. Hmong/Mong Americans tend to hold unskilled, low-paying, and manufacturing jobs. For example, the top five categories of occupational distribution by percentage of the Hmong/Mong American population in 2005 are production, transportation, and material moving occupations (41.7 percent); sales and office occupations (20.6 percent); management, professional, and related occupations (17.1 percent); service occupations (15.6 percent); construction, extraction, and maintenance occupations (4.5 percent); and farming, fishing, and forestry occupations (0.4 percent). The median annual income of Hmong/Mong American families, which was among the lowest of all Asian Americans, was $32,400, compared with $59,300 for Asian American families, $70,849 for Japanese American families, and $50,000 for general U.S. families.[31] In 2010, Asian Americans as a group had lower than average poverty rates (12 percent, compared to 15.1 percent for the national rate), but several Asian nationalities had higher than average rates of poverty. The poverty rate among Hmong/Mong was 37.8 percent, Cambodians 29.3 percent, Laotians 18.5 percent, and Vietnamese 16.6 percent.[32]

Economic Progress

There have been public concerns that refugees will be a burden on American taxpayers. The U.S. refugee program has therefore focused on promoting refugee self-sufficiency through early employment and minimal reliance on public assistance. Research based on longitudinal data sources indicates that Southeast Asian refugees have higher rates of labor force participation and lower rates of unemployment over time than the general U.S. population. Analyzing annual aggregate data from the Internal Revenue Service on income received and tax paid by Southeast Asian Americans, researchers found that arrival cohorts displayed very low rates of labor force participation and high rates of unemployment during their first year in the United States. However, the rates of labor force participation began climbing in the succeeding years, especially for the 1975 to 1978 cohorts, who have shown the highest rates of labor force participation (71–80 percent) within their first four years in the country, exceeding the rate for the general U.S. population (64 percent).[33]

A study of refugee use of public assistance based on 1983 to 1988 national longitudinal survey data found that 18 percent of all Southeast Asian households were economically self-sufficient after their first year in the United States, some of whom have never used public assistance. Among those who used public assistance, 41 percent had left public assistance programs within their second year in the United States, 57 percent by their fifth year. However, the study also showed significant differences between refugee households in California (home to over 40 percent of the total Southeast Asian population) and those in the rest of the country. In California, only 7 percent of the Southeast Asian households were financially independent after their first year and only 18 percent after their second year, compared to 26 percent and 57 percent, respectively, outside of California.[34] One of the strong determinants for the higher reliance among California Southeast Asian residents was the number of dependent children in the family: family income from public assistance grew by 10 percent for each dependent child. In addition, concern over medical coverage was a decisive factor for large refugee families remaining on public assistance (including Medicaid) rather than taking low-wage jobs that provide no health care insurance at all.[35]

Challenges Facing Southeast Asian Americans

Unlike the voluntary immigrants who chose to leave their homelands and search for a better life in the new country, Southeast Asian refugees were thrown into a strange land by war, political turmoil, and other unforeseeable events, through horrific flights, hardships, and physical sufferings. These traumatic experiences often affect their mental health. In addition, the drastic differences between the socioeconomic conditions in their homelands and those in the United States have made their adaptation and acculturation more difficult than those of other immigrants. Around 90 percent of Hmong/Mong and 55 percent of Cambodians lived in rural areas prior to emigration. Vietnamese and ethnic Chinese from Vietnam, though mostly from urban settings in South Vietnam, also experienced maladjustment upon arrival in the United States. Studies have shown the major challenges facing Southeast Asian American families to be mental health issues, children's education, and bicultural and generational conflicts.

First, mental health has posed a major challenge to Southeast Asian Americans. A national survey of the general American adult population by the National Center for Health Statistics in 1980 found that 74 percent of Americans scored in the positive well-being range, 16 percent in the moderate demoralization rage, and only 9.6 percent in the severe demoralization range (indicating "clinical significant distress"). By contrast, Southeast Asian refugees scored 34 percent positive well-being, 38 percent moderate demoralization, and 28 percent severe demoralization in a 1984 survey. The rate of severe demoralization for the Southeast Asian refugees was three times higher than that for the general American population. The demoralization rates were highest for Cambodians, who had experienced the most traumatic contexts of exit, followed in descending order by Hmong/Mong and Vietnamese. Research also found that the process of psychological adaptation appears to be temporally and socially patterned. The first several months after arrival in the United States tended to be a relatively hopeful period, but this was followed by a period of "exile shock" during the second year when depressive symptoms reached their highest levels, and finally a psychological recovery occurring after the third year.[36]

Second, Southeast Asian American children often faced problems at schools. As most Southeast Asian American families initially settled in low-income neighborhoods, their children generally attended schools with other children from similar socioeconomic backgrounds. Research has shown that native minorities and immigrants are heavily concentrated in urban public schools that are suffering from rapid deterioration as members of the middle class continue to abandon inner cities for the suburbs. The Los Angeles metropolitan area, site of the largest Vietnamese concentration in the country, exhibits this pattern. In the mid-1990s, the Los Angeles Unified School District identified 87 percent of the students in the district as "minority" and 40 percent as having limited English proficiency.[37]

Statistics also show that Southeast Asian American adolescents were disproportionally more likely than their other Asian counterparts to be institutionalized, mostly in correctional facilities. According to 1990 census data, Vietnamese adolescents ranked second among racial minority groups (210 incarcerated per 100,000), after Blacks (695 per 100,000), and higher than all other Asian groups (93 per 100,000). Youth gangs have been a serious problem plaguing Vietnamese communities throughout the country.[38]

Despite these socioeconomic disadvantages, Southeast Asian American youth nevertheless attained remarkable educational progress. A study of the educational attainment for Southeast Asian American students in San Diego schools in 1990 showed that despite a higher proportion of limited English proficiency (LEP), their academic grade point averages (GPAs) were 2.47, significantly exceeding the district average (2.11) and that of whites (2.24).[39]

In addition, bicultural and generational conflicts between Southeast Asian American adolescents and their parents are a common occurrence. Many immigrant children, born or raised in the United States, tend to compare themselves with native-born American children rather than with foreign-born children. They long to fit in with and gain acceptance from their American peers, and their values are more likely to be influenced by those around them and by the American mass media than by their parents. They seem to be attracted more easily than their parents to material gains, immediate gratification, and conspicuous consumption. By contrast, their parents tend to focus more on survival and economic mobility than on instantaneous material gains. Immigrant parents often possess a dual frame of reference, in which the norms of the home society, not those of the host society, provide a measure for assessing their accomplishments. These different ways of looking at the world and looking at their own lives can result in conflicts between immigrant parents and their children.

In exercising guidance over the goals to which their children aspire, immigrant parents are often handicapped by their lack of English-language ability. Immigrant children who learned English much faster than their parents often serve as interpreters for their parents when interacting with American society. The ability to speak English and familiarity with the American environment tend to make immigrant children sometimes contemptuous of their parents, as exemplified in a Vietnamese youth's comment: "I don't see why I should listen to her [his mother]. Like, she needs me a lot more than I need her. She can't even talk to anybody that calls on the phone. So I just do what I like. Who's going to tell me I can't?"[40]

PLIGHTS AND POTENTIALS OF UNDOCUMENTED IMMIGRANTS

The economic prosperity in America during the postwar era attracted not only immigrants with legal documents but also undocumented immigrants who crossed borders without legal papers or entered the country with legal documents for a temporary stay or short visit but overstayed the duration of their visa. By 2009, an estimated 12 million people without legal status resided in the country.[41] However the number dropped to 10.5 million in 2017 due to the tightened immigration regulations and practices of the federal government during this period.[42] While the overwhelming majority of undocumented immigrants are from Mexico and Caribbean countries, many from Asia are also smuggled into the country or have overstayed their legal documents.[43] As of 2009, Filipinos and Asian Indians counted for the highest number of undocumented immigrants among Asian Americans, about 270,000 and 200,000, respectively. They were followed by Koreans (200,000) and Chinese (120,000).[44] According to a study by the Pew Research Center, Mexican-born immigrants accounted for only 47 percent of the 10.5 million undocumented immigration population in 2015. Overstayers represented about 46 percent of the 10.5 million undocumented immigrants in the United States. Although the largest number of overstayers—about 1 million—hailed from Mexico, many were from countries in Asia and South America. Between 2010 and 2017, the number of Indian undocumented immigrants in the country alone grew by over 60 percent, from 330,000 to 525,000—about 5 percent of the total undocumented immigrant population. Large numbers of people from China, Venezuela, the Philippines, Brazil, and Colombia also overstayed.[45]

Little research has been done on undocumented immigrants from Asia, except those from China.[46] The 1990 census estimated that there were 70,000 undocumented residents from China living in the United States. A decade later the number had jumped to 115,000.[47] Among the undocumented Chinese in America, Changle immigrants from Fujian province exemplify both the plight and potential of those living without a normalized residency status in the United States.

Causes of Undocumented Immigration

Located on the south bank of the Min River and along the southeast coast of China, across from the Taiwan Strait, Changle is the homeland to most of the Chinese Fujianese in New York. It is close to Fuzhou, the provincial capital of Fujian province and one of China's established trading ports. Like Guangdong province, Fujian, with its seafaring tradition and busy ports, has been known as a hub for Chinese emigrants around the world. In the 1950s and 1960s, very few Chinese succeeded in emigrating due to strict

FIGURE 6.6 An asylum seeker crossing the U.S.-Canadian border illegally from the end of Roxham Road in Champlain, New York, is directed to the nearby processing center by a Mountie, August 14, 2017. Courtesy Daniel Case.

governmental control under the Mao regime. Those who did make it to the United States were the "ship jumpers" who served as crew on merchant vessels and absconded when reaching New York or California. These Fujianese ship jumpers formed a small seed community in New York, making the city a preferred destination for later immigrants from Fujian. During the 1970s many Fujianese wanted to leave their villages and migrate to Hong Kong; this demand prompted the earliest "snakeheads" (nickname for smugglers or operators of human trafficking) to start their operations. They would ferry customers to Fuzhou, then to Shenzhen, a rapidly expanding new city adjacent to Hong Kong, and then to Hong Kong. Once the migrant had established residence in the British colony, it was possible to emigrate to Taiwan, Japan, Europe, and the United States.

In the late 1970s the privatization of rural land under China's economic reforms contributed to large-scale domestic migration as well as emigration overseas. As the amount of land owned by individual households was not very large, able-bodied young villagers sought to migrate to cities or overseas for economic opportunities. When less educated Fujianese found their upward mobility in larger Chinese cities limited, they began emigrating overseas. As those who prospered in the United States began remitting money home for the construction of family mansions or conspicuous consumption, the resulting jealousy was transformed into a peer pressure that pushed even more young villagers to emigrate. The large and ever-increasing pool of aspiring emigrants enabled the snakeheads to charge steeper fees of $18,000 per person, and thus the undocumented Fujianese in New York were called "eighteen-thousand-dollar-men" by the city's traditionally Cantonese community. The continued and increasing demand pushed the fees to $35,000 in the mid-1990s, $50,000 in the early 2000s, and $80,000 since the mid-2000s. In comparison, Indians paid up to $28,000 in the early 2000s to be smuggled to the United States. These exorbitant fees were way above individual incomes in rural Fujian (a worker's monthly income in urban Fujian was $40 in the 2000s, thus the smuggling fee equals 125 years' salary of a Fujianese in China); families and relatives of the prospective emigrants often had to pool money together or take loans at 30 percent interest from snakeheads. Prospective emigrants were asked to pay several thousand dollars each as a down payment (later it increased to half of the total cost, and in the 2000s many snakeheads demanded full payment up-front); their families and relatives would pay the balance once the emigrant reached their destination.

In the 1990s, after most of the able-bodied male villagers in the Fuzhou area had departed for overseas, human smuggling activities shifted to Wenzhou (in Zhejiang province, which has replaced Fuzhou as the top sending place of undocumented Chinese immigrants), Shanghai, Beijing, Tianjin, Qingdao (in Shandong province), Shenyang (in Liaoning province), and other port cities in China.[48]

The Mechanisms of Human Smuggling

From the initial years of the industry, snakeheads have exploited a dizzyingly ingenious array of routes to deliver their customers. The industry evolved roughly through three stages. In the 1980s, the initial stage, the travel route generally followed a Fuzhou–Hong Kong–Bangkok–South America pattern. Snakeheads bribed local Chinese officials to obtain exit visas to Hong Kong, then through further briberies secured visas to Thailand and then visas to various Latin American countries. These visas could be used to board flights bound for Latin America that had layovers in New York. Once the flight landed in New York, the passenger was instructed to disembark and request asylum at the airport. As the backlog of pending asylum cases was so extensive, it often took more than a year to wait for claims to be processed. During this waiting period, the applicants were released into the city, where they immediately began working in Chinese restaurants or garment shops. Another popular method of operation was "photo-sub" passports. Snakeheads would purchase genuine passports belonging to Asian men or women and replace the original photos with those of their customers. These passports could be recycled several times for more profit, and snakeheads would instruct those who successfully gained entry to the United States via this method to mail the passport to China for the next customer.

In 1991, the demand in Fujian province for passage to America exceeded snakeheads' capacity to produce fake documents. Coincidentally, the government of Taiwan issued a ban on drift-net fishing, making a fleet of oceangoing vessels available for other businesses. Soon dozens of Taiwanese fishing boats were crisscrossing oceans with hundreds of passengers in their holds. Recognizing the larger profits available from using boats to transport migrants and the unquenchable demand for their services from the Fujianese, the snakeheads shifted their business model from retailing to wholesaling passengers. Shiploads of undocumented passengers were delivered to Japan, Taiwan, and Thailand; to Guatemala and Mexico; to Hawaii, San Francisco, New Bedford, and New York. Most undocumented Chinese immigrants were smuggled into America during the peak years of this illicit industry, between 1989 and 1993. In the initial years, snakeheads usually accompanied their customers at each stage of the trip. As business rapidly grew, big snakeheads subcontracted to a series of local guides and fixers who operated as a relay throughout the trip. After customers traveled from Changle to Kunming, the western city near China's border with Burma, they would be escorted by local guides in Kunming over the border and handed over to Burmese guides, who would lead them over the jungle-covered mountains and malarial swamps to the Golden Triangle. There Thai guides would bring them over the border to Thailand and then to Bangkok, where they would be taken either to the airport to board a plane using phony documents or south to the Gulf of Thailand, where Taiwanese ships were waiting to ferry them to the United States. Many of the passengers never made it to their destinations: some were arrested at one border or another and jailed or sent back to China; others perished in the Burmese mountains when their guides deserted them; still others died when their ships capsized in storms.

The horrific *Golden Venture* incident brought smuggling by boat to an end. On the morning of June 1993, a run-down Honduran-registered forty-two-year-old freighter ran aground on the Rockaway Peninsula in the borough of Queens, New York, forcing 286 Chinese passengers to swim to shore, with 10 drowning in the rushing currents. The tragedy originated in an internal dispute within the Fuk Ching gang (Fu Qing Bang) over the dividing up of the huge profits they were earning from their trade in migrants. An intragang shootout resulted in the death of all the gang members responsible for offloading the undocumented Fujianese and the subsequent arrest and incarceration of their killers, the faction whose task was to pick up the passengers and collect money from them. As a result, nobody turned up to conduct the disembarkation of the frightened passengers. The tragedy was a media sensation, eliciting public anger and FBI investigations into the ringleader of the transnational crime industry—Zheng Cuiping (Cheng Chui Ping), known as Sister Ping, a Chinese version of Tony Soprano who made $40 million from the illicit business over a two-decade span and was finally arrested in Hong Kong in 2000 and sentenced to thirty-five years in prison.

The *Golden Venture* calamity appears to have been a turning point as the international crime syndicate abandoned human smuggling by boat and entered a new stage of smuggling that involves elaborate and sophisticated transnational operations utilizing the most advanced communication technologies for coordination and models its operations on multinational corporations' efficient global supply chains. A partial listing of the routes that law enforcement agencies have unearthed during these years reveals the dizzying complexity of the world tour: Fuzhou–Hong Kong–Bangkok–Moscow–Havana–Managua–Tucson or Fuzhou–Hong Kong–Bangkok–Kuala Lumpur–Singapore–Dubai–Frankfurt–Washington. Most of all, the human smuggling industry relies heavily on global corruption in international regulatory architecture, offering an illicit back door into the licit international system. These "geopolitical black holes" served as durable hubs in the international networks of the snakeheads. For instance, in Bangkok, corrupt officials at the airport would overlook paperwork inconsistencies and allow Fujianese passengers to board flights to North America. Immigration and customs officials in the United States were not immune to corruption either. Jerry Stuchiner, the top U.S. immigration official posted to Hong Kong and later Honduras, was arrested in Hong Kong in 1997 for attempting to sell Honduran passports to Chinese customers. In August 2000, two Chinese women applying for political asylum accused an immigration official in Los Angeles of soliciting bribes and sexual services from them in return for approving their applications.[49]

The Plights of the Undocumented Immigrants

Once they are beyond the customs controllers or released by immigration officers, new arrivals are picked up by the snakeheads' subcontractors and then soon disappear into the masses of their compatriots who are busily making a living for themselves in the multiethnic metropolis. They immediately start working in a Chinese restaurant or a garment shop in Chinatown. Without legal status and with no knowledge of English, they can work only at low-wage jobs, often making less than $1,000 a month, just enough to pay the interest on their loans. It is not uncommon that even after three years many remain indebted. Yet the debts have to be paid. One common practice is for the snakeheads to hire "enforcers" to violently wrest the money out of the debtors or to threaten relatives with the debtor's imminent execution in order to exact a quick cash payment. There are cases of undocumented immigrants having been made into the virtual slaves of the snakeheads: they worked during the day in restaurants affiliated with crime syndicates, and at night they were brought back to prison-like dorms where they had to hand over their daily earnings and were locked up.

In the early 2000s, undocumented immigrants who worked in garment factories as seamstresses would make only thirty dollars a day after toiling for twelve hours. Even such low-paying jobs were hard to get. Seamstresses in New York's Chinatown have to line up outside the factory long before the doors open to be the first ones to begin work. It is not unknown for some seamstresses to refrain from drinking anything during the day so as to avoid going to the bathroom and thereby interrupting their piecework. In the slower months, from November to the end of the year, seamstresses make less than twenty dollars a month. The most egregious practice at Chinese garment factories is the withholding of workers' legitimate wages; this can be for anything from three weeks to as much as several months. The length of the wage-withholding period has become the standard by which female garment workers choose the factory in which they will work.

A substantial number of undocumented immigrant women also worked as domestic workers in middle-class Chinese American families. In Southern California it is common for Chinese American women with newborn babies to have a *yuezi gong*, or "monthly live-in nanny." Chinese tradition encourages a new mother to be bound to her bed for a month while she recuperates from the delivery of a baby. Middle-class women whose parents or in-laws are unavailable during the month would hire a live-in nanny to care for them and their infant babies.[50]

Many young undocumented immigrant women were coerced into prostitution by snakeheads. In 1997, New York–based sociologist Peter Kwong, disguised as a client with a hidden camera, interviewed prostitutes including some who were made sex slaves by snakeheads after failing to pay off the balance of the smuggling fee, and filmed some of the activities inside nine massage parlors in New York's Chinatown and one in North Carolina. Many of these women were brought to brothels from the airport directly upon their arrival in the United States. One young girl from Beijing was immediately transported to a brothel in North Carolina from Los Angeles, her place of entry. She was confined in a dimly lit room and forced to take customers continuously, without having a chance to know anything of the outside world. Generally, these sex slaves could make fifty dollars from each customer, but they had to hand their average monthly income of three thousand dollars to snakeheads. Kwong estimated that there were at least twenty to thirty underground brothels in New York's Chinatown.[51]

Others being unable to pay off debts by toiling in garment factories have opted for the skin trade. In San Gabriel Valley, California, many Asian massage parlors or acupuncture clinics are operated by middle-aged businessmen or -women usually of Chinese descent who could make thirty thousand dollars a month. Women who ply sex-for-sale activities are in their twenties, thirties, and forties from Shanghai, Beijing, Tianjin, or Shenyang. They could take home at least half of their untaxed cash "tips."[52]

> ### STORY OF AN UNDOCUMENTED CHINESE WOMAN
>
> Ms. Wang who came to America by smuggling told [the reporter] how she fell into prostitution. She grew up in a rural area of Fujian province. From the Tiananmen Incident in Beijing in 1989 to *Golden Venture* incident in 1993, the smuggling of passengers from China reached its peak time; these passengers spent months on high seas, enduring hardships and even risking their lives, in order to chase their American dream. In 1992, Ms. Wang decided to jump into the waves of smugglers, to join her husband who smuggled to America in 1991, only a few months after their marriage.
>
> In a murky evening, Ms. Wang boarded a freighter at the mouth of Min River sailing to sea. Over forty passengers crowded in the dilapidated cabin, which was closed during the journey, with only a few small holes on both sides of the boat for ventilation. Ms. Wang was one of the few females among the passengers. After a few days of chopping sail, the male passengers began sexually assaulting the female passengers. One male fellow villager volunteered to be her "protector"; they told other passengers that they were relatives. During the over two-month journey, Ms. Wang was repeatedly raped by the man and got pregnant.
>
> When the pregnant Ms. Wang finally joined her husband, who scorned her, beat her frequently, and asked her to pay back the entire smuggling fee. Without any relatives and means in New York, Ms. Wang entered the skin trade after a female fellow villager introduced her to an underground brothel.
>
> *Source*: "Huabu maichunnu, tongshi tianya lunluoren" [Chinatown prostitutes, all falling souls in the world], *Shijie Ribao* [World journal], March 5, 1998, translation by the author.

The Potentials of the Undocumented Immigrants

Despite the uncertainties and hardships facing Fujianese immigrants, most of them remain optimistic and hopeful, looking forward to the day when they pay off their debts, obtain legal status, and bring their families to the United States. With hard work and a frugal lifestyle, most undocumented Fujianese immigrants could pay off their debts within three to five years. This is the primary reason why Fujianese are willing to risk their lives and endure the hardships of being smuggled to the United States. However, the path to their American dream is strenuous. What helps the Fujianese surmount the obstacles is the *Changle Jingshen*, or "spirit of Changle," unique characteristics possessed by Changle natives.

The historian Xiaojian Zhao encapsulates these characteristics. First, Changle people are loyal to each other. Their strong bond to their native place is manifested in mutual support in the American environment. Most Changle business owners have hired fellow villagers because that is regarded as a service and obligation to their community. Second, Changle people are willing to take risks and able to endure extreme hardships. Changle people are aware that, unlike most immigrants who start life in America with little or nothing, they actually start from a point of negative assets because most of them are heavily in debt upon arriving in America and start from zero only after they have paid off that debt. They are prepared to toil extremely hard even at humble work. It is common for new arrivals to work sixty to seventy hours a week, and Changle people often choose high-crime neighborhoods to start a business. They believe that the higher risks they take, the greater the returns. Third, Changle natives are flexible, able to move up and down the socioeconomic ladder, in order to make it in America. Ronghua Chen's story exemplifies such flexibility. A child prodigy who started publishing poems in China at the age of twelve, Chen endured a six-month journey to America—a plane trip and a sea voyage followed by crossing mountains and rivers on foot spanning more than ten countries, before he was instructed to swim ashore near New York. He started in Chinatown by working at the lowest job in a restaurant where he was bossed around and bullied by everyone. He learned to be humble and flexible, which enabled him to find ways to survive and succeed. Over time, he became the manager of a big restaurant before he opened his own. After his wife joined him, he began composing poems again and had the opportunity to lecture on Chinese calligraphy at American University in Washington, D.C.[53]

Changle immigrants' insistence on solidarity, willingness to endure hardships, and flexibility have enabled them to utilize collective resources and overcome seemingly insurmountable obstacles. By 2004, around 70 percent of Changle immigrants were involved in food service, ranging from street venders to mom-and-pop takeout places and large restaurants. The mode of illegal immigration led many Fuzhou immigrants to work in menial jobs such as food service, construction, and garment manufacturing that rely on undocumented migrants for cheap, nonunionized, and exploitable labor. However, in recent years, the flight of garment factories from Chinatown and the decline of construction in New York resulted in the concentration of Fuzhouness in the restaurant businesses.[54]

Two-thirds of the 200,000 Changle natives in America have gained legal status. Chinese banks in Changle estimate that annual remittances from Changle people in America amount to more than $300 million. These remittances have transformed the formerly dilapidated Changle county capital into a bustling boulevard lined with glittering shops and high-rise apartment buildings.[55]

The incessant waves of undocumented immigrants have also pushed some Fujianese immigrants, both documented and undocumented, to other states, mostly in the Midwest and South, such as Indiana, Virginia, and Georgia, that are collectively known as *waizhou*, Mandarin for "out of state." For the Fujianese, waizhou is more than a geographic description; it is crisscrossed by Greyhound bus routes and dotted with little towns that already have or could use more Chinese restaurants. Waizhou symbolizes owning one's own restaurant and spacious house and sending children to better schools than they could have afforded in New York. Small towns are also much safer than New York, where stories of Chinese men being beaten or killed while delivering Chinese food are common. Mr. Long Chen's story exemplifies the trend. A handsome and easygoing young Changle man, Chen came to the United States in 1990 as a tourist. He overstayed his tourist visa, worked in restaurants in New York, and hired a lawyer to help him obtain legal status after he saved enough money. Once legalized, he brought his bride from home. The couple scouted out various places and eventually settled in 2000 in a midwestern university town, where they bought a restaurant and sent their two young sons to private schools, piano lessons, and taekwondo classes after school.[56] Mr. Chen is not alone; an overwhelming majority of Chinese restaurants in midwestern and southern small towns are owned and operated by Chen's fellow Fujianese, mostly Changle people.[57]

Similarly, the undocumented South Asian immigrants employed at Dunkin' Donuts stores share many common traits. Most of them came from one region in India, Gujarat, many from the same village or district. They were encouraged to contact former villagers about immediate employment at Dunkin' Donuts, entered the country as visitors or as part of an entertainment or cultural troupe, but soon disappeared under the authorities' radar. The contacts or agents demanded a hefty price for the service. In the 1990s, the fee for going to America was around Rs. 600,000, or approximately $15,000. In 2004, after the 9/11 clampdown on South Asian immigrants, the price skyrocketed to Rs. 2,500,000, about $55,000. It is difficult to estimate the exact number of undocumented immigrants employed in donut franchises, but the owners themselves have acknowledged that without the labor of undocumented immigrants they could not continue operating the business.[58]

Many of the undocumented Indian immigrants, however, do not fit into the stereotypical profile of the working-class undocumented immigrants. In the heart of Silicon Valley, Sunnyvale, California, the high-tech giant Google hired a large number of engineers and technicians trained in India under the H-1B visa program. About a quarter of the workforce are visa overstayers from Asia who remained "in the shadows" of the valley's socioeconomic life, being unnoticed by news media and the general public.[59]

"Children of the Killing Fields"—Deportation of Cambodian Americans

During the late 1970s and early 1980s, thousands of Cambodians fleeing the Khmer Rouge regime arrived at refugee camps in Thailand and were eventually granted asylum by the United States. Many of them settled in places like Lowell, Massachusetts, and Long Beach,

California. Among the 275,000 Cambodians living throughout America, up to 2,000 are now under the threat of deportation back to their homeland, and 300 have been deported to Cambodia since 2002.

What happened to these Cambodian American deportees was the culmination of U.S. antiterrorist policy since the 9/11 attacks. The Antiterrorism and Effective Death Penalty Act and the Illegal Immigration Reform and Immigrant Responsibility Act were enacted in 1996 by the Clinton administration during a period of heightened anti-immigration sentiment. In the wake of the 9/11 attacks, these laws were vigorously enforced. In 2011, there were 216,000 "criminal aliens" deported from the country, compared to 71,000 in 2001. But those forced deportations did not affect Cambodian Americans until 2002, when the U.S. and Cambodian governments signed a repatriation agreement. No statute of limitations or judicial review were included in the agreement. Critics speculated that the U.S. government threatened to cut back its international aid to Cambodia if the deal was not struck.

Typical Cambodian American deportees were young men in their twenties or thirties who were born in Cambodia or in refugee camps in Thailand and came to the United States as small children with their refugee parents. Although they were granted green cards, many never applied for citizenship due to barriers such as lack of English ability, legal knowledge, and education and were thus subject to deportation for criminal activities. Many children of the Cambodian refugees were not even aware of their alien status since they were born or grew up in America and assumed that they were Americans. Most Cambodian refugees were placed in urban settlement sites, lived in housing projects in dilapidated neighborhoods, and found menial jobs in factories and construction. Their children often fell into a cycle of street gangs, drug abuse, and robbery, typical urban crimes. Statistics show that 70 percent of Cambodian American youths had only a high school education and faced bleak employment prospects. The typical deportees, who had committed some felonies years ago and had served the penalty but were arrested under the provisions of the 2002 repatriation agreement, were placed on planes by the immigration authorities with only the clothing they were wearing and little money. They landed in a country that they had never visited and that is troubled by an economic recession and rampant corruption, as illuminated in the story of Mout Iv (see sidebar).[60]

"THE QUIET MIGRATION": TRANSNATIONAL TRANSRACIAL ADOPTION

Among the waves of Asian immigration to the United States in the post–World War II period, there existed a "quiet" and "overlooked" group of newcomers—Asian American adoptees. Although still a small fraction of the Asian American population, the group's

THE CHILDREN OF THE KILLING FIELDS

I met Mout Iv two summers ago in his barber shop in north Philadelphia. A hip-hop version of a Norman Rockwell illustration, this cocoon from the city's hardscrabble streets came complete with a revolving barber's pole, talcum powder, a steady flow of light-hearted banter and a vast collection of memorabilia from Mout's beloved Phillies baseball team. "Sports was something that got me into the American way," Mout tells me. "We learned basketball from the blacks and baseball from the whites."

Business was steady, steady enough that Mout owned the store as well as the apartment above it where he lived with his fiancée and his daughter. Another child was on the way. Following enough upheaval, setbacks and stumbles to last several lifetimes it appeared the 33-year-old barber might finally be getting ahead.

One month later he was taken into custody by immigration officials. He spent nine months in a county prison and was then put on a plane to Cambodia for a crime he committed almost a decade ago and for which he already had been punished. Mout has little or no possibility of ever returning to his family in the United States. . . .

Mout Iv had become one of about 300 Cambodians from around the United States to be deported under strict US anti-terrorism and immigration laws mandating deportation for non-citizens who have committed even relatively minor and non-violent crimes. . . .

In 1998 Mout was convicted of aggravated assault after a street fight and spent three and a half years in jail. Had he been able to tell his story before a judge he would have told the same one he recounted to me in his barber shop.

When he was two years old, Mout, his mother and two sisters fled Cambodia and spent the next seven years in a camp inside the Thai border. In 1986 they were accepted as refugees in the United States and came to live in Philadelphia. Like most of the refugees being taken in at this time, Mout's family came from a rural background with little or no formal education. They couldn't speak any English.

The urban blight into which they moved in Philadelphia was among the worst in the United States. The city was in the midst of a recession and government assistance was minimal. As Mout recounts: "It was real hard. My mom was raising me. It was just me, my mom and two sisters. We struggled to have a bowl of rice sometime." . . .

Mia-lia Kiernan [a Cambodian American activist-author] has visited Mout Iv in the Cambodian capital Phnom Penh and says his and the other deportees' plight is bleak: "It's difficult. It's hard to find jobs and there's a lot of division between the local population and the returnees."

Source: Michael Maher, "The Children of the Killing Fields," *Global Mail*, February 8, 2012, http://www.theglobalmail.org/feature/the-children-of-the-killing-fields/39/.

rapid increase in size and potential impact on Asian America have attracted academic and public attention.[61]

The Genesis of Transnational Transracial Adoption

The transnational transracial adoption of Asian children in the United States began with the adoption of the Korean War orphans. Although generally referred to as Korean War orphans, they comprised children of Korean women and U.S. servicemen and those who were born into impoverished families or born out of wedlock. In 1953, an evangelical Oregonian couple, Bertha and Harry Holt, acting out of their belief in Christian charity, adopted eight war orphans from Korea. This action became an instantaneous media sensation and prompted the founding of the Holt Agency, which rapidly expanded from a family project to an international adoption agency.[62] Most of those orphans had mixed-race parentage, their mothers typically unwed Korean women and their fathers American GIs, and therefore were stigmatized in Korea as "filthy" and unwelcome. It was widely believed that it was Americans' responsibility to "rescue" these children from misery. These emotions of sympathy and compassion and sentiments of duty, national pride, and convenience together sustained the Korean transnational transracial adoptions as the first and largest adoptee population up until the 1990s when it was replaced by the mostly female adoptees from China.

The transnational adoption not only was a product of U.S. overseas military interventions but also had its roots in domestic transracial adoption. In 1948, the first domestic transracial adoption of an African American child into a white family took place in Minnesota. Campaigns in the 1950s for transracial adoption inspired more white Americans to inquire about adoptions of African American children. Pressured by the difficulty of finding enough same-race parents for all the African American and mixed-race children in need, a few adoption agencies began placing these children into white families. However, transracial adoption took a turn in 1972 when the National Association of Black Social Workers issued a statement opposing the practice and labeling it as "unnatural" and "unnecessary," thus reducing the transracial adoption of African American children by white families to a trickle.[63]

Nevertheless, domestic transracial adoption provided the precedent for transnational transracial adoption. Approximately 15,000 transnational adoptions took place between 1953 and 1962. The following years more transnational adoptions occurred, with 37,469 cases from 1965 to 1976.[64] In 1986, the peak year for Korean transnational adoption, 6,138 children from Korea were adopted in the United States. In the decade from 1989 to 1998, transnational adoption dramatically changed both in numbers and in sending countries: the number of transnational adoptions doubled to 15,744, and more countries, such as China, Russia, Guatemala, Columbia, India, the Philippines, Vietnam, Romania, and

Cambodia, have developed programs for transnational adoption to the United States. Since 1990, China has replaced Korea as the leading source of transnational adoptions in the United States, involving more than 5,000 children annually. In 2006, 20,679 children from overseas were adopted by American families, among whom 5,454 came from China, 4,728 from Guatemala, 2,310 from Russia, 1,255 from Ethiopia, and 939 from South Korea.

Socioeconomic and demographic changes in the United States since the 1960s also increased the acceptability of and demand for transnational transracial adoption. The number of white infants available for adoption decreased due to a dramatic increase in family planning. The demand for adoptive children was further increased when baby boomers entered the age of parenthood. The civil rights movement also made white Americans more comfortable with the idea of multiculturalism and more willing to share their fortunes with underprivileged races. As the number of adoptive children decreased, adoption agencies also became more selective in their placements, making screening criteria stricter, including the standards for age and income and proof of infertility. Since the 1980s, the supply of adoptive children decreased in the United States as the American child welfare system preferred the temporary removal of children from the custody of their parents rather than adoption as the primary remedy for families experiencing such problems as substance abuse, the negligence or abuse of children, and incarceration. At the same time, prospective adoptive parents, who were more likely to be better-educated and middle-class white families, shunned the children from "problem" families for domestic adoption. Since the 1990s, increased globalization further transformed transnational adoption into another type of global commercial transaction, making transnational adoption more accessible and convenient. All of these factors contributed to the growth of transnational transracial adoption in the United States.

While changes in the United States have rendered it a favorable market for transnational transracial adoptions, factors including socioeconomic conditions and governmental adoption policies in the sending countries have helped supply children to meet the demand in the United States. In China, the one-child policy implemented since the late 1970s resulted in a growing problem of female infant abandonment. The tradition that only a male heir could pass down the family name and continue its genealogical line, combined with advances in reproductive technologies' ability to predict the gender of the fetus, exacerbated the problem. Infant babies were often left at police stations, hospitals, or markets, sites where the birth parents hoped the baby would be discovered quickly and be taken care of afterward. To deal with the problem, many orphanages were established by state and local governments or private agencies. In 1991, the Chinese government passed a national adoption law. The law codified a highly restrictive adoption policy that required adoptive parents to be childless and over age thirty-five. Scholars believe this policy has limited the domestic adoption pool as thirty-five is an unacceptably advanced age to become adoptive parents, thus it has favored international adoption over domestic adoption. In fact the adoption law has helped China establish a new nationwide adoption system to facilitate the placement of children through international adoption, to regulate the exchange of documents and foreign currency and the movement of children across international borders.

This policy, however, led to criticism from human rights watchers that the Chinese government was using children as another source of export to garner foreign currency for its growing capitalistic economy since an international adoption generates $3,000 per capita as a mandatory orphanage donation plus an additional $1,000 to $2,000 for fees and expenses from the adoptive parents. But in the broad context of China's economy these funds are insignificant, although undeniably the donations to orphanages have greatly helped improve their conditions and services at a time when there is a shortage of funds from governmental sources. In 1998, the Chinese government revised its adoption law to encourage domestic adoption. It lowered the age of adoptive parents to thirty and also allowed families with children with birth defects to adopt healthy foundlings. Better government regulation and a larger pool of healthy babies have made international adoptions rise rapidly from 61 in 1991 to 5,053 in 2000, according to U.S. State Department statistics based on adoptee visas issued. China became the leading supplier of children for transnational adoption, constituting 80 percent of the total transnational adoptions in the United States.[65]

Comparisons of Korean and Chinese Adoptions

Transnational transracial adoptions from Korea and China are different in a number of ways. First, the motivations for adoptions differ. The adoptions of Korean orphans, and later Operation Babylift, the recusing of about 3,300 Amerasians (children of American servicemen and Vietnamese women) from Vietnam between April 3 and 26, 1975, on the eve of the fall of Saigon, were products of U.S. neocolonial overseas involvements, while transnational transracial adoption from China grew because of multiple factors related to socioeconomic changes and government policies in both the receiving and sending countries, as discussed earlier.

Second, the adoption procedures also differ. Transnational transracial adoption from Korea had been influenced by the mainstream adoption practices of secrecy (there was no disclosure of identity and information of birth mother, and the adoptees were handed to adoptive parents by Korean adoption agents at U.S. airports) and isolation (adoptees were dispersed throughout the country, and there are few social support groups for adoptees and adoptive parents). On the contrary, adoptions from China are often "open adoptions" in which agencies disclose information (though very little in reality) regarding birthplaces or sites where the adoptees were found, and the American adoptive families are often organized in groups of a dozen families who stay in China for a couple of weeks while waiting for adoption papers, seeing sites of interests, and getting acquainted with their newly adopted babies/children and who often organize reunions and form post-adoption support groups.

Third, the initial framework of Korean adoption being a combination of humanitarian action and evangelical mission has impacted Korean and other transitional adoptions. Korean adoptees and other transnational adoptees have been regarded as recipients of charitable, often Christian, actions. Both the adoptive parents and American society focused on assimilating them into American culture. Few adoptive parents had ever visited Korea, although since the 1990s Korean adoptees and their families have been more actively engaging in community development. For example, in 1998 the Korean Adoptee/Adoptive Family Network (KAAN) held its first conference to discuss adoption issues and to develop adoption community. In contrast, the adoptive parents of Chinese girls tend to be older, more liberal, and more diverse—perhaps "Jewish mommy," "single mommy," or "two mommies"—and are obsessed with learning about the culture of their adoptive children. They have been actively involved in organizing various support groups, including Families with Children from China (FCC), with over one hundred branches across the country, adoption listservs, and activities celebrating Chinese culture, such as China Days, culture camps, and trips to visit orphanages in China.

Asian American adoptees' relationships with the Asian American community, however, have remained uneasy. Asian American community activists have been concerned that the celebratory activities of Asian American adoptees and families have overemphasized the exoticism of Asian culture while overlooking the issues of race, class, gender, and inequality that Asian Americans have to negotiate in their daily life. Meanwhile Asian American adoptees also found it difficult when engaging in relationships with the Asian American community. Which part of the community would be accessible and receptive to them? Speakers of Mandarin or Cantonese? Students, workers, or second- or third-generation professionals?

Further, these celebratory activities have been largely organized by adoptive parents as the majority of the Chinese adoptees are still minors. Matthew Salesses, a Korean adoptee and blogger, has vocalized adoptees' feelings on their "genealogical bewilderment" and the futility of such cultural celebratory activities as return journeys and traveling "culture camps."

> Adoption isn't simple. It's the most complicated thing I know. Answers are not easy and not firm and don't answer the questions you're really asking—or, as the case may be, *not* asking. Adoptees may wonder about their real birthday, or what it was like where they grew up, or even why they were abandoned (getting closer), but what they are really asking is much more complex than that. I have asked those questions both out loud

FIGURE 6.7 A Korean girl adopted by American parents, ca. 1940s. Courtesy National Archives and Records Administration.

and in my head my entire life. And underneath those questions are further questions—like how has adoption made me who I am, and who is that, and how would I be different if I knew my birth family. . . .

Why didn't you ask adoptees? Why didn't you ask adoptees who had grown up a little since then, who have some perspective and could tell you what those trips meant to them? I wish I had gone to Korea when I was 14, or younger. I went when I was 24. And I learned a lot. I learned so much. And I have even more questions for all the "answers" I found. It was great and eye-opening and important to me to go to Korea, but I can tell you that no trip is going to answer what being adopted means.[66]

NEW WAVES OF IMMIGRANTS IN HISTORICAL PERSPECTIVE

The postwar new immigrants are more diverse in their socioeconomic conditions prior to emigration, the means of their journeys to America, and their post-migration experiences. A few important pieces of immigration legislation in the postwar era have transformed the gender lopsidedness of Asian America into a more gender-balanced component of multiethnic America. The Immigration and Nationality Act of 1965, the first nonracist immigration and naturalization legislation, helped alter the composition of Asian Americans; more educated and moneyed newcomers have contributed to the overall improvement of Asian Americans' socioeconomic conditions. The sudden dislocation and relocation as a result of wars and political persecutions in their homelands made adjustment and adaptation to their new home more challenging for Southeast Asian refugees. The undocumented immigrants, like their counterparts with legal status, have proven to be able to work extremely hard and contribute to the economic developments of their homelands as well as the host country. Transnational transracial adoptions contributed a new demographic group to the Asian American population. As Asian American adoptees are coming of age, in addition to the generic concerns of race, class, gender, and equality, they face a new set of issues—their longings to know their birth mother and birth culture and their searches for self-identity and for belonging, issues similar and dissimilar all at once to those of their non-adoptee Asian American counterparts.

KEY TERMS

War Brides Act (1945)
G.I. Fiancées Act (1946)
Displaced Persons Act (1948)
Refugee Relief Act (1953)
war brides
Filipino nurses
Exchange Visitor Program (EVP, 1961)
Immigration and Nationality Act of 1965

settlement of Southeast Asian refugees
Refugee Act (1980)
Immigration Reform and Control Act (IRCA, 1986)
Immigration Act of 1990
undocumented immigrants
transnational transracial adoption

REVIEW QUESTIONS

1. Name two pieces of legislation that enabled more Asian women to enter the United States.
2. Describe how the Immigration and Nationality Act of 1965 helped change the profile of Asian Americans.
3. Identify major problems/challenges facing Southeast Asian refugees.
4. Illustrate the plights and potentials of undocumented immigrants during their journeys to America and after their arrival. Relate the issue to continued national debates on immigration reforms.
5. Discuss the circumstances for transnational transracial adoption from Asia. Compare adoptions from Korea and from China. What are the unique concerns of Asian American adoptees? What are their relationships with the Asian American community?

FILMS

Chiang, S. Leo. *A Village Called Versailles*. 54-minute documentary about Versailles, a Vietnamese community in New Orleans, in the aftermath of tragedy. 2010.

Cohn, Peter (writer/producer/director). *Golden Venture*. Documentary on struggles of passengers who were aboard the *Golden Venture* in 1993. 2006.

Depaepe, Tim (director). *Quiet Passages: The Japanese American War Bride Experience*. 26-minute documentary on Japanese war brides in the Midwest (study guide). 1991.

Egan, Candace Lee (director). *Voice of Challenge: Hmong Women in Transition*. 39-minute documentary on the realities faced by Hmong refugees and their children in America. 1996.

Jang, Lindsey, and Robert C. Winn (producers/directors). *Saigon USA*. 56-minute documentary on the Vietnamese community of Little Saigon in Orange County, CA. 2004.

Knowlton, Linda Goldstein (director/producer). *Somewhere Between*. 88-minute documentary on four teenagers as they meet and bond with other adoptees—some journey back to China to reconnect with the culture and some reach out to the orphaned girls left behind. 2012.

Mallozzi, Julie (director). *Monkey Dance*. 56-minute documentary on children of Cambodian refugees in Lowell, MA, shadowed by their parents' nightmares of the Khmer Rouge. 2004.

Nakasako, Spencer (producer/director). *Refugee*. 60-minute documentary on a Cambodian youth's reunion with his father and younger brother in Cambodia (in English and Cambodian with English subtitles and study guide). 2003.

Tsuno, Keiko (producer/director). *The Story of Vinh*. 60-minute documentary on Vinh Dinh, the son of a U.S. serviceman and a Vietnamese mother, who immigrates to the United States as part of a group of repatriated Amerasian children. 1990.

FURTHER READING

Chan, Sucheng, ed. *Hmong Means Free: Life in Laos and America*. Philadelphia: Temple University Press, 1994.

———, ed. *The Vietnamese American 1.5 Generation: Stories of War, Revolution, Flight, and New Beginnings*. Philadelphia: Temple University Press, 2006.

Chin, Ko-lin. *Smuggled Chinese: Clandestine Immigration to the United States*. Philadelphia: Temple University Press, 1999.

Choy, Catherine Cenaza. *Empire of Care: Nursing and Migration in Filipino American History*. Durham, NC: Duke University Press, 2003.

———. *Global Families: A History of Asian International Adoption in America.* New York: New York University Press, 2013.

Espiritu, Yen Le. "Toward a Critical Refugee Study." *Journal of Vietnamese Studies* 1, no. 1–2 (February/August 2006): 410–433.

Freeman, James M. *Hearts of Sorrow: Vietnamese American Lives.* Stanford, CA: Stanford University Press, 1989.

Glenn, Evelyn Nakano. *Issei, Nisei, War Bride: Three Generations of Japanese American Women in Domestic Service.* Philadelphia: Temple University Press, 1986.

Harvey, David. *A Brief Introduction to Neoliberalism.* New York: Oxford University Press, 2009.

Hing, Bill Ong. *Defining America through Immigration Policy.* Philadelphia: Temple University Press, 2004.

Keefe, Patrick Radden. *The Snakehead: An Epic Tale of the Chinatown Underworld and the American Dream.* New York: Doubleday, 2009.

Kibria, Nazli. *Family Tightrope: The Changing Lives of Vietnamese Americans.* Princeton, NJ: Princeton University Press, 1995.

Kim, Eleana J. *Adopted Territory: Transnational Korean Adoptees and the Politics of Belonging.* Durham, NC: Duke University Press, 2010.

Kwong, Peter. *Forbidden Workers: Illegal Chinese Immigrants and American Labor.* New York: New Press, 1997.

Kyle, David, and Rey Koslowski, eds. *Global Human Smuggling: Comparative Perspectives.* Baltimore: Johns Hopkins University Press, 2001.

Ling, Huping. *Emerging Voices: Experiences of Underrepresented Asian Americans.* New Brunswick, NJ: Rutgers University Press, 2008.

———. *Voices of the Heart: Asian American Women on Immigration, Work, and Family.* Kirksville, MO: Truman State University Press, 2007.

Nelson, Kim Park Nelson. "Mapping Multiple Histories of Korean American Transnational Adoption." U.S. Korea Institute at SAIS, 2009.

Ngai, Mae M. *Impossible Subjects: Illegal Aliens and the Making of Modern America.* Princeton, NJ: Princeton University Press, 2004.

Passel, Jeffrey S., and D'Vera Cohn. "Trends in Unauthorized Immigration: Undocumented Inflow Now Trails Legal Flow." Washington, DC: Pew Hispanic Center, October 2, 2008.

Portes, Alejandro, and Rubén G. Rumbaut. *Immigrant American: A Portrait.* Berkeley: University of California Press, 1996.

Shah, Bindi V. *Laotian Daughters: Working toward Community, Belonging, and Environmental Justice.* Philadelphia: Temple University Press, 2012.

Vang, Chia Youyee. *Hmong America: Reconstructing Community in Diaspora.* Chicago: University of Illinois Press, 2010.

Yang, Kao Kalia. *The Latehomecomer: A Hmong Family Memoir.* Minneapolis: Coffee House Press, 2008.

Yang, Philip Q. *Asian Immigration to the United States.* Cambridge: Polity, 2011.

Zhao, Xiaojian. *The New Chinese America: Class, Economy, and Social Hierarchy.* New Brunswick, NJ: Rutgers University Press, 2010.

Zhou, Min, and Carl Bankston III. *Growing Up American: How Vietnamese Children Adopt to Life in the United States.* New York: Russell Sage Foundation, 1998.

7

MOVING UPWARD

CHAPTER OUTLINE

Educational Attainments
New Patterns of Employment and Economic Potentials and Constraints
Political Incorporation
Myth and Reality of "Model Minority"
Asian American Upward Mobility in Historical Perspective

SIGNIFICANT EVENTS

1966	William Petersen publishes an article in the *New York Times Magazine* to praise Japanese Americans' successful entry into the American mainstream; *U.S. News & World Report* features a story hailing the socioeconomic achievements of Chinese Americans, prompting the "model minority" stereotype
1980s	Admissions controversy as elite universities place a cap on Asian American enrollment
1982	Vincent Chin is mistaken for a Japanese and killed in Detroit by two white Americans
1984	In a speech delivered to a group of Asian Americans, President Ronald Reagan congratulates Asian Americans on their success and recognizes its significance
1989	Ming Hai Loo is mistaken for a Vietnamese and killed in Raleigh, North Carolina, by two white brothers, whose third brother was killed in the Vietnam War
1992	Jeong H. Kim founds Yurie Systems, a telecommunication company
1996	Gary Locke is elected as governor of Washington, becoming the first Chinese American governor in U.S. history

2001	Taiwanese-born immigrant Elaine Chao is appointed secretary of labor by President George W. Bush, becoming the first Chinese American and the first Asian American woman to serve in a presidential cabinet
2001	Dr. Sanjay Gupta joins CNN as its chief medical correspondent
2005	Steve Chen cofounds the internet video file-sharing site YouTube
2007	Bobby Jindal is elected governor of Louisiana, becoming the Asian Indian American governor in U.S. history
2009	President Barack Obama appoints Steven Chu, a Nobel Prize–winning physicist, as secretary of energy and former Washington State governor Gary Locke as secretary of commerce; Judy Chu is elected as a congresswoman representing California's 32nd congressional district with 62 percent of the vote, becoming the first Chinese American woman elected to Congress
2011	Gary Locke is appointed as the U.S. ambassador to China
2012	Congress acknowledges the injustice of the discriminatory laws against Chinese immigrants with the passage of the Judy Chu Resolution for Regret of Chinese Exclusion Act of 1882

THE EMPHASIS ON EDUCATION and hard work in Asian values has contributed to the educational achievements and occupational successes of Asian American children. While new economic opportunities have been presented to Asian Americans, obstacles such as uneven occupational distribution among different groups of Asian Americans and the "glass ceiling" against Asian Americans in managerial areas remained. The newer and smaller groups of Asian Americans are still struggling with poverty and unemployment. Furthermore, educational and occupational successes have prompted the media to portray Asian Americans as a "model minority" and to triangulate the complex racial relations of the United States.

EDUCATIONAL ATTAINMENTS

Since the 1960s, Asian Americans' educational achievements have attracted much media attention. The *San Francisco Chronicle*, for instance, made the following comments: Asian Americans are held to be among "the most economically successful minority group in the country . . . exceeding all other groups in income and education. . . . Ethnic Asians are the state's [California's] fastest growing minority and have begun to influence the state's education system, economy and government out of proportion to their numbers."[1]

Asian Americans' educational achievements have been remarkable not only in California but throughout the United States. According to the 1970 U.S. census, the school enrollment rates of the Chinese and Japanese compared favorably with those of the total U.S. population. The high enrollment rates of both men and women between eighteen and twenty-four are particularly impressive. In 1980, for the dominant college-bound ages of twenty and twenty-one, more than 50 percent of Asian Americans were enrolled in school, compared to 30 percent of whites of the same age. For specific Asian American groups, the percentages enrolled were 62 percent for Japanese, 74 percent for Chinese, 38 percent for Filipinos, and 55 percent for Koreans. A decade later, the rates of Asian American males and females who had completed high school or obtained a bachelor's degree or higher were greater than those of their white, Black, and Hispanic American counterparts. This trend continued in the following decades. In 2000, 44 percent of Asians had earned at least a bachelor's degree, compared to 24 percent of the total U.S. population.[2] According to the 2010 census, 50 percent of single-race Asians age twenty-five or older had a bachelor's degree or higher, in comparison to 28 percent for all Americans of the same age (see table 7.1).[3]

It is important to note that U.S. censuses lump Asian Americans and Pacific Islanders together on their educational attainment. The statistical data produced by such a method do not accurately reflect the actual educational status of each Asian American and Pacific Islander ethnic group, nor the disparities between the Asian American groups with much higher than national average rates (such as Chinese, Japanese, and Asian Indians) and those with much lower than national average rates. In other words, the lower than national average rates among those Asian Americans who mostly came to the country as refugees, such as Vietnamese, Cambodians, Laotians, and Hmong/Mong, have been concealed by such lumping. The data generated by this method thus only reinforce the myth of Asian Americans as a "model minority."[4]

The extraordinary level of Asian American educational attainment is further supported by a wide array of other evidence, such as school reports on classroom behavior, test scores, and an overrepresentation in higher education.[5] At Ivy League universities, especially, the high percentage of Asian Americans present is disproportionate to their population size (Asian American students composed 10 to 30 percent of the student body at these elite universities in the 1980s, while the Asian American population constituted only 2 percent and 2.75 percent of the total population. In the 1980s and 1990s, Asian Americans constituted the largest racial group on seven of the nine University of California campuses and the largest racial group of undergraduates in the UC system in 2009.[6]

The discriminatory backlash against Asian American overrepresentation at elite universities is exemplified in the admissions controversy of the 1980s, when Asian American activists charged that campus administrators had placed a cap on Asian American

TABLE 7.1 EDUCATIONAL ATTAINMENT BY RACE, 1970–2010

	All races[a]		White[b]		Black[b]		Asian and Pacific Islander[b]		Hispanic[c]	
Year	Male	Female	Male	Female	Male	Female	Male	Female	Male	Female
High school graduate or more[d]										
1970	51.9	52.8	54.0	55.0	30.1	32.5	61.3	63.1	37.9	34.2
1980	67.3	65.8	69.6	68.1	50.8	51.5	78.8	71.4	45.4	42.7
1990	77.7	77.5	79.1	79.0	65.8	66.5	84.0	77.2	50.3	51.3
2000	84.2	84.0	84.8	85.0	78.7	78.3	88.2	83.4	56.6	57.5
2010	86.6	87.6	86.9	88.2	83.6	84.6	91.2	87.0	61.4	64.4
College graduate or more[e]										
1970	13.5	8.1	14.4	8.4	4.2	4.6	23.5	17.3	7.8	4.3
1980	20.1	12.8	21.3	13.3	8.4	8.3	39.8	27.0	9.4	6.0
1990	24.4	18.4	25.3	19.0	11.9	10.8	44.9	35.4	9.8	8.7
2000	27.8	23.6	28.5	23.9	16.3	16.7	47.6	40.7	10.7	10.6
2010	30.3	29.6	30.8	29.9	17.7	21.4	55.6	49.5	12.9	14.9

Sources: U.S. Census Bureau, "U.S. Census of Population, 1970 and 1980, Vol. 1; Current Population Reports P20-550, and Earlier Reports"; and U.S. Census Bureau, "Educational Attainment," http://www.census.gov/population/www/socdemo/educ-attn.html; U.S. Census Bureau, "Statistical Abstract of the United States: 2012. Table 230—Educational Attainment by Race, Hispanic Origin, and Sex" (2012).

[a] Includes other races not shown separately.
[b] Beginning in 2005, for persons who selected this race group only. See footnote 2, Table 229.
[c] Persons of Hispanic origin may be any race.
[d] Through 1990, completed 4 years of high school or more and 4 years of college or more.
[e] Starting in 2005, data are for Asians only, exclude Pacific Islanders.

enrollment at elite universities such as Brown, Yale, Princeton, Cornell, Stanford, the University of California, Los Angeles (UCLA), and the University of California, Berkeley. Asian American applicants were quite able, these universities' spokespersons responded, but their large numbers would upset the racial "balance" and diversity they sought for their student body.[7]

Despite criticism from the Asian American community and other observers, the discriminatory admissions policies and practices remain a persistent problem at a handful of Ivy League schools. A 2011 report by Jesse Washington of the Associated Press notes that as Asian Americans meet Ivy League schools' admission standards at rates far out of proportion to their 6 percent representation in the U.S. population, they often need test scores hundreds of points higher than applicants from other ethnic groups to have an equal chance of admission. These numbers, along with the fact that some top colleges with race-blind admissions policies have doubled the Asian percentage of Ivy League schools, prove the existence of anti-Asian discrimination. For instance, the California Institute of Technology chooses not to consider race, and consequently its student body

SOME ASIANS' COLLEGE STRATEGY: DON'T CHECK "ASIAN"

Lanya Olmstead was born in Florida to a mother who immigrated from Taiwan and an American father of Norwegian ancestry. Ethnically, she considers herself half Taiwanese and half Norwegian. But when applying to Harvard, Olmstead checked only one box for her race: white.

"I didn't want to put 'Asian' down," Olmstead says, "because my mom told me there's discrimination against Asians in the application process."

For years, many Asian-Americans have been convinced that it's harder for them to gain admission to the nation's top colleges.

Studies show that Asian-Americans meet these colleges' admissions standards far out of proportion to their 6 percent representation in the U.S. population, and that they often need test scores hundreds of points higher than applicants from other ethnic groups to have an equal chance of admission. Critics say these numbers, along with the fact that some top colleges with race-blind admissions have double the Asian percentage of Ivy League schools, prove the existence of discrimination.

The way it works, the critics believe, is that Asian-Americans are evaluated not as individuals, but against the thousands of other ultra-achieving Asians who are stereotyped as boring academic robots.

Now, an unknown number of students are responding to this concern by declining to identify themselves as Asian on their applications.

For those with only one Asian parent, whose names don't give away their heritage, that decision can be relatively easy. Harder are the questions that it raises: What's behind the admissions difficulties? What, exactly, is an Asian-American—and is being one a choice?

Olmstead is a freshman at Harvard and a member of HAPA, the Half-Asian People's Association. In high school she had a perfect 4.0 grade-point average and scored 2150 out of a possible 2400 on the SAT, which she calls "pretty low."

College applications ask for parent information, so Olmstead knows that admissions officers could figure out a student's background that way. She did write in the word "multiracial" on her own application.

Still, she would advise students with one Asian parent to "check whatever race is not Asian."

"Not to really generalize, but a lot of Asians, they have perfect SATs, perfect GPAs . . . so it's hard to let them all in," Olmstead says.

Source: Jesse Washington, "Some Asians' College Strategy: Don't Check 'Asian,'" Associated Press, December 3, 2011, http://news.yahoo.com/asians-college-strategy-dont-check-asian-174442977.html.

is about one-third Asian. The University of California, Berkeley, which is forbidden by state law to use race in admissions, is 40 percent Asian, up from 20 percent before the law was passed. As a result, an unknown number of Asian American applicants have opted not to identify themselves as Asian in their applications (see sidebar).[8]

It is also worth noting that there is a great disparity in higher educational attainment among Asian Americans depending on socioeconomic and ethnic backgrounds and geographical locations. Nearly half of Asian American students in higher education were enrolled at two-year community colleges, while Asian American students were publicly perceived as being overrepresented at elite universities. A 1992 study revealed that 40 percent of Asian American college students were enrolled at two-year community colleges. A 2005 study found that according to the 2000 census, Asian American students made up 15 percent of all students enrolled in two-year institutions, a much higher percentage than their share of the total population. A study conducted in 2007 by the Asian American Studies Center at UCLA found Pacific Islanders lagging behind in higher educational attainment. Among those twenty-five years and older, single-race Pacific Islanders are only about half as likely (15 percent) as non-Hispanic whites (30 percent) to have a bachelor's degree. The gap is even wider when compared to the general Asian American population (49 percent with a bachelor's or higher degree). The levels of higher educational attainment for Pacific Islanders are similar to those of African Americans (15 percent vs. 17 percent). Pacific Islanders in Hawaii have lower educational attainment than those in the other forty-nine states.[9]

Reasons for Asian American Educational Achievements

What are the reasons for Asian Americans' extraordinary educational achievements? Educators and researchers have long been studying and debating the issue, producing a large body of academic literature. The wide array of interpretations present in that literature can be categorized into two general sets—cultural theories focusing on Asian values and theories that emphasize American socioeconomic conditions. The former interpretation holds that the values of hard work and respect for authority are the more compelling reasons behind Asian American educational achievements. The latter interpretation maintains that a more favorable socioeconomic climate in America during and after World War II mainly contributed to the educational success of Asian Americans. However, even among the scholars in the latter camp, most also agree that Asian values are key to understanding Asian American educational achievements. Meanwhile, researchers have also cautioned that the Asian American population is composed of ethnically diverse constituent parts, so any generalized and monolithic model for explaining educational success would do a disservice to the Asian American community as well as the general public.[10] In this section, we will investigate the various arguments and then come to a conclusion on what factors Asian American educational success can be attributed to.

Cultural Thesis: Asian Values

A dominant interpretation of Asian American educational success has been the cultural thesis. According to this interpretation, successful minorities place a premium on ambition, persistence, and deferred gratification and exhibit a strong desire for intergenerational social upward mobility. They believe there is significant overlap between the value systems of traditional Japanese society and those of the American middle class, with both emphasizing education. Similarly, the fact that traditional Chinese culture cherishes family unity, respect for the elderly and authority, education, industry, and self-discipline has been regarded as a cause of Chinese Americans' success. To reinforce this argument, theorists maintain that even under the least favorable socioeconomic climate in the first decades of the twentieth century, Asian Americans consistently performed well in educational attainment thanks to their salient cultural values. As exemplified in a study by sociologists Charles Hirschman and Morrison G. Wong, writers from this theoretical camp emphasize the deep historical roots of Asian American educational success. Hirschman and Wong found that native-born Chinese and Japanese Americans attained educational parity with the white majority population during the first three decades of the nineteenth century, when second-generation Asian Americans reached school age.[11]

American Socioeconomic Conditions: Impact of Immigration

There are, however, theoretical interpretations of Asian American educational attainment that are more comprehensive and more measurable by empirical investigation with extensive data. Some studies have suggested that Asian values in interaction with the broader socioeconomic environment and opportunity structure influence Asian American educational success. Here, multiple factors contribute to Asian American educational success. First, the process of migration works as a self-screening mechanism, which selects the most driven and determined individuals to immigrate to the new land. Second, the often strenuous long-distance international migration and the severance of past ties seem to create an intense drive and commitment to achieve in the new environment. Third, this strong desire for success, coupled with difficulties of finding employment due to discrimination, language difficulty, and lack of skills relevant to the larger labor market, prompted many immigrants into the small business or self-employment sector. Although these features are common to all immigrant communities, Asian Americans, as a "middleman minority," have possessed most of these characteristics as an immigrant community.[12]

Finally, the impact of restrictive immigration policies on Asian immigrant settlement and adaptation also influences the quality and composition of the Asian American population. A series of restrictive immigration laws, extending from the 1882 Chinese Exclusion Act to the 1908 Gentlemen's Agreement halting Japanese immigration, the 1924 Quota Act barring all Asian immigrants, and the 1934 Tydings-McDuffie Act against Filipinos, made the stream of immigration more selective. The selectivity of Asian immigrants could lead to the high educational expectations for their children.[13]

In summary, both the cultural thesis and the American socioeconomic conditions thesis have their merits and validity, thus a balanced and more complete perspective should consider elements of both interpretations, looking for further evidence that may reinforce either or both interpretations or inspire more nuanced interpretations.

NEW PATTERNS OF EMPLOYMENT AND ECONOMIC POTENTIALS AND CONSTRAINTS

The primary goal for most immigrants has been improving their economic status, therefore finding and holding jobs have been crucial and essential to most if not all Asian Americans. As the cultural, economic, and educational backgrounds of Asian immigrants differ, there have been various patterns of employment among Asian immigrants and their American-born offspring. Many studies have pointed out that the prevalent employment pattern among Asian Americans has been a *dual structure* of professional jobs and small businesses. An overwhelming percentage (50 to 80 percent depending on the regions) of foreign-born and native-born Asian Americans are concentrated in the areas of professional, managerial, and small-business operation, as illustrated by census statistics.[14]

Professionals and Entrepreneurs

Figures from the censuses of the past decades indicate the following patterns. In general, older and more established Asian Americans—the Chinese, Japanese, and Asian Indians—are distributed in more prestigious and better-paying occupations than the newly arrived Pacific Islanders and Southeast Asians. In 1990, 31 percent of Asians worked in managerial and professional specialty, and 33 percent in technical, sales, and administrative support; in contrast, 26 and 32 percent of all Americans worked in these two categories.[15] In 2000, 45 percent of Asian Americans were employed in management, professional, and related occupations, compared with 34 percent of the total population. However, the proportions employed in these jobs varied from 60 percent for Asian Indians, 52 percent for Chinese, 50 percent for Japanese, and 44 percent for Pakistanis

> ### STEVE CHEN, THE LOCAL BOY THAT CREATED YOUTUBE
>
> The co-founder of YouTube, 27-year-old Steve Chen (陳士駿), left Taiwan for the US during his first year in high school.
>
> After completing high school, Chen attended the University of Illinois at Champaign-Urbana before becoming an employee of PayPal, where he met future YouTube partners Chad Hurley and Jawed Karim.
>
> Chen and Hurley were at a dinner party in January last year when they realized there was no easy way to share online video, the way people can with photos.
>
> At the time, they were both between jobs and carrying substantial credit card debt. They founded YouTube in February.
>
> The website was officially launched in December 2005. Since then, the service has grown rapidly in popularity.
>
> *Source:* "Steve Chen, the Local Boy That Created YouTube," *Taipei Times*, October 8, 2006, 2.

to 27 percent for Vietnamese, 18 percent for Cambodians, and 13 percent for Laotians.[16] In 2010, 48 percent of Asians worked as financial managers, engineers, teachers, or registered nurses and 22 percent in sales and office occupations.[17]

The stories selected for the sidebars feature a few successful Asian American professionals in the information technology and health industries, providing examples from one point of the spectrum of Asian American employment patterns.

Certain employment models also exist among certain groups of Asian Americans. For example, the Japanese, Filipinos, Koreans, Hawaiians, and Guamanians are usually in the technical sector, the Chinese and Indians in the professional sector, and the Vietnamese and Laotians/Hmong in the laborer sector.

The overrepresentation of Asian Americans in the small-business sector continues as a pattern. Among Asian American businesses, 76 percent did not hire paid employees; that means these businesses were operated solely by family members. Of all Asian American businesses, 87 percent are in retail, food service, health service, or construction.[18]

In addition, occupational monopolies exist among certain Asian American groups. For instance, Korean Americans are predominant in the grocery business; Vietnamese American manicurists are ubiquitous; Asian Indians are so noticeable in the motel business that the saying of "motel, hotel, Patel" has been circulated, as a large number of motel and hotel operators share this common Hindu surname. In the following sections, we further discuss these phenomena.

YURIE SYSTEMS: HIGH-TECH HOT ROD

Jeong H. Kim has always been in a hurry. The 36-year-old Korean immigrant took just three years to complete college. He later finished his Ph.D. in reliability engineering in just half of the typical four years. And he did it while working as a full-time engineer.

So it's no surprise that Yurie Systems Inc., the Lanham (MD) company Kim founded five years ago is moving just as fast. Topping BUSINESS WEEK's 1997 Hot Growth list. Yurie—named after one of Kim's two daughters—has seen revenues an average of 385% annually over the past three years, to $21.6 million in 1996. Earnings have been even stronger, rising 410% annually to hit $3.2 million last year.

Creativity. The secret behind the spurt: The company makes equipment that transmits voice, video, and data over phone lines as well as satellite and wireless networks. "I would never be content to sit on the sidelines," says Kim, "I wanted to create technology."

So far that creativity has been a hit with Uncle Sam. Last year, 96% of Yurie's sale went to the U.S. government or government contractors. In part, that's because Kim, who served as a nuclear submarine officer in the U.S. Navy, knew what the military needed. And Yurie's products—known as asynchronous transfer mode (ATM) access equipment—have proven particularly useful at speeding military communicating systems in such places as Bosnia. Yurie also got a big hand: most were sold through AT&T, which has extensive government sales. To gain quick entrée, Kim signed an exclusive deal with AT&T in 1995 to market Yurie's product to the government.

But Kim figures Yurie doesn't need a middleman to sell commercial buyers, so he has begun pitching his products to telecommunication carriers for use in their networks and those of corporate customers. In 1997's first quarter, commercial sales hit $3.6 million, up from $800,000 in the previous quarter.

Still, it's likely to be a tough fight. Yurie is facing off against such stars as 3Com Corp, and Cisco Systems Inc. "They are going to have to fight the battle of gaining recognition," warns Thomas L. Nolle, president of telecom consultant CIMI Corp. "The next year to 18 months will be critical."

. . . With no formal training in the area, Kim taught himself the technology. He financed Yurie almost completely by himself, going as far as $400,000 in the hole by borrowing his house and on credit cards.

Not anymore. With Yurie stock hovering around its February initial public offering price of $12, Kim's 56% stake is worth some $168 million. And he has wooed an all-star board that includes former CIA chief R. James Woolsey, ex–Secretary of Defense William J. Perry, and Kenneth D. Brody, onetime head of the Export/Import Bank. Despite his success, Kim is a pragmatist who does not rule out a sale of Yurie. "The Force of consolidation is very strong in this industry," he notes. But for now, Kim is gunning for the big boys.

Source: Amy Barrett, "Yurie Systems: High-Tech Hot Rod," *Business Week*, May 26, 1997, 92–93.

> ### DR. SANJAY GUPTA
>
> Dr. Sanjay Gupta is the Emmy®-award winning chief medical correspondent for CNN. Gupta, a practicing neurosurgeon, plays an integral role in CNN's reporting on health and medical news for American Morning, Anderson Cooper 360°, CNN documentaries, and anchors the weekend medical affairs program Sanjay Gupta, MD. Gupta also contributes to CNN.com and CNNHealth.com. His medical training and public health policy experience distinguish his reporting on a range of medical and scientific topics including brain injury, disaster recovery, health care reform, fitness, military medicine, HIV/AIDS, and other areas.
>
> In 2011, Gupta has reported from earthquake- and tsunami-ravaged Japan, adding clarity and context to the human impact and radiation concerns. In 2010, Gupta reported on the devastating earthquake in Haiti and unprecedented flooding in Pakistan.
>
> Based in Atlanta, Gupta joined CNN in the summer of 2001. He reported from New York following the attacks on the U.S. on Sept. 11, 2001. In 2003, he embedded with the U.S. Navy's "Devil Docs" medical unit, reporting from Iraq and Kuwait as the unit traveled to Baghdad. He provided live coverage of the first operation performed during the war, and performed life-saving brain surgery five times himself in a desert operating room.
>
> Gupta's passion for inspiring Americans to lead healthier, more active lives led him to launch "Fit Nation," CNN's multi-platform anti-obesity initiative. In 2011, "Fit Nation" follows the progress of Gupta and six CNN viewers as they inspire each other while training for a triathlon.
>
> Before joining CNN, Gupta completed separate neurosurgical fellowships at the Semmes-Murphey Clinic in Tennessee, and the University of Michigan Medical Center. In 1997, he was selected as a White House Fellow, serving as a special advisor to First Lady Hillary Clinton.
>
> Gupta received his undergraduate degree from the University of Michigan and a doctorate of medicine from the University of Michigan Medical School.
>
> *Source:* CNN, "Anchors & Reporters," n.d., http://www.cnn.com/CNN/anchors_reporters/gupta.sanjay.html.

Korean Small Businesses "Caught in the Middle"

Korean entrepreneurs are predominantly found in the grocery business; about 1,000 out of the 1,200 independent grocery stores in New York City were run by Koreans in the 1980s.[19] A significant proportion of Korean businesses are located in low-income Black neighborhoods and their customers are primarily African Americans and Caribbean Americans. Thus, Korean entrepreneurs, as indicated by researchers, play a "middleman minority" role in the United States. They found a niche in operating grocery and liquor stores in low-income neighborhoods, where the large corporate supermarket chains are unwilling to open stores for lack of security but business property rents are also much

FIGURE 7.1 The kitchen of a Chinese restaurant in Kirksville, Missouri, 1997. Huping Ling Collection.

lower. Benefiting from the absence of corporate competitors and the cheaper rent, Korean American entrepreneurs have been able to launch businesses with much less capital. The ethnic resources of Korean immigrants facilitated their business development. They could collect capital and utilize laborers through ethnic and kinship networks. While the middleman minority in traditional societies filled the status gap between the elite and the masses, in post-1965 America where the white-Black status gap is no longer conspicuous but the economic gap between white American society and the inner-city minority underclass is still large, the highly entrepreneurial Korean American businessmen filled the needs of inner-city minorities for daily consumer goods.

As a middleman minority, however, Korean small businesses are constrained by both ends of the commercial chain, or "caught in the middle." On one end, they have to depend on large corporations for their supplies. On the other, they need the residents of the low-income neighborhoods as their customers. A boycott from either end would affect their business margins. Meanwhile, they are constantly facing resentment from both ends of the social scale. The negative stereotypes of Korean small businessmen as being clannish, disloyal, and unscrupulous outsiders often serve to identify and isolate them as scapegoats in racial conflicts, particularly Korean-Black conflicts. In New York City in the 1980s, the city's Korean community encountered four long-term Black boycotts of Korean stores and several arson attacks. The conflicts climaxed in Los Angeles on April 29, 1992, when anti-Korean rioting caused 2,300 Korean-owned stores to be looted, burned, or both. Black nationalist rhetoric that emphasized the importance of economic autonomy

FIGURE 7.2 Roy Choi from Koji BBQ at Aspen Food & Wine Fest 2010. Roy Choi was born in Seoul, Korea, and raised in Los Angeles, California. Choi is known as one of the architects of the modern food truck movement through Kogi BBQ. Courtesy Wikimedia.

in African American communities and opposed non-Black businesses operating in their neighborhoods has been identified as the major cause behind these conflicts.[20]

Kinship networks have been identified by numerous scholars as the critical factor contributing to Asian American entrepreneurship. Studies of Korean American entrepreneurship recognize the importance of personal and family savings, usually ranging from 60 to 80 percent of the initial investment for the business.[21] Works on Chinese Americans have agreed on the vital role of ethnic networks in starting and operating Chinese American businesses.[22] A similar pattern is also present among Asian businesses in Canada and Southeast Asia. In Canada, kinship networks have been crucial to starting traditional Chinese businesses, such as food services and retail.[23] Similarly, in Southeast Asia new immigrants rely heavily on ethnic networks in finding housing and jobs.[24]

Vietnamese in Nail Care Service

Vietnamese Americans are closely associated with the development and growth of professional manicures. Traditionally nail care was a secondary service provided by hair salons to well-to-do clientele. It was only in the 1980s that specialized nail salons began to proliferate in the beauty sector. Vietnamese immigrants in particular were concentrated in the nail care business. Less than 1 percent of Vietnamese manicurists are U.S.-born, and more Vietnamese than other immigrants worked in the beauty sector in the 2000s. In 2000, 34 percent of foreign-born Vietnamese were employed in the beauty industry, compared with only 2 percent of Korean and 3 percent of Dominican immigrants, the second and third largest immigrant groups working in the sector. In 2009, Vietnamese accounted for 40 percent of all manicurists, up from 34 percent seven years earlier, while white manicurists accounted for 37 percent, down from 50 percent in the same time period. According to the industry magazine *Nails*, Vietnamese in 2012 made up 80 percent of California's licensed manicurists and 40 percent of manicurists nationwide.

How can we explain the Vietnamese gravitation to this niche in nail care and their dominance in the sector? A variety of factors may help answer the question. The initial leadership from both native-born Americans and foreign-born Vietnamese was credited with the Vietnamese association in nail work. Actress Tippi Hedren, who starred in several of Alfred Hitchcock's movies in the 1960s, was instrumental in helping Vietnamese immigrants to California get started in the nail industry. Hedren served as an international relief coordinator with the organization Food for the Hungry. After Saigon fell, she worked in a refugee camp in Sacramento. Concerned with the plight of Vietnamese refugees, she hired her manicurist to teach refugee women the necessary skills and further persuaded a beauty school to train the refugees for free and to help them find work. Among those who had acquired the skill, Kien Nguyen and her husband Diem Nguyen, who was a navy commander in South Vietnam prior to seeking refuge in 1975, opened the first Vietnamese American–owned beauty salon. They then opened a beauty training school, the Advanced Beauty College (ABC), in the Vietnamese enclave in Orange County, California, known as Little Saigon and the emerging hub of the Vietnamese community in the United States. The school offered training in a range of specialized beauty services including manicuring. The classes were conducted in Vietnamese, and the ethnic enclave provided social and economic capital for these newly minted Vietnamese beauty technicians. They hired employees trained by the school, and the salon and school served as models for other Vietnamese. Vietnamese women responded to these early initiatives as they were faced with limited job options. The cluster of nail businesses in Southern California formed the foundation for the ethnic niche.

More importantly, the Vietnamese association with nail care is attributable to their creation of a broad-based demand for professional manicures. They "stretched" the market demand by broadening the customer base and by diversifying the range of nail-care offerings. The lower prices they charged made manicures affordable for the first time to women from a wider variety of socioeconomic backgrounds. Innovative Vietnamese entrepreneurs not only adopted newer products for nails and more efficient electronic nail files but also established the stand-alone nail salon that transformed professional nail care into a mass service, called the "McNailing of America," a revolution of manicuring similar to how McDonald's revolutionized fast food. Vietnamese manicurists also incorporated inexpensive spa-style pedicures and nail art in their services.

At the same time, Vietnamese nail technicians expanded in response to growing demands for commercial nail care. Government regulations contributed to the Vietnamese concentration in manicuring. The requisite number of hours in training is mostly minimal and varies by state, from zero in Connecticut to 750 in Alabama. The states also allowed the training and licensing exam to be conducted in the Vietnamese language. The ethnic social capital of the Vietnamese also helped them enter and sustain the business. Many salons are family business ventures; they garnered capital from family members and relatives and rely on family members to minimize labor costs. Vietnamese salon owners can also easily recruit employees through Vietnamese training schools. Vietnamese media such as newspapers and magazines further provide both Vietnamese entrepreneurs and technicians with employment information available only to Vietnamese speakers.[25]

In short, the initial leadership role played by a Hollywood star and Vietnamese entrepreneurs in training Vietnamese manicurists, the innovative drive of the Vietnamese manicuring industry, the limitations of the larger labor market, and favorable government regulations have combined to make Vietnamese American manicurists dominant in the nail care business.

Indian American Motel and Dunkin' Donuts Outlet Owners

The construction of the American Interstate Highway System resulted in the appearance of motels (motor hotel) along the highways as early as the 1940s. The "hotel, motel, Patel" phenomenon began in the 1960s when Indian immigrants from Gujarat applied their business acumen to the U.S. hotel industry. Today, Indian Americans own approximately 50 percent of the motels in the country. Motels owned and operated by Indian Americans can be found in all corners of the nation. The overwhelming majority of Indian owners in the United States came from Gujarat or are the descendants of Gujaratis. Further, most descended from only a few regions in central and southern Gujarat, with a common surname, Patel.

According to sociologist Pawan Dhingra's recent study on Indian American motels, most Indian American motel owners operate low- to middle-budget motels. The low-budget motel is typically an independent, mom-and-pop establishment. About one-third of Indian American–owned motels are independents. They are usually located off interstate highways, often in the downtown or high-crime areas. They offer very low rates but very few amenities and cheap supplies, which can be easily replaced in case stolen. They are normally small (thirty rooms or fewer) and serve truckers and long-term stays (guests staying for a week or month at a time).

Many Indian American motel owners are concentrated in the low-middle-budget franchise motels such as Days Inn, Econo Lodge, Motel 6, Super 8, and Travelodge. Their

> ### FROM "HOTEL, MOTEL, PATEL" TO "CORNELL HOTEL PATELS"*
>
> A 2004 *New York Time* story complemented the growth of motels owned by first- and second-generation (that is, immigrant parents and their U.S.-born children) Patels by profiling a typical owner, saying:
>
>> Morning and night, Mr. Patel, an immigrant from the Indian state of Gujarat, manned the front desk and did repairs on a 60-room EconoLodge in Bordentown, New Jersey, while his wife, Indu, and two children hauled suitcases, made up beds, and vacuumed rooms. And the work paid off. At age 57, Mr. Patel owned not only the EconoLodge, but, with relatives, four other hotels. . . . At hotel schools like those at Cornell University, New York University, and San Diego University, as well as more general business schools, the children are study how to manage chains of hotels, work in corporate offices of name-brand franchisors, and acquire more upscale properties like Marriott and Hilton. Call them the Cornell hotel Patels.
>
> Source: Pawan Dhingra, *Life Behind the Lobby: Indian American Motel Owners and the American Dream* (Stanford, CA: Stanford University Press, 2012), 2.
>
> * Titled added by the author.

rates are economical, but they offer more amenities and up-to-date equipment. They are often off interstate highways, attracting more tourists, people on temporary contracts with nearby companies, and some truckers. They may have a small staff, including a few housekeepers, desk clerks, and possibly a maintenance person. However, like the low-budget motels, the owner has to be available and often lives on site with his or her family if allowed by the franchise motel.

Indian Americans also own middle-budget franchise motels such as Best Western, Comfort Inn and Suites, and Ramada Inn, and higher-middle-budget hotels such as Country Inn and Suites, Hampton Inn, and Holiday Inn / Holiday Inn Express. These middle-budget motels usually cater to business travelers and offer higher-end amenities such as hot breakfast, in-room coffee makers, and internet connections. They often employ ten to fifteen people. Only a fraction of Indian American motel owners operate high-budget motels: Courtyard by Marriott, Hilton Garden Inn, and the like. They are very well maintained, with ample amenities and numerous employees.

By running a niche sector of the hospitality industry, Indian Americans achieved their American dreams, yet ironically they still lived with inequalities. They may accrue profit, but doing so requires exploiting themselves. Business strains come from competition as well as long working hours and having to live at the work site.[26]

Like in the motel business, Asian Indian Americans also dominate Dunkin' Donuts outlets. This niche originated from the post-1965 immigration of skilled professionals who first bought into the business in the early 1980s when they saw little opportunity for upward mobility in professional jobs. It grew as a legitimate use of the family reunification law that allowed earlier immigrants to sponsor less-educated relatives and employ them in the business. According to a recent study, an estimated 50 percent of the nation's Dunkin' Donuts stores are owned by South Asians. The ownership patterns vary from region to region; for example, in the Midwest about 95 percent of Dunkin' Donuts stores are owned by Indians and Pakistanis, but on the East Coast Dunkin' Donuts are still mostly owned by white Americans, although South Asians are making inroads, while in California some 90 percent of donut store owners are Cambodian Americans and their stores are independently owned and family-run. The Dunkin' Donuts story, like that of the motel industry, is a paradoxical one of success and failure, of millionaire owners and exploited workers, of seized opportunities and unrealizable dreams.[27]

POLITICAL INCORPORATION

Scholars have generally divided Asian American political participation into three categories: electoral politics, mass protest politics, and coalition politics.[28] Their involvement in electoral politics can be traced back to the 1920s when a Hawaiian Republican Nisei, James Hamada, ran for office in the territorial legislature. Since the 1960s, Asian Americans have gradually become more visible in electoral politics. Up to 2001, more than 300 Asian and Pacific Islander Americans had been elected to public offices, including 2 U.S. senators, 5 U.S. representatives, 2 governors, 49 state representatives, 89 city council members, 26 city mayors, 133 school board or higher education board members, and 210 judges. In addition, more than two thousand appointed officials at the state, federal, and territorial levels also were of Asian Pacific background.[29] These figures rapidly increased in less than a decade. By 2008, there were 2 U.S. senators (both from Hawaii), 4 U.S. representatives, 5 state governors, 62 state senators, 85 state representatives, 121 city council members, 275 school board or higher educational board members, and 306 judges (see table 7.2).[30]

Asian American political incorporation has some unique characteristics. Asian American voters are generally concerned about issues of immigration, language access (the ability of nonnative English speakers to obtain critical services in their native language), discriminatory treatment against Asian Muslims in the wake of the 9/11 terrorist attacks, and U.S. foreign policy toward their native countries. Yet Asian Americans have had smaller levels of voter turnout than any other ethnic group, with normally 1 to 2 percent in most states, 6 percent in California, and 33 percent in Hawaii in the 2000s and 2010s.[31] Further, the cultural, religious, and political diversity of Asian Americans made their political participation fragmented, as they are divided along nationality lines.[32] Moreover, the challenges facing Asian American political incorporation are not only numbers but also distribution—where they live. While in the past Asian Americans were more likely to be found in significant numbers only in Hawaii, California, and New York, in

TABLE 7.2 ASIAN AMERICAN REPRESENTATION BY STATE, 2007

State	Positions
Alabama	City councilmember (1)
Alaska	State representative (1), judge (1)
American Samoa	Federal representative (1), state senator (18), state governor (1), lieutenant governor (1), school board (7)
Arizona	City councilmember (1), judge (4), school board (2)
Arkansas	
California	Federal representative (2), state representative (9), state elected official (4), city mayor (18), city councilmember (76), judge (96), school board (142)
Colorado	Judge (4), school board (1)
Connecticut	State representative (1), city councilmember (1), school board (1)
Delaware	
District of Columbia	Judge (2)
Florida	School board (3)
Georgia	State representative (1), city councilmember (1), judge (3), school board (1)
Guam	State senator (14), state governor (1), lieutenant governor (1), judge (11), school board (11)
Hawaii	Federal senator (2), state senator (18), state representative (50), lieutenant governor (1), city mayor (3), city councilmember (20), judge (81), school board (19)
Idaho	
Illinois	City mayor (1), city councilmember (2), judge (6), school board (5)
Indiana	Judge (1), school board (1)
Iowa	State representative (1), judge (1)
Kansas	
Kentucky	
Louisiana	City councilmember (1)
Maine	
Maryland	State representative (3), judge (3), school board (2)
Massachusetts	City councilmember (3), judge (2), school board (4)
Michigan	State representative (2), city councilmember (3), school board (2)
Minnesota	State senator (2), state representative (3), judge (5), school board (5)
Mississippi	
Missouri	School board (1)
Montana	
Nebraska	Judge (1)

(continued)

TABLE 7.2 (continued)

State	Positions
Nevada	State representative (1)
New Hampshire	State representative (1)
New Jersey	State representative (1), city mayor (1), city councilmember (5), judge (3), school board (10)
New Mexico	Judge (1)
New York	State representative (1), judge (15), school board (20)
North Carolina	
North Dakota	
Northern Marianas Islands	State senator (9), state governor (1), lieutenant governor, judge (8)
Ohio	Judge (1)
Oklahoma	
Oregon	Federal representative (1), judge (1), school board (1)
Pennsylvania	State representative (1), judge (1)
Puerto Rico	
Rhode Island	
South Carolina	State representative (1)
South Dakota	
Tennessee	
Texas	State representative (1), city councilmember (4), judge (16), school board (2)
Utah	State representative (1), city councilmember (4), judge (5)
Vermont	State representative (1), judge (1)
Virginia	Judge, school board (2)
Virgin Islands	
Washington	State senator (1), state representative (3), state governor (1), city mayor (1), city councilmember (4), judge (22), school board (24)
West Virginia	State representative (1)
Wisconsin	School board (2)
Wyoming	

Source: Don T. Nakanishi and James S. Lao, eds., *2007–2008 National Asian Pacific American Political Almanac* (Los Angeles: UCLA Asian American Studies Center, 2007), 82–83.

the recent presidential votes, especially in 2008, Washington, Nevada, Virginia, Oregon, and Minnesota were among the competitive states where Asian Americans could form an important voting bloc. However, Asian Americans in these states did not force most presidential candidates to address their concerns, unlike the Cuban Americans who happen to be concentrated in the highly competitive and populous state of Florida.

Mass protest politics emerged as another form of Asian American politics in the 1980s when two major Asian American mass protests took place. In June 1982, Vincent Chin, a twenty-seven-year-old Chinese American draftsman in Detroit, was killed by two European American men, Ronald Ebens and his stepson, Michael Nitz, who mistook Chin for a Japanese at a time when many Detroit autoworkers were being laid off due to competition from the Japanese auto industry. A Wayne County circuit judge sentenced both men to three years' probation and a fine of $3,000 each plus $700 in fees. Asian Americans in Detroit and around the country were outraged by the light sentence and organized a campaign to demand a retrial of the two murderers. Although the retrials failed to put the murderers in prison, the lesson learned in the Chin case was used in a later protest. In late July 1989, Ming Hai Loo (also known as Jim Loo), a twenty-four-year-old Chinese American, was killed in Raleigh, North Carolina, in a situation similar to that of Vincent Chin. Loo was mistaken for a Vietnamese by two European American brothers, Robert and Lloyd Piche, who had lost a third brother in Vietnam. Loo died of head injuries from the attack by the Piches. Chinese Americans in the city immediately organized the Jim Loo American Justice Coalition to represent Loo's parents, who spoke little English. Although Lloyd, the younger of the two Piche brothers, was given a light sentence of six months for assault and disorderly conduct, the Chinese American campaign succeeded in securing a thirty-seven-year prison sentence for Robert Piche.

However, "protest is not enough," according to scholars who specialize in the examination of coalition politics; coalitions between ethnic minorities and whites and the need for political integration have become compelling components of urban ethnic politics.[33] The history of Asian Americans and multiracial political coalitions started as early as 1949 when Mexican American Edward Roybal was elected as the first Latino member of Los Angeles City Council in the twentieth century; he depended on an alliance consisting of Latinos, African Americans, Asian Americans, and European Americans.[34] Scholars such as George Lipsitz and Leland Saito believe that racialized government policies that have forced African Americans, Asian Americans, Mexican Americans, and Native Americans into similar occupational, residential, and political urban spaces have created common interests and concerns among these minority groups and made such a multiracial political coalition possible.[35]

Asian Americans' political participation entered a new stage in the new millennium, as more Asian American politicians have filled high-profile positions in the presidential cabinet and in Congress or as top executives within state government.

In 2001, Taiwan-born immigrant Elaine Chao was appointed secretary of labor by President George W. Bush, becoming the first Chinese American and the first Asian American woman to serve in a presidential cabinet. Born in Taipei in 1953, Chao immigrated to the United States with her parents at the age of eight. With an MBA from Harvard University, she worked at several banks. In 1983, after an intense competition, she was selected as a "White House Scholar" and began her government career. Due to her achievements, she was chosen as one of the ten most outstanding youths in the United States in 1987. On April 19, 1989, Chao was appointed assistant secretary of transportation. This appointment made her the highest-ranking female official, the first Chinese American federal secretary, the highest-ranking federal government officeholder among first-generation immigrants, and the youngest such departmental officer. After her appointment, she became an active and powerful spokeswoman for Asian Americans. For instance, she strongly opposed the "quota system" in the hiring practices of government agencies and educational institutions. She claimed that the prejudiced quota system was against the basic principles of the U.S. Constitution and created false equality. She also stated that well-qualified women and minority professionals did not need the protection of a quota system.[36]

Upon his inauguration in 2009, President Obama appointed Chinese Americans Steven Chu, a Nobel Prize–winning physicist, as secretary of energy, and former Washington State governor Gary Locke as secretary of commerce. Born into a Taiwanese immigrant family in St. Louis in 1948, Steven Chu taught at the University of California, Berkeley, as a professor of physics and professor of molecular and cell biology, and he also held positions at Stanford University and AT&T Bell Laboratories. Prior to his appointment, Chu was the director of the Department of Energy's Lawrence Berkeley National Laboratory, where he led the center's pursuit of alternative and renewable energy technologies. Chu's research in atomic physics, quantum electronics, polymers, and biophysics includes tests of fundamental theories in physics, the development of methods to laser cool and trap atoms, atom interferometry, the development of the first atomic fountain, and the manipulation and study of polymers and biological systems at the single molecule level. While at Stanford he helped start Bio-X, a multidisciplinary initiative that brings together the physical and biological sciences with engineering and medicine. In announcing Chu's selection, President Obama said, "The future of our economy and national security is inextricably linked to one challenge: energy. Steven has blazed new trails as a scientist, teacher, and administrator, and has recently led the Berkeley National Laboratory in pursuit of new alternative and renewable energies. He is uniquely suited to be our next Secretary of Energy as we make this pursuit a guiding purpose of the Department of Energy, as well as a national mission." Chu was sworn into office as the twelfth secretary of energy on January 21, 2009.[37]

Born into an immigrant family on January 21, 1950, Gary Locke worked in his father's grocery store, became an Eagle Scout, and graduated with honors from Seattle's Franklin High School in 1968. Through a combination of part-time jobs, financial aid, and scholarships, Locke attended Yale University, earning a bachelor's degree in political science in 1972. After receiving his law degree from Boston University in 1975, he worked for several years as a deputy prosecutor in King County, Washington, prosecuting felony crimes. In 1982, Locke was elected to the Washington State House of Representatives, where he served on the House Judiciary and Appropriations committees, with his final five years spent as chairman of the House Appropriations Committee. Locke was elected as Washington's twenty-first governor on November 5, 1996, making him the first Chinese American governor in U.S. history. On November 7, 2000, he was reelected to a second term. In 2004, Locke willingly stepped out of public life, deciding against running for a third term in which he would have been heavily favored.

FIGURE 7.3 Official portrait of the U.S. secretary of commerce, 2009. Courtesy U.S. Department of Commerce.

Locke's nomination as the secretary of commerce came after Obama's two previous candidates—New Mexico governor Bill Richardson and Senator Judd Gregg from New Hampshire—withdrew. Locke was known for his squeaky-clean political record and for being a successful governor who presided over tough economic times, worked with large Washington businesses that have national policy concerns, including Boeing, Starbucks, and Microsoft, and nurtured trade relations with China. It was little surprise that in March 2011 the Obama administration appointed Locke as the U.S. ambassador to China when Jon Huntsman stepped down from the post.[38] This appointment was hailed as a symbol of not only the rising Asian American political profile in U.S. national and international politics but also the increasing importance of China in American politics.

In July 2009, Judy Chu was elected as congresswoman representing the 32nd congressional district, earning 62 percent of the vote and becoming the first Chinese American woman elected to Congress. Born in Monterey Park, California, in 1963, Chu developed her work ethic from watching her grandfather and father toil in their Chinese restaurant and her mother, an immigrant from Guangzhou, go through the aches and pains of working in a cannery. Chu attended UCLA, where she earned a bachelor's degree in math and became interested in civic issues. She later received a doctoral degree in psychology from the California School of Psychology and taught at East Los Angeles Community College for thirteen years before she was beckoned into politics. In 1985, Chu was elected board member of the Garvey School District in the San Gabriel Valley, where she took a key role in fighting racism. Between 1988 and 2001, she served on the Monterey Park City Council, where she was appointed as the city's mayor for three terms during this period. In 2001, she won a California State Assembly seat and stayed there until 2006. Her victory in the congressional race in July 2009 opened the national stage for her political activism. In the 112th Congress, Chu served on the House Judiciary Committee, where she was a member of the Crime, Terrorism, and Homeland Security and the Intellectual Property, Competition, and the Internet subcommittees. She was also a member of the House Small Business Committee, where she led the Contracting and Workforce Subcommittee as the ranking Democrat and served on the Economic Growth, Tax and Capital Access and Agriculture, Energy and Trade subcommittees. In 2011, she was elected as the chair of the Congressional Asian Pacific American Caucus (CAPAC).[39]

She focused on immigrant issues in the House, and one of her major political achievements was the unanimous passage of the Judy Chu Resolution for the Regret of Chinese Exclusion Act of 1882 in the House of Representatives on June 18, 2012. The resolution marked the first time that Congress had acknowledged the far-reaching injustices of the discriminatory laws against Chinese immigrants.[40]

Indian American Bobby Jindal's rise in American politics exemplifies the importance of personal drive and dedication. Jindal was born in Baton Rouge on June 10, 1971, into a family of Asian Indian immigrants. He graduated from Baton Rouge High School in 1988 and went on to attend Brown University, where he graduated with honors in biology and public policy. He then attended Oxford University as a Rhodes Scholar, having turned down admissions to medical and law schools at both Harvard and Yale. In 1994, Jindal went to work for McKinsey and Company as a consultant for *Fortune* 500 companies before entering public service. In 1996, he was appointed secretary of the Louisiana Department of Health and Hospitals (DHH). During Jindal's tenure as DHH secretary, he rescued Louisiana's Medicaid program from bankruptcy, childhood immunizations increased, Louisiana ranked third best nationally in health care screenings for children, and new and expanded services for elderly and disabled persons were offered. In 2004 he was elected to the 109th U.S. Congress representing the first district of Louisiana. He was elected governor of Louisiana on October 20, 2007, garnering 54 percent of the vote in the primary. During his term as governor, Jindal was known for his successes in cutting red tape, reducing taxation, and reforming the state's health care, education, and transportation systems as well as encouraging workforce development and continuing recovery efforts in areas devastated by hurricanes.[41]

While celebrating these high-profile Asian American politicians, one has to keep in mind that the successes of a few "token" minorities or elite politicians should not overshadow the general underrepresentation of Asian Americans at all levels of government and the much lower rate of political participation among Asian Americans—their electoral participation rate is only 2 to 3 percent in most states and 6 percent in California. Meanwhile, the rise to prominence of high-profile Asian American politicians and activists also coincided with the globalization of capitalism. As China and India have emerged as fast-growing economies, Asian Americans of Chinese and Indian ancestries have been incorporated into the U.S. political system to reflect the new global balance of power.

MYTH AND REALITY OF "MODEL MINORITY"

Asian Americans have experienced drastic cultural, political, and emotional changes and have achieved remarkable educational, occupational, and political accomplishments since the 1960s. As a result, a popular press image of them as a "model minority" emerged.[42]

In January 1966, William Petersen published an article in the *New York Times Magazine* praising Japanese Americans' successful entry into the American mainstream. In December of the same year, *U.S. News & World Report* also featured a story hailing the socioeconomic achievements of Chinese Americans.[43] Promoted by the popular press, the model minority image has since become a stereotype describing the socioeconomic success achieved by Asian Americans through hard work, respect for traditional values, and accommodation.

Two decades later, the model minority thesis resurfaced in the press. In the 1980s, national television networks and popular magazines vied to report stories of Asian American success. American politicians responded in a timely fashion. In a speech delivered to a group of Asian Americans in 1984, President Ronald Reagan congratulated Asian Americans on their success and recognized its significance.[44]

The model minority image did not emerge from a vacuum. Various statistics proved that Asian Americans had made significant socioeconomic progress. According to the 1970 census, the median family income of Chinese and Japanese Americans surpassed that of white Americans. The Japanese American median family income was $3,000 higher and Chinese American income was $1,000 higher than the U.S. median family income.[45] The 1980 census also indicated that a higher percentage of Asian Americans had completed a four-year college education than did Black, Hispanic, and white Americans: Filipino (21.7percent), Korean (21.2percent), Chinese (15.8percent), Japanese (15.6percent), Asian Indian (14.1), white (9.4) Black (4.9), and Hispanic (3.5).[46] As noted earlier, since U.S. census data do not include refugees and their children, they clearly reinforce the model minority stereotype.

The Asian American model minority image is alluring yet troubling. Although the model minority thesis recognizes Asian Americans' socioeconomic achievements since World War II, its appearance in the 1960s served certain political purposes. The Asian American success story of upward mobility relying on hard work and Asian values was used against Black and Hispanic civil rights activists who were engaging in militant activities to improve their social conditions. The model minority thesis further underscored the notion that America was still a land of opportunity and American democracy had continued to guarantee individual success. Here, Asian American success was used as a shining example to subtly criticize African and Hispanic Americans in failing to achieve their American dreams under the same circumstances. The model minority theory has been proven to be a useful and effective tool to triangulate race politics in America.

SUCCESS STORY, JAPANESE-AMERICAN STYLE

Asked which of the century's ethnic minorities has been subjected to the most discrimination and the worst injustices, very few persons would even think of answering: "The Japanese Americans." Yet, if the question refers to persons alive today, that may well be the correct reply. Like the Negroes, the Japanese have been the object of color prejudice. Like the Jews, they have been fear and hated as hyperefficient competitors. And, more than any other group, they have been seen as the agents of an overseas enemy. Conservatives, liberals and radicals, local sheriffs, the Federal Government and the Supreme Court have cooperated in denying them their elementary rights—most notoriously in their World War II evacuation to internment camps.

Generally this kind of treatment, as we all know these days, creates what might be termed "problem minorities." Each of a number of interrelated factors—poor health, poor education, low income, high crime rate, unstable family pattern, and so on and on—reinforces all of the others, and together they make up the reality of slum life. And by the "principle of cumulation," as Gunnar Myrdal termed it in "An American Dilemma," this social reality reinforced by them. When whites defined Negroes as inherently less intelligent, for example, and therefore furnished them with inferior schools, the products of these schools often validated the original stereotype.

Once the cumulative degradation has gone far enough, it is notoriously difficult to reverse the trend. When new opportunities, even equal opportunities, are opened up, the minority's reaction to them is likely to be negative—either self-defending apathy or a hatred so all-consuming as to be self-destructive. For all the well-meaning programs and countless scholarly studies now focused on the Negro, we barely know how to repair the damage that the slave traders started.

The story of Japanese Americans, however, challenges every such generalization about ethnic minorities. And for this reason alone deserves far more attention than it had been given. Barely more than 20 years after the end of wartime camps, this is a minority that has risen above even prejudiced criticism. By any criterion of good citizenship that we choose, the Japanese Americans are better than any other group in our society, including native-born whites. They have established this remarkable record, moreover, by their own almost totally unaided effort. Every attempt to hamper their progress resulted only in enhancing their determination to succeed. Even in a country whose patron saint is the Horatio Alger hero, there is no parallel to this success story. . . .

The Japanese . . . could climb over the highest barriers our racists were able to fashion in part because of their meaningful links with an alien culture. Pride in their heritage and shame for any reduction in its only partly legendary glory—these were sufficient to carry the group through its travail.

Source: William Petersen, "Success Story, Japanese-American Style," *New York Times Magazine*, January 9, 1966, 20–43.

Moreover, the model minority thesis, with its rosy picture of Asian American success overlooked the factors that contradict the all success "model" experiences. First, an increasing number of Chinese and other Asian Americans entered the middle-class social stratum, resided in suburban white neighborhoods, and enjoyed mainstream lifestyles. However, the majority of Asian Americans, especially newcomers, were still confined to inner-city ghettos. They struggled with problems of limited job opportunities, unhealthy and hazardous working conditions, crowded and substandard housing, and emotional stress. These problems were overlooked despite being well documented.[47]

Second, although more Chinese and Asian Americans attained higher education than Black, Hispanic, and white Americans, they earned lower incomes than their Black, Hispanic, and white counterparts with the same levels of education. According to the 1980 census, with the exception of Japanese Americans, all Asian Americans with a college degree had lower annual earnings than Black, Hispanic, and white American college graduates.[48]

Third, the typical "model" Chinese and Asian Americans were well-educated professionals: professors and teachers, doctors and nurses, librarians and technicians. Few Asian Americans climbed to the managerial and administrative levels due to the glass ceiling that projected Asian Americans as "quiet" and "uncomplaining" and therefore unfit for leadership positions. Only 0.3 percent of the senior male executives in *Fortune* 1,000 industrial companies and *Fortune* 500 service industries were Asian Americans in the 1990s.[49]

Fourth, more Chinese and other Asian Americans worked full-time to supplement family income. In 1970, about 60 percent of all Chinese and Japanese American families had more than one income earner, while only 51 percent of all American families had more than one earner.[50] In 1989, 56 percent of native-born and 50 percent of foreign-born Chinese American families had two workers, while 41.7 percent of all American families had two workers.[51] This pattern of multiple income earners within Asian American families is more evident in the recent decades, as indicated in table 7.3.

The model minority thesis not only misrepresented the reality of Asian Americans but also impeded their socioeconomic progress. For instance, about one-third of San Francisco's poor who qualified for public assistance were Asians, but only 6 percent of the city's social welfare program funds were granted to help them in the 1990s.[52] The limited political participation of Asian Americans certainly contributed to this unfair distribution of public assistance. Doubtless, the model minority stereotype also affected many decision makers who saw less need to assist a minority group that was believed to have achieved socioeconomic success. Therefore, the model minority thesis in fact has worked as a new form of racial and cultural prejudice against Asian Americans, as it impedes rather than facilitates access to various opportunities and results in discrimination and social indifference regarding the needs of Asian Americans. Writers have

TABLE 7.3 NUMBER OF WORKERS IN FAMILY BY RACE, 2000–2010

	2000		2010	
	Total population	Asian American	Total population	Asian American
Total	72,261,780 (100%)	2,616,085 (100%)	114,567,419 (100%)	3,587,927 (100%)
No workers	9,148,427 (12.7%)	188,424 (7.20%)	31,183,644 (27.2%)	233,859 (6.52%)
1 worker	16,114,172 (22.3%)	786,087 (30.0%)	45,082,026 (39.3%)	1,127,898 (31.4%)
2 workers	36,433,010 (50.4%)	1,186,968 (45.4%)	31,560,302 (27.5%)	1,667,645 (46.5%)
3 or more workers	8,610,842 (11.9%)	454,579 (17.4%)	6,751,447 (5.90%)	530,010 (14.8%)

Sources: American FactFinder, PCT084, "Family Type by Number of Workers in Family in 1999, Total Population"; American FactFinder, PCT084, "Family Type by Number of Workers in Family in 1999, Asian Alone or in Combination with One More Other Races (400–499) & (100–299) or (300, A01–z99) or (400–999)"; American FactFinder, B23009, "Presence of Own Children under 18 Years by Family Type by Number of Workers in Family in the Past 12 Months, Asian Alone or in Combination with One More Other Races (400–499) & (100–299) or (300, A01–z99) or (400–999); American FactFinder, B08202, "Household Size by Number of Workers in Household, Total Population."

urged educators to be cognizant of the "myth" of the model minority and discard the stereotype to describe Asian American students.[53] In his May 2012 speech addressed to members of Congress and prominent Asian Americans at an awards gala in Washington hosted by the Asian Pacific American Institute for American Studies, President Obama recognized that the treatment of Asian Americans must go beyond viewing them as the "model minority" to better understand the challenges faced by many ethnic groups, especially recent immigrants.[54]

ASIAN AMERICAN UPWARD MOBILITY IN HISTORICAL PERSPECTIVE

While Asian Americans have achieved educational and occupational success and are realizing their American dreams through running restaurants, grocery stores, and souvenir shops, polishing nails, and manning motels and donut shops, they are still confined by educational, economic, racial, and cultural inequalities. While moving upward socioeconomically, they still have to battle racial discrimination and social prejudice. The segmentation and monopoly of ethnic Americans in certain businesses are by-products of the racial structure and racial relations of the United States. This is the paradox of Asian Americans living in a classed and racialized society. Although Asian Americans have made great strides in participating in American politics, there remain many obstacles in their path—fragmentation and divisions along lines of ethnic differences, nationality, homeland politics, and occupational gaps within Asian America as well as cultural and racial prejudice against them from the larger society.

KEY TERMS

William Petersen
glass ceiling
admissions controversy
dual structure of Asian American employment
middleman minority theory
Jeong H. Kim
Sanjay Gupta
Korean grocery
Vietnamese nail care service
South Asian motel owners
Vincent Chin
Ming Hai Loo
Elaine Chao
Steve Chen
Steven Chu
Gary Locke
Bobby Jindal
Judy Chu
model minority theory and its assessments

REVIEW QUESTIONS

1. Why do many Asian Americans avoid checking the category of "Asian" when applying for college admissions?
2. What are the major reasons for Asian Americans' educational achievements?
3. Explain the dual structure of the employment pattern among Asian Americans. What is the "middleman minority" theory? List the factors that explain Vietnamese gravitation to the nail care niche and their dominance of the industry. How did Indian Americans realize their American dreams in the motel industry?
4. How have Asian Americans slowly and steadily become incorporated into American political life?
5. How would you evaluate the model minority theory?

FILMS

Dalzell, Liam (director). *Punjabi Cab*. 20-minute documentary on Sikh taxi drivers in the San Francisco Bay Area after 9/11. 2004.

Kim-Gibson, Dai Sil (writer/director/producer/narrator). *Sa-I-Gu: From Korean Women's Perspectives*. 36-minute documentary on Sa-I-Gu, literally April 29, the Los Angeles riots, from the perspectives of Korean women shopkeepers (in English and Korean with English subtitles). 1993.

Kim-Gibson, Dai Sil (producer/director). *Wet Sand: Voices from L.A.* 57-minute documentary on the aftermath of the 1992 LA civil unrest. 2004.

Sakya, Sapana, Donald Young, and Kyung Yu (directors). *Searching for Asian America*. 90-minutes documentary with study guide. Center for Asian America and KVIE, 2003.

Tajima-Peña, Renee (director). *Labor Women*. 30-minute documentary on activism, labor, and lesbian, gay, and bisexual women. 2002.

FURTHER READING

Bonacich, Edna. "A Theory of Middleman Minorities." *American Sociological Review* 37, no. 5 (1973): 583–594.

Bonacich, Edna, and John Modell. *The Economic Basis of Ethnic Solidarity: Small Business in the Japanese American Community*. Berkeley: University of California Press, 1980.

Chang, Gordon H., ed. *Asian Americans and Politics: Perspectives, Experiences, Prospects*. Stanford, CA: Stanford University Press, 2001.

Choy, Catherine C. *Empire of Care: Nursing and Migration in Filipino American History*. Durham, NC: Duke University Press, 2003.

Davé, Shilpa S. *Brown Voice and Racial Performance in American Television and Film*. Urbana: University of Illinois Press, 2013.

Dhingra, Pawan. *Life Behind the Lobby: Indian American Motel Owners and the American Dream*. Stanford, CA: Stanford University Press, 2012.

Espiritu, Yen Le. *Home Bound: Filipino American Lives across Cultures, Communities, and Countries*. Berkeley: University of California Press, 2003.

Garrod, Andrew, and Robert Kilkenny, eds. *Balancing Two Worlds: Asian American College Students Tell Their Life Stories*. Ithaca, NY: Cornell University Press, 2007.

Lam, Andrew. *Birds of Paradise Lost*. Pasadena, CA: Red Hen Press, 2012.

Lien, Pei-te, M. Margaret Conway, and Janelle Wong. *The Politics of Asian Americans: Diversity and Community*. New York: Routledge, 2004.

Ling, Huping. *Emerging Voices: Experiences of Underrepresented Asian Americans*. New Brunswick, NJ: Rutgers University Press, 2008.

———. *Voices of the Heart: Asian American Women on Immigration, Work, and Family*. Kirksville, MO: Truman State University Press, 2007.

Min, Gap Pyong. *Ethnic Solidarity for Economic Survival: Korean Greengrocers in New York City*. New York: Russell Sage Foundation, 2011.

Park, Lisa. *Consuming Citizenship: Children of Asian Immigrant Entrepreneurs*. Palo Alto, CA: Stanford University Press, 2005.

Takagi, Dana. *Retreat from Race: Asian Admissions and Racial Politics*. Piscataway, NJ: Rutgers University Press, 1992.

Valverde, Kieu-Linh Caroline. *Transnationalizing Viet Nam: Community, Culture, and Politics in the Diaspora*. Philadelphia: Temple University Press, 2013

8

NEW FORMATIONS OF ASIAN AMERICAN COMMUNITIES

CHAPTER OUTLINE

Urban Enclaves (1850s)
Transnational Urban and Suburban Communities and Cyber Communities (1990s)
Asian American Communities in Historical Perspective

SIGNIFICANT EVENTS

1880s	First Asian ethnic urban enclave, a Chinatown, is formed in San Francisco
1960s	Asian American suburban communities appear; Asian American cultural communities emerge
1975	Southeast Asian refugees and immigrants settle in the United States
1990s	Asian American virtual communities are formed
2004	Facebook is launched by Mark Zuckerberg and his college roommates and friends

THE GEOGRAPHIC, ethnographic, and socioeconomic landscape of America has changed dramatically since the 1960s. Asian American communities, reinforced by newcomers from Asian countries and regions, have undergone profound transformation. While traditional and long-established ethnic enclaves are renewed and revitalized by the influx of new immigrants, other different types of urban or suburban communities have also emerged as a result of the socioeconomic upward mobility of native-born Asian Americans and the changing profiles of the new immigrants from Asia since the 1960s. Many of them, such as professionals and entrepreneurs, are better equipped with human, monetary, and social capital. They are responsible for the formation of the new Asian American communities: global cities, suburban ethnic communities, cultural communities, and cyber communities—communities without geographical or cultural/social boundaries. At the same time, refugees and immigrants coming from Southeast Asia (Vietnam, Laos, and Cambodia) since the end of the Vietnam War in 1975 have also constructed communities that resemble the urban enclaves of the traditional ethnic communities in the initial years following their settlement in America, some of whom have been able to move out of their urban enclaves and dwell in a variety of suburban Asian American communities. Rapid global economic development and internet technological innovations since the 1990s have given birth to transnational urban and suburban communities as well as cyber communities through social networks.

This chapter presents a comprehensive picture of contemporary Asian American communities. It includes discussions of Asian American communities not only in coastal metropolises but also in the hinterland; not only the commercial/residential neighborhoods but also communities with commercial centers only; not only those that can be defined as urban enclaves but also suburban communities; and not only geographical formations but also culturally/socially bounded communities. In presenting a comprehensive and broad picture of Asian American communities, the chapter explores the profound and complex socioeconomic and cultural elements present in the formation of varying Asian American communities in the contexts of capitalism, transnationalism, and globalization. It examines how Asian Americans have challenged and altered the conventional borders and boundaries of a community and formed the communities best suited for their present socioeconomic needs. We will examine and analyze the different forms of Asian American communities in accordance with their evolution in three historical periods, although the discussions may overlap or go beyond specific time frames in some places since various forms of Asian communities crisscross the eras covered: (1) prior to the 1960s most Asian American ethnic neighborhoods were *urban enclaves* encompassing both commercial and residential areas; (2) in the post-1960 era Asian American communities have become more diverse, including commercial/tourist-centered urban communities as well as *suburban ethnic communities and cultural communities*; (3) since the early 1990s when transnationalism, globalization, and rapid internet technological developments have dramatically transformed socioeconomic and cultural conditions in the world, two new trends in Asian American communities have emerged, one being *transnational* in both urban and suburban communities and the other the formation of *cyber communities* through internet social networks.

URBAN ENCLAVES (1850s)

Asian immigrants, like all newcomers, first faced the challenge of survival on foreign soil. However, due to racial prejudice the New World was more hostile to Asian immigrants than to their European counterparts. Survival in a strange and unfriendly land thus resulted in the formation of the first type of Asian community—urban *ghettos* or *enclaves*. Two factors are believed to be primarily responsible for the construction of Asian ethnic urban enclaves: the external discriminatory legislature and practices against Asian immigrants and the internal drive of the Asian immigrants to survive and succeed in the New World by utilizing ethnic networks and resources. The external factor (for instance, in the forms of the Foreign Miners' License Tax passed in 1850 and 1852 and the alien land laws passed between 1885 and 1921, and various discriminatory practices in the labor market) restricted the socioeconomic opportunities of Asian immigrants in the larger society and pushed them into limited and often service-oriented occupations (laundry, dry cleaning, restaurants, wholesale and retailing, garment manufacturing, and domestic service) and dilapidated urban neighborhoods where rents were low. There they could survive and prosper largely through the practical means of mutual aid and ethnic networks (as discussed in the chapter on labor). Historically such ethnic communities have in general been defined as ethnic "ghettos" or "enclaves"; in particular they have been dubbed Chinatown, Japantown (J-Town), Koreatown (K-Town), Little India or as replicas of the ethnic groups' original cultures symbolized by the names of capital cities of the homelands, such as Little Manila or Little Saigon. There are two types of urban ethnic enclaves. Prior to the 1960s, Asian urban enclaves were mostly ethnic neighborhoods with both commercial and residential areas. Since the 1960s, when the socioeconomic conditions of Asian Americans improved and they consequently moved into suburban neighborhoods, Asian urban enclaves have become more commercial and tourist-centered districts, often in the forms of strip malls and mixed with businesses of other ethnic groups. In this section, we examine these two types of ethnic enclave separately.

Urban Enclaves as Commercial and Residential Centers

CHINATOWNS. Chinatowns are most illustrative in exhibiting the formation of Asian ethnic urban enclaves. Chinese communities in America have largely been an urban phenomenon since the early twentieth century. In the 1930 census, 64 percent of the 74,954 Chinese resided in urban centers. A decade later, the Chinese population totaled 77,504 and 71 percent of them lived in major American cities. By the 1950 census, more than 90 percent of the Chinese population resided in cities, and the trend continues upward.[1] The pronounced presence of Chinese Americans in cities undoubtedly warrants the view that research on urban centers constitutes a significant focus within Asian American studies.

Like other immigrant groups, Chinese immigrants predominantly settled in gateway cities and major urban centers, where they established communities known as Chinatowns. The first Chinatown in the United States emerged in the 1850s in San Francisco, referred to as the First City by the Chinese. The Chinese quarter there, as it was commonly known by both academics and the mass media in the late nineteenth and early twentieth centuries, was formed "to protect" the Chinese and "to make themselves at home."[2] Chinatowns have generally been understood as confined urban commercial and residential districts where Chinese could find employment, housing, and cultural comfort, virtually without interacting with the larger society.[3] By 1856, there were thirty-three Chinese-owned grocery shops, fifteen pharmacies, five doctor offices, three boardinghouses, three tailors, and five restaurants in San Francisco's Chinatown. In 1876, Chinatown covered about nine blocks, comprising Sacramento, Clay, Washington, Jackson, Pacific, Kearny, Stockton, and DuPont streets, hosted a population of around 30,000 between 1870 and 1900, and provided various goods and services to local residents as well as visitors.[4]

The anti-Chinese movement, compounded by the economic depression on the West Coast in the final decades of the nineteenth century, contributed to the redistribution of the Chinese immigrant population in the United States, which dispersed throughout the East, Midwest, and South. In New York, the opening of a Chinese general goods store at 34 Mott Street store run by Wo Kee in 1873 was considered the beginning of New York's Chinatown. The 1880 census reported 748 Chinese living in Manhattan. New York's Chinatown, where Chinese-Irish families persisted as a dominant pattern, became the largest east of the Sierra Nevada. The typical Chinese laborers in New York were, in descending order, cigar makers, sailors, retailers, stewards, and candy makers.[5] By 1890, the Chinese population had increased to 2,559. In 1920, most of the 5,042 Chinese in the city were engaged in hand laundries and restaurants.[6]

In Chicago, the "Second City" of the United States since 1890, the Chinese also formed their Chinatown in the 1870s. Centrally located and a node of land, water, rail—and later air—transportation, Chicago served as a hub for Chinese immigrants in North America. Encouraged by the relatively more accommodating reception in Chicago, Moy Dong Chow, one of the Chinese pioneers in Chicago, wrote to his compatriots in San Francisco in 1880 asking them to join him. As a result, there were one hundred Chinese in the city by 1880. Moy Dong Chow also continuously sent for his family members from the homeland. By 1885, forty members of the extended Moy family from his native village were living in Chicago. By the end of 1890, there were more than five hundred Chinese living on South Clark Street, the first Chinatown in Chicago. Laundries, grocery stores, and restaurants made up the early Chinatown. Two Chinese laundries in 1870 in the Loop (the downtown business district coinciding with the old cable car service area), a few businesses, and a Chinese church in the mid-1870s provided the early structure of the Chinatown. The anti-Chinese sentiments prevalent in the country affected relations between the Chinese and the larger society. In the 1910s, downtown property owners raised rents, making it difficult for Chinese businesses to survive, forcing the vast majority of the over two thousand Chinese to move to the South Side, where property was cheaper. On the South Side, the Chinese soon established a new Chinatown, known as South Chinatown today, which remains a major tourist attraction of the city.[7]

In St. Louis, another metropolis in the Midwest, the Chinese established their urban enclave community in the 1860s. In 1857, Alla Lee, a twenty-four-year-old native of Ningbo, China, seeking a better life, came to St. Louis, where he opened a small shop on North Tenth Street selling tea and coffee. As the first and probably the only Chinese there for a while, Alla Lee mingled mostly with immigrants from Northern Ireland and married an Irish woman. A decade later, Alla Lee was joined by several hundred of his compatriots from San Francisco and New York, who were seeking jobs in mines and factories in and around St. Louis. Most of the Chinese workers lived in boardinghouses located near a small street called Hop Alley. In time, Chinese hand laundries, merchandise stores, herb shops, restaurants, and clan association headquarters sprang up in and around that street; thus, Hop Alley became synonymous with Chinatown. Local records indicate that Chinese businesses, especially hand laundries, drew a wide clientele and thus the businesses run by Chinese immigrants contributed disproportionally to the city's economy. They provided 60 percent of the services for the city during the late nineteenth and early twentieth centuries, although Chinese composed less than 0.1 percent of the city's total population of about 300,000 in the 1890s. Despite frequent police raids and bias among other residents, Hop Alley survived with remarkable resilience and energy until 1966, when urban renewal bulldozers completely leveled the area to construct a parking lot for Busch Stadium.[8]

JAPANTOWNS. While Chinese urban enclaves have been renewed and revitalized by an incessant stream of new immigrants and thus still maintain one of the dominant forms of Chinese American community, Japanese urban enclaves, different from their Chinese counterparts, are gradually vanishing. Their enclaves had never been a dominant part of Japanese American communities. In 1940, when 90 percent of Chinese Americans were urban dwellers, more than one-half (51.4 percent) of all the male Japanese workers in the three West Coast states were employed in agriculture, forestry, and fishing, as were one out of every three Japanese working women. Only less than one-fourth (23.6 percent) of all working Japanese were employed in wholesale and retail trade, and the remainder (17.1 percent) worked in personal service and were considered urban residents.[9]

As postwar Japanese Americans have "structurally" assimilated into the larger society,[10] most Japanese Americans live in predominantly European American neighborhoods, work for mainstream companies, participate in the social and political activities of the larger society, and intermarry with European Americans in significant numbers. For instance, in 1979, 50 percent of new marriages involving Japanese in Los Angeles were with non-Asians.[11] These characteristics of Japanese Americans, combined with other factors, such as the lower rate of postwar Japanese immigration to the United States, consequently resulted in the erosion, dissolution, and even extinction of Japantowns or Little Tokyos in the United States.

For instance, the Little Tokyo in downtown Los Angeles had been home to more Japanese Americans than anywhere else since 1910. But since the late 1950s, the Japanese American population in Southern California has dispersed; by the 2000s, there were only about a thousand residual Japanese Americans in the neighborhood. It mainly served as a nexus for international tourism and the display of artworks. It is home to institutions such as the Japanese American Culture and Community Center, the Japanese American National Museum, and the Union Center for the Arts.[12]

For this reason, we will discuss Japanese American communities in the later section on Asian American communities with cultural/social boundaries.

KOREATOWNS. It is necessary here to summarize briefly the Korean immigration history. Korean immigrants came to the United States in three major waves. The first major wave of immigration brought 7,226 Koreans to Hawaii as contract laborers between 1903 and 1905 to replace Japanese workers who demanded higher wages and initiated strikes. Approximately two thousand of these Korean laborers later migrated to the American mainland, mostly settling on the West Coast. This early wave was halted by the Korean government in 1905 when the country lost its independence to Japan. The Japanese government intended to stop the anti-Japanese resistance movement among overseas Koreans and to eliminate the competition with Japanese immigrants from Koreans. The second wave of Korean immigration came between the Korean War (1950–1953) and 1965. The majority of these immigrants, numbering 14,027, were war orphans or wives and relatives of American servicemen who had been stationed in Korea.[13] The third wave of Korean immigration to the United States reached the country under the 1965 Hart-Celler Act, also known as the 1965 Immigration Act. The new wave of Korean immigration was characterized by a significant shift in the socioeconomic profile of the immigrants who were largely middle-class professionals in their homeland.[14]

While most scholarship on the new Korean immigrants has focused on entrepreneurship and Black-Korean tensions in inner-city neighborhoods,[15] a few studies have explored the community structure. These studies indicate that Korean immigrants possessed the qualities of hard work and frugality, strong family and kinship ties, and ethnic solidarity; and such qualities helped many succeed in ethnic enterprises. Korean communities in the major metropolises of Los Angeles and New York tend to be commercial centers only.

In Los Angeles, officially designated as Koreatown by the Los Angeles City Council in 1980, the Korean American community is located in the Wilshire Center district, roughly bounded by Arlington Avenue on the west, Melrose Avenue on the north, Hoover Street on the east, and Pico Boulevard on the south. Korean influence in the area increased rapidly in the 1970s when most businesses in the district became Korean-owned. Signs in Hangul, the Korean alphabet, appeared in strip malls, shopping centers, liquor stores, and restaurants. The Korean media, including newspapers, magazines, radio, and television, further reinforced the area's Koreanness. The race riot on April 29, 1992, caused widespread destruction in Koreatown (see the discussion in chapter 6), but the economic recovery of the community was evident by the early 2000s. The area is well known for its many restaurants and lively nightclub scene. Two popular shopping centers, Koreatown Galleria and Koreatown Plaza, are located in the district. This new boom was driven by foreign investment and an increasingly affluent immigrant population.[16]

In New York, Korean immigrant businesses revitalized the major business strips in Flushing, Elmhurst and nearby Jackson Heights, Woodside, and Sunnyside, in the borough of Queens during the 1980s. The diverse Korean-run small businesses included supermarkets and groceries, delicatessens, bakeries, restaurants, general merchandise stores, specialty stores, dry cleaners, beauty salons, real estate offices, driving schools, language schools, insurance and travel agencies, car repair shops, doctors' offices, accountants, lawyers, medical clinics, pharmacies, Korean herb doctors and acupuncturists, and garment factories.[17] A comparative study of Korean, Chinese, and Vietnamese American communities in Philadelphia also depicts a similar picture. While most Korean immigrants worked in small businesses located in Koreatown on North Fifth Street, they maintained ethnic solidarity through preserving their ethnic language, holidays and rituals, participating in ethnic organizations, and running ethnic media.[18]

Thus, the Korean urban enclaves are characterized by the separation of commercial and residential lives. The post-1965 Korean immigrants, although working in the small businesses, garment factories, or services of the inner-city districts, have lived in apartment complexes outside of the business precincts and formed an "associational community," a community created through occupational, residential, and religious associations.[19] Therefore, the separation of the commercial and residential lives of Korean immigrants distinguishes Koreatowns from Chinatowns, which typically possess both commercial and residential properties.

LITTLE INDIAS AND OTHER SOUTH ASIAN COMMUNITIES. It is also necessary to briefly describe the immigration history of South Asians. South Asian immigration to the United States also came in three waves. The first wave comprised Sikh men from

Punjab in India during the late nineteenth and early twentieth centuries. They worked in railroads, farms, and canneries in California and Washington. Between 1881 and 1917, about 7,000 Asian Indians entered the country. They were mostly bachelors or married men who left families behind in India; but in the agricultural areas in Southern California, they formed Punjabi-Mexican families in the 1920s.

The second wave following the 1965 Immigration Act consisted of mostly Indians and Pakistanis and a relatively small number of immigrants from other South Asian countries. They were overwhelmingly middle-class professionals, with 83 percent entering under the occupational category of professional and technical workers between 1966 and 1977.

The third wave of South Asian immigration began in the 1980s and continues to the present. While most immigrants of this period still came under the legal framework of the 1965 Immigration Act, the category of immigration shifted from the occupational one in the second wave to the one of family reunification. The newcomers were mostly family members and relatives of the 1966–1977 cohorts. In addition to the change in modes of entry, another shift of this period is a greater diversity in national origins. Along with Indians and Pakistanis who are still the majority of the influx, increasing numbers of immigrants from Bangladesh, Nepal, and Sri Lanka have also been admitted to the United States. The entrance of the latter reflected the decline of the labor migration to the Middle East countries in the early 1990s. Some of them were also admitted as refugees or applicants for political asylum. Still more benefitted from the 1990 Diversity Visa Program or green card lottery (see the discussions on immigration legislation in chapter 6).

South Asian Americans formed their communities primarily in major metropolises. The top six metropolitan statistical areas for the Asian Indian population in 2000 were New York (400,194), San Francisco (144,231), Chicago (116,868), Los Angeles (104,482), Washington, D.C. (88,211), and Philadelphia (53,280), consisting of about 50 percent of the total South Asian population of 1.8 million. A decade later, the order of the list changed— New York–New Jersey–Long Island (526,133), Chicago (171,901), Washington, D.C. (127,963), Los Angeles (119,901), San Francisco (119,854), and Dallas (100,386)—indicating a South Asian population shift to the Midwest and South. In the New York–New Jersey area, there are over twenty "Little Indias" where ethnic South Asian grocery stores, jewelry shops, restaurants, and other service businesses are concentrated. In addition to serving the needs of South Asian Americans, the ethnic economy of South Asian Americans has also provided services to the larger U.S. population. While Gujarati Indians generally engaged in the motel industry across the country, South Asian Americans also carved out other niche businesses, such as subway newsstands, retail discount stores, auto shops, and taxicabs in large cities. About 70 percent of New York's cabbies are from South Asian countries.[20]

LITTLE MANILAS. Although Filipinos have been entering the United States since the 1700s, the majority have come following the Immigration Act of 1965. The number of Filipinos entering the United States has been increasing annually since the passage of the liberalizing law. In 1973, 30,000 Filipinos were admitted to the United States. By the end of the 1980s, over 50,000 Filipinos were entering the country annually. In 1990, there were 1.5 million Filipinos in the United States.[21] Ten years later, the figure jumped to 1.8 million, making Filipinos the second largest Asian American group, behind the Chinese, in the United States. In 2010, the Filipino American population further increased to 3.4 million, continuing as the second largest Asian American population.[22]

The 1965 Immigration Act alone cannot explain the influx of Filipino immigrants; the U.S. presence in the Philippines propelled and shaped this movement of human migration. The 1898 Treaty of Paris—ending the Spanish-American War and forcing Spain to cede the Philippines to the United States—and the subsequent U.S. annexation of the Philippines (1899–1913) complicated the polity, economy, and culture of the Philippines. Prior to the passage of the 1965 Immigration Act, most Filipinos came to America as laborers or *pensionados* (students). Many Filipino men were also recruited by the U.S. Navy to fight during the two world wars. Two of the largest American military installations overseas, Clark Air Base and Subic Bay Naval Base, are located in the Philippines, and most of their needs in terms of military personnel are served by Filipinos. Although the two bases were closed in 1991 and 1992 respectively, the U.S. Navy had resumed using the latter from 2012 onward. In addition, the United States serves as the Philippines' major trading partner, and American investment accounts for half of the country's foreign investment.[23] The military and socioeconomic ties between the United States and the Philippines have profoundly impacted Filipino society in many ways. Academics assert that Filipino immigration to the United States has been a result of the "Americanization" of Filipino culture through American colonization.[24] The Americanization of Filipino culture has been embodied in the government structure, educational system, language, customs, and values. The Filipino government was set up based on the American model, as was its educational system. English is the language used in public and private schools, and Filipino television channels are inundated with American movies and soap operas.

Filipinos were also pushed out of the country by its grave political, economic, and social conditions. Although the martial law presidency of Ferdinand Marcos was terminated in 1986, the successive democratic government under President Corazon Aquino was plagued with political instability. As a result of the Philippines' economic policy that rested completely on U.S. involvement in the Vietnam War, the country's economy tanked in the 1980s. The problems of inflation and foreign debt were compounded by heavy unemployment, dependency on agricultural exports, and inequality in the distribution of income and wealth.[25]

The oversupply of educated people in the Philippines since the 1960s also contributed to the Filipino exodus. In 1970, 25 percent of college-age Filipinos was enrolled in colleges and universities, a national proportion that trailed behind only the United States. However, the country could not provide its educated people with adequate employment and pay. For instance, Filipina nurses in the United States could earn twenty times more than their counterparts in the Philippines. Since the 1960s, professional Filipinas/os have migrated to the United States in large numbers, and the majority of them are physicians, nurses, and other health practitioners as a result of aggressive U.S. recruitment policies to fill the shortage of trained personnel in the healthy industry. Two-thirds of Filipino immigrants to the United States in the 1960s were women, many of whom were nurses. By the late 1980s, 50,000 Filipino nurses were working in the United States.[26]

California has the largest number of Little Manilas. Meanwhile, many Filipino enclaves also exist in Hawaii and in at least seventeen states on the mainland, in Washington, D.C., and in each of the five boroughs of New York City. In California, Filipino communities share a common history of settlement and development. They were generally formed in the 1920s when Filipino migrants searched for jobs under racial discrimination and prejudice. The stability of present Little Manilas varies from place to place. While some remain prosperous and continue to grow, others are gradually losing their Filipino identity as middle-class Filipino families move out of the ethnic neighborhoods and the local population is replaced by other ethnic groups. Still others are under the threat of dissolution due to urban development projects.

In Los Angeles, the Filipino community, known as Historic Filipinotown (Hi-Fi), to the northeast of downtown, is located between Westlake and Echo Park. It originated from the Filipino settlement of the 1920s and flourished in the 1940s when more Filipino businesses and homes were established. Presently, Hi-Fi represents the heart of the Filipino community in Southern California. However, its 6,900 residents—out of the total 100,000 Filipinos in Los Angeles—are overshadowed by the larger Mexican and Central American populations. Filipinos also built a community in the Navy town of San Diego. While the pre-1965 Filipino community was small, numbering 5,123 people who were predominantly connected to the Navy, post-1965 immigrants were largely middle-class professionals who swelled the community to 121,000 in 2000.[27]

In Northern California, most Little Manilas have to fight for their survival. In San Francisco, as most Filipinos moved into the suburbs in the 1960s and 1970s, Manilatown declined. When the International Hotel on Kearny Street, the remaining original structure of the community, was torn down and its elderly tenants were evicted in 1981, the community was about to go extinct. With the efforts of the Manila Heritage Foundation, construction for a new senior residence building on the site of the old hotel began in 2002. Another ongoing struggle for the preservation of Little Manila occurs in Stockton, site of one of the oldest Filipino migrant worker settlements. In the early twentieth century, when they were banned from living in white neighborhoods, Filipino agricultural laborers established their community in downtown Stockton. The community evolved to a four-block district with more than sixty businesses and institutions, including restaurants, hotels, union offices, auto repair shops, churches, and news agencies. During the 1960s and 1970s, a city development plan in the form of the Crosstown Freeway endangered Little Manila and nearby Chinatown. In 1999, a new urban development initiative—the Gateway Project—further threatened the Filipino neighborhood. Filipino activists launched a campaign called the Little Manila Project to preserve what little remained of the district. In 2000, the Stockton City Council voted unanimously to designate four blocks as the Little Manila Historic Site.

In New York, the largest Filipino American concentration is in the borough of Queens. Near half of the city's 220,000 Filipinos reside in the community. A subway stop on the 7 Line provides easy access to Little Manila. It hosts many restaurants, shipping centers and freight services, the Philippine National Bank, and numerous medical offices. In Manhattan, one can also find a small Filipino district on First Avenue between Eleventh and Fifteenth streets, with a large number of Filipino medical professionals. In addition, Lower Manhattan also hosts some high-end Filipino restaurants and the Chapel of San Lorenzo Ruiz, a popular church serving a large Filipino American congregation.[28]

Urban Commercial/Tourist Centers and Suburban Ethnic and Cultural Communities (1960s)

Since the 1960s, many Asian American urban enclaves throughout America have transformed from ethnic enclaves for immigrants and Asian Americans into tourist attractions to satisfy the curiosity of people from diverse backgrounds and commercial centers for Asian cooking ingredients and the culinary enjoyment of Asian Americans and others alike. In San Francisco, New York, Los Angeles, Chicago, St. Louis, Washington, D.C., Philadelphia, and other large cities, Asian ethnic enclaves have evolved, often with the encouragement of municipal governments, into tourist-oriented commercial centers. Most gift stores and restaurants are patronized by visitors motivated by cultural curiosity. To attract tourists for the development of the ethnic economy, local businesses and community organizations have exploited the exotic features of Asian culture, especially in architectural designs making them appealing to the curious visitors. With reference to such tourist-centered commercial efforts, scholars have expressed concerns about the "overuse" of architectural ethnic symbols, contending that it gives them a flavor of superficiality rather than conveying Asian Americans' sense of community. Further, scholars are concerned that the exoticism of these tourist-oriented ethnic commercial centers could unintentionally reinforce the "otherness" of Asian Americans, thus promoting rather than combatting racism in America.[29] Nevertheless, commercial-centered Asian

FIGURE 8.1 A double-decker at Grant Street, Chinatown, San Francisco, April 19, 2014. This is an example of combining tourism and ethnic commerce practiced in the larger ethnic centers of many American major cities. Huping Ling Collection.

ethnic enclaves continue to prevail and prosper, serving as an enduring form of Asian American urban community.

LITTLE SAIGONS. In 1975, when South Vietnam fell to the communists, over two million refugees fled Vietnam, Laos, and Cambodia, forming waves of refugees escaping the turmoil. The Southeast Asians constitute the most recently formed ethnic group. Unlike the earlier Asian American groups, Vietnamese, Laotian, and Cambodian Americans are refugees and their American-born children. Their immigration pattern and their life in America are thus inevitably intertwined with the refugee experience.

Orange County, California, hosts the largest concentration of Vietnamese refugees. The population of Vietnamese Americans in the area swelled to over 400,000 out of the 1.2 million total Vietnamese Americans across the country in 2000.[30] Over two to five thousand Vietnamese businesses in the Little Saigon area cater to the ethnic community. Different from the earlier urban ethnic enclaves that served as both commercial and residential areas and were located in downtown districts, Little Saigon consists of

FIGURE 8.2 South Chinatown, Chicago, the primary Chinese American urban commercial and residential area of the city. 2008. Huping Ling Collection.

ethnic commercial belts located on arterial thoroughfares. It provides Vietnamese Americans with commercial goods, services, as well as a sense of community. Meanwhile, its commercial wealth also attracts tourists of diverse backgrounds, which diminishes the sense of community. Today, it is home to about 88,000 Vietnamese Americans. The community is also known for its conservative, "anti-communist" politics, as most Vietnamese refugees escaped the communist takeover in Vietnam in 1975. However, with the capitalistic reforms and the rapid economic development in Vietnam since the 1990s, more Vietnamese Americans have participated in transnational economic and cultural activities in the Pacific Rim, including visiting and investing in Vietnam (see sidebar).[31]

In the Midwest, Chicago became one of the major points of settlement for Southeast Asian refugees. When Vietnamese refugees first set foot in Chicago in the mid-1970s, Chinatown, the traditional point of entry for new immigrants, was already overwhelmed by an influx of post-1965 newcomers mostly from Hong Kong and was unable to provide adequate housing, social service, and employment opportunities, thus forcing these new Southeast Asian refugees to look for alternative areas of settlement. They quickly found refuge in an emerging new Chinatown located on Argyle Street between Sheridan Road

FIGURE 8.3 Devon Avenue, an Indian American neighborhood in Chicago, 2012. Huping Ling Collection.

and Broadway, on Chicago's North Side. In 1974, the federal government acquired the Hip Sing (a traditional community organization in the Midwest and on the East Coast) property on Clark Street under eminent domain in order to construct a jail and a parking garage. With assistance from the Nationalist government in Taiwan, Hip Sing purchased several buildings along Argyle Street on the city's North Side and made ambitious plans for a beautiful mall complete with fountains and pagodas. Although this new Chinatown in Argyle was less successful than the leaders of Hip Sing had envisioned, it did attract the nexus of a new Chinese American community and thus enticed the ethnic Chinese and other refugees from Southeast Asia to settle there and to revitalize the neighborhood. The resident Chinese Americans and Southeast Asian refugees together transformed Argyle Street into a productive Asian business district, now referred to as North Chinatown in Chicago. It is also often referred as Little Saigon.[32] A similar revitalization of an old ethnic district by Southeast Asian refugees also occurred in other urban centers across the country.

CAMBODIAN AMERICAN COMMUNITIES. After the fall of Phnom Penh to the communist Khmer Rouge in 1975, a few Cambodians, mostly elite members of the military

FIGURE 8.4 Indian Square in Jersey City, New Jersey, looking east along Newark Street (India Square) toward JFK Boulevard, April 14, 2010. Courtesy Wikimedia.

government, relocated to the United States. The overthrow of the Khmer Rouge in 1979 produced a large wave of Cambodian refugees to Vietnam and Thailand. Among the roughly 600,000 Cambodian refugees, about 150,000 were admitted to the United States. To encourage their rapid assimilation and to spread their economic impact, the U.S. government dispersed the Cambodian refugees throughout the country. However, the remigration that took place after the refugees had become established enough to communicate with each other and travel within the United States brought Cambodian Americans to various localities with warmer climates, concentrations of friends and relatives, and greater job opportunities and government benefits. Large Cambodian communities can be found in Long Beach, Fresno, and Stockton in California, Providence in Rhode Island, Cleveland in Ohio, Lynn and Lowell in Massachusetts, Seattle in Washington, and Portland in Oregon. In 2000, there were 206,052 Cambodian Americans, and their number increased to 276,667 in 2010.

FIGURE 8.5 A multilingual welcome sign on Main Street, Flushing, New York, indicates the multiethnic residents of the area, April 7, 2007. Huping Ling Collection.

Most Cambodian refugees came from poor rural regions, as many of the better-educated and better-off Cambodians had been persecuted by the Khmer Rouge regime. Lacking education, English ability, and the skills requisite for an industrial world, they suffer from poverty, high rates of unemployment, and mental health issues. To help ease their assimilation into American life, Cambodian Americans have established community organizations. The most prominent organizations with national reach include the Cambodian American National Council (CANC), the Cambodian Humanitarian Organization for Peace on Earth (C-HOPE), and Cambodian American Heritage, Inc. (CAHI). CANC, founded in 1988 in Philadelphia, provided legal, advocacy, and other professional services to local Cambodian organizations. It also organized national conventions to exchange ideas about educational, cultural, and economic development within Cambodian American communities. C-HOPE, founded in 1998 and headquartered in the largest Cambodian American population center in the United States—Long Beach, California—attracts largely college-educated Cambodian Americans, encouraging their participation and leadership in community initiatives.[33]

FIGURE 8.6 A commercial square of various Asian American businesses, along with H-Mart, a popular Korean Super Market in Santa Clara, California, May 27, 2018. Huping Ling Collection.

HMONG AMERICAN COMMUNITIES. The first wave of about 30,000 Hmong refugees from 1975 to 1978 went mostly to Montana and California. Four years later, the second wave came as a result of the Refugee Act of 1980 permitting entry to the families of the Secret Army, a Hmong militia hired by the CIA. By 2000, the 186,310 Hmong were living in every state except Wyoming. In 2010, 260,073 Hmong Americans resided in the United States, and the ten states with the largest estimated Hmong American populations were California (91,224), Minnesota, (66,181), Wisconsin (49,240), North Carolina (10,864), Michigan (5,924), Colorado (3,859), Georgia (3,623), Alaska (3,534), Oklahoma (3,369), and Oregon (2,920).[34]

Scholars have periodized the development of the Hmong American community into three stages: the refugee years (1975–1991), the turning point period (1992–1999), and the Hmong American era (2000–present). During the refugee years, both Hmong and the general public perceived them as "refugees," while the Hmong themselves were experiencing cultural shock and making drastic adjustments from a life in rural and mountainous Laos to the modern American environment. The election of Choua Lee in 1992 to the board of education in Saint Paul, Minnesota, marked the beginning of a turning point period when Hmong transformed from refugees to Hmong Americans. Starting from 2000, many young Hmong Americans began identifying themselves as Hmong Americans. They established Hmong media, Hmong professional journals, Hmong archives, the Center for Hmong Studies, the Center for Hmong Arts and Talents, and other cultural establishments.

LITTLE SAIGON, ORANGE COUNTY

In the mid-1970s, when the first group of Vietnamese refugees arrived, the area that would become Little Saigon was a bedroom community populated mainly by elderly whites and was known for its aging tract homes, trailer parks, small farms, auto yards, and open lots. The area experienced a population growth in the post–World War II era when service personnel stationed in local military bases decided to settle permanently; however, younger generations abandoned this suburb for better opportunities elsewhere. Many of the early Vietnamese came through "Operation New Arrival[s]"* and were processed in the resettlement center at El Toro Marine Corps Air Station in Orange County, while others came from nearby Camp Pendleton, a marine base in northern San Diego County, where the first wave of refugees were temporarily housed in 1975. Attracted by the warm weather and educational and occupational opportunities, along with affordable housing and commercial space, second and third waves of refugees joined this first group, quickly enlarging the population and revitalizing the area. . . .

Little Saigon has become the largest Asian business district in the county and rivals those in nearby Los Angeles. Vietnamese from surrounding Los Angeles, San Bernardino, Riverside, and San Diego counties flock to this area for their shopping and social needs, but it also attracts a fair number of regular out-of-state visitors, who come to socialize with relatives and friends as well as to buy ethnic goods. While in flight from Hawaii, commercials on television monitors encourage airline passengers to visit Little Saigon. Mainstream tourist guidebooks and travel or food sections of local periodicals on Southern California direct visitors to this ethnic "treasure," where they can shop and eat in Little Saigon. The area cannot be defined solely as an "ethnic enclave" that caters just to Vietnamese "refugees," but attracts other Asian ethnics and non-Asians interested in finding a bargain meal and affordable groceries or those interested in exploring an ethnic community.

Source: Excerpt from Linda Trinh Võ, "Transforming an Ethnic Community: Little Saigon, Orange County," in *Asian America: Forming New Communities, Expanding Boundaries*, ed. Huping Ling (New Brunswick, NJ: Rutgers University Press, 2009), 88–89.

* Operation New Arrivals (April 29–September 16, 1975) was the military operation that airlifted more than 120,000 Vietnamese refugees to camps around the United States before they were placed in permanent settlements in the country.

During the four decades of Hmong American history, the Hmong American community leadership has been instrumental in the transition of Hmong from refugees to Americans. Hmong community leadership has evolved from the beginning of the Hmong American experiences. The initial leadership mostly came from previous military officers and government officials, known as "older, traditional" leaders. For example, former general Vang Pao organized the Lao Family Community in 1977 and the Hmong National Council in the early 1980s. Since 1981, a more diverse Hmong leadership has emerged. Hmong women formed the Association for the Advancement of Hmong Women in Minnesota in 1981. By the end of the 1980s, more mutual assistance associations were established and mostly led by middle-aged leaders. By the early 1990s, a third group of leaders, mostly professionals, joined the Hmong leadership.[35]

TRANSNATIONAL URBAN AND SUBURBAN COMMUNITIES AND CYBER COMMUNITIES (1990s)

Ethnic Suburban Communities

The influx of new immigrants from Asia since 1965 resulted in a profound transformation of Asian American communities. As many of the new arrivals were better educated, better skilled, and better financed and had a better English-speaking ability, they tended to be better assimilated into the host country socioeconomically and dwell in suburban middle- or upper-middle-class neighborhoods.

In Los Angeles, many of the suburban-bound Chinese Americans in the 1950s and 1960s moved to Monterey Park. They commuted to downtown for work and shopped in downtown ethnic grocery stores for their cooking ingredients. Suburbs functioned mostly as bedroom communities until the early 1970s when a Chinese shopping center, DiHo, was built by a Taiwanese developer, along with a few Chinese restaurants in Monterey Park.[36] Between 1980 and 1990, immigrants from China, Taiwan, Hong Kong, and elsewhere in Asia more than doubled the Chinese population in Los Angeles County, from 93,747 to 245,033. They formed multinuclear concentrations in suburban communities in the San Gabriel Valley. Different from the earlier immigrants, these newcomers came with financial capital and were heavily investing in Los Angeles. While the Chinese population counted for only 2.8 percent of the total population of Los Angeles County, they purchased 20 percent of the homes in the county in 1992. Further, they transformed Los Angeles into the city with the largest number of Chinese-owned firms, replacing San Francisco. The inflow of capital and entrepreneurs from the Chinese diaspora has made the valley's economy an integral part of the Pacific Rim economy.[37]

On the East Coast, similar changes also occurred. Chinese Americans in the New York City area formed a "satellite city" or "global town," reflecting the rapid growth of Asian economies since the 1980s and the higher degree of globalization in the world. From 1965 to 1985, between 200,000 and 600,000 Asian Americans settled in New York City. These new arrivals helped the Chinatown in Manhattan expand from four streets in 1890 to more than twenty commercial streets in the 1980s. Manhattan's Chinatown became a commercial center of Asian goods for New York, New Jersey, Connecticut, and other eastern states. A striking new feature of the newcomers since 1970 was that they brought massive capital from Asia and invested it in manufacturing, banking, real estate, and other services. The new immigrants from Asia also joined some of the older immigrants and second-generation Chinese Americans by choosing to settle in Queens, as Manhattan's Chinatown was already overcrowded and had poor housing and sanitary conditions. Many of them followed the path of the IRT No. 7 Line, dubbed the Oriental Express, into Flushing in Queens,[38] where they intermingled commercially and residentially with other Asian Americans and immigrants from Korea, India, Pakistan, and other Asian countries. The strong business and cultural connections these Asian ethnic neighborhoods had with their homelands earned them such nicknames as Satellite City and Global Town.[39]

In the heartland of the country, Chinese Americans have also accelerated the suburbanization around the city of Chicago, mostly in surrounding Cook County and its suburbs. In 1980, there were 721 Chinese residents recorded in Skokie Village, north of Chicago. Nine other cities, towns, and villages in Cook County each had 100 or more Chinese residents. By 1990, twenty-one cities, towns, and villages in Cook County had a sizable Chinese population. The western suburb of Naperville in nearby DuPage County had over 1,000 Chinese residents. Together there were 20,700 Chinese living in the suburbs, nearly half of the Chinese population reported by the 1990 census.[40] According to the 2000 census, the Chinese American population in Illinois increased by 54 percent, rising from 28,597 in 1980 and 49,936 in 1990 to 76,725 in 2000. The largest number of Chinese Americans, 48,058 in total, reside in Cook County, representing 0.9 percent of the county's entire population.[41]

Occupationally, most Chinese American suburbanites are American-educated professionals from Taiwan and mainland China employed by the area's high-tech industries and research institutions, such as Argonne National Laboratory, Fermi Lab, Abbott Laboratories, Motorola, the University of Chicago, Northwestern University, the Illinois Institute of Technology, and many other such research institutions, universities, and colleges located in the western, northwestern, and northern suburbs surrounding Chicago. Their stable income, human capital, and class resources afford them the lifestyle associated with suburban communities. Gravitating toward new housing developments, better school systems, and newly emerging ethnic supermarkets and services in the suburbs, Chinese American suburbanites readily blend into the dominant American suburban culture. They are complacent with their suburban living conditions and rarely depend on the traditional Chinatown for employment, services, or entertainment, except for sporadic visits on special occasions. As the Chinese American suburban population climbed, ethnic shops and supermarkets soon sprang up in or around these population centers to serve the needs of this fast-growing population. The most illuminating example is the DiHo Supermarket complex in the suburb of Westmont, which attracts a large number of Chinese American residents from nearby areas.[42]

Cultural Communities

While transnational ethnic urban and suburban communities developed on the coastal metropolitan areas, a different form of suburban community—cultural communities—simultaneously emerged in the hinterland and other areas of the country. The cultural community has emerged as a new form of Asian American suburban community since the 1960s. While both urban enclaves and suburban Asian American communities focus on the construction of the physical or geographical space of a given community with identifiable territorial boundaries, cultural communities center on the construction of cultural/social space and are defined by the cultural boundaries of a given ethnic culture rather than geographical borders.

Generally, a cultural community does not necessarily have particular physical boundaries; rather it is defined by the common cultural practices and beliefs of its members. A cultural community is normally constituted by the Asian language schools, Asian religious institutions, Asian American community organizations, Asian American cultural agencies, Asian American political coalitions or ad hoc committees, and the wide range of cultural celebrations and activities facilitated by the aforementioned agencies and groups. A cultural community can also be identified by its economy and demography. Economically, the overwhelming majority of the population of a cultural community are professionally integrated into the larger society; therefore, the ethnic economy of the community does not significantly affect the security of its members and the community as a whole. Demographically, a cultural community contains a substantial percentage of professionals and self-employed entrepreneurs whose economic well-being is more dependent on the larger economy than on an ethnic economy. The former are mostly employed by mainstream not minority employers, and the latter, though self-employed, also depend on the larger society for their economic success.

Cultural community was first identified in St. Louis. Unlike the Chinese suburban communities in Flushing (New York), Monterey Park (California), or Vancouver (Canada) and Toronto (Canada), where Chinese Americans/Canadians invest substantially in banking, manufacturing, real estate, and service industries, Chinese American community in St. Louis primarily consists of professionals employed mostly by mainstream companies and agencies, and their economic well-being does not depend on an ethnic economy. Therefore, economic interest and economic networking are less likely the dominant motives for the formation of the St. Louis Chinese community. Since the inner-city Chinatown, Hop Alley, was leveled in 1966 by urban revival projects, there had been attempts to reestablish an urban Chinatown. The continued urban revival projects and the lack of support from the Chinese community subsequently reduced the Chinese ethnic urban community to a limited commercial strip along Olive Boulevard that is lined with Asian grocery stores, restaurants, real estate offices, Chinese medical clinics, and

FIGURE 8.7 A Korean bride and her American husband, Seoul, South Korea, December 1978. Huping Ling Collection (Courtesy Huang-Suk Harrington).

other service agencies. However, ethnic businesses on Olive Boulevard constitute only 6 percent of all Chinese businesses in the greater St. Louis area. Chinese St. Louisans congregate more frequently in cultural institutions like Chinese language schools, Chinese Christian churches and Buddhist temples during weekends, and cultural activities organized by various community organizations on special occasions and traditional holidays. The over forty community cultural organizations have functioned as the infrastructure of the cultural community there.[43]

The suburban Chinese American communities in Chicagoland (the metropolitan areas of Chicago) are strikingly similar to their counterparts in St. Louis. The members of these communities work largely in American companies and reside in dispersed suburban neighborhoods. They sporadically visit the inner-city Chinatowns only for dining or ethnic grocery shopping; even the latter needs can be sufficiently met by the large suburban Asian supermarkets, such as the DiHo in suburban Westmont. While maintaining their distance from the inner-city Chinatowns, the Chinese American suburbanites regularly and frequently congregate among themselves in cultural and social activities. The Chinese language and heritage schools serve as fundamental community structures among the Chinese American suburban population. Although mostly well-educated biculturally and bilingually, having higher education degrees from both their homeland and the host country, and speaking English fluently at work and Mandarin or Taiwanese at home, they are eager to have their children preserve Chinese linguistic and cultural heritage. This strong desire for linguistic and cultural preservation motivates them to form weekend Chinese languages schools, usually on Saturdays. In 1971, Chinese American professionals from Taiwan founded the Cooperative Chinese Language School in the western suburbs. While the earlier Chinese American suburbanites from Taiwan formed Chinese language schools teaching the "classic" or old style Chinese characters, the newer residents from mainland China founded schools—such as the seven Chinese schools throughout Chicago's suburbs founded in 1989 by the Xilin Association—that teach the new "simplified" Chinese characters used in the PRC since 1954. The 1998–1999 Chicago Chinese Yellow Pages listed thirty-five Chinese language schools, among which eight were in South Chinatown, one in North Chinatown, and twenty-one in the Chicagoland suburbs, not counting the seven Xilin schools.[44]

FIGURE 8.8 An Indian bride at her wedding prior to coming to America to join her student husband, Patna, Bihar, India, 1981. Huping Ling Collection (Courtesy the bride).

The cultural community model is not limited only to St. Louis or Chicago. It is also applicable to communities where physical concentration of the ethnic minority groups is absent, such as when a minority group has economically and professionally integrated into the larger society but culturally has remained distinct from it. The model is especially applicable to communities where the members of ethnic minority groups are overwhelmingly professionals. Further, the cultural community model has been found among other Asian groups or other ethnic Americans in communities across the country.

FIGURE 8.9 Filipino national dresses, 1998. Huping Ling Collection (Courtesy Kit Hadwiger).

Japanese Americans have managed to maintain their community life through preserving cultural and social relationships, a model similar to cultural community. Writers believe that the persistence of Japanese American ethnicity stems from elements in traditional Japanese culture that structure social relationships between group members. They explain why contemporary Japanese Americans are able to retain a high level of involvement in their ethnic community while the vast majority of them have become structurally assimilated into mainstream American life. The answer lies in their ability to perceive all members of their ethnic group as "quasi kin."[45] Similarly, cultural institutions, such as Christian churches and community organizations, are pivotal in stabilizing the Korean American communities in New York.[46] In Koreatown in Los Angeles, the 1.5-generation-run Korean American community organizations cultivate and maintain ethnic political solidarity despite increasing spatial dispersion, class polarization, and ideological differences within the community.[47]

These "less-territory-centered" and more "fluid" spaces are also found among the other Asian American communities.[48] For instance, "Oriental" stores, social halls, community

FIGURE 8.10 Tinikling Dance, a native folk dance in the Philippines, 1999. Huping Ling Collection (Courtesy Kit Hadwiger).

centers, and community newspapers have constituted the "alternative community spaces" among Filipino American communities in Los Angeles and San Diego and have defined ethnic identities and transformed communities.[49] In San Francisco's Excelsior District, a working-class neighborhood bordering San Francisco and Daly City, the Filipino Community Center serves as an "intentional" community to the Filipino residents in the district.[50] A 2000 study also concurs that architecture, daily social interaction, and public ritual events in Little Saigon can "create and sustain a sense of place, foster community identity, and structure social relations."[51]

Cyber Communities through Social Networks

The advancement in information technology and the increase of internet users since the 1990s have created a new type of Asian American community—the cyber community, dubbed as "virtual states," "cybersociety," or "virtual community" by various writers.[52] Various surveys indicate that in the 1990s and 2000s, more than 60 percent of Chinese Americans and Chinese Canadians owned a home PC and had internet access.[53] The launching of the China News Digest (CND) in 1989, for instance, generated a global virtual community for its Chinese language users. The members of the cyber community could work in any occupation and reside in any geographical locality, yet still form a spatial community through internet. The concept of cyber community appears to present a plausible explanation for the many presently IT-savvy Asian Americans, especially Asian

FIGURE 8.11 Thai New Year Celebration, St. Louis, Missouri, April 25, 1999. Huping Ling Collection.

American professionals, whose professional and emotional well-being is closely tied with the internet. Like cultural communities, a cyber community possesses no geographical space, yet it spans the globe and provides broad cyber space for commercial, social, academic, cultural, and recreational activities to its users, who depend on these services/activities to various degrees and derive a sense of community from such activities.

Facebook, a social networking service, is one of the most popular cyber communities that emerged in the 2000s. In February 2004, Mark Zuckerberg, a Harvard student majoring in computer science, with his college roommates and fellow students Eduardo Saverin, Andrew McCollum, Dustin Moskovitz, and Chris Hughes, founded Facebook. Initially, Facebook was intended to be a website providing social networking only for Harvard students. It soon was expanded to other colleges in the Boston area, the Ivy League, and Stanford University. It later added support for students at colleges across the country, to high school students, and eventually to anyone aged thirteen and over. According to *Social Media Today*, 128.9 million or 41.6 percent of the American population had a Facebook account by April 2010.[54] Facebook purchased fb.com in January 2011 and bought Instagram, a photo sharing website, for $1 billion in 2012, thus securing its dominance in the social networking service industry. By May 2012, it was estimated that Facebook had over 900 million active users.[55] By August 2013, Zuckerberg, the CEO of Facebook, claimed the service had over five billion users.[56]

Researchers have analyzed the connections between a large subset of more than a billion users of Facebook to reveal that the system has a very strong structure, resembling

> ### DECODING OUR NETWORK COMMUNITIES
>
> A new way of finding community structure within networks—anything from social networks such as Facebook, to power grids, political voting networks, and protein interaction networks in biology—could help us understand how people are connected and how connections change over time. The new technique, developed by a team from the University of North Carolina, University of Oxford, and Harvard University, aims to be more realistic than conventional approaches, which only capture one type of connection or a network at only one moment in time.
>
> The new approach captures the totality of connections within a network and could be used to examine the different ways communities form; for example, analyzing relationships between university students and staff across many different connections such as Facebook friendship, college affiliation, and subject studied. Alternatively, it could be used to track how one type of connection—such as Facebook friendship—changes over time.
>
> The technique is not limited to social networks as community detection has the potential to find important groups in many other applications, such as protein-protein interaction networks, transportation networks, and political voting networks.
>
> A report of the team's work, advancing the theory of community detection, was recently published in the journal *Science*.
>
> "Capturing the complexity of people's relationships through networks such as Facebook and how these relationships change over time is a huge challenge," said Dr. Mason Porter of Oxford University's Mathematical Institute, an author of the report. "Our new approach, which can be applied to any type of network, is potentially much better than existing methods at identifying what makes a 'community' within a network and at tracking how such groupings evolve over time."
>
> Source: "Decoding Our Network Communities," *Science Daily*, May 24, 2010, http://www.sciencedaily.com/releases/2010/05/100521210128.htm.

a community. Emilio Ferrara of the Department of Mathematics at the University of Messina, Italy, anonymized Facebook data and used two sophisticated algorithms to disclose the hidden network structure among one million users of Facebook. His research displays that Facebook has three common properties of the social networks in the everyday world and networks found in the future. First, it demonstrates the "small world" effect, known as "six degrees of separation," meaning that it is possible to connect the majority of members of a network with all the other members through a number of links of mutual friends or connections. Second, Facebook follows the power law degree distribution where there are many users with a small number of connections and only a very small number of people with a huge number of connections. Third,

Facebook manifests as a community of interacting users rather than a collection of individuals.[57] Similar research could also apply to other social networks, such as Twitter and LinkedIn, to spot the similarities and differences.

Surveys have noted that young Asian Americans are the most likely Facebook users. For instance, a Nielsen report shows that the profile of the type of internet user who is most likely to use Facebook is an Asian American female aged between eighteen and thirty-four who lives in New England, has at least a bachelor's degree, and makes less than $50,000 a year.[58] As indicative or misleading as it may be, the report nevertheless points out the importance of Facebook as a social networking community to the younger and socially and technologically more connected generations of Asian Americans and the general American population. While there has not been research available on the topic, it is reasonable to assume that Facebook constitutes a community-like social structure on the internet, as indicated in the sidebar article.

Compared to Facebook, WeChat probably is a more popular software among Asian Americans, especially Chinese Americans. WeChat (literally "micro message" in Chinese) is a multifunctional application created by Tencent (Tengxun in Chinese, named after Huateng Ma, the CEO of the company) in 2010 and launched in 2011. It soon became the single most used application worldwide due to its wide range of functions including messaging, social media, and online payment, with over one billion monthly active users in 2018.[59] However, the most concerning issue on WeChat has been its usage as a "mass surveillance network" in China, as users' activities are analyzed, tracked, and shared with Chinese authorities. Even data transmitted by accounts registered outside China are surveilled, analyzed, and used to build up censorship algorithms in China.[60]

Despite concerns regarding its security function, most of the Chinese studying, traveling, or working in the United States and Chinese Americans with familial and social connections largely Chinese have to or are accustomed to use WeChat in their daily economic and social life because of its convenience and versatility.

The hostility between India and China in recent years resulted in the banning of WeChat along with all applications made in China.[61] Former U.S. president Donald Trump also sought to ban U.S. "transactions" with WeChat through an executive order, but it was blocked by a preliminary injunction issued by the U.S. District Court for the Northern District of California in September 2020.[62]

Individuals, agencies, and organizations have employed social media networks to disseminate news and mobilize the communities. Many Asian Americans remain connected with their colleagues, friends, and relatives whom they don't normally meet in the locale of their workplace or residence. Professional and community organizations also utilize social media in disseminating information to members and therefore a wider audience through the ripple effect of social media. The Association for Asian American Studies, for instance, posts job listings, conference announcements, calls for papers and conferences, blurbs about new publications and accomplishments of its members, news updates, debates, and discussions with its members through the organization's Facebook page; the members of the association further pass on the information to individuals of other circles with which they are involved.

Similarly but more effectively, Chinese American communities used WeChat to organize their economic and social life through transforming various WeChat groups into emergency networking structure during the COVID-19 pandemic (2020–2023). For instance, the various groups of parents of schoolchildren are voluntarily turned into shopping networks connecting around ten families, whose members would share the shopping responsibilities, along with other economic and social activities. Members of each such group have formed tight bonds resembling the traditional Chinese *baojia* system in which ten families were organized into a *bao*, and ten of such *baos* in turn formed a *jia*. This voluntary yet very effective social networking has been extremely popular in California, New York, and other areas with significant Chinese American population. The most illuminous example is found in South Chinatown in Chicago. When almost all Chinese commercial areas in the major U.S. cities had been inflicted with robberies, looting, and arsons associated with the George Floyd protests during late May 2020 and the following months, Chicago's South Chinatown was the only Chinese American commercial and residential community spared. One of the primary reasons behind the miracle lies in the diligent daily patrolling of South Chinatown by the Chinese Gun-owners Association in Chicago organized through WeChat.[63]

ASIAN AMERICAN COMMUNITIES IN HISTORICAL PERSPECTIVE

History tells us that an immigrant or ethnic group's advancement in America generally follows three stages: physical concentration for economic survival, cultural congregation for ethnic identity, and political participation for a sense of democracy and justice. The transformation of Asian American communities from ethnic urban enclaves to suburban communities with physical spaces, or cultural communities or cyber communities with social spaces, demonstrates Asian Americans' upward social mobility. The population shift from inner-city ethnic enclaves to dispersed suburban communities or cultural communities, where residents own their homes and automobiles, indicates a higher level of socioeconomic integration into the majority society for Asian Americans.

Meanwhile, urban enclaves are often devastated by continuous urban development projects for freeways, shopping malls, and other infrastructure and facilities. Asian American communities have developed various strategies to preserve Asian ethnic heritage and to promote the ethnic economy. Collaborating with municipal governments and developing tourist-centered ethnic commercial districts has been a common strategy to preserve ethnic heritage and to promote ethnic economies and cultural diversity, as demonstrated in Chinatowns in San Francisco, Manhattan, and New York and South Chinatown in Chicago, as well as Little Saigon in Orange County and many other tourist/commercial-oriented ethnic urban communities. Mobilizing community financial resources and applying political pressure on city councils to designate historic districts for Asian ethnic communities is another effective method, as illustrated by the examples of Little Tokyo, Koreatown, and Hi-Fi in Los Angeles and Little Manila in Stockton, California.

Social networks such as Facebook offer a community-like structure, which forges a strong sense of community and common identity and can be used as an effective means of mass communication and political participation. Numerous Asian American community organizations have used Facebook as one of the fastest ways to disseminate news and to mobilize the communities. As the cyber communities are still a relatively new form of Asian American community, studies on its strengths and challenges are still yet to appear.

KEY TERMS

urban enclaves
ethnic suburban communities

cultural communities
cyber communities

REVIEW QUESTIONS

1. List the internal and external factors that impacted the formation of ethnic urban enclaves.
2. What are the similarities and dissimilarities of the various Asian American urban communities?
3. How do you define a community with social or cultural boundaries?
4. Give examples of cyber communities and explain their functions as a community.

FILMS

Chiang, S. Leo (producer/director). *A Village Called Versailles*. 54-minute documentary on a Vietnamese community in eastern New Orleans in the aftermath of Hurricane Katrina. 2010.

Cho, Michael (producer/director). *Another America*. 56-minute documentary on Korean and African American conflict as exemplified by the 1992 Los Angeles riots and Michael Cho's family history. 1996.

Choy, Curtis (producer/director). *The Fall of the I-Hotel*. 58-minute documentary on the eviction of the International Hotel's tenants, mostly Filipino Americans. 1993.

Jang, Lindsey, and Robert C. Winn (producers/directors). *Saigon USA*. 56-minute documentary on the Vietnamese community in Little Saigon in Orange County, CA. 2004.

Nair, Mira (producer/director). *The Namesake*. 122-minute drama about the American-born son of Indian immigrants who feels pulled between his ethnic heritage and his desire to assimilate. 2007.

FURTHER READING

Chan, Sucheng. *Survivors: Cambodian Refugees in the United States*. Urbana: University of Illinois Press, 2004.

Chung, Angie Y. *Legacies of Struggle: Conflict and Cooperation in Korean American Politics*. Palo Alto, CA: Stanford University Press, 2007.

España-Maram, Linda. *Creating Masculinity in Los Angeles's Little Manila: Working Class Filipinos and Popular Culture, 1920s–1950s*. New York: Columbia University Press, 2006.

Espiritu, Yen Le. *Home Bound: Filipino American Lives across Cultures, Communities, and Countries*. Berkeley: University of California Press, 2003.

Fong, Timothy P. *The First Suburban Chinatown: The Remaking of Monterey Park, California*. Philadelphia: Temple University Press, 1994.

Fugita, Stephen. *Japanese American Ethnicity: The Persistence of Community*. Seattle: University of Washington Press, 1991.

Ignacio, Emily Noelle. *Building Diaspora: Filipino Cultural Community Formation on the Internet*. New Brunswick, NJ: Rutgers University Press, 2005.

Kim, Claire Jean. *Bitter Fruit: The Politics of Black-Korean Conflict in New York City*. New Haven, CT: Yale University Press, 2003.

Kim, Sharon. *A Faith of Our Own: Second-Generation Spirituality in Korean American Churches*. New Brunswick, NJ: Rutgers University Press, 2010.

Kurashige, Scott. *The Shifting Grounds of Race: Black and Japanese Americans in the Making of Multiethnic Los Angeles*. Princeton, NJ: Princeton University Press, 2008.

Kwong, Peter. *The New Chinatown*. New York: Hill & Wang, 1987.

Li, Wei. *Ethnoburb: The New Ethnic Community in Urban America*. Honolulu: University of Hawai'i Press, 2009.

Ling, Huping, ed. *Asian America: Forming New Communities, Expanding Boundaries*. New Brunswick, NJ: Rutgers University Press, 2009.

———. *Chinese Americans in the Heartland: Migration, Work, and Community*. New Brunswick, NJ: Rutgers University Press, 2022.

———. *Chinese Chicago: Race, Transnational Migration, and Community since 1870.* Stanford, CA: Stanford University Press, 2012.

———. *Chinese St. Louis: From Enclave to Cultural Community.* Philadelphia: Temple University Press, 2004.

———, ed. *Emerging Voices: Experiences of Underrepresented Asian Americans.* New Brunswick, NJ: Rutgers University Press, 2008.

Lyman, Stanford. *Chinatown and Little Tokyo: Power, Conflict, and Community among Chinese and Japanese Immigrants in America.* Millwood, NY: Associated Faculty Press, 1986.

Min, Gap Pyong. *Caught in the Middle: Korean Communities in New York and Los Angeles.* Berkeley: University of California Press, 1996.

Nakamura, Lisa. *Cybertypes: Race, Ethnicity, and Identity on the Internet.* New York: Routledge, 2002.

Okamura, Jonathan. *Imaging the Filipino Diaspora: Transnational Relations, Identities, and Communities.* New York: Taylor & Francis, 1998.

Park, Kyeyoung, and Jessica Kim. "The Contested Nexus of Los Angeles Koreatown." *Amerasia Journal* 34, no. 3 (2008): 127–150.

Ray, Krishnendu. *The Migrant's Table: Meals and Memories in Bengali-American Households.* Philadelphia: Temple University Press, 2004.

Spickard, Paul. *Japanese Americans: The Formation and Transformations of an Ethnic Group.* New Brunswick, NJ: Rutgers University Press, 2009.

Valverde, Kieu-Linh Caroline. *Transnationalizing Viet Nam: Community, Culture, and Politics in the Diaspora.* Philadelphia: Temple University Press, 2012.

Võ, Linda Trinh. *Mobilizing an Asian American Community.* Philadelphia: Temple University Press, 2004.

Zhou, Min. *Chinatown: The Socioeconomic Potential of an Urban Enclave.* Philadelphia: Temple University Press, 1992.

PART IV

The Future of Asian America, 2020s–

9

THEORIZING ASIAN AMERICA
Significant Theories and Issues

CHAPTER OUTLINE

Asian American Movement and the Construction of Pan-Asian Ethnicity
Challenges of Asian American Identities in Recent Decades
Asian American Panethnicity in Historical Perspective

SIGNIFICANT EVENTS

1968	Asian American movement begins; a panethnic term, "Asian American" emerges unifying various groups of Americans with Asian ancestry; the founding of the Asian American Political Alliance (AAPA), the first group to call itself Asian American, at UC Berkeley; the establishment of the first ethnic studies program at San Francisco State College
1968–1969	Third World strikes at San Francisco State College from November 6, 1968, to March 27, 1969, and at UC Berkeley from January 19, 1968, to March 14, 1969, demand the establishment of autonomous ethnic studies programs on campus
1969	In January, the AAPA, the Chinese Students Club, and Nisei Student's Clubs sponsor a conference called "Asian American Experience in America—Yellow Identity," with about 900 Asian Americans attending; conference participants adopt the panethnic term "Asian American" as their identity
1970s	Asian Americans for Action (Triple A) is formed on the East Coast; Asian Union in Madison, Asian American Alliance in Illinois, and Asian American Political Alliance in Minneapolis are formed in the Midwest
1968–1973	First wave of institutionalization of Asian American studies: programs or individual Asian American studies courses are created at colleges and universities mainly on the West Coast

1980s	Interracial marriage and dating become more acceptable
1990s	Transnationalism theory is formulated; "hemispheric approach" picks up momentum; queer Asian American studies become noticeable
1990s–2000s	Second wave of institutionalization of Asian American studies: Asian American studies programs are developed in locations outside of California, such as the East Coast, Midwest, and South
2000s	Under "the Great Third Coast" approach, the Midwest and South are incorporated into Asian American studies; studies of underrepresented Asian Americans (newer and smaller groups) are incorporated into the field
2001	September 11 terrorist attacks; the USA PATRIOT Act of 2001 passes to secure the land and its people; the enforcement of the law leads to numerous detentions and deportations of innocent Muslim immigrants and American citizens of Middle Eastern, South Asian, and African ancestries
2002	The Department of Homeland Security is created

THE CIVIL RIGHTS, Black Power, and women's liberation movements in the 1960s and 1970s propelled the rise of the Asian American movement. Inspired and encouraged by their civil rights experience, and supported by its rapidly increasing population following the reform of U.S. immigration policy in 1965, Asian community activists and scholars created a new collective panethnic identity—*Asian American*—to claim their lot and to assert their equal rights in America. The Asian American movement sired Asian American studies academic programs and courses at colleges and universities across the country to serve the Asian American community and to develop research agendas on the history and current conditions of Asian Americans. Within nearly five decades of struggle and striving since its creation in 1968, Asian American studies has established itself as a well-developed academic discipline. It embraces degree-granting graduate and undergraduate programs and course offerings on university and college campuses across the United States and has a national organization with annual meetings, regional sub-organizations, and an official journal—the *Journal of Asian American Studies*. Asian American community activists and academics are continuously working to connect "campus" and "community," exploring the ever-evolving meaning of *Asian America*.

ASIAN AMERICAN MOVEMENT AND THE CONSTRUCTION OF PAN-ASIAN ETHNICITY

The Asian American movement consists of a range of radical political activities initiated by Asian American students in the late 1960s and early 1970s spontaneously across the country. The major goal of the movement was to gain political power on U.S. college campuses for the benefit of the growing Asian American community since the 1960s. It set an agenda for the articulation of Asian American political consciousness and resulted in the institutionalization of Asian American studies. In the movement, a pan-Asian ethnic identity for all Americans with Asian ancestries was conceived and has since become the core concept of Asian American studies.

Origins of the Movement

The birth of the Asian American movement was prompted by multiple forces in a tumultuous period in post–World War II history. Internationally, revolutions throughout the Third World (a term coined during the Cold War era that refers to countries not allied with either NATO or the Eastern Bloc but has often been used for countries in Africa, Asia, and Latin America that have struggled to attain steady economic development), the Zengakuren (All-Japan League of Student Self-Government) Student Movement in Japan, and the Great Proletarian Cultural Revolution in China provided revolutionary energy to the movement. Domestically, the civil rights movement, anti–Vietnam War activities, and the Black Power movement influenced the thinking of many Asian Americans, who rose to question the nature of American democracy. While participating in the civil rights movement, Asian Americans realized that the struggle for social justice in America was more than an African American and European American issue, and it also involved other people of color. The influx of the new immigrants since the 1965 Immigration Act on the one hand reinforced the Asian American population, on the other further complicated the already deteriorating working and housing conditions in many gateway Asian American communities. Asian American community conditions—garment sweatshops, substandard and overcrowded housing, poor schools, and evictions caused by urban development—all became rallying points for expanding the movement's influence.

Student activism was pivotal to the movement. On the West Coast, student strikes spearheaded the movement. In 1968, graduate students at the University of California, Berkeley and civil rights veterans Yuji Ichioka and Emma Gee formed a small Asian American caucus, which became a forerunner of the Asian American Political Alliance (AAPA), the first group to call itself Asian American, a term coined by Ichioka. The AAPA also adopted a key facet of Black Power ideology—militant self-reliance. Soon, Asian

American became a term unifying various groups of Americans with Asian ancestry. The AAPA inspired many Asian Americans to participate in the social movement. Asian American students and other students of color took part in the Third World strikes at San Francisco State College from November 6, 1968, to March 27, 1969, and at UC Berkeley from January 19, 1968, to March 14, 1969. As part of the Third World Liberation Front (TWLF), they demanded self-determination for themselves and their communities. Their immediate goal was to establish autonomous ethnic studies programs on campus to reflect the demographical changes in Asian American communities and to address the pressing issues concerning Asian Americans.

Indirectly influenced by the Berkeley AAPA, Asian American students at Yale and Columbia also formed an East Coast AAPA. In 1969, activists Kazu Iijima and Minn Matsuda, two Nisei women with a history of fighting social injustice, formed one of the first pan-Asian organizations on the East Coast, Asian Americans for Action (Triple A). They were soon joined by college students, peace activists, and Japanese American internment camp survivors. Triple A placed the Vietnam War in the larger context of imperialism and racism and called for U.S. withdrawal from Vietnam and an end to the U.S.-Japan Security Treaty. In the Midwest, the civil rights, antiwar, and United Farm Workers movements influenced the formation of Madison's Asian Union, Illinois's Asian American Alliance, and Minneapolis's Asian American Political Alliance in the early 1970s.

Contents of the Movement

YELLOW IDENTITY CONFERENCE AND IDENTITY CONSTRUCTION. Student conferences and symposiums were important in developing Asian American identity and culture. Emulating the Black Power movement, Asian American activists launched their own Yellow Power movement. On January 11, 1969, the AAPA, the Chinese Students Clubs, and the Nisei Student's Clubs sponsored a conference called "Asian American Experience in America—Yellow Identity." About 900 Asian Americans, mainly Chinese and Japanese Americans from the West Coast, attended the conference. Organizers identified important issues for Asian American activism, including identity consciousness, Asian American studies, community organizing, student organizing, and support for the Third World Liberation Strike at San Francisco State College (SFSC).

However, the "Yellow" reference was dropped when Filipino Americans rejected the term, claiming that they were brown, not yellow. Meanwhile, other pan-Asian community organizations used the term "Oriental" to define their organizations. But Asian American activists also objected to the term, as it provoked stereotypical images of Asians as seductive sex objects, such as Susie Wong, or wily and even sinister characters such as Charlie Chan or Fu Manchu. The term also reflected a Eurocentric colonialist and imperialistic connotation: Oriental means "East," and Asia was the "East" only when viewed from the Europeans' perspective, thus the term "Oriental" suggests the passivity and submission of Asians. To define their Asian heritage and their American identity, they adopted the term "Asian American."

SERVICE-ORIENTED COMMUNITY ACTIVISM. The Asian American Movement prompted the establishment of local community-based organizations. Asian American activists spilled into local communities to establish community centers and organizations that endeavored to "serve the people," a term adopted from the Chinese communist ideology, to provide services that met the community's needs. In San Francisco, they formed the Asian Community Center, Asian Legal Services, the Chinese Progressive Association, the International Hotel Tenants Association, the Japanese Community Youth Center, J-Town Collective, and the Kearny Street Workshop. In New York Chinatown, Asian American activists established the Basement Workshop to provide space for community media projects as well as English as a second language (ESL), citizenship, and youth programs.

Significance of the Asian American Movement

The most significant legacy of the Asian American Movement was its construction of Asian American panethnicity, which enabled and empowered Asian Americans to build their sociopolitical base in ethnic communities and brought about the establishment of Asian American studies as an interdisciplinary academic field, which in turn helps strengthen the Asian American ethnic communities by producing generations of Asian American professionals, scholars, and social activists.

Institutionalization of Asian American Studies

Following the establishment of the first ethnic studies program at San Francisco State College in 1968, by the early 1970s scores of programs and individual Asian American studies (AAS) courses were created at colleges and universities across the country. According to a survey conducted in 1978, at least fourteen universities established AAS programs, including four campuses of the University of California: Berkeley, Los Angeles, Davis, and Santa Barbara; five campuses of the California State University: San Francisco, Fresno, San Jose, Sacramento, and Long Beach; the University of Southern California; the University of Washington; the University of Colorado; the University of Hawai'i; and City College of New York.[1] Most of the AAS programs focused on teaching, relating to the socialization of Asian American students, and increasing their ethnic consciousness and self-awareness. The second priority was involvement in Asian American community organizations and activities. The third emphasized the development and dissemination of new social and political perspectives and research on Asian Americans.

Before the 1990s, the majority of AAS programs were concentrated on the West Coast, especially in California. In the 1990s, a second wave of the student movement focused on AAS issues developed outside of California. The rapid Asian American population increase in the 1980s and 1990s led to a dramatic increase in Asian American student enrollment in colleges nationwide. Meanwhile, there was a lack of sufficient courses in the discipline. The demand for Asian American courses prompted the establishment of AAS programs on campuses on the East Coast, in the Midwest, and further in the South in the 2000s. While some universities, such as the University of Pennsylvania, were able to establish an AAS program peacefully, many other universities faced formidable obstacles in complying with the desire of Asian American students, which led to student protests on campuses.[2]

Among the obstacles faced by AAS programs across the country, the lack of support or resistance in some cases from university administrations has been a universal challenge. Student and faculty requests for AAS curricula often fell on unsympathetic ears when they reached university administrators. To overcome the barriers created by less supportive administrative bodies, Asian American specialists have developed a variety of strategies for establishing AAS programs. On campuses located in communities with relatively sizeable Asian American populations, Asian American activists could succeed in creating independent AAS programs. At institutions with small Asian American populations, faculty members specializing in AAS had to rally with colleagues from Asian studies or from ethnic studies to form joint Asian and AAS programs or to be incorporated into the broader ethnic studies programs.[3]

CHALLENGES OF ASIAN AMERICAN IDENTITIES IN RECENT DECADES

In the first two decades following its birth, the field was preoccupied with the tasks of justifying its very existence and of institutionalizing its academic programs. Scholarly discourses of this period focused on the nature and scope of AAS and its core theories. Interdisciplinary and multidisciplinary in nature, it focused on history, identity, and community in both curricular development and research. Scholars applied various theoretical approaches—Marxism, racial formation, colonialism, imperialism, postcolonialism, postmodernism, among others—in their investigations of assimilation and adaptation, identity, and consciousness. Meanwhile, being keenly aware of its existence as the product of a social movement, AAS consciously linked itself with the community and activism. It served as a training center for future community leaders and connected academics and students with grassroots community organizations.

With the rapid development of AAS programs in the 1990s, institutional legitimization of AAS has in general decreased as an urgent agenda, although in some states numerous politicians remain less sympathetic to AAS. The field is pressed to reflect increasingly more diverse constituencies. Expanding the agenda of AAS has thus become the new focus. Since the 1990s, in terms of new paradigms interpreting Asian American experiences, transnationalism and hemispheric perspective have been employed by writers; new locales of AAS in the Midwest and South have emerged to reflect the rapid Asian American population growth in those regions; new demographic groups such as lesbian, gay, bisexual, and transgender (LGBT or LGBTQIA+) groups have been incorporated into the field;[4] underrepresented Asian American ethnic groups (smaller and/or less visible groups, such as Burmese, Cambodian, Hmong, Indonesian, Mong, and Thai) have also begun to proclaim their voices. Meanwhile, neo-exclusionism—hate crimes or discriminatory treatment of Asian Muslims—has also alarmed Asian American communities, which have diligently worked on developing strategies and programs to educate its constituencies and the general public.[5]

Transnational and Hemispheric Perspectives

TRANSNATIONALISM. Since the 1990s, a growing number of scholars have noted that immigrants have lived their lives across geographical borders and maintained close ties to homelands. A number of social scientists have begun to use the term "transnational" to describe such cross-national, cross-cultural phenomena. A group of anthropologists have analyzed and conceptualized transnational migration in more precise language in their coedited work in 1992. They define transnationalism as "the emergence of a social process in which migrants establish social fields that cross geographic, cultural, and political borders. Immigrants are understood to be transmigrants when they develop and maintain multiple relations—familial, economic, social, organizational, religious, and political—that span borders.... The multiplicity of migrants' involvements in both the home and host societies is a central element of transnationalism."[6] Since then, writers from various disciplines have further delineated and evaluated the theorization of transnationalism.[7] As the concept of transnationalism has become a compelling theoretical framework for interpreting manifestations of international migration, a number of Asian American historians have also endorsed the idea in their monographs.[8]

HEMISPHERIC APPROACH. Scholars have also challenged the sole focus of AAS on the "east-west threads" of migration, insisting that migrants moved not only east and west but also north and south and that AAS should pay close attention to Asian migration throughout the Americas. For instance, 42 percent of prewar Japanese migration to the Americas (1868–1941) was to Latin America. During the World War II era,

33 percent of Chinese in the Americas resided in Latin America, while 46 percent lived in the United States and 21 percent in Canada. The broadening of AAS to include the "inter-American dynamics" of Asian migration would help "situate the history of Asian Americans in local, regional, and global contexts."[9] Since the 1990s, scholarly work on Canadian Chinese and Chinese in Latin America has expanded and contributed to our understanding of Asian American experiences.[10]

"The Great Third Coast" of Asian American Studies: South and Midwest

In recent decades, a new demographic trend has occurred among Asian Americans; southern and midwestern states experienced more rapid population growth than California, Hawaii, and New York, the states with the highest Asian American population. As the 2010 census for the first time counted the Asian alone and Native Hawaii and Other Pacific Islander (NHOPI) alone populations separately, we will list them accordingly in table 9.1. From 2000 to 2010, the fastest Asian alone and NHOPI alone population growth occurred in the South and Midwest. Twelve states in the South (as defined by the Census Bureau) experienced growth greater than 50 percent in both or either of the two groups: Arkansas (78.5), Alabama (71.0), Delaware (75.6), Florida (70.8), Georgia (81.6), Kentucky (64.5), Maryland (51.2), North Carolina (83.8), South Carolina (64.0), Tennessee (61.0), Texas (71.5), and Virginia (68.5). Eight states in the Midwest—Indiana, Iowa, Kansas, Minnesota, Missouri, Nebraska, North Dakota, and South Dakota—and one state in the Northeast (Vermont) experienced growth greater than 50 percent in their Asian alone and NHOPI alone populations. In comparison, the growth of Asian alone or NHOPI alone populations in California, Hawaii, and New York fell below 36 percent (see table 9.1).

This demographic change prompts the Asian American community and academia to call for the field to expand beyond its traditional scope—that is, a focus on the West and East Coasts and Hawaii—to incorporate "the Great Third Coast"—the South and Midwest—into the Asian American experience.

The growth of AAS academic programs in the Midwest and South is witness to the expansion of the field. AAS at the University of Illinois Urbana-Champaign was founded in 1997. It is currently one of the largest AAS programs in the Midwest, with fourteen core and ten affiliated faculty members. The history of Asian American student organizations at the University of Illinois is diverse. Several originated as clubs for Asian international students (e.g., the Indian Students Association and the Philippine Students Association) and later evolved into organizations for Asian American students, whereas several others were conceived primarily for Asian American students (e.g., the Asian American Association and the Taiwanese American Students Club). Regardless of the origins of these student groups, it was the collaborative efforts of the various Asian

TABLE 9.1 ASIAN AMERICAN POPULATION CHANGE IN SOUTHERN AND MIDWESTERN STATES IN COMPARISON WITH CALIFORNIA, HAWAII, AND NEW YORK, 2000–2010

	Asian alone		Native Hawaiian and other Pacific Islander alone	
	% of population	% change	% of population	% change
Southern states				
Alabama	1.1	71.0	0.1	117.0
Arkansas	1.2	78.5	0.2	251.5
Delaware	3.2	76.0		
Florida	2.4	70.8	0.1	42.4
Georgia	3.2	81.6	0.1	42.4
Kentucky	1.1	64.5	0.1	71.3
Maryland	5.5	51.2	0.1	37.1
North Carolina	2.2	83.8	0.1	65.8
South Carolina	1.3	64.0	0.1	66.2
Tennessee	1.4	61.0	0.1	65.2
Texas	3.8	71.5	0.1	50.0
Virginia	5.5	68.5	0.1	51.5
Midwestern states				
Indiana	1.6	73.3		
Iowa	1.7	44.9	0.1	98.5
Kansas	2.4	44.8	0.1	70.4
Minnesota	4.0	50.9		
Missouri	1.6	59.2	0.1	97.0
Nebraska	1.8	47.2	0.1	53.0
North Dakota	1.0	91.6		
South Dakota	0.9	73.8		51.0
Wisconsin				
Northeast				
Vermont	1.3	52.3		
California	13.0	31.5	0.4	23.4
Hawaii	38.6	3.2	10.0	19.3
New York	7.3	35.9		−0.6

Source: Compiled by Huping Ling according to U.S. Census Bureau, "2010 Census Result, Population Change by State: 2000–2010" (2010), http://2010.census.gov/2010census/data/.

American student organizations and the faculty, staff, and administration that resulted in the formation of the program in AAS. In fall 1997, the Asian American Studies Committee was organized, with the charge to build an academic program in AAS. George Yu became AAS's first director and served a five-year term. This academic program was created in fall 2000, with six faculty lines filled. In fall 2002, the minor in AAS became available, and Kent Ono was hired as director of the program.[11]

The AAS program at the University of Minnesota followed suit. A state with a reputation for its pronounced German and Scandinavian presence (Americans of German ancestry consisted of 38 percent of the state's residents and Americans of Scandinavian ancestry 32 percent on the 2010 U.S. census), Minnesota has become a magnet for immigrants from countries throughout Asia since the 1970s when Chinese, Japanese, and Filipinos migrated to the state. In the late 1970s and the 1980s, Southeast Asians including Hmong, Lao, Cambodians, and Vietnamese further helped the state's Asian population growth. In the past few decades, refugees from Tibet, Burma, and Thailand have also made Minnesota home. The 2010 U.S. census demonstrated that Minneapolis and Saint Paul have the greatest concentration of Asian Americans in the interior of the United States (7.2 percent).[12]

The burgeoning Asian American population makes Minnesota an exciting research site for studying and addressing the challenges faced both by new refugees and immigrants and by earlier generations of Asian Americans. Beginning in 1998, faculty, staff, graduate and undergraduate students, and artists, leaders, and activists in the Twin Cities organized the Asian American Studies Initiative at the University of Minnesota. They recognized a need to reframe for Minnesota a discipline traditionally centered on the East and West Coasts and sought to establish an academic presence on campus. In 2003, those efforts became a reality when the regents of the University of Minnesota voted to establish the AAS program and undergraduate studies minor.[13]

While the larger land-grant universities in the Midwest established independent AAS programs, universities and colleges with fewer resources in the Midwest also established joint AAS programs, in connection with ethnic studies or Asian studies, in the 1990s. For instance, Truman State University, a public liberal arts institution in Kirksville, Missouri, launched a number of courses on AAS in 1991 and finally established a joint degree-granting program of Asian studies in 2000, with three concentrations on AAS, East Asian studies, and South/pan-Asian studies, respectively.

In the South, student protests prompted the establishment of a Center for Asian American Studies at the University of Texas at Austin. The power and strength of the Asian American community have been first reflected in the growth of the Asian American student population at UT Austin, which doubled every six to eight years, reaching 6,236 in 2000. The rapidly increasing Asian American student body soon discovered that their image in the educational mirror was missing and consequently initiated the movement to create an AAS program in 1992. The student initiative finally propelled the founding of the center in 2000, making the center the first AAS program in the nation as a creation of student activism.

The Association of Asian American Studies (AAAS) has recently held its annual conference more frequently in the South and Midwest, to reflect the demographic change. The AAAS annual conference was held in Atlanta in 2006, Chicago in 2008, Austin in

2010, and New Orleans in 2011. These conferences brought scholars and community activists to the rapidly expanding Asian American population centers, learning about the development and concerns of the local Asian American communities, discussing strategies to address these concerns, and laying out research agendas for the field.

Scholarly work on the Midwest has also appeared to mirror the new demographic transformation of Asian America. Three monographs feature the two major midwestern metropolises—St. Louis and Chicago. *Chinese St. Louis: From Enclave to Cultural Community*, published in 2004, hails the triumph of ordinary Chinese men and women in the city despite hardship and adversity and defines the nature, scope, and applicability of a "cultural community" model, which employs cultural institutions, such as Chinese language schools, churches, and community organizations as the infrastructure and social boundaries of the community. *Chinese Chicago: Race, Transnational Migration, and Community since 1870*, released in 2012, chronicles the Chinese American communities since 1870s and their significance as centers for regional, national, and transnational socioeconomic developments. *Chinese Americans in the Heartland: Migration, Work, and Community*, published in 2022, draws rich evidences from various government records, personal stories and interviews, and media reports, and sheds light on the commonalities and uniqueness of the region, as compared to the Asian American communities on the East and West Coast and Hawaii.[14] A more recent anthology edited by Sook Wilkinson and Victor Jew in 2015 offers a close glimpse into Michigan's Asian American communities.[15]

Queer Asian America

Although queer Asian America appears to be a recent phenomenon since the 1990s, it actually has a longer history, and its presence is attributed to the continued efforts from Asian American lesbian/gay activists, writers, and scholars in the last decades of the twentieth century. They worked and organized both within and outside of various social movements—feminism, civil rights, Third World liberation, anti–Vietnam War protests, Black Power, and gay liberation. During this period, two historic developments made the rise of queer AAS possible. The first development occurred in the 1980s, which witnessed the formation and proliferation of various Asian American lesbian/gay organizations in metropolitan centers. These included Boston Asian Gay Males and Lesbians (1979), Asian Pacific Lesbians and Gays (Los Angeles, 1980), the Association of Lesbian and Gay Asians (San Francisco, 1981), Asian Lesbians of the East Coast (New York, 1983), Asian Pacific Lesbians and Friends (Los Angeles, 1983), Gay Asian Rap (Los Angeles, 1984), Gay Asian Pacific Alliance (San Francisco, 1988), Gay Asian Pacific Support Network (Los Angeles, 1988), Asian Pacific Sisters (San Francisco, 1989), and Gay Asian Pacific Islander Men of New York (1990). The second development was the

FIGURE 9.1 Aqua DC gaysian—DC Gay Pride Parade 2012. Courtesy Tim Evanson.

publication of books by various Asian American lesbian writers, such as Willyce Kim (*Curtains of Light*, 1970), Barbara Noda (*Strawberries*, 1979), Kitty Tsui (*Words of a Woman Who Breathes Fire*, 1986), and Merle Woo (*Yellow Woman Speaks*, 1986) during the late 1970s and 1980s. These works ushered the Asian American lesbian subject into mainstream feminist writings.[16]

In the 1990s, scholars of queer AAS began to break new ground in AAS by incorporating the LGBTQIA+ Asian American experience into the public discourse. *Amerasia Journal*, then the sole scholarly and advocacy periodical on AAS, published a special issue on Asian American gay, lesbian, and bisexual identities and orientations in 1994, containing a series of scholarly discussions, narratives of interviews, gay and lesbian community studies, literary critiques, roundtable discussions, and cultural creations. Among the collections, Dana Takagi's essay injected the topic of sexuality, particularly lesbian, gay, and bisexual identity, into the landscape of Asian America. Takagi challenged the rather static cultural nationalist concept of racial identity of Asian America and urged scholars to situate and think about both sexual and racial identities in AAS.[17]

The political activism, cultural productions, organizational network, and scholarly discourse of queer Asian America encouraged the community to grow more rapidly in the first decades of the twenty-first century. In 1990, the census counted only 2,195 Asian and Pacific Islander households in which same-sex partners lived together, representing 4.9 percent of the 45,000 unmarried, same-sex households of all races. By the 2000 census, the number of same-sex partner households of all races had grown to 594,000, of which about 17,000 included at least one Asian partner. The largest numbers of same-sex households were concentrated in a few major metropolitan areas—New York (2,653), Los Angeles (2,534), and San Francisco (2,366).

Interracial Marriages

Along with the improvement of Asian Americans' socioeconomic conditions in recent decades, interracial marriage has become more visible. A study based on 1980 census statistics relating to the interracial marriage patterns of six subgroups of Asian Americans—namely Chinese, Filipino, Japanese, Korean, Asian Indian, and Vietnamese—produced the following findings: first, Asian men showed greater propensity to marry within their own group than Asian women (78 percent vs. 64 percent), with the exception of Asian Indians, in which case the men were less likely than women to be in-married; second, Japanese were the most likely to be intermarried—49 percent of men and 60 percent of women married non-Japanese—while Korean and Filipino women also exhibited higher rates of intermarriage, 50.5 percent and 43 percent, respectively (see table 9.2).[18] In the San Francisco Bay Area, American-born Asians were more likely to marry outside their own ethnic group. In some ethnic groups, the interracial marriage rate was as high as 80 percent in 1990.[19] Other studies indicate similar trends in the successive decades. The rise of interracial marriage among Asian Americans is most evident in the 2000s, as demonstrated by the census. A recent report by the Pew Research Center indicates that among the newly married in 2010, 9 percent of whites, 17 percent of Blacks, 26 percent of Hispanics, and 28 percent of Asians married out.[20] Among all the racial groups in America, Asian Americans are most likely to marry outside of their group.

What has caused Asian Americans to have a higher level of interracial marriage? Scholars have analyzed interracial marriages among Asian Americans since World War II. Milton Gordon's classic work, *Assimilation in American Life*, spearheaded *assimilation theory*. This theory praised interracial marriage as a sign of the growing acceptance of a minority group by the majority group, although Gordon's assimilation model was based on European immigrants.[21] Most studies of assimilation theory have suggested that interracial marriage served as an indicator of the assimilation of Asian Americans into American majority society.

Meanwhile, an alternative theory of *hypergamy* (meaning "marrying up") has emerged. Originally a concept used in studies of marriage patterns in India, hypergamy has examined the intermarriage between higher-caste males and lower-caste females.[22] Challenging the assimilation theory view of intermarriage, hypergamy theory has seen the phenomenon as a function of the inequality existing within a class and racially stratified society. In India, a high-class male could trade his social status for beauty, intelli-

TABLE 9.2 DISTRIBUTION OF SPOUSE'S ETHNICITY FOR SIX GROUPS OF ASIANS BY GENDER (PERCENTAGE), 1980

Asians by gender	Ethnicity of spouse				Total	
	Same group	Other Asians	Anglo	Other	N	%
Japanese						
Husbands	51.56	5.73	34.46	6.25	384	100
Wives	39.21	5.94	46.93	7.92	505	100
Chinese						
Husbands	82.41	4.80	10.70	2.09	813	100
Wives	76.22	1.71	18.43	3.64	879	100
Filipino						
Husbands	77.01	2.80	16.26	3.93	539	100
Wives	56.91	3.45	32.04	7.6	724	100
Korean						
Husbands	92.83	0.98[a]	5.21	0.98[a]	307	100
Wives	49.31	3.29	39.27	8.13	578	100
Asian Indian						
Husbands	79.60	0.50[a]	17.22	2.68	598	100
Wives	89.81	0.19[a]	7.55	2.45	530	100
Vietnamese						
Husbands	85.83	3.94	7.87	2.36[a]	127	100
Wives	79.56	4.38	13.14	2.92[a]	137	100
All Asians						
Husbands	77.79	3.15	16.03	3.04	2,764	100
Wives	64.12	2.86	27.32	5.7	3,353	100

[a] Percentages are based on 5 or fewer cases.
Source: Sean-Shong Hwang, Rogelio Saenz, and Benigno E. Aguirre, "Structural and Assimilationist Explanations of Asian American Intermarriage," *Journal of Marriage and Family* 59, no. 3 (August 1997): 758–772.

gence, youth, and wealth through intermarriage. Similarly, interracial marriage in the United States also allowed both partners of the marriage to mutually benefit, as a minority male with higher socioeconomic status but lower racial status might upgrade his racial position by marrying a female with the opposite characteristics.[23] After a decade or two of unpopularity, hypergamy theory has reemerged in more recent scholarship. Drawing upon this theory, Larry Hajime Shinagawa and Gin Yong Pang have argued that intermarriage was more likely determined by the marital partners' nativity, gender, age, education, and socioeconomic characteristics.[24]

Similar to the hypergamy thesis, Paul Spickard, in *Mixed Blood*, analyzed intermarriage from various dimensions, including social structure, demography, class status, and intermarriage behavior. Spickard contended that class, generation, and ethnic concentration in the surrounding population have shaped intermarriage patterns. He further claimed that there was a distinct hierarchy of intermarriage preferences.[25] Along the same lines, Colleen Fong and Judy Yung's study emphasizes the factors that play a role in Asian American interracial marriage—aversion to Asian patriarchy, overbearing Asian mothers, cultural and economic compatibility (particularly with Jewish Americans), upward mobility, and media representations of beauty and power—thus asserting that interracial marriage is tied to the racial and gender power relations of American society.[26]

Both assimilation and hypergamy theories have provided meaningful interpretations of intermarriage. Yet each alone could not explain intermarriage completely. Assimilation theory has hailed intermarriage as an indicator of a minority's acceptance by the majority and asserted that love and attraction were primary motives of such marriage. However, it has failed to explain why minority members (both male and female) with higher socioeconomic status and native-born minority members were more likely to marry outside of their group. The hypergamy model has viewed intermarriage as a deal in which the white marital partner traded their higher racial status for the advantages of physical attraction, youth, or higher socioeconomic status brought to the marriage by the partner of a racial minority. It has excluded the factors of love and romance in intermarriage.

In reality, most marital partners of intermarriages (with the exception of picture brides) have claimed that love or attraction was the major reason to draw them together. Clearly, the role of love and mutual attraction in intermarriage should not be overlooked. However, few individuals fell in love at first sight; love grew gradually during the interaction between the two partners. The interaction often occurred among individuals with similar educational, occupational, and socioeconomic experiences. Therefore, intermarriage should be understood in terms of the marital partners' education, occupation, and socioeconomic conditions. When a minority member moved to the socioeconomic setting (often an institution of higher education or a professional occupation) in which they had the possibility to meet a prospective marital partner of the majority group, their status was already upgraded regardless of an intermarriage, since the majority group tended to enjoy better socioeconomic conditions. Therefore, a minority member's assimilation into the majority society was more determined by their education, occupation, and class status than by intermarriage.[27]

Underrepresented Asian American Groups

The personal quotes in the sidebars give examples of the specific socioeconomic and political experiences prior to their immigration to the United States of the Asian Americans traditionally underrepresented in scholarship and of some of the issues and problems they confronted after their arrival in this country. While a growing number of popular and scholarly works on Asian Americans reflect and interpret the experiences of the Chinese, Japanese, Korean, Filipino, and Asian Indian Americans—the earlier and larger groups of Asian Americans—many newer and smaller groups, such as the Burmese, Hmong, Indonesians, Kashmiri, Laotians, Mong, Romani, Thai, Tibetans, and many more, have remained underrepresented and understudied in both popular and academic literature, with the Hmong as the only exception. Even in the case of the Hmong, most work is still in the data collection stage.[28] Therefore, Americans are not very informed about the critical issues of emigration, ethnic identity, gender, class, work, religion, family, and education as they pertain to underrepresented Asian Americans.

Unlike the earlier and larger groups of Asian immigrants, many of whom made the choice to come to America to seek better economic opportunities, underrepresented Asian Americans were often forced to make the drastic transition to America, with little physical and psychological preparations, by the threat of war or political persecution in their homelands. Thus, upon their arrival in the United States, they are frequently faced with questions such as "Why am I here?" "Where is home?" "Who am I?" and "Why am I discriminated against?" Because the population and socioeconomic power of these groups of Asian Americans are growing, it is important to reflect upon the paramount issues that face them today.

Other than the fact that these groups have been underrepresented, there are multiple significant reasons for studying them. These reasons are closely associated with more profound factors, such as how we conceive of Asian Americans; the recent demographic changes within these groups; the connections between emigration and America's foreign policies in the homelands of these groups; and their cry for new identities.

> I'm a first Hmong generation to America. I came to Omaha, Nebraska in July 1979 at the age of 12. I am now living in Fresno, California. . . . It is unfortunate that many Americans still refuse to understand us, the Hmong, and the struggles we endured. They must realize that we didn't come to America for economic reasons. We came to America because we had only two choices—go to a third-world country or go back to Laos and possibly face persecution. Which would you choose, especially when you had just fought with the communists for the last ten years?
>
> —SCHWA YANG
>
> *Source:* Jeff Lindsay, "The Hmong People in the U.S.," http://www.jefflindsay.com/Hmong_tragedy.html.

ASIAN AMERICANS AS A DYNAMIC AND EVOLVING CONCEPT. As discussed in the previous section, the terminology of Asian Americans emerged from the civil rights movement in the 1960s to reflect a consciousness and awareness of Americans of Asian ancestry and their increasing population in the United States since that time. AAS as an academic field consequently developed and has ever since produced a growing body of scholarship. Early on, academic programs in Asian American or ethnic American studies

> In Tibet, my family opposed the Chinese occupation of Tibet, and for that we suffered harsh persecution for many years. . . . Because of my activities, the Chinese government arrested and imprisoned me for three years and four months. During those years, they tortured me. Fortunately, I managed to escape to this country, and arrived in November 1995. . . . I won asylum in 1997. In 2000, lawyers at the firm of Latham & Watkins helped me to found Song Tsen Tibetan Community Outreach, a Tibetan community organization based in New York. As President of Song Tsen, I work to inform the Tibetan refugee community about the 1996 immigration law's asylum filing deadline. In a survey that Song Tsen conducted with 600 Tibetan refugees in New York City, we found that more than half did not know that it exists.
>
> —AMCHOK THUBTEN
>
> ---
>
> *Source:* Human Rights First, "Asylum in the United States," http://www.humanrightsfirst.org/asylum/stories/storie-0.1.htm.

were largely focused on the earlier and larger Asian American groups—the Chinese, Japanese, Korean, Filipino, and Asian Indian Americans. In recent decades, programs and scholarship have expanded to include the newer groups—the Vietnamese, Laotian, and Cambodian Americans. Yet many newer or smaller groups—the Burmese, Hmong, Indonesians, Kashmiri, Laotians, Mong, Romani, Thai, Tibetans, and many more—still remain understudied.

NUMBERS, FACTS, AND BEYOND. The 1990 census counted 6,908,638 Asian Americans, a 99 percent increase over the 1980 census figure of 3,466,847. While Chinese (24 percent of Asian American population), Filipino (20 percent), and Japanese (12 percent) remained as the largest groups, the newer immigrant groups—Burmese, Hmong, Indonesian, Kashmiri, Laotian, Mong, Romani, Thai, and Tibetan—each accounted for 2 percent or less of the Asian American population.[29] The 2000 census counted more than 11 million Asian Americans including at least twenty-eight ethnic groups, a 63 percent increase over the 1990 census count. Among the Asian American population, Chinese, Filipino, Indian, and Korea ranked as the largest four groups. Hmong ranked as the tenth largest group, numbering 186,310; Thai as the eleventh, numbering 150,263; Indonesians as the thirteenth, numbering 63,073; and Burmese as the seventeenth, numbering 16,720.[30] In 2010, the largest Asian American groups were Chinese, Filipino, Indian, and Vietnamese. The Bhutanese, Nepalese, Burmese, and Mongolian ethnic groups experienced the largest population increases, expanding by 532.9, 499.3, 212.6, and 156.6 percent, respectively (see table 9.3 for complete figures).[31] These numbers indicate rapid demographic change among underrepresented Asian Americans.

As with population increase, the geographical distribution of Asian Americans across the United States has been uneven, with approximately 66 percent of Asian Americans concentrated in the five states of California, New York, Hawaii, Texas, and Illinois. While

TABLE 9.3 ASIAN POPULATION BY NUMBER OF DETAILED GROUPS, 2010

Detailed group	Asian alone		Asian in combination with one or more other races		Detailed Asian group alone or in any combination[a]
	One detailed Asian group reported	Two or more detailed Asian groups reported[a]	One detailed Asian group reported	Two or more detailed Asian groups reported[a]	
Total	14,327,580[b]	346,672	2,429,530	217,074	17,320,856
Asian Indian	2,843,391	75,416	240,547	23,709	3,183,063
Bangladeshi	128,792	13,288	4,364	856	147,300
Bhutanese	15,290	3,524	442	183	19,439
Burmese	91,085	4,451	4,077	587	100,200
Cambodian	231,616	23,881	18,229	2,941	276,667
Chinese[c]	3,347,229	188,153	334,144	140,588	4,010,114
Chinese, except Taiwanese[d]	3,137,061	185,289	317,344	140,038	3,779,732
Taiwanese[d]	196,691	2,501	15,781	468	215,441
Filipino	2,555,923	94,050	645,970	120,897	3,416,840
Hmong	247,595	4,728	7,392	358	260,073
Indonesian	63,383	6,713	22,425	2,749	95,270
Iwo Jiman	1	1	7	3	12
Japanese	763,325	78,499	368,094	94,368	1,304,286
Korean	1,423,784	39,690	216,288	27,060	1,706,822
Laotian	191,200	18,446	19,733	2,751	232,130
Malaysian	16,138	5,730	3,214	1,097	26,179
Maldivian	98	4	25	0	127
Mongolian	14,366	772	2,779	427	18,344
Nepalese	51,907	5,302	1,941	340	59,490
Okinawan	2,753	2,928	3,093	2,552	11,326
Pakistani	363,699	19,295	24,184	1,985	409,163
Singaporean	3,418	1,151	645	133	5,347
Sri Lankan	38,596	2,860	3,607	318	45,381
Thai	166,620	16,252	48,620	6,091	237,583
Vietnamese	1,548,449	84,268	93,058	11,658	1,737,433
Other Asian, not specified[e]	218,922	19,410	366,652	18,777	623,761

Source: U.S. Census Bureau, 2010 census special tabulation.

Note: This table shows more detailed Asian groups and response types than tables in "2010 Census Summary File 1." As a result, some numbers do not match those shown in "2010 Census Summary File 1." For information on confidentiality protection, nonsampling error, and definitions, see www.census.gov/prod/cen2010/doc/sf1.pdf.

[a] The numbers by detailed Asian group do not add to the total Asian population. This is because the detailed Asian groups are tallies of the number of Asian *responses* rather than the number of Asian *respondents*. Respondents reporting several Asian groups are counted several times. For example, a respondent reporting "Korean" and "Filipino" would be included in the Korean as well as Filipino numbers.

[b] The total of 14,327,580 respondents categorized as reporting only one detailed Asian group in this table is higher than the total of 14,314,103 shown in Table PCT5 (U.S. Census Bureau, "2010 Census Summary File 1"). This is because the number shown here *includes* respondents who reported "Chinese" and "Taiwanese" together as a single detailed group, "Chinese," whereas PCT5 *excludes* respondents who reported "Chinese" and "Taiwanese" together.

[c] *Includes* respondents who reported "Chinese" and "Taiwanese" together.

[d] *Excludes* respondents who reported "Chinese" and "Taiwanese" together.

[e] Includes respondents who checked the "Other Asian" response category on the census questionnaire or wrote in a generic term such as "Asian" or "Asiatic."

the Asian American population has been highly concentrated in California, New York, and Hawaii, the concentration varies by groups. According to the 2000 census, the top five states for foreign-born Hmong are California, Minnesota, Michigan, Wisconsin, and North Carolina, and the top five metropolitan areas for foreign-born Hmong are Minneapolis–Saint Paul, Minnesota; Fresno, California; Sacramento-Yolo, California; Milwaukee-Racine, Wisconsin; and Merced, California.[32] About one-half of the nation's 50,000 or more Indonesians reside in California, of whom around three-fourths live in Southern California.[33] Kashmiri Hindu Americans largely concentrate in the San Francisco Bay Area, New York City, Washington, D.C., and Fresno, California, along with smaller populations in the metropolitan areas of Atlanta, Philadelphia, Miami, and Houston.[34] The top ten states for Thais are California, Texas, Florida, New York, Illinois, Washington, Virginia, Nevada, Maryland, and Georgia, and the top ten cities are Los Angeles, New York, Chicago, San Francisco, Houston, Seattle, San Diego, Las Vegas, San Jose, and Long Beach, California.[35] The top five places in North America for Tibetans in 2000 are New York City and New Jersey, Toronto, Minnesota, Northern California, and Wisconsin.[36] In 2010, counties that experienced the fastest growth in the Asian population were primarily located in the South and the Midwest. Of the detailed Asian groups that numbered one million or more within the Asian alone or in any combination population, the highest proportion of each group lived in California. The Filipino population (43 percent) had the highest proportion that lived in California, followed by Vietnamese (37 percent), Chinese (36 percent), Japanese (33 percent), and Korean (30 percent). Asian Indians (19 percent) had the lowest proportion living in California relative to all groups shown. The places with the largest Asian populations were New York and Los Angeles. The place with the greatest proportion of the Asian population was urban Honolulu, Hawaii.[37]

While the many Asian American success stories have broadly influenced Americans' conception of Asian Americans, Asian Americans and Pacific Islanders overall have a higher rate of poverty than the general U.S. population. Thirteen percent of Asian Americans and 17 percent of Pacific Islanders live below the federal poverty line, compared to 12 percent of the general population, according to the 2000 census.[38] Among Asian Americans, many of the underrepresented groups have an even higher rate of poverty. Thirty-eight percent of the Hmong population, for instance, was living below the federal poverty line in 2010.[39] Of all Asian Americans, this is the poorest group.

Such statistics have multiple implications. First, the Asian American community is becoming increasingly diversified, as the experiences of these groups are far more complex than can be conveyed by the notion of "model minority." This development needs to be documented. Second, this diversity poses new challenges not only to the communities affected but also to the academic field of AAS. Third, new directions in the study of fast-changing Asian American groups will have an impact on federal and local policies, as issues affecting these minorities are negotiated.

IMMIGRATION AND AMERICAN FOREIGN POLICY. The immigration of underrepresented Asian Americans is in part a consequence of American foreign policy, as is mostly evident in the case of the Hmong. Since the end of the Indochina War in 1975, over one million refugees and immigrants from Vietnam, Cambodia, and Laos arrived in the United States. The Southeast Asian refugees are a product of the longest war in modern history—the thirty-year Vietnam War (1945–1975)—and its metastasis into Laos and Cambodia in the 1960s and early 1970s. In Laos, the Hmong, an ethnic minority of the mountainous highlands who had originally migrated from southwest China, were recruited by the CIA to fight a "secret war" against the Pathet Lao and endured most of the war's casualties, with 400,000 Hmong killed, thousands more injured and disabled, and countless people missing. By 1975, about one-third of the Hmong population had been uprooted by war. In addition to Hmong, Mong emigrants from Laos also came to the United States under similar circumstances.

Tibetan immigration is also the result of American foreign policy. In 1951, the U.S. government urged the Dalai Lama to renounce an agreement made between his negotiators and Beijing and encouraged him to go into exile. The U.S. commitment to Tibet had been presented in a series of proposals to the Dalai Lama: "The first concerned the official position of the Dalai Lama and the legal status of Tibet with the consequences this would have for any appeals made to the United Nations; the second provided guarantees for the maintenance and political support of the Dalai Lama and his entourage while they remained in exile; the third was a pledge of support for the resistance hedged by what limitations Indian policy might impose."[40] These guidelines formed the basis of the relationship between Tibetans and the U.S. government for decades to follow.

America's close relationship with the noncommunist nations in Southeast Asia is in part responsible for the exodus from these countries. For instance, Christian organizations, backed by the U.S. government, have penetrated Indonesia and converted natives to the religion. Most of the Indonesia migrants, either Chinese Indonesians or native Indonesians, are Christians who were already Christianized in Indonesia.[41]

ETHNIC IDENTITY: OLD LABELING AND NEW CONSCIOUSNESS. The ethnic identity of underrepresented groups of Asian Americans also challenges the conventional perception. The underrepresented Asian Americans have been previously conveniently grouped in "East Asian" (in the case of Tibetan), "South Asian" (Kashmiri), and "Southeast Asian." In the "Southeast Asian" group, Burmese, Hmong, Laotian, Mong, and Thai are from the states within "mainland region," while Indonesian "maritime region."[42] The Romani, who originated from northern India but departed in the eleventh century, have been excluded from any of the groupings. Examining the Indian ethnic origin of the Romani people would shed light on the interpretation of their identity; Romani culture may have been more influenced by Indian and more generally Asian culture than by the Middle Eastern and European traits acquired later.[43] Furthermore, the inclusion of Romani also timely reflects the currently heated scholarly debate on the inclusion of Arab Americans of Central and West Asian heritage into AAS.[44] Therefore, emphasis on either their Asian or their Middle Eastern heritage would make it worthwhile to explore the Romani identity. As the field of AAS is steadily developing and evolving, it embraces more previously uncharted areas.

THE MEANING OF THE TERM "UNDERREPRESENTED ASIAN AMERICANS." The term "underrepresented Asian Americans" reveals these groups' conditions in America on the multifaceted fronts of ethnicity, education, employment, religion, social class, and scholarship. Ethnically, most of these groups are small, each accounting for 2 percent or less of the Asian American population. Furthermore, the countries or regions of their origins have been economically devastated, politically unstable, and ethnically marginalized. As newer and smaller groups, some of the underrepresented Asian American groups, such as the Laotians and Hmong, have lower rates of educational attainment and employment, while groups such as the Thai and Indonesian Americans have enjoyed more educational and occupational successes. Yet overall their successes and achievements have been overshadowed by those of the earlier and larger groups of Asian Americans. Most of the underrepresented Asian American groups came from countries or regions with strong religious influence, and subsequently religion has been a vital component of their American life. However, there have been limited studies on the importance and impact of religion on these groups. A large number of the underrepresented Asian Americans fall into the underprivileged social classes and are living with limited means. Examining the social conditions and the placement of each group of underrepresented Asian Americans in contrast to those of the general population and the earlier and larger groups of Asian Americans would depict a fuller and more complex tapestry of the Asian American experience.

Neo-Exclusionism

SEPTEMBER 11 ATTACKS AND THEIR EFFECTS ON SOUTH ASIANS. On September 11, 2001, the world was shocked when the dreadful images of the fallen Twin Towers of the World Trade Center in Manhattan, New York City, appeared on television screens. It was part of the coordinated attacks on New York City and Washington, D.C., organized by the Islamic militant group al-Qaeda. Four American airplanes were hijacked by nineteen al-Qaeda terrorists. Two of the airplanes, American Airlines Flight 11 and United Airlines Flight 175, intentionally flew into the Twin Towers; both buildings collapsed within two hours. The third hijacked airplane hit the Pentagon in Arlington, Virginia. The fourth airplane was intended to attack the U.S. Capitol but crashed into a field near Shanksville, Pennsylvania. These attacks resulted in the deaths of more than 2,900 innocent men and women.

The United States responded by launching the War on Terror and by invading Afghanistan to depose the Taliban, a fundamentalist Muslim military organization that harbored al-Qaeda. Domestically, President George W. Bush signed the USA PATRIOT Act into law on October 26, 2001. The law dramatically reduced restrictions on law enforcement agencies' ability to collect intelligence within the United States, expanded the secretary of the treasury's authority to regulate financial transactions, and broadened the discretion of law enforcement and immigration authorities in detaining and deporting immigrants suspected of terrorist acts. The United States enacted the Homeland Security Act of 2002, which created the Department of Homeland Security and the new cabinet-level position of secretary of homeland security.

The enforcement of the USA PATRIOT Act led to numerous detentions and deportations of innocent Muslim immigrants and American citizens of Middle Eastern, South Asian, and African ancestries. The Immigration and Naturalization Service and other government agencies also secretly detained Muslim immigrants. By late November 2001, 1,200 Muslims or people who were suspected to fit the profile of terrorists had been detained.[45]

The government legislation and initiatives enacted after September 11 have further enflamed the general public's suspicion and stereotyping of Muslims of Middle Eastern and South Asian origins. There were increased hate crimes targeting Muslims and South Asians, largely because many Americans cannot distinguish South Asians from Arabs as a result of the media stereotyping of these groups. Sikhs in particular were assaulted because their turbans and beards made them look like Osama bin Laden in the eyes of some Americans. Numerous incidents of harassment and hate crimes against Muslims and South Asians were reported in the wake of 9/11. The FBI found an increase of 1,600 percent in hate crimes against Muslims or people believed to be Muslims between 2000 and 2001, from 28 cases in 2000 to 481 in 2001.[46] The most illustrative incident of the kind is the murder of Balbir Singh Sodhi, a Sikh mistaken for a Muslim, who was fatally shot on September 25, 2001, in Mesa, Arizona (see sidebar).

American Muslim organizations quickly responded to the terrorist attacks and their aftermath. The Islamic Society of North America, the American Muslim Alliance, the American Muslim Council, the Council on American-Islamic Relations, the Islamic Circle of North America, and Shari'a Scholars Association of North America condemned

THE FIRST 9/11 BACKLASH FATALITY: THE MURDER OF BALBIR SINGH SODHI

FIGURE 9.2 The murder of Balbir Singh Sodhi (1949–2001). Courtesy Wikimedia.

Summary: On September 15, 2001, Balbir Singh Sodhi was shot and killed outside of his Mesa, Arizona, gas station by Frank Roque. Mr. Roque wanted to "kill a Muslim" in retaliation for the attacks on September 11. Mr. Sodhi was the first murder victim due to post-9/11 backlash. Mr. Roque was convicted of first-degree murder and sentenced to life in prison for the hate crime.

Just a few months before the tenth anniversary of his death and the attack on America, the Arizona legislature decided to remove Mr. Sodhi's name from the state 9/11 memorial because he was not deemed "a victim of 9/11." After advocacy by community groups, Governor Jan Brewer would veto the bill and continue to honor the memory of Mr. Sodhi.

The events of September 11, 2001, affected each and every American in pointed and distinct ways. Many thousands perished during the attack, others lost loved ones. Many reacted with fervent patriotism for their country in order to overcome the devastation in progressive and constructive ways, while others lashed out with fear and hate towards the unknown and who they perceived to be "the enemy." Despite the myriad reactions to that day, it is clear that the tragedy and loss of 9/11 did not end on that fateful Tuesday. It is still very real for the families of those that were lost in the attacks, for the families of those that were attacked in the backlash, and those that still fear for their safety in America.

Balbir Singh Sodhi was shot and killed on Saturday, September 15, 2001 in Arizona. It was the first fatal act of hate violence resulting from 9/11. Mr. Sodhi was a 49 year old Sikh American man, who owned a Chevron gas station in Mesa, Arizona. He was shot while arranging American flags in front of his gas station. His assailant, Frank Roque, wanted to "kill a Muslim" in retaliation for the terrorist attacks. He selected Mr. Sodhi simply because he had a beard and wore a turban in accordance with his Sikh faith. Mr. Roque shot at Mr. Sodhi three times, then shot at another service station owned by a Lebanese American, and finally shot at a home of a family of Afghan descent. Fortunately, no one else was injured.

Source: Excerpt from Sikh American Legal Defense and Education Found, "The First 9/11 Backlash Fatality: The Murder of Balbir Singh Sodhi," August 30, 2011, http://www.saldef.org/issues/balbir-singh-sodhi/.

the terrorist attacks, launched blood drives, and provided medical assistance, food, and shelter for victims.

At the same time, Asian American activism focused on developing new strategies in the post-September 11 era. Some immigrant rights activists in the San Francisco Bay Area developed programs educating their constituents on the similarities between the methods of the U.S. government has used in the recent involuntary deportation cases against Filipinos and South Asians, in which a group of Filipinos from San Francisco and a group of South Asians from New York were deported and were handcuffed and chained to one another on their flight to the Philippines and India. They warned their constituencies of the lack of due process and the violation of human rights in these cases in the wake of 9/11 due to heightened nationalistic fervor within the United States.[47]

Asian American activists and scholars were also actively engaged in educating the Asian American community and the general public by connecting the violation of civil rights in the past and the present. In times of war and situations of emergency, the U.S. government and the general public have often tried to scapegoat enemy-like people in the country. The foremost violation of individual liberty was the internment of more than 120,000 Japanese immigrants and their American-born children in relocation camps following the Pearl Harbor attack by the Japanese Imperial Navy on December 7, 1941. *Amerasia Journal*, the prime voice of advocacy among Asian American campuses and communities, devoted a double special issue (2001–2002) to document discriminatory and violent reactions to the September 11 attacks, drawing comparisons with the Pearl Harbor and Japanese internment experiences.

ASIAN AMERICAN PANETHNICITY IN HISTORICAL PERSPECTIVE

The need for Americans of Asian ancestries to embrace a panethnicity resembles that for African Americans and Latino Americans. Panethnicity as a generalization of solidarity among ethnic subgroups was first a product of categorization by the general public, while some of the literature demonstrates that panethnicity was initially a product of government's racial lumping. The categorization generally neglects the subgroup boundaries and lumps diverse people together in a single "ethnic" framework. Africans were brought to America from diverse and distinct ethnic groups and nationalities, yet the slavery experience erased their original ethnic diversity, and made them into generic "Africans." Similarly, diverse Latino populations in America have also been treated as a unitary group with common characteristics and problems. Asian immigrants and their American-born children have been perceived as "Mongolian," "Oriental," or "foreigner" by the American public, regardless of their diverse linguistic, cultural, and religious backgrounds.

At the same time, the categorization or lumping together also helps the diverse ethnic minorities form a large and solidified social force in a racialized society. When facing racial violence, racial categorization necessarily leads to protective panethnicity. Experiencing a common discriminatory treatment in America, different ethnic groups of Asian immigrants and American citizens of Asian descent have realized that they need to put aside historical rivalries and intergroup differences to participate in a panethnic movement.[48]

KEY TERMS

Asian American movement
Yuji Ichioka
Asian American studies
transnationalism
hemispheric approach
the Great Third Coast
queer Asian America

debates on interracial marriage
underrepresented Asian Americans
September 11 terrorist attacks
USA PATRIOT Act
Department of Homeland Security
hate crimes

REVIEW QUESTIONS

1. What were the origins of the Asian American movement? What were its contents, scope, and significance?
2. How do you define Asian American panethnicity? What factors necessitated the formation of panethnicity?
3. List major challenges to the Asian American identity and explain the circumstances for each of them.

FILMS

Bautista, Pablo (producer). *Fated to Be Queer*. 25-minute documentary on four charming and articulate Filipino men that illuminates some of the issues and concerns of gay people of color in San Francisco. 1992.

Dalzell, Liam (director). *Punjabi Cab*. 20-minute documentary on harassment and violence against Sikh taxi drivers in the San Francisco Bay Area since 9/11. 2004.

DaSilva, Jason (producer/director). *Lest We Forgot*. 80-minute documentary that connects the imprisonment of Japanese Americans after the Pearl Harbor attack with the incarceration and racial profiling of Arab and Muslim Americans after 9/11. 2003.

Fulbeck, Kip (producer/director). *Split Banana.* 37-minute documentary on identity and biracial (Chinese/European) ethnicity. 1990.

Gee, Deborah (producer/director). *Slaying the Dragon.* 60-minute documentary on Asians and Asian Americans as depicted in American media productions. 1988.

Nakasako, Spencer, and Sokly Ny (producer/director). *A.K.A. Don Bonus.* 55-minute documentary on a Cambodian refugee family. 1995.

Okazaki, Steven (writer/director). *American Sons.* 28-minute documentary on how racism shapes the lives of Asian American men. 1995.

Shiekh, Irum (director). *On Strike! Ethnic Studies 1969–1999.* 30-minute documentary that provides a historical and political overview of what it took to establish and sustain ethnic studies at one of the nation's leading universities.1999.

Tajima-Pena, Renee (director). *Labor Women.* 30-minute documentary on activism, labor, and lesbian, gay, and bisexual women Asian Americans. 2002.

Yeager, Tami (producer/director). *A Dream in Doubt.* 57-minute documentary on Rana Singh Sodhi, a Sikh American who fights the hate threatening his family and community after 9/11. 2009.

FURTHER READING

Chan, Sucheng. *In Defense of Asian American Studies: The Politics of Teaching and Program Building.* Urbana: University of Illinois Press, 2005.

Dhingra, Pawan. *Managing Multicultural Lives: Asian American Professionals and the Challenge of Multiple Identities.* Stanford, CA: Stanford University Press, 2007.

Eng, David, and Alice Hom, eds. *Q & A: Queer in Asian America.* Philadelphia: Temple University Press, 1998.

Espiritu, Yen Le. *Asian American Panethnicity: Bridging Institutions and Identities.* Philadelphia: Temple University Press, 1992.

Hune, Shirley. "Asian American Studies and Asian Studies: Boundaries and Borderlands of Ethnic Studies and Area Studies." In *Color-Line to Borderlands: The Matrix of Ethnic Studies*, edited by J. Butler, 227–239. Seattle: University of Washington Press, 2001.

Kibria, Nazli. *Muslims in Motion: Islam and National Identity in the Bangladeshi Diaspora.* New Brunswick, NJ: Rutgers University Press, 2011.

Koshy, Susan. *Sexual Naturalization: Asian Americans and Miscegenation.* Stanford, CA: Stanford University Press, 2005.

Koshy, Susan, and R. Radhakrishnan, eds. *Transnational South Asians: The Making of a Neo-Diaspora.* New York: Oxford University Press, 2008.

Leonard, Karen Isaksen. *Muslims in the United States: The State of Research.* New York: Russell Sage Foundation, 2003.

Leong, Russell, ed. *Asian American Sexualities: Dimensions of the Gay and Lesbian Experience*. New York: Routledge, 1996.

Ling, Huping. *Chinese Americans in the Heartland: Migration, Work, and Community*. New Brunswick, NJ: Rutgers University Press, 2022.

———. *Chinese Chicago: Race, Transnational Migration, and Community since 1870*. Stanford, CA: Stanford University Press, 2012.

———. *Chinese St. Louis: From Enclave to Cultural Community*. Philadelphia: Temple University Press, 2004.

———, ed. *Emerging Voices: Experiences of Underrepresented Asian Americans*. New Brunswick, NJ: Rutgers University Press, 2008.

Lowe, Lisa. "Heterogeneity, Hybridity, Multiplicity: Marking Asian American Differences." *Diaspora* 1, no. 1 (1991): 24–44.

Maira, Sunaina. *Youth, Citizenship, and Empire after 9/11*. Durham, NC: Duke University Press, 2009.

Manalansan, Martin. *Global Divas: Filipino Gay Men in the Diaspora*. Durham, NC: Duke University Press, 2003.

Masequesmay, Gina, ed. *Embodying Asian/American Sexualities*. New York: Lexington Books, 2010.

Okihiro, Gary Y. *Margins and Mainstreams: Asian in American History and Culture*. Seattle: University of Washington Press, 1994.

Ong, Aihwa. *Flexible Citizenship: The Cultural Logics of Transnationality*. Durham, NC: Duke University Press, 1999.

Parrenas, Rhacel, and Lok Siu. *Asian Diasporas: New Formations, New Conceptions*. Stanford, CA: Stanford University Press, 2007.

Prashad, Vijay. *Uncle Swami: South Asians in America Today*. New York: New Press, 2012.

Rumbaut, Rubén G., and Alejandro Portes, eds. *Ethnicities: Children of Immigrants in America*. Berkeley: University of California Press, 2001.

Spickard, Paul. *Mixed Blood: Intermarriage and Ethnic Identity in Twentieth-Century America*. Madison: University of Wisconsin Press, 1989.

Srikanth, Rajini. *Constructing the Enemy: Empathy/Antipathy in U.S. Literature and Law*. Philadelphia: Temple University Press, 2012.

Tuan, M. *Forever Foreigners or Honorary Whites? The Asian Ethnic Experience Today*. New Brunswick, NJ: Rutgers University Press, 1998.

Wei, William. *The Asian American Movement*. Philadelphia: Temple University Press, 1993.

THE FUTURE OF ASIAN AMERICA UNDER GLOBALIZATION

CHAPTER OUTLINE

China Rise / Asian Rise versus the U.S. Decline
Importance of Global Collaboration and Various Prescriptions
New Trends of Migration and Assimilation under Globalization
The COVID-19 Pandemic and Asian American Communities
Asian Americans under Globalization in Historical Perspective

WHAT LIES AHEAD for Asian Americans in the next few decades? The rapid speed of globalization, assisted by incessant developments in the information technology industry, has ushered a new era for the world. In this new era, two superpowers, the United States, often seen as a "declining" power, and China, widely hailed as an "ascending" power with a "gravity-defying economy," have attracted much attention from experts, observers, pundits, and laymen when looking into the future of the world. How does one understand the China ascent versus U.S. decline dichotomy? How will the new power balance impact Asian Americas? And how will Asian Americans, and everyone else, reposition themselves in the globalized world? When the unprecedented global COVID-19 pandemic hit the country, how did Asian Americans who suffered not only the pandemic but more anti-Asian hate crime respond to the new challenges? This chapter explores these intriguing questions.

CHINA RISE / ASIAN RISE VERSUS THE U.S. DECLINE

Although China has achieved an astonishing economic "miracle" in the past three decades, the phenomenal "rise of China" in recent years has been used more likely as a scare tactic in the Western world, especially in America. Here, media, politicians, demagogues, and extremists have joined hands to effectively arouse the public anxiety and anger toward an external threat, real or imaginary, to be blamed for domestic problems such as the economic downturn, budget deficit, trade deficit, unemployment, and health care.

When looking into history, one finds this paranoia toward China's rise quite parallel with other historical phenomena. For instance, in the thirteenth century, the "yellow peril" of the Mongol power that swept Asia and Europe shook the world and left deep imprints in the collective memories of Europeans. More recently, the "red scare" of communism spreading in Asia and Europe following World War II turned the United States hysteric and its government thus devised a "containment" policy to fend off communist influence and spread during the Cold War era. This containment mentality helped breed the madness of McCarthyism and the country's involvement in wars in Korea and Vietnam. Meanwhile in China, the "rise of China" has also been a popular buzzword in the recent decades, initially promoted by academics who have studied the rise of various industrial and military powers in the past, including Great Britain, Germany, the United States, Japan, and now China, and then propagated by the government propaganda machine to incite nationalistic sentiments among the Chinese populace.[1] It seems that the governments on both sides of the Pacific Ocean have employed China's rising economic power to serve a common need: maintaining domestic stability.

The Rise of China

How fast China is rising and how rapidly the United States is declining thus become the growing concerns among increasingly anxious Americans. It is important to explore the dichotomy—China rising and the United States declining. First, the rise of China is real and rapid, but not as threatening as described by the media, demagogues, and extremists. Since the 1980s, China's annual GDP growth had been maintained at about 10 percent for over three decades. There has been a slow economic recovery from the worldwide recession since 2008 in the United States, Europe, and Japan and a slowdown of China's economic growth since 2012. Even so, according to a recent study, "China 2030: Building a Modern, Harmonious, and Creative High-Income Society," a 468-page document compiled by the World Bank and the influential Chinese government research organization, the Development Research Center in Beijing, China will surpass the United States as the largest economic power by 2030. The document forecasts that China's economy could grow by about 8 percent a year in the next few years and could sustain an average annual growth about 6.6 percent for nearly twenty years. The annual growth is more likely to slow down eventually to about 5 percent in the years leading to 2030. This growth margin, however, is more than enough for China to surpass the United States, which would have 2 to 3 percent annual growth during the same time period, as the world's biggest economy.[2]

Other signs of development further indicate China's rapidly growing economic power. China now has the longest high-speed rail (HSR) trunks and the fastest trains in the world, with about 37,900 kilometers (23,549 miles) of routes in service as of the end of 2020.[3] The notable HSR lines such as the Beijing-Shanghai High-Speed Railway, a dedicated passenger trunk line opened in June 2011, reduced the 1,318-kilometer (819 miles) journey between the two largest cities in China to under five hours, with a top speed of 300 kilometers per hour (186 mph) for the entire trip. The Shanghai Maglev Train, an airport rail link service between Pudong International Airport and the business district of Shanghai, began operating in 2004 and travels 30 kilometers (19 miles) in seven minutes, averaging 240 kilometers per hour (149 mph) and reaching a top speed of 431 kilometers per hour (268 mph).

Other miraculous feats are the prefabricated buildings built by the Broad Sustainable Building Company (BSB) in China, which boasts the ability to construct high-rises in days. The company, established in 2009 and headquartered in Changsha, Hunan province, shocked the world by assembling a fifteen-story hotel in two days for the Shanghai World Exposition in 2010. In January 2012, the same company finished a thirty-story five-star hotel in Changsha in fifteen days, a stunning example of China's construction boom. Even though most parts of the building (90 percent) are premade in factory, the efficiency rendered its Western architectural counterparts speechless. It includes a swimming pool and a helicopter pad, as well as being earthquake proof and environmentally friendly. The company employed technologies already used in Western countries for some time, using the concept of factory-made building components, but with unique adaptations. BSB's system of prefabrication requires constructing segments of a building in advance in an indoor factory. The basic building blocks of a modern building, such as ventilation, water pipes, and electrical wiring, are preinstalled and then uniformly stacked at the construction site and assembled like Lego blocks. The system promises to revolutionize construction by reducing the building schedule by one-third or half, allowing a decrease of 20 to 30 percent in construction costs through reduced construction times and greater efficiencies.[4]

In education, Chinese students stand out as the top performers in international standardized tests. On December 7, 2010, the Paris-based Organisation for Economic Co-operation and Development (OECD), which represents thirty-four countries, released the 2009 Program for International Student Assessment (PISA). PISA is conducted every three years and studies fifteen-year-old students in the participating countries. The OECD Executive Summary on each assessment is regarded as the most authoritative evaluation of the participating countries' effectiveness of educational systems. The PISA 2009 test results indicate that the fifteen-year-olds from the Shanghai region of China topped every country in all academic categories of mathematics, science, and reading. Singapore and Hong Kong–China ranked second and third, respectively, while the fifteen-year-olds in the United States ranked twenty-fifth among their peers from thirty-four countries on a math test and scored seventeenth in science and reading.[5] The results shocked American educational policy makers and educators. American education secretary Arne Duncan gasped that the results were a "massive wake-up call" and alerted that American students must improve to compete in a global economy. President Obama's administration also vowed to promote national curriculum standards and to revamp teacher pay, stressing performance rather than credentials and seniority.[6]

Despite these shining promotional efforts, economists have sharply pointed out the complexity and uniqueness of the Chinese economy. China's economy bears a duality in a number of ways. Although over 90 percent of China's economy has been subjected to market forces, which economists normally would categorize as "capitalistic," the strategic sectors and infrastructure of China's economy are still held within the tight grasp of the state or state-owned conglomerate corporations. The Chinese government has insisted that China's economy is a type of "socialism with Chinese characteristics," while foreign observers have called it "bureaucratic capitalism" or "capitalism without liberty." Regardless of the names, this heavy government control of the economy has successfully guarded China from the recent regional and international economic crises including the Asian financial tsunami in 1997 and the worldwide recession beginning in 2007. For this reason, Western observers have regarded the Chinese economy as a "gravity-defying" "Chinese model" or a "third-way" between socialism and capitalism that is worth emulating.[7]

The drawbacks of the state monopoly, however, are also noticeably severe, ranging from rampant corruption, bribery, fraud, and nepotism among all levels of government bureaucracy to inequity of wealth distribution—wide gaps between coastal areas and hinterland regions, urban centers and rural villages, and the top one percent elite class and the massive populace. While China's economy has ranked as the second largest in the world, valued at $7.3 trillion as of 2011 (trailing the United States' $15 trillion), the per capita income of China was $5,184, which ranked 90th of the world.[8]

Furthermore, the United States and China are the two largest economies globally in both Nominal and PPP methods. United States is at the top in nominal, whereas China is at the top in PPP since 2017 after overtaking the United States. However, The per capita income of the United States is 5.78 and 3.61 times higher than that of China in nominal and PPP terms, respectively. The United States is the 5th richest country in the world, whereas China comes at 63rd rank. On a PPP basis, the United States is on 8th position, and China is at 76th.[9] China is still a midlevel income country.

The Fall of the United States

Meanwhile, the fall of the United States is true but not as appalling as described and fanned by the demagogues. There are clear and undeniable signs of the fall of the United States. The average annual GDP increase was 2.9 percent between 2002 and 2007, 2.2 percent in 2008, 1.1 percent in 2009, and 1.2 percent in 2010, according to the Bureau of Economic Analysis of the Department of Commerce in December 2011.[10] As of March 5, 2012, U.S. national debt was approximately $15 trillion and the annual budget deficit was about $1.3 trillion, or 8.7 percent of the total national budget.[11] The unemployment rate was 9.6 percent in 2010, the highest in the post–World War II era, and remained at 8.2 percent in 2012.[12] President Barack Obama called for world-class education in the United States in order to compete in a globalized world (see sidebar).

In international affairs, the influence of the United States is gradually fading. One of the landmark events of the decline of American power occurred during the Libyan Revolution in February 2011, when the opposition force called for the ousting of dictator Muammar Gaddafi and the latter's security force fired on the crowd, thus leading to the Libyan Civil War. The Obama administration decided not to take America's traditional role as a world leader in pressuring the Gaddafi government but instead called for a "shared responsibility" of leading nations of the world. This action has been dubbed as the "Obama Doctrine" by the Republican Party and has been used as evidence of the weakness of the Obama administration's foreign policy. In fact, facing a huge government deficit and with Americans weary of further military involvement in the world, the Obama administration had no option but choosing multilateralism in world affairs.

Regardless of all the alarming signs, writers have maintained that the fall of any superpower is a political, historical, biological, and natural cycle. Retrospectively, the talk of the fall of the United States is nothing new and has always been used as a scare tactic by politicians and the media in the context of international competitions, real or imaginary. In the wake of the socialist Bolshevik Revolution in Russia in 1917, communism, an ideology believed to be contagious and potentially dangerous, seemed to pose a challenge to the United States and the values of individual freedom and democracy cherished by Western countries. Thus the threat led to a crusade

> A world-class education is the single most important factor in determining not just whether our kids can compete for the best jobs but whether America can out-compete countries around the world. America's business leaders understand that when it comes to education, we need to up our game. That's why we're working together to put an outstanding education within reach for every child.
>
> —PRESIDENT BARACK OBAMA, JULY 18, 2011
>
> Source: http://www.whitehouse.gov/issues/education.

against communist influence in the United States. Under such a "red scare" mentality, the Communist Party and the leftist movement in the country were crushed, the union movement suffered a backlash, and individuals, especially Eastern and Southern European immigrants, suspected to be communist spies or sympathizers, were raided, persecuted, and denied access to an impartial justice system (as in the case of Sacco and Vanzetti).

From the moment the United States arose as the leader of the free world and an absolute superpower by the end of World War II, it has never let its guard down against the communist camp led by the Soviet Union. The potential threat of communism continuously fanned cries of the fall of the United States during the Cold War. As ample studies and media reports revealed the educational, cultural, athletic, and scientific advances made by the Soviet Union, political and academic discussions were preoccupied with talks of the signs of U.S. decline.

The fear of the decline of the United States was directed not only to the Soviet Union, which dissolved in 1991, but also to Japan, which emerged as a potential enemy and a real trade foe of the United States in the 1980s. Consequently, the decades of the 1980s and 1990s were devoted to studies of Japan and especially its business management "secrets." Throngs of students and scholars of business management traveled to Japan, looking for the reasons behind its economic success, and then produced academic essays on how to compete with the Japanese upon returning to the United States.[13] Unfortunately, the country of the Rising Sun turned into a falling sun after the burst of its bubble economy following the Asian financial tsunami in the early 1990s and has never truly recovered. The devastating Fukushima Daiichi nuclear crisis triggered by the Tohoku earthquake and then subsequent tsunami on March 11, 2011, threw the country once again into another economic recession.

On the other hand, China has enjoyed uninterrupted, over four-decade-long economic growth, with an annual GDP growth rate of 10 percent. This unprecedented economic surge not only uplifted its population of billions out of poverty but also let China past Japan in GDP in 2009, officially making China the world's second largest economy. As discussed earlier, even with a slower annual economic growth rate of 5 percent, China could surpass the United States in 2030 or earlier (one estimate is 2025) by Western observers' predictions. Now the fall of the United States is real and imminent!

What shall we do? The United States may fall, but the sky is not falling. The United States can still survive and even bounce back from the fall. All empires, as Stanford historian Niall Ferguson notes, no matter how magnificent and powerful they might have been, are inclined to decline and fall. Like all empires, the United States cannot escape the rule, despite the wishful belief of American "exceptionalism." Any civilization, like a seasonal cycle, always ends in bitter winter. Ferguson further maintains that neo-cyclical theories find that a few conditions lead to the fall of a superpower. First, when leaders fail to respond to challenges, empire declines. Second, when great powers overstretch, they collapse. Ferguson argues that a "self-organizing complexity system" is the major cause of the fall of the United States. The huge U.S. fiscal deficits have resulted not from the country's international military actions but from the heavy domestic burdens of its Medicaid/Medicare and Social Security programs.[14] It has been widely circulated knowledge that for every dollar of the federal budget in 2010, 59 cents were spent on entitlement programs, including unemployment (16 cents), Medicaid (8 cents), Medicare (16 cents), and Social Security (19 cents), while 18 cents were spent on defense spending, including overseas operations, leaving only 23 cents for everything else.[15]

Other Emerging Economies in Asia

In addition to China, a number of other Asian countries have also experienced rapid economic growth in recent decades. India, the other major emerging economy in Asia, also poses challenges to the United States. Before 1991, the Indian government had practiced socialistic protectionist economic policies. In 1991, an acute balance payment crisis forced the government to liberalize its economy and move toward a free-market system. With its average annual GDP growth rate of 5.8 percent over the past two decades, India is one of the world's fastest growing economies, and its GDP of $1.848 trillion in 2011 was the tenth largest in the world.[16] However, with its 1.2 billion population, the country ranks 140th in the world in nominal GDP per capita. India ranks 17th in financial market sophistication, 24th in the banking sector, 44th in business sophistication, and 39th in innovation, ahead of several advanced economies, as of 2010.[17] With seven of the world's top fifteen information technology outsourcing companies based in India, the country is viewed as the second most favorable outsourcing destination after the United States as of 2009. India's consumer market is expected to become fifth largest by 2030.

The communist government in Vietnam has undergone a series of economic and political reforms since 1986. These reforms have led the country to be integrated into the world economy, and its economic growth has been among the highest in the world since 2000. In 2011 it had the highest Global Growth Generators Index among eleven major economies.[18] However, Vietnam is still plagued with problems of income, gender, and health care inequalities.

Positive and Negative Consequences of Globalization

The rise of China and other emerging economies in Asia and the decline of the United States are direct consequences of globalization. Many writers have eloquently outlined both the positive and negative impacts of globalization. On the positive side, globalization makes the world flatter and smaller. Cultural and economic gaps between peoples and nations become narrower—though globalization does benefit developed countries more than developing ones. Meanwhile, globalization also causes negative consequences, such as global economic crises, economy downsizing and outsourcing, widespread public anxiety, the rise of extremist movements in developed countries (such as the Tea Party and Birthers movements in the United States), and polarization in developing countries due to corruption, lack of democratic governing structure, lack of effective legal system and civic sense, and cultural baggage.[19]

IMPORTANCE OF GLOBAL COLLABORATION AND VARIOUS PRESCRIPTIONS

Globalization has also made countries more dependent on one another, and the big powers need each other. Princeton professor of political science Aaron L. Friedberg eloquently argues about the importance of the global collaboration between the big powers, especially between the United States and China (see sidebar). However, he cautions that the relationship between the two superpowers will continue to be "constrained competition," as both are preparing for a possible future confrontation.

One of the most provocative prescriptions is "Chinmerica," a term coined by then Harvard professor Niall Ferguson in 2007. It emphasizes collaboration of the two economic powers, as globalization makes economies of nations interconnected, interactive, and entangled. According to this theory, the relationship between China and America will be the most important factor in understanding the world economy, and China and America will be considered as one economy—Chinmerica. Chinmerica accounted for a quarter of the world's population, a third of its gross domestic product, and over half of global economic growth between 2003 and 2009.[20] The mutual benefits and mutual engagements between the two countries will determine the relationship between the two major powers.

> ### IMPORTANCE OF U.S.-CHINA RELATIONS*
>
> If tensions between the two Pacific powers worsen, the whole of eastern Eurasia could become divided in a new cold war, and the prospects for confrontation and conflict would seem certain to rise. On the other hand, a deepening U.S.-China entente could bring with it increased possibilities for sustained worldwide economic growth, the peaceful resolution of outstanding regional disputes, and the successful management of pressing global problems, including terrorism and the proliferation of weapons of mass destruction. Whether for good or ill, the most significant bilateral international relationship over the course of the next several decades is likely to be that between the United States and the PRC.
>
> Source: Aaron L. Friedberg, "The Future of U.S.-China Relations: Is Conflict Inevitable?," International Security 30, no. 2 (Autumn 2005): 7–45.
>
> * Title added by the author.

Yale senior researcher Immanuel Wallerstein, an internationally renowned analyst, has made a similar observation. The realization of the need for geopolitical power balance from both China and the United States directs both sides to be cautious in maintaining a positive relationship. He summarizes the China-U.S. relationship pointedly in a commentary he wrote on January 15, 2012: "Are China and the United States rivals? Yes, up to a point. Are they enemies? No, they are not enemies. Are they collaborators? They already are more than they admit, and will be much more so as the decade proceeds."[21]

Furthermore, the need for world peace (curb global imbalance) is making collaboration of multilateral powers more important, thus replacing the past bipolar geopolitical confrontations between two opposing international alliances or two superpowers, such as Alliance versus Axis during World War II and the capitalist camp versus the communist camp during the Cold War. The rise of Asia and fall of the United States would make power balance depend more on cooperation and collaboration among the multiple powers in Asia (China, Japan, and India), in Europe (Russia and the European Union), and in North America (the United States and Canada). The latter two powers constitute the "Greater West." The Greater West should have a positive relation with Asia, especially with China.[22] Writers also have noted that America's leadership in geopolitical affairs can succeed only through collaboration with other nations.[23] Thus, multilateralism has become a much hailed approach in dealing with international conflicts, as opposed to unilateralism, which the United States practiced and enjoyed in the post–Cold War era until September 11, 2001.

Award-winning author Thomas Friedman analyzes globalization through contrasting it with the Cold War. Globalization, he believes, is a new world system following the Cold War era. While the Cold War's overarching feature was division and its structure of power balance was between the United States and the Soviet Union, the globalization system has its own overarching feature of integration and its own defining structure of power, but which is much more complex than the Cold War structure. While the Cold War system was built exclusively around the nation-state, globalization is driven by free-market capitalism and built around *three balances*—the traditional balance between nation-states, the balance between nation-states and global markets, and the balance between individuals and nation-states.[24]

Friedman's three balances theory offers guidance when we think about how to position the United States as a nation-state under globalization. As globalization has its own inherently empowering and humanizing aspects and its inherently disempowering and dehumanizing aspects, it is important to make certain that the world is aware that the advancement of human life in some aspects and some areas is leading to declines in some other aspects and other areas. No nation has a greater responsibility and opportunity to ensure this than the United States. According to Friedman, to maintain balances, the

United States needs to develop a politics for the age of globalization, that is, to understand globalization as a technology-driven phenomenon (not a trade-driven one) and then develop a new "social bargain" between workers, financiers, and governments, which would ensure sustainable globalization by democratizing globalization—making it work for more and more people all the time. Friedman terms the system as "Integrationist Social-Safety-Nettism."[25] This system sounds wonderful in theory, but it is nearly impossible in practice. As noted in an earlier section, already under heavy debts of $15 trillion, how does the U.S. government fund, let alone expand, these entitlement schemes?

NEW TRENDS OF MIGRATION AND ASSIMILATION UNDER GLOBALIZATION

There have been a number of new trends of migration and assimilation under globalization. First, in terms of immigration destinations, the United States will continue as a major receiving country but face competition from other developed countries. Second, China, India, Pakistan, the Philippines, and Vietnam will remain as major sending countries. Third, competition for highly skilled immigrants among the immigration destination countries has intensified. Fourth, new patterns of residence and citizenship have emerged, as assimilation to American identity becomes less important. And finally, globalization poses both new opportunities and new challenges to Asian Americans.

Immigration Destinations: The United States Continues as a Major Immigrant-Receiving Country, but Faces Competition

Globalization and the current international geo-economic-political conditions will, as always, determine the new magnets of the global human movement. It is highly likely that the United States will continue to be the top choice of new immigrants, but it will face competition from Canada, Australia, New Zealand, and a number of European countries.

Immigration in general is a deliberate and planned individual action responding to the deteriorating socioeconomic conditions in the sending countries and the perceived better socioeconomic conditions and immigration laws in the receiving countries. As the United States remains the strongest economic and military power in the world, with vast territory and rich natural resources, higher living standards, a cleaner environment, a quality education, advanced communication systems, and a stable democratic political system, it continues to be one of the most desirable immigration destinations. However, other developed countries such as Canada, Australia, and New Zealand that are comparable in these attributes have in the recent decades competed with the United States as desirable migration destinations. In 2008, about 1.9 million Chinese immigrants were admitted to the United States, 1.5 million to the European countries, 850,000 to Canada, and 600,000 to Australia and New Zealand, according to Chinese government estimates.[26] On April 20, 2012, Gallup released its survey on world potential migration. The survey shows that 13 percent of the world's adult population, or 640 million people, intend to emigrate, among whom 23 percent, or 150 million, are interested in migrating to the United States. Potential migrants, who said they would like to move to the United States, were most likely to come from populous countries such as China (22 million), Nigeria (15 million), India (10 million), Bangladesh (8 million), and Brazil (7 million). Gallup's Potential Net Migration Index (PNMI) suggests that Singapore, New Zealand, Canada, Australia, and the United States lead the ranks of the most desirable destinations for migration. Since 2007, when Gallup started polling the potential migration trend, the United States has remained as a top desired destination. However, it has continued to place further down the list, after Singapore, Canada, and several other developed nations. It is important to keep in mind that a country's population size affects how high or low its index score is and its ranking.[27] In addition, the less restrictive immigration and naturalization policies in these countries have also made them equally appealing as if not more attractive than the United States. These countries have either points system for immigrant admission and work visa programs that are not subject to immigration quotas.

Meanwhile, globalization has broadened the choices of migration destinations. Chinese immigrant communities can be found in every corner of the world. In 2008, there were approximately 10 million Chinese who emigrated from China. Among them, Southeast Asian countries, due to their proximity to China, hold the largest number, 2.5 million, or 25 percent of the total Chinese emigrants in that year. The United States (1.9 million), Canada (850,000), Japan (750,000), Australia, and New Zealand (600,000) were the preferred destinations for students and professionals as well as unskilled laborers. European countries attracted primarily entrepreneurs and unskilled laborers (1.5 million). Meanwhile, Latin American countries (750,000) and Russia (200,000) also drew substantial numbers of Chinese small entrepreneurs. African countries attracted 500,000 Chinese small entrepreneurs, technicians, and unskilled laborers.[28]

Immigration Sources: China, India, Pakistan, the Philippines, and Vietnam as Major Sending Counties

In the next decades, Asia will continue as a major source of immigration to the United States. Since 1965, more Asian immigrants have entered the United States, trailing only their counterparts from Latin America. The number of Asian immigrants had increased steadily, from 201,412 in the 1960s to 1.3 million in the 1970s, 2.4 million in the 1980s, 2.6 million in the 1990s, and 3.1 million in the 2010s.[29] This trend will likely to continue thanks to a number of factors. First, the economic disparity between many of the Asian countries and the United States remains a major pushing force behind the exodus from Asia. At the same time, Asian countries have few emigration restrictions. Furthermore, the continued need in the United States for skilled laborers, especially highly trained professionals, and capital from overseas will attract immigrants from many Asian countries with surpluses of highly trained professionals. The ongoing military, diplomatic, commercial, and cultural interactions between many Asian countries and the United States will also facilitate Asian immigration to America. Thus, new immigrants will continue to come from the populous Asian countries of China, India, Pakistan, Philippines, and Vietnam, including working-class immigrants, students, and "investment immigrants" with capital.

Competition for Highly Skilled Immigrants Intensified

Competition for skilled immigrants in the recent decades has most notably intensified between the two major immigrant-receiving countries in the North America—the United States and Canada. While U.S. immigration policies since 1965 have been primarily based on the principle of family reunification, as 74 percent of the annual immigration quota goes to preferences pertinent to family reunification, Canadian policies are based on four principles—demographic, economic, social, and humanitarian, admitting economic class, family class, and refugee migrants. The establishment of the points system in 1967 in particular has placed the primary focus on certain categories when valuing human capital, categories such as age, education, credentials, official language proficiency, and Canadian experiences and connections. These policies have placed more emphasis on skilled migration than family reunification.

Further, to address the declining economic performance of the skilled immigrants in Canada, the Canadian government passed the Immigration and Refugee Protection Act in 2002 to adjust the selection criteria for skilled immigrants. The new law consists of two major changes: it raises the total number of points required for entry from 70 to 75 (out of 100), and it emphasizes language, formal education, and prior experience in the labor market. These new criteria contributed to the increased number of skilled immigrants from India, which remained the top immigrant-sending country to Canada between 2008 and 2010, when the Philippines surpassed the former.[30]

To respond to the global competition for talent, the United States tripled the worldwide annual quota for employment-based immigrants to 140,000 in its 1990 Immigration Act. It also created the H-1B visa category as a three-year temporary work visa program for skilled immigrants with college and postgraduate education; H-1B visa holders are eligible to apply for permanent residency. This program has been quickly utilized mostly by Chinese and Indian immigrants. Ongoing immigration reform debates in the United States have discussed possibilities to revamp the immigration admission system to better serve the nation's need for highly skilled migrants by adopting the Canadian-, Australian-, and New Zealand-style points system.[31]

A more recent development further and explicitly reveals the urgency to compete for the highly trained professionals. On November 30, 2012, Congress overwhelmingly passed the STEM Jobs Act of 2012, by a 245–139 vote. The bill proposes to reserve 55,000 permanent residence visas each year for foreign students with advanced degrees from American universities in the STEM fields (science, technology, engineering, and mathematics). But the bill was opposed by Democrats as they believed it would replace the Diversity Immigrant Visa Program established in 1990, which allows less-trained immigrants from Africa and elsewhere to enter the country. Therefore, the bill would less likely be taken up in the Democratic-controlled Senate.[32] Nevertheless, the act indicates the heightened struggle for highly trained immigrants in an increasingly competitive world.

On the other shore of the Pacific Ocean, the Chinese government has also sped up its efforts in the global race for brains. The Changjiang xuezhe jiangli jihua, or Yangtze River Scholar Award Program, the most prestigious scholarship program under the authority of the Chinese Ministry of Education, with matching funds from the Hong Kong Li Jiacheng (Li Ka-shing) Foundation, was initiated in August 1998 to recruit preeminent Chinese scholars overseas. Yangtze River Scholars are promised attractive compensation and research funds to teach and conduct research at Chinese universities, where they are hired for a three-year term as a Changjiang Scholar. From its inception to the end of 2008, 1,308 Chinese scholars overseas, primarily from the United States, Canada, Australia, the United Kingdom, and the major European countries, and mostly in the STEM fields, had been hired by 115 universities in China.[33]

Since the mid-1990s, with China's remarkable economic success and steady rise on the global geopolitical stage, increasing numbers of overseas Chinese students turned professionals have returned to China, commonly nicknamed as *haigui* in Chinese (meaning "overseas returnees," but it puns with "sea turtle" in Chinese, therefore being called *haigui*, "sea turtles" in Chinese). In 1990, 1,593 Chinese students who received advanced training overseas returned to China. The number increased to 5,750 in 1995, 9,121 in 2000, 34,897 in 2005, and 108,300 in 2009. The number of returned students and scholars reached more than 632,000 in 2010.[34] Moreover, a large number of student migrants returned without settling in China, but frequently traveling between China and the country of their immigration; they are commonly known as *kongzhong feiren*, meaning "astronauts." A 2008 survey of Chinese returnees reveals that 34 percent of them held American permanent residency or citizenship, indicating a changing meaning of immigration and assimilation.[35]

New Patterns of Residence and Citizenship: Assimilation to American Identity Becomes Less Important

As discussed in the previous section, assimilation to American culture may have become less attractive to transnational world citizens. Laws and practices of dual citizenship would enable new immigrants to reside, work, and participate in voting in more than one country. Scholars have consequently proposed such concepts as "flexible citizenship" or "selective citizenship" to delineate the new phenomenon. They maintain that "the multiple-passport holder is an apt contemporary figure; he or she embodies the split between state-imposed identity and personal identity caused by political upheavals, migration, and changing global markets" and further suggest that "nationality is a simple product of the political world in which one is to be registered and administered (*guanxia*), and it is not identical with their personal identity and cultural belonging."[36]

In fact, the attractiveness of assimilation was already under attack in the 1970s, when ethnicity and multicultural identities grew more prominent. For instance, in Southeast Asia, many Chinese have identified themselves as local nationals of Chinese descent since World War II, and they have been expected to be assimilated into the local societies. However, since the 1970s many individuals, who once identified themselves linguistically and culturally as Thai, Filipino, or some other Southeast Asian nationalities, have increasingly emphasized their Chinese identity, joined Chinese cultural associations, and tried to teach their offspring Mandarin.[37] Numerous studies have noted the similar situation among Chinese communities in North America, New Zealand, Europe, Africa, and everywhere else.[38]

Further, more individuals will enter the United States as tourists but overstay their visas and become undocumented migrants. In 2000, 700 million tourist entries were recorded, compared to 480 million in 1990 and 300 million in 1980.[39] Distinctions between travel and migration have become increasingly blurred. Still more new immigrants continue to maintain citizenship of the sending countries and residences in both the United States and sending countries and in third countries. A recent demographic trend also indicates that many Asian American retirees have relocated to their Asian sending countries for better and less expensive medical care, cheaper housing, and cheaper domestic services.[40]

New Opportunities and Challenges Facing Asian Americans

It is very likely that the rapid development in the information technology (IT) industry prompted by computer technology and globalization has presented Asian Americans with more socioeconomic opportunities. In the so-called knowledge economy, Asian Americans are finding more employment. With a higher concentration in college degrees associated with STEM fields, Asian Americans in recent decades have found more employment in the IT industry.[41] The number of Asian Americans working in IT increased from 170,771 in 2000 to 171,150 in 2010, while the general American population employed in IT declined from 3,996,564 to 3,015,521 during the same period.[42] The popular image of Asian Americans as academic and occupational successes is further strengthened.

On the cultural front, the rapid expansion of Confucius Institutes in the United States and Canada indicates growing interest in Chinese culture and a consequential friendlier socioeconomic climate for Chinese Americans. Confucius Institutes are Chinese government-sponsored nonprofit public institutions that aim to promote Chinese language and culture and facilitate cultural exchanges. The first Confucius Institute was opened in Seoul on November 21, 2004. The same year an institute opened at the University of Maryland. In their initial years, the institutes were usually opened at state universities or regional colleges in the United States. However, following Chinese president Hu Jintao's October 2007 speech to the Seventeenth Chinese Communist Party Congress, in which he said China must enhance its culture as "part of the soft power" of the country, the program grew rapidly in scope and ambition. Under the auspices of the Chinese Ministry of Education, a special agency called the Office of Chinese Language Council International, colloquially Hanban, was established and directly involved in the management of the program. Hanban generally promises each Confucius Institute in the United States $100,000 a year, along with teaching materials, to promote the teaching of the Chinese language as well as cultural exchange.

The economic downturn since 2008 made the Chinese offer associated with the establishment of Confucius Institutes more attractive. Many private universities have joined the ranks to approve the opening of institutes. The University of Pennsylvania, once a staunch critic, passed the proposal to open a Confucius Institute in 2012. At the same time, Stanford University welcomed it on campus, as did Columbia University and the London School of Economics. By early 2012, there were 350 Confucius Institutes worldwide among 96 nations or regions, but mostly located in North America and Europe. In the United States, there were 70 institutes as of 2012. It is estimated that about 30 million non-Chinese people are learning Chinese language around the world. However, critics remain suspicious and worry about the influence of the Chinese institute on campuses.[43] Since 2017, 104 of the 118 total Confucius Institutions in American universities and colleges had been shut down.[44] The rapid economic development in Asia also increased the chances for Asian Americans to have greater voices in American politics. Recent decades have seen increased Asian American representation at all levels of politics. The appointment of two Asian American cabinet members during the Obama administration, Steven Chu as secretary of energy and Gary Locke as secretary of commerce in 2009, and the latter as American ambassador to China in 2011, represented only the most high-profile political participation of Asian Americans. At the state and

TABLE 10.1 ASIAN AMERICAN REPRESENTATION, 2007 TOTALS

Federal senators	2
Federal representatives	4
State senators	62
State representatives	85
State elected officials	4
State governors	5
Lieutenant governors	4
City mayors	24
City councilmembers	121
Judges	306
School board and higher education officials	275

Source: Don T. Nakanishi and James S. Lao, eds., *2007–2008 National Asian Pacific American Political Almanac* (Los Angeles: UCLA Asian American Studies Center, 2007), 82–83.

local levels, many Asian Americans have been incorporated into the mainstream political structure, as indicated in table 10.1.

Globalization at the same time has also posed new challenges to Asian Americans. To better position themselves in the increasingly globalized socioeconomic environment and the rising economies in Asia, Asian Americans have realized the importance of knowing Asian culture and the ability to speak one's ancestral language, especially Chinese, as it is becoming the official language of Asia. As documented in numerous studies, learning Chinese in a non-Chinese-speaking environment is a formidable task for Asian American children and their parents. Even following years of study at weekend ethnic language schools, many Asian American youth found themselves nonproficient in their ancestral languages and had to relearn them by enrolling in Asian language classes at college.[45]

The increased opportunities for working and traveling between the United States and other countries have produced many transmigrants, or so-called astronauts, individuals flying back and forth between the United States where their families dwell and Asian countries where they work. The transnational split family life has in recent decades presented challenges to the generally more stable family structure of many Asian American families. Although no statistics are available yet, there has been evidence of a rise in the divorce rate and growing numbers of extramarital affairs among transnational split families. Numerous real or fictional stories of marriage dissolutions are circulating in the Asian media and in the circle of transmigrants and their virtual communities such as the Chinese News Digest and haiguinet.com.[46]

Furthermore, the transnational lifestyle also raises issues concerning transmigrant children's education, dual/multiple residences, dual citizenship/nationality, and split identity/loyalty to sending country / receiving country. Many returnees found themselves frustrated by the problem of lack of appropriate schooling for their children in Asian countries. They further face challenges from government administrative restrictions. Without local registration identity, they are constrained in myriad aspects of life, including housing, children's education, and limited access to research facilities and funding. To deal with the situation, many Chinese returnees, while holding American passports or permanent resident cards, continue to maintain and renew their Chinese Registration Identity Card, thus having virtual dual citizenship. Meanwhile, many transnational Asian Americans with legitimate dual citizenship participate in the vote in both countries, practicing a "flexible citizenship" and remaining loyal to both host and sending countries.[47]

Economic difficulties resulting from outsourcing and the economic downturn since 2008 may have also caused feelings of anxiety and anger toward Asian Americans, which would lead to violence or hate crimes against Asian Americans, and there might be possible repeats of Vincent Chin, a Chinese American in Detroit who was beaten to death by two European Americans in June 1982. The death of Danny Chen proves the concern legitimate. On October 3, 2011, Private Chen, a nineteen-year-old Chinese American from New York, was found dead (apparently by suicide) in a guard tower on an American outpost in Afghanistan. The officials revealed that Private Chen had been subjected to physical abuse and ethnic slurs such as "chink," "dragon lady," and "gook" by his supervisors, who one night dragged him out of bed and across the floor when he failed to turn off a water heater after showering.[48]

On June 23, 2012, the thirtieth anniversary of the Vincent Chin murder, Asian American communities in over thirty cities organized a mega "Google Hangout" to commemorate the event and to call for Asian Americans to be vigilant against hate crimes and discriminatory reactions to them under globalization. Featuring a number of high-profile Asian American politicians and activists, the event discussed hate crimes and bullying. In light of recent tragedies like the extreme hazing and subsequent death of Private Chen and the continuing effects of 9/11, the event asked what Asian Americans and Pacific Islanders could do to stand up against racism and discrimination.

THE COVID-19 PANDEMIC AND ASIAN AMERICAN COMMUNITIES

COVID-19, the unprecedented global pandemic, has profoundly changed life for all human beings and their physical, geopolitical, socioeconomic, and psychological environments. To Asian Americans, however, the blow of the pandemic and its ripple waves were much more detrimental than to other populations. Frustrated and devastated by the multifaceted consequences of the crisis, angry individuals targeted Asians as they vented their frustrations; criminals also took advantage of the situation and robbed, looted, and destroyed property owned by Asian Americans. Numerous incidents occurred where Asians or Asian Americans were spat on, punched, kicked, and assaulted.[49] In addition, Asian restaurants, stores, and private properties were looted, robbed, torched, and destroyed.[50] Starting as a public health issue, COVID-19 has triggered the long-existing racial tension and forced Asian Americans to reorganize and realign their socioeconomic infrastructures to face new challenges.

COVID-19's Impacts on Asian American Businesses and Communities

ECONOMIC LOSS. A survey indicated that 51 percent of the Chinese restaurants in the United States had closed because of the COVID-19 pandemic, as "a result in part of consumer prejudice and misperceptions," by mid-April 2020. The closure rate in descending order was sandwich restaurants (23 percent), Indian restaurants (21 percent), and burger specialists (20 percent). In contrast, delivery and takeout chicken wing specialists had the lowest (8 percent) mortality rate.[51]

Consequently, restaurants turned to delivery and takeout but faced hefty charges from online ordering companies: up to 30 percent of the cost of each order, along with other expenses of rent, utility, and labor. For each dollar of online ordering, a restaurant operator received only 30 cents. Facing challenges, many Asian restauranteurs tried to be flexible to survive the crises and modified their operations. A restaurant in New York, for instance, converted its business to catering health care providers from a nearby hospital with reduced prices and boxed food delivery. 888 Seafood Restaurant in New York purchased two laminating machines to seal delivery orders. This service earned the trust of customers and attracted more orders. Some other restaurant owners turned to social media vloggers (video bloggers), making cooking videos to promote sales.[52]

HATE CRIMES: FROM HOSTILITY TO VERBAL ABUSE, PHYSICAL ASSAULTS, ROBBERY, AND KILLING. On February 9, 2021, Stop AAPI Hate reported over 2,808 cases of hate crimes against Asian Americans from March 19 to December 2020 in forty-seven states and Washington, D.C. Among the cases, physical assaults constituted 8.7 percent of the cases, spitting 6.4 percent, verbal abuse 70.9 percent, and avoidances 21.4 percent (see sidebar).[53]

On February 19, 2021, Ethnic Media Services, an organization founded by Sandy Close in 2017, headquartered in San Francisco, promoting the voices of ethnic media, and influencing about one-half of the ethnic minority residents in California, hosted a media briefing. The leaders of the major ethnic community organizations in California urged the ethnic community to unite to combat anti-Asian violence.[54]

On March 16, 2021, anti-Asian crime crashed to a new low in Atlanta. Around five o'clock in the afternoon, twenty-one-year-old Robert Aaron Long stormed into three Asian-owned massage spas, killing eight people who were mostly female workers. Six of the eight victims were women of Asian ancestry—four South Korean, two Chinese. Long admitted that he had "sex addiction" and was angry about it.[55] The Atlanta spa shooting turned into a catalyst mobilizing Asian Americans and the general population to form a united front to combat the accelerating anti-Asian hate crime. In the following days, various Asian American community organizations condemned the anti-Asian hate and organized candlelight vigils and peaceful rallies. Asian American politicians, activists, and scholars publicly aired their anger and concern, connecting the current events to historical and systemic racial discrimination and exploitation in the country and pressing federal, state, and local authorities for new legislations.[56]

PSYCHOLOGICAL TRAUMA: IDENTITY CRISIS / LOYALTY QUESTIONED. Asian Americans began to feel less of a sense of "belongingness" and greater "otherness." They wondered if they were Americans anymore when facing more frequent and blatant discrimination and inhospitality. Korean American actor John Cho's cry well represented such feelings (see sidebar). Others became resentful to their Asian heritage. A second-generation Chinese American complained about his Asian background, "I could have been admitted to a better college if I were not Chinese," despite the fact

---

RECENT ANTI-ASIAN VIOLENCE RELATING TO COVID-19*

A family celebrating a birthday at a restaurant is yelled at with racist remarks by a tech executive: "F–k you Asians. Trump is going to F–k you . . . f–king Asian piece of s–t."

An Asian American resident physician is berated by a black patient for allegedly being a carrier of coronavirus. A middle school child is punched in the head twenty times in his schoolyard by a bully who accuses him of having COVID-19 and tells him to go back to China.

A rash of brutal crimes targeting Asian Americans highlights deepening racism related to the arrival of COVID-19 in the country. In recent weeks, videos on social media in which vulnerable elderly people are pushed on the sidewalks or physically attacked, have aroused not only the concern of those who have been tracking this racial violence but also the solidarity of other ethnic minorities.

Source: Jenny Manrique, "Ethnic Communities Unite to Combat Anti-Asian Violence," *Ethnic Media Services*, February 23, 2021, https://ethnicmediaservices.org/immigration/ethnic-communities-unite-to-combat-anti-asian-violence/.

* Title added by the author.

that he went to the best high school in New York City.⁵⁷

INNER-CITY ASIANS SUFFER MORE CASUALTIES OF PANDEMIC. The pandemic caused an exodus from New York and other coastal metropolises to the Midwest and small towns elsewhere. As individuals with better financial means ran away from New York to less populated localities, residents engaged in essential services or with limited resources had to stay put. Poor Asians suffered higher rates of pandemic-related sickness and death. In New York, pandemic patients of Asian ancestries were 50 percent higher than that of Euro-Ancestries according to the Ethnic Media Services briefing on February 12, 2021.⁵⁸

FEWER CHINESE STUDENTS COME TO THE UNITED STATES. As COVID-19-related anti-Asian hate crimes grew in the United States, many Chinese parents opted for international schools in China rather than sending their children overseas. Consequently, growth rates in the once-booming industry slowed drastically. In 2020, the growth in the Chinese students studying in the United States plunged to less than one percent, according to a report by a Beijing-based think tank.⁵⁹

> **CORONAVIRUS REMINDS ASIAN AMERICANS LIKE ME THAT OUR BELONGING IS CONDITIONAL**
> John Cho
>
> The pandemic is reminding us that our belonging is conditional. One moment we are Americans, the next we are all foreigners, who "brought" the virus here.
> ... And because the stereotypes may be complimentary (hard-working, good at math), it makes people—including us—think that anti-Asian sentiment is somehow less serious, that it's racism lite. That allows us to dismiss the current wave of Asian hate crimes as trivial, isolated and unimportant. Consider the comedians who mock Asians, but restrain themselves when it comes to other groups.
> ... You can't stand up for some and not for others. And like the virus, unchecked aggression has the potential to spread wildly.
>
> *Source*: John Cho, "Coronavirus Reminds Asian Americans Like Me That Our Belonging Is Conditional," *Los Angeles Times*, April 22, 2020.

Responses from Asian American Communities

COUNT ANTI-ASIAN AMERICAN RACISM CAMPAIGNS. Following the surge of anti-Asian hate sentiments, Asian Americans launched a series of campaigns to count anti-Asian hate crimes. On March 19, 2020, in response to increased racially motivated violence against Asian peoples as a result of the COVID-19 pandemic in the country, the Asian Pacific Planning and Policy Council (A3PCON), Chinese for Affirmative Action

FIGURE 10.1 Vigil against Asian hate in Union Square, San Francisco, California, March 19, 2021. On March 16, 2021, the Atlanta spa shooting where suspect Robert Aaron Long killed eight people, six of whom were Asian women, prompted mass protests against anti-Asian violence in cities across the United States during the COVID-19 pandemic. Courtesy Andrew Ratto.

(CAA), and the Asian American Studies Department of San Francisco State University, launched the Stop AAPI Hate reporting center. This nonprofit social organization tracks incidents of discrimination, hate, and xenophobia against Asian Americans and Pacific Islanders (AAPIs).[60]

Recognizing Asian American heritage month and urging "Advocate Not Hate," PBS produced a 5-part docuseries titled *Asian Americans*, which aired on May 11 and 12, 2020. It highlights the role of Asian American community in shaping American history and identity.[61] Meanwhile, various Asian American politicians, activists, and civil rights organizations sponsored public workshops providing legal advice and information on how to defend oneself when facing verbal/physical assaults.[62] At the national and local levels, many Asian American studies specialists made presentations educating the public on Asian American history, denouncing anti-Asian hate crimes, and calling for partnership in combatting systemic racism.[63]

In February 2021, the racially motivated anti-Asian violence heightened around and after the Lunar New Year on February 12. In New York, San Francisco, and Rowland Heights, California, elderly Asians and women were attacked and robbed.[64] Angry community leaders and local residents could no longer remain silent. They organized #StopAsianHate rallies in New York, San Francisco, and Oakland, declaring, "This isn't an Asian fight. This is a human fight."⁶⁵ On April 22, 2021, the Senate overwhelmingly (94–1) passed the Stop Asian Hate Crimes bill, sponsored by Senator Mazie Hirono of Hawaii and Representative Grace Mong of New York.⁶⁶ The bill encourages Asian American communities with various innovative responses as follows.

MUTUAL AID

1. *Collective actions.* Across the country in many major Asian American communities, residents took collective actions and organized diverse group activities. For example, social groups of roughly ten families or so evolved from the varieties of social media groups, especially through WeChat, a Chinese social media application used by the majority of Chinese Americans that originated from mainland China, These groups, quite similar to the local mutual collective Bao Jia System (保甲制, ten families form a *jia*, ten *jias* form a *bao*) in Chinese history. Members of such groups alternated shopping responsibilities—shopping for the group and then dividing the goods among member families in order to reduce exposure to the COVID-19 virus.⁶⁷

2. *Maintain positive images.* In New York City, many Chinese American individuals and organizations donated facial coverings and other personal protection equipment to hospitals throughout the city.⁶⁸ In St. Louis, Asian American restaurants and community organizations including the Chinese Chamber of Commerce, Chinese language churches, and Asian American organizations jointly delivered hundreds of boxed-food meals to area hospitals.⁶⁹

3. *Volunteer patrols to maintain neighborhoods safety.* In places where Asians suffered the most anti-Asian violence such as New York City, San Francisco, Oakland, and Rowland Heights, local residents and business owners jointly organized volunteer patrols. In New York, volunteers cleaned and patrolled neighborhoods beginning in mid-2020. In Oakland, where a number of Asian elderly people were physically assaulted by criminals around the Lunar New Year, Chinese small business owners and volunteers formed the Oakland Chinatown Volunteer in February 2021 to patrol Chinatown. In Rowland Heights, where Asians, especially women, had been targeted by criminals, local resident Chuck Sun, a newly retired engineer, founded a volunteer patrol group, garnering support from area residents and the local police force.⁷⁰

In many major cities with substantial Chinese populations, Chinese organized gun-owner clubs. Members took turns patrolling commercial areas. The Chicago Chinese Gun-Owners Club, for instance, routinely cruised the Chinatown business district and effectively discouraged criminal activities and therefore contributed to the fact that Chicago's Chinatown was the only Chinatown in the country that escaped looting, robberies, and major destruction.⁷¹

ASIAN AMERICANS UNDER GLOBALIZATION IN HISTORICAL PERSPECTIVE

The rise of China and other Asian countries as emerging economic powers and the decline of the United States are inevitable consequences of globalization, which helps equilibrate the distribution of wealth around the world. Globalization is gradually removing the natural and artificial barriers causing gaps between the developed and developing countries and between the one-percenters and the ninety-nine-percenters. The rise of both China and other Asian countries with fast-growing economics and the decline of the United States will slow down until they reach their proper places in the world's equilibrium. Although the situation remains murky, it will become clear in the decades to come. In the meanwhile, governments and individuals should reposition themselves to best adjust to the new world system. The COVID-19 pandemic and the subsequent economic, social, and psychological difficulties facing Americans intensified long-existing racial tensions in the country, prompting Asian Americans to adopt new strategies to survive and further thrive in the new era.

KEY TERMS

China rise
U.S. decline
Program for International Student Assessment (PISA)
Obama doctrine
globalization
Chinmerica

three balances theory
astronauts
flexible citizenship
Confucius Institute
Danny Chen
STOP AAPI hate

REVIEW QUESTIONS

1. What is your understanding of the Asian ascent and U.S. decline phenomenon? What is your assessment of the world in the next twenty to thirty years?
2. How would you interpret globalization and its positive and negative impacts?
3. Identify the new trends of migration and assimilation under globalization. How would you reposition yourself in order to better negotiate the increasingly globalized environment?
4. What types of damage did Asian American communities endure during the COVID-19 pandemic? What were the strategies or responses of Asian American communities when facing multifaceted challenges during the pandemic?

FILMS

Crichton, Kelly (series producer). *China Rises.* Discovery Channel. 2 DVDs (4 ours, 24 minutes). Documentary on the rapidly developing economic power, from a factory to a pop concert, an Olympic volleyball court, and the red carpet at the Shanghai Film Festival. 2008.

Gulati, Sonali (writer/director/producer). *Nalini by Day, Nancy by Night.* 27-minute documentary on the outsourcing of American jobs to India. 2005.

FURTHER READING

Ferguson, Niall. *Colossus: The Rise and Fall of the American Empire.* New York: Penguin, 2005.

Friedman, Thomas L. *The Lexus and the Olive Tree: Understanding Globalization.* New York: Anchor Books, 2000.

Helweg, Arthur W. *Strangers in a Not-So-Strange Land: Indian American Immigrants in the Global Age.* Belmont, CA: Thomson Wadsworth, 2004.

McKeown, Adam. *Melancholy Order: Asian Migration and the Globalization of Borders.* New York: Columbia University Press, 2008.

Omi, Michael A. "The Changing Meaning of Race." *America Becoming: Racial Trends and Their Consequences* 1 (2001): 243–263.

CHRONOLOGY

1784	The *Empress of China* becomes the first U.S. merchant ship to arrive in China, inaugurating trade between the two countries.
1785	Individual Chinese reported in Pennsylvania.
1790	The U.S. Congress passes the Naturalization Act, restricting naturalized citizenship to white persons only; the law bars naturalized citizenship for Asian immigrants until the mid-twentieth century.
1818	The first Chinese students to attend a U.S. institution of higher education enroll at the Foreign Mission School in Cornwall, Connecticut.
1829	The Siamese twins Chang and Eng are the first Thais to arrive in the United States; they are granted citizenship in 1839.
1835	Americans establish the first sugar plantation in Hawaii.
1830s	The first Chinese immigrants begin working on sugar plantations in Hawaii.
1848	Gold is discovered in California, leading to the immigration of tens of thousands of Chinese in the late 1840s and 1850s.
1849	100,000 immigrants, mostly male, flock to California.
1850	California legislature passes the Foreign Miners' Tax, initially targeting Latin Americans, but soon affecting Chinese; Hawaii passes the Masters and Servants Act and sets up the Royal Hawaiian Agricultural Society to recruit plantation workers for its rapidly developing sugar plantations.
1851	Chinese in San Francisco form the Sam Yup (or San Yi, meaning "three counties": Namhoi [Nanhai], Punyi [Panyu], and Shuntak [Shunde]) and Sze Yup (Si Yi, meaning "four counties": Sunwui [Xinhui], Toishan [Taishan], Hoiping [Kaiping], and Yanping [Enping]) regional associations.
1852	The first group of 195 Chinese contract laborers arrives in Hawaii; 20,000 arrive in San Francisco; missionary William Speer opens a Presbyterian mission for Chinese immigrants in San Francisco; Chinese first begin to appear in court. Chinese immigrants found America's first Buddhist temple in San Francisco. The first Chinese secret society, or *tong*, is founded in San Francisco.
1854	Yung Wing graduates from Yale College, becoming the first person of Chinese ancestry to graduate from a U.S. institution of higher learning. The Convention of Kanagawa is signed between the Japanese government and Commodore Matthew Perry, establishing formal relations between the two countries; Perry is representing the United States on his second expedition to open up Japan to the outside world.

1856	The *Chinese Daily News* is launched in Sacramento, California, becoming the first Chinese language daily newspaper in the world.
1858	Joseph Heco, a stranded Japanese fisherman and translator for Commodore Matthew Perry on his pioneering visit to Japan in 1854, becomes the first person of Japanese ancestry to gain U.S. citizenship.
1859	San Francisco opens the Chinese School, America's first public school for Asian immigrants.
1860	Chinese children are banned from California public schools.
1862	Chinese American businessmen in San Francisco found the Chinese Six Companies, later the Chinese Consolidated Benevolent Association, an umbrella organization for various mutual aid societies.
1863	The first Chinese Americans are hired by the Central Pacific to lay track on the transcontinental railroad; by the time the project is finished in 1869, about ten thousand will be hired.
1868	The governments of the United States and Imperial China sign the Burlingame Treaty, guaranteeing fair treatment and residency rights for each other's immigrants; the treaty will be abrogated as a result of the Chinese Exclusion Act of 1882.
	The first Japanese plantation workers arrive in Hawaii, lured to what was then an independent kingdom by an American businessman there.
1869	The first significant contingent of Japanese immigrants to the U.S. mainland arrive in California and form the first Japanese American settlement, in the gold country of the Sierra Nevada foothills.
1871	Rioting in Los Angeles leads to the deaths of twenty-one Chinese at the hands of white mobs.
1873	San Francisco passes the Laundry Ordinance, shutting down Chinese-owned laundries in the city; the U.S. Supreme Court overturns the law as unconstitutional in *Yick Ho v. Hopkins*, the first time it rules in favor of the rights of Asian American immigrants.
1875	Congress passes the Page Act, requiring potential Chinese immigrants to win approval of U.S. consul representatives before immigrating to the United States; the act represents the first legislation aimed at restricting Chinese immigration.
	White Californians found the Native Sons of the Golden West as a fraternal society aimed at preserving the state's gold rush heritage; by the early twentieth century, the Native Sons had become one of the most influential anti-Asian immigrant organizations in the country.
1876	The San Francisco municipal government enacts the Queue Ordinance, banning Chinese men from wearing their characteristic queues, or long pigtails.
1880	California becomes the first state to include Asian Americans under its anti-miscegenation statutes.
	Whites riot in Denver, killing one Chinese and leaving much of the city's Chinatown in ruins.
1882	Congress passes the first Chinese Exclusion Act, banning the immigration of Chinese laborers for ten years; the law is extended in 1892 and 1902.
	The United States and Korea sign the Treaty of Amity and Commerce, establishing diplomatic relations between the two countries.
1883	Ya Giljun becomes the first Korean to study in the United States when he enrolls at the Dammer Academy in Massachusetts.

1885	Twenty-eight Chinese laborers are killed by white miners in the town of Rock Springs, Wyoming.
1885	Local government officials order the expulsion of Chinese from the Puget Sound region of Washington Territory, resulting in gun battles over the next two years between Chinese, whites, and police.
1888	Congress amends the Chinese Exclusion Act of 1882 to include all persons from China, with a limited number of exemptions for students and teachers; it also passes legislation preventing Chinese who return to their home country on visits to return to the United States.
1893	American planters and businessmen seize control of Hawaii from Queen Liliuokalani, the last native ruler of an independent Hawaii.
1895	In response to anti-Chinese discrimination and to promote opportunity within the Chinese American community, the predecessor organization of the Chinese American Citizens Alliance is founded in San Francisco.
1898	The California Supreme Court rules in the case of *Tape v. Harley* that Chinese children are permitted to attend public schools in their neighborhoods if there are no schools set up specifically for them. With Hawaii's annexation by the United States in 1898, thousands of Japanese and other Asian workers there migrate to the continental United States. The United States gains possession of the Philippines and Guam as a result of the Spanish-American War. Congress passes the Pensionado Act to train Filipino students at U.S. colleges and universities.
1899	Part of the Samoan island chain is annexed by the United States, eventually becoming the territory of American Samoa.
1900	Mainland labor recruiters begin bringing Japanese agricultural workers from Hawaii to California and the West Coast.
1901	The U.S. Navy begins to recruit Filipino sailors, of whom some 6,000 will serve in World War I.
1902	Congress passes the Geary Act, making the Chinese Exclusion Act permanent.
1903	Federal legislation establishes an "Asiatic barred zone," prohibiting immigration from British India (including Burma), French Indochina, and parts of the Middle East, Central Asia, Oceania, and Russia's Far East. The Japanese Mexican Labor Association is founded in Oxnard, California, becoming the first farm workers union in California. The first organized group of Korean laborers arrives in Hawaii. Some of them found Sin-Min-Hoi, dedicated to fighting Japanese imperialism in their home country; it is the first organization of Koreans in the United States. Filipino students with U.S. government scholarships, known as *pensionados*, begin to study at American universities.
1905	White labor leaders in San Francisco found the Asiatic Exclusion League, aimed at preventing immigration from Japan, Korea, and later India.
1906	A massive earthquake and fire level San Francisco's Chinatown, the largest Chinese enclave in the United States. San Francisco school board attempts to segregate Asians from white students through the creation of the Oriental School. The first Filipino laborers arrive in Hawaii to work on sugar plantations.

1907	The first large contingent of Indian immigrants enters the United States; coming via British Columbia, they settle in California's Sacramento River Valley.
	The Hawaiian Sugar Planters Association begins to recruit unskilled workers from the Philippines.
1907–1908	President Theodore Roosevelt negotiates and signs the Gentlemen's Agreement with the government of Japan, an informal understanding that the latter will severely restrict its citizens from immigrating to the United States.
1910	The Angel Island immigration station is opened in San Francisco Bay, largely to process immigrants from Asia; the station will remain in operation until it is partially destroyed by fire in 1940.
1912	Sikh immigrants found their first temple the United States, located in Stockton, California.
	The first U.S. branch of the Khalsa Diwan (Free Divine) Society, the first social and political organization of Asian Indians in North America—founded in Vancouver, British Columbia, in 1906—is established in Stockton, California.
1913	The California legislature passes the Alien Land Law, restricting and/or prohibiting the lease or sale of land to "aliens ineligible for citizenship"; the measure primarily affects Asian Americans.
	The Ghadr Party, or Hindi Association of the Pacific Coast, is launched by Indian immigrants in Astoria, Oregon; the party pushes for Indian independence from Britain.
1915	Chinese farmers and merchants found the predominantly Chinese American community of Locke, California, the largest nonurban Asian American town in the continental United States.
1916	The first Tongans of modern times arrive in Hawaii.
1919	The Filipino Federation of Labor, America's first Filipino labor union, is founded by sugar workers in Hawaii.
1920	California voters pass a referendum further restricting the leasing of land to Asian aliens in the United States, closing loopholes in the 1913 Alien Land Law that permitted Asian immigrants to own land under the names of their native-born children; eleven other states pass similar laws between 1917 and World War II.
	Bengali guru Paramahansa Yogananda arrives in the United States and lectures on yoga, helping to introduce that discipline and Indian spirituality to Americans.
1920	White Californians organize the Japanese Exclusion League to advocate a ban on Japanese immigration into the United States.
1922	Congress passes the Cable Act, nullifying the citizenship of all U.S.-born women who marry someone ineligible for citizenship; the law primarily affects Asian Americans.
	The U.S. Supreme Court rules in *Takao Ozawa v. United States* that Japanese immigrants are not eligible for citizenship.
1923	In *United States v. Bhagat Singh Thind*, the U.S. Supreme Court rules that immigrants from India are not "free white persons," and therefore not eligible for citizenship under the Naturalization Act of 1790.
1924	The omnibus National Origins Act, which includes the Asian Exclusion Act, establishes strict national quotas for immigration, limiting newcomers from Asian countries and colonial possessions, among others, to token numbers.
	A gun battle between striking Filipino sugar plantation workers and police in Hanapepe, Hawaii, results in the deaths of sixteen Filipino workers and four police officers.

1925	The Chinese Hospital, the first in the United States devoted to the health needs of Chinese immigrants, is founded in San Francisco.
	The Filipino Federation of America, a leading mutual aid society, is founded in Los Angeles.
1927	In *Farrington v. Tokushiga*, the U.S. Supreme Court rules that efforts to close private Japanese language schools are unconstitutional.
1929	The Japanese American Citizens League, the leading advocacy organization for Japanese Americans, is founded in California.
	White mobs, angered by interracial mingling between Filipino men and white women at local dance halls, attack Filipinos in Watsonville, California, leading to dozens of injuries and the death of one Filipino.
1934	The Tydings-McDuffie Act provides limited self-government for the U.S. colony of the Philippines, setting it on the road to independence; the measure also sets strict limits on the number of Filipinos entering the United States.
1935	The Filipino Repatriation Act is passed by Congress and signed into law; the measure helps Filipinos residing in the United States return to their native islands.
1937	In response to Japan's invasion of China, Chinese Americans establish the China War Relief Association of America in San Francisco to coordinate aid to their homeland. The Bank of Canton, the first Chinese American–owned bank, opens in San Francisco.
1941	On December 7, military forces of Imperial Japan attack the U.S. naval base at Pearl Harbor, Hawaii, triggering a declaration of war against Japan and U.S. entry into World War II.
1942	In response to the Japanese attack on Pearl Harbor, President Franklin Roosevelt issues Executive Order 9066, calling for the incarceration of more than 120,000 West Coast Japanese Americans in "internment camps" for the duration of World War II.
	An armed confrontation between internees and guards at Manzanar, California, over informants results in the deaths of two Japanese American internees; it is the worst incident of violence in any wartime internment camp for Japanese Americans.
1943	Congress repeals the Chinese Exclusion Act of 1882, though still limiting Chinese immigration to about 100 persons per year.
	The U.S. government organizes the 442nd Regimental Combat Team and 100th Infantry Battalion of Japanese American soldiers; the two units see action in Italy.
	Japanese American Ikiko Toguri, better known as "Tokyo Rose," begins her English language propaganda broadcasts from Tokyo aimed at U.S. servicemen. In 1949, she receives a ten-year federal prison sentence for treason; released in 1955, she was granted a pardon in 1977.
1943–1944	In three *coram nobis* ("error before us") cases—*Hirabayashi v. United States* (1943), *Yasui v. United States* (1943), and *Korematsu v. United States* (1944)—the U.S. Supreme Court upholds wartime laws and rules requiring Japanese Americans to obey curfews or turn themselves over to authorities for incarceration, per Executive Order 9066 in 1942.
1944	In a rare wartime ruling, the U.S. Supreme Court declares in *Ex Parte Endo* that the federal government could not incarcerate a Japanese American woman whose loyalty it had already conceded.
	The Heart Mountain Fair Play Committee is established at the Japanese American relocation center of the same name in Wyoming to resist U.S. efforts to draft Japanese Americans for service in the military. Arrested for conspiring to violate the Selective Service Act, several leaders of the committee are granted pardons in 1946.

1944–1945 U.S. forces seize much of Micronesia from the Japanese, establishing a protectorate that will continue into the 1990s and, in the case of the Northern Marianas, to the present day.

1946 The United States grants independence to the Philippines. With passage of the Filipino Naturalization Act, or Luce-Celler Act, the U.S. Congress grants naturalization rights to immigrants from India and the newly independent Philippines.

1947 Congress passes the War Brides Act, permitting U.S. military personnel to marry and bring into the United States brides from Japan, China, the Philippines, and Korea, exempting them from the national quotas of the Immigration Act of 1924. Several thousand women enter the country under the law.

California removes segregation clauses from its education code, allowing for the integration of Asian and non-Asian students in public schools.

1948 In the case of *Oyama v. California*, the Supreme Court declares California's Alien Land Law of 1913 unconstitutional under the Fourteenth Amendment's "equal protection" clause.

Congress passes the Displaced Persons Act, accelerating the immigration of World War II refugees; following the communist takeover of China the following year, the act is used to allow in thousands of refugees fleeing the new communist regime in mainland China.

The Evacuation Claims Act, aimed at providing compensation to Japanese Americans for financial losses suffered during their incarceration in World War II, is passed by Congress and signed into law by President Harry Truman.

Korean American Sammy Lee becomes the first Asian American to win an Olympic gold medal, in platform diving at the London games.

1949 After more than twenty years of warfare, communist forces emerge victorious in mainland China; the United States refuses to recognize the new communist government, backing the nationalist forces on Taiwan instead.

1950 The United States leads an international military force to turn back a North Korean invasion of South Korea; the war continues through 1953.

Communist China invades Tibet, sending tens of thousands of refugees to India, Nepal, and other countries; several thousand eventually settle in the United States.

1951 Chinese-born immigrant Wang An founds Wang Laboratories, which will become one of the country's leading early computer hardware and software companies.

1952 The Immigration and Nationality Act, better known as the McCarran-Walter Act, reverses earlier laws that banned Asian immigrants from gaining U.S. citizenship.

1953 Though aimed at European refugees of World War II and communism, the Refugee Relief Act allows some 2,000 Chinese and 3,000 other Asian refugees to enter the United States.

1954 In the landmark *Brown v. Board of Education* decision, the U.S. Supreme Court declares racially segregated public schools unconstitutional; while aimed primarily at African American students, the ruling affects Asian students as well.

1956 The Immigration and Naturalization Service launches its Confession Program, allowing Chinese immigrants who came into the country under false pretenses to regularize their status and put them on the road to citizenship.

Democrat Dalip Singh of California becomes the first Asian American elected to U.S. Congress.

1957 Tsung-dao Lee and Chen Ning Yang become the first Asian Americans to win a Nobel Prize, in physics.

1959	Hawaii is admitted to the Union as the fiftieth state. With its large Asian American population, it becomes the first state with a nonwhite majority; its representative, Daniel Inouye, becomes the first Japanese American to serve in the U.S. Congress.

The American Federation of Labor creates the Agricultural Workers Organizing Committee to organize Filipino grape pickers in California. |
| 1963 | President John F. Kennedy establishes the Chinese Refugee Relief Committee, to aid persons fleeing Communist China; he appoints Anna Chenault, the first Chinese American to serve in a high-level White House position, to head the committee. |
| 1965 | The United States begins sending combat troops to defend the South Vietnamese government against indigenous communist forces backed by North Vietnam. Direct American involvement in the war continues until 1973; South Vietnam falls to communist forces in 1975, ending near continuous warfare in the country since the late 1940s.

President Lyndon Johnson signs into law the Immigration and Nationality Act, ending the small national quotas established under the Immigration Act of 1924. Emphasizing family reunion, education, and job skills as criteria for immigration, the law opens the possibility of immigration to millions of Asian immigrants over the subsequent decades.

The East West Players, a leading showcase for Asian American theater, is founded in the Little Tokyo neighborhood of Los Angeles.

Japanese American Patsy Mink of Hawaii becomes the first Asian American woman, and the first nonwhite woman, to serve in the U.S. Congress. |
1966	Sociologist William Petersen coins the term "model minority" to describe Asian Americans as an educationally and economically successful ethnic minority. Many Asian Americans would come to resent the term, saying it allowed non-Asian Americans to overlook the problems and prejudice facing many Asian Americans.
1967	In *Loving v. Virginia*, the U.S. Supreme Court declares the anti-miscegenation laws of Virginia and thirty-seven other states unconstitutional, allowing for interracial marriages between, among others, Asians and non-Asians.
1968	The federal Bilingual Education Act mandates and funds bilingual education for non-English-speaking students.
1970	In pursuit of Vietnamese communist sanctuaries, the United States launches an invasion of neighboring Cambodia.
1971	The first advocacy group for Pakistani Americans, the Pakistan League of America, is founded in New York City.
1972	President Richard Nixon visits the communist People's Republic of China, beginning a rapprochement between Washington and Beijing.
1974	The Asian American Dance Theatre is founded in New York City.

The U.S. Supreme Court rules in the precedent-setting case of *Lau v. Nichols* that San Francisco must provide bilingual education to its Chinese American students. |
| 1975 | The fall of Cambodia, Laos, and South Vietnam to communist forces leads to a mass exodus of Vietnamese, Hmong, and, later, Cambodian refugees to the United States.

The Khmer Rouge seize power in Cambodia, leading to four years of genocide that results in the deaths of up to one-third of the country's population and sending tens of thousands of refugees abroad, many eventually settling in the United States. |

Chinese American assemblywoman March Fong Eu is elected California's secretary of state, becoming the first Asian American to hold statewide office anywhere in the United States.

1976　Chinese immigrant Charles Wang cofounds Computer Associates International, which later becomes one of the nation's largest software firms.

1978　The first so-called boat people, seagoing refugees from the communist government of Vietnam, set sail. Over the next several years, more than a million Vietnamese refugees will leave the country, though not all by sea; about half ultimately settle in the United States.

1979　The United States and the communist People's Republic of China normalize relations; Washington shifts diplomatic recognition from Taiwan to mainland China, though it maintains its commitment to defense of the former.

Vietnam invades Cambodia, putting to an end the genocidal Khmer Rouge regime and setting off a vast wave of refugees to the United States and other Western countries.

1980　Congress passes the Refugee Act, bringing the U.S. definition of refugees into line with that of the United Nations; the law will help pave the way for the entry of hundreds of thousands of Southeast Asians fleeing communist regimes in Cambodia, Laos, and Vietnam.

The Los Angeles City Council declares part of the Mid-City neighborhood Koreatown, reflecting its importance as the largest Korean community outside Asia.

Los Angeles–area activists found Asian/Pacific Lesbians and Gays, the first advocacy organization for gay and lesbian Asian American and Pacific Islanders.

1982　Chinese American immigrant Vincent Chin is murdered by two unemployed autoworkers in Detroit who mistake him for Japanese; resentment against Japanese imported cars, which are perceived to be undermining the U.S. car industry and causing job losses, had been running high in the Motor City. The minimum sentence received by the perpetrators, three years' probation and a $3,000 fine, outrages the Asian American community.

The Vietnam Veterans Memorial, designed by Chinese American artist Maya Ying Lin, opens on the National Mall in Washington, D.C.

The American Association of Physicians of Indian Origin is founded in Dearborn, Michigan.

1983　The Korean American Coalition, a nonprofit, nonpartisan organization whose mission is to facilitate the Korean American community's participation in civic, community, and legislative affairs, is founded in Los Angeles.

1984　Taiwanese immigrant Roger Chen launches the 99 Ranch Market supermarket chain, the largest U.S. retail chain dedicated to Asian Americans.

Indian businesspersons in the San Francisco Bay Area found the Indo American Bank, the first lending institution formed specifically to aid the Indian American community.

1987　Asian American activists found the Washington-based National Network Against Anti-Asian Violence, partially in response to the 1982 racially motivated murder of Chinese American immigrant Vincent Chin.

1988　President Ronald Reagan signs the Civil Liberties Act, offering a formal apology and $20,000 in reparations to Japanese Americans survivors of incarceration during World War II.

1989	Playwright David Henry Hwang becomes the first Asian American to win a Tony Award for Best Play, for his drama *M. Butterfly*.
1990	Chinese-born Chang-lin Tang becomes chancellor of the University of California, Berkeley; he is the first Asian American to head a major university in the United States.

Chinese American Vera Wang, one of America's premier wedding gown designers, opens her first design salon in New York. |
| 1992 | The Los Angeles riots result in some $350 million in damages to Korean American–owned businesses, though only one Korean American is killed in the violence.

Choua Lee becomes the first Hmong American elected to public office when she wins a seat on the Saint Paul, Minnesota, Board of Education.

Tony Lam is elected to the city council of Westminster, California—the heart of Orange County's "Little Saigon" community—becoming the first Vietnamese American elected to public office. |
| 1993 | Asian American lawyers and others found the National Asian Pacific American Legal Consortium in Washington, D.C., to protect the civil and legal rights of the Asian American and Pacific Islander communities.

President Bill Clinton selects Japanese American congressman Norman Mineta of California as his secretary of commerce; Mineta becomes the first Asian American to serve in a presidential cabinet. |
| 1994 | The American Broadcasting Company (ABC) begins airing the first regularly scheduled program—*All-American Girl*, starring Korean American comedian Margaret Cho—to feature a primarily Asian American cast; the show proves unsuccessful and is taken off the air the following year.

Taiwanese-born immigrant Jerry Yang co-founds the web portal and internet search engine Yahoo! in Silicon Valley. |
| 1996 | Democrat Gary Locke of Washington is elected as the first Asian American state governor in U.S. history.

Time magazine chooses Taiwan-born immigrant David Ho as its "Person of the Year" for research that led to successful drug therapies for persons with HIV/AIDS. |
| 1997 | Thai / African American golfer Tiger Woods becomes the first person of Asian background, and the youngest player ever, to win the prestigious Masters Tournament. |
| 1998 | California voters pass Proposition 227, requiring English-only instruction in public schools, with a one-year immersion course in English for non-English speakers. |
| 1999 | U.S. authorities arrest Wen Ho Lee, a Taiwanese-born nuclear physicist working at the Los Alamos National Laboratory, for allegedly selling U.S. nuclear secrets to the People's Republic of China. Lee is released from jail a year later after pleading guilty to a single minor count of unlawfully gathering national defense information.

Street protests against a video store owner who displayed portraits of Vietnamese communist leaders in his shop window roils the Little Saigon neighborhood of Orange County, California, attesting to the community's intense anticommunist politics. |
| 2000 | For the first time, the U.S. census allows people to register as members of more than one race. Statistics gathered in the decennial census show that some 7.3 percent of Asian Americans consider themselves multiracial. |

The U.S. Census Bureau counts 10,171,820 persons of Asian and Pacific Islander background living in the United States, as well as another 1,687,626 of mixed Asian and other race background; the former figure is up from 202,970 in 1970.

2000s — Under "the Great Third Coast" approach, the Midwest and South are incorporated into Asian American studies; the studies of underrepresented Asian Americans (newer and smaller groups) are incorporated into the field.

2001 — September 11 terrorist attacks; the USA PATRIOT Act of 2001 passes to secure the land and its people.

Taiwanese-born immigrant Elaine Chao is appointed secretary of labor by President George W. Bush, becoming the first Chinese American and the first Asian American woman to serve in a presidential cabinet.

2002 — The Department of Homeland Security is created. Its enforcement of the USA PATRIOT Act of 2001 leads to numerous detentions and deportations of innocent Muslim immigrants and American citizens of Middle Eastern, South Asian, and African ancestries.

2005 — Chinese American Steve Chen co-founds the internet video file-sharing Web site YouTube.

2009 — President Barack Obama appoints Chinese Americans Steven Chu, a Nobel Prize–winning physicist, and former Washington State governor Gary Locke as secretary of energy and secretary of commerce, respectively.

Judy Chu elected as Congresswoman representing 32nd congressional district with 62 percent of the vote, becoming first Chinese American woman elected to Congress.

2010 — The U.S. Census statistics see the AAPI population more than 18 million, among which 14 million are as Asians Alone, and 2.6 million as Asian in combination with one or more additional races.

2011 — President Barack Obama appoints Gary Locke as the Ambassador of the United States to China.

2012 — Congress passes H. Res. 683 drafted by Congresswoman Judy Chu expressing the regret of the House of Representatives for the passage of laws that adversely affected the Chinese in the United States, including the Chinese Exclusion Act.

2014 — U.S. Labor Department inducts the Chinese Railroad Workers of 1865–1869 into the Labor Hall of Honor on May 9.

2019 — From 2011 to 2019, the Asian American population climbed from about 18.2 million to 23.2 million people, according to the census, an increase of 27 percent.

2020 — Chinese American entrepreneur Andrew Yang runs as presidential candidate on a Democratic ticket.

2020–2022 — Unprecedented worldwide COVID-19 pandemic hits America, causing more anti-Asian hate crimes against Asian Americans.

NOTES

1. ROOTS OF ASIAN MIGRATION TO AMERICA

1. See Huping Ling, *Surviving on the Gold Mountain: A History of Chinese American Women and Their Lives* (Albany: State University of New York Press, 1989).
2. Dorothy Ko, *Cinderella's Sisters: A Revisionist History of Footbinding* (Berkeley: University of California Press, 2005); John King Fairbank, *East Asia: Tradition and Transformation* (Boston: Houghton Mifflin, 1973), 142–143; Ling, *Surviving on the Gold Mountain*, 19; and Xu Xishan, "San-cun JinLian" [Bound feet], *World Journal*, March 8–10, 1997.
3. John King Fairbank, *East Asia: Tradition and Transformation*, rev. ed. (Belmont, CA: Wadsworth, 1989), 300–302.
4. Fairbank, *East Asia* (1989), 268.
5. Gail Lee Bernstein, *Recreating Japanese Women, 1600–1945* (Berkeley: University of California Press, 1991), 8.
6. Michael Molly, *Experiencing the World's Religions: Tradition, Challenge, and Change* (Boston: McGraw-Hill, 2005).
7. Christmas Humphreys, *Buddhism: An Introduction and Guide* (New York: Penguin, 1991).
8. Khushwant Singh, *The Illustrated History of the Sikhs* (Oxford: Oxford University Press, 2006).
9. Karen Isaksen Leonard, *The South Asian Americans* (Westport, CT: Greenwood, 1997), 24.
10. Karen Armstrong, *Islam: A Short History* (New York: Modern Library, 2002).
11. Joy Hendry, *Understanding Japanese* (London: Routledge, 1995), 116–119.
12. Ian Gillman and Hans-Joachim Klimkeit, *Christians in Asia before 1500* (London: Routledge Curzon, 1999).
13. See Immanuel Hsu, *The Rise of Modern China* (New York: Oxford University Press, 1990).
14. See, for example, Roger Daniels, *Asian America: Chinese and Japanese in the United States since 1850* (Seattle: University of Washington, 1988), 9–12.
15. Tael is a Chinese unit of weight. It was also used as a unit of Chinese silver currency during imperial China, equivalent of 1.3 ounces. In the late eighteenth and early nineteenth centuries, a tael was approximately equal to a Spanish dollar.
16. See, for example, Fairbank, *East Asia* (1973); Hsu, *Rise of Modern China* (1990).
17. Ronald Takaki, *Strangers from a Different Shore: A History of Asian Americans* (Boston: Little, Brown, 1989), 79.
18. Elmer C. Sendmeyer, *The Anti-Chinese Movement* (Urbana: University of Illinois Press, 1973), 16.
19. Moon-Ho Jung, *Coolies and Cane: Race, Labor, and Sugar in the Age of Emancipation* (Baltimore: Johns Hopkins University Press, 2006), 19–20; see also Lisa Yun, *The Coolie Speaks: Chinese Indentured Laborers and African Slaves in Cuba* (Philadelphia: Temple University Press, 2009).

20. See Albert M. Craig, *The Heritage of Japanese Civilization* (Upper Saddle River, NJ: Prentice Hall), 2011.
21. Sucheng Chan, *Asian Americans: An Interpretive History* (Boston: Twayne, 1991), 12.
22. See, for example, Chan, *Asian Americans*, 11–12; and Takaki, *Strangers from a Different Shore*, 44.
23. Chan, *Asian Americans*, 12.
24. Chan, *Asian Americans*, 12; and Eiichiro Azuma, *Between Two Empires: Race, History, and Transnationalism in Japanese America* (New York: Oxford University Press, 2005), 29.
25. See Michael J. Seth, *A History of Korea: From Antiquity to the Present* (New York: Rowman & Littlefield, 2011).
26. Wayne Patterson, *The Korean Frontier in America: Immigration to Hawaii, 1896–1910* (Honolulu: University of Hawai'i Press, 1988), 19–30; Chan, *Asian Americans*, 13.
27. Patterson, *Korean Frontier in America*, 31–37; and Chan, *Asian Americans*, 15.
28. Chan, *Asian Americans*, 18. See also Yen Le Espiritu, *Home Bound: Filipino American Lives across Cultures, Communities, and Countries* (Berkeley: University of California Press, 2003), and Barbara M. Posadas, *The Filipino Americans* (Westport, CT: Greenwood, 1999).
29. Marina E. Espina, *Filipinos in Louisiana* (New Orleans: A. F. Laborde, 1988), 1–18.
30. See John Keay, *India: A History* (New York: Grove, 2000).
31. Roger Daniels, *A History of Indian Immigration to the United States: An Interpretive Essay* (New York: Asia Society, 1989), 11; Harry H. L. Kitano and Roger Daniels, *Asian Americans: Emerging Minorities* (Upper Saddle River, NJ: Prentice Hall, 2001), 104.
32. Ling, *Surviving on the Gold Mountain*, 88–89.
33. Karen I. Leonard, *Making Ethnic Choices: California's Punjabi Mexican Americans* (Philadelphia: Temple University Press, 1992).

2. RESTRICTIONS AND RESISTANCES

1. Stuart Creighton Miller, *The Unwelcome Immigrant: The American Image of Chinese, 1785–1882* (Berkeley: University of California Press, 1969), 16–80.
2. Moon-ho Jung, "Seditious Subjects: Race, State Violence, and the U.S. Empire," *Journal of Asian American Studies* 14, no. 2 (June 2011): 221–247, and *Coolies and Cane: Race, Labor, and Sugar in the Age of Emancipation* (Baltimore: Johns Hopkins University Press, 2006).
3. Alexander Saxton, *The Indispensable Enemy: Labor and the Anti-Chinese Movement in California* (Berkeley: University of California Press, 1971); and Lisa Low, *Immigrant Acts* (Durham, NC: Duke University Press, 1996), 4–5.
4. Sue Fawn Chung, *In Pursuit of Gold: Chinese American Miners and Merchants in the American West* (Urbana: University of Illinois Press, 2011), 33.
5. Mary R. Coolidge, *Chinese Immigration* (New York: Henry Holt, 1909; reprint, New York: Arno Press, 1969), 69–73.
6. Douglas W. Nelson, "The Alien Land Law Movement of the Late Nineteenth Century," *Journal of the West* 9 (1970): 46–59.
7. Roger Daniels, *Asian America: Chinese and Japanese in the United States since 1850* (Seattle: University of Washington, 1988), 143–147.
8. *People v. Hall*, 4 Cal. 399 (1854).

9. Information in the past two paragraphs is derived from Jean Pfaelzer, *Driven Out: The Forgotten War against Chinese Americans* (New York: Random House, 2007), 32–37.
10. *Los Angeles Star*, October 25, 26, 27–30, 1871; *Los Angeles News*, October 28, 1871; Scott Zesch, *The Chinatown War: Chinese Los Angeles and the Massacre of 1871* (New York: Oxford University Press, 2012), 122–150.
11. Pfaelzer, *Driven Out*, 61–69.
12. Descriptions in the above three paragraphs are drawn from Coolidge, *Chinese Immigration*, 271, and Daniels, *Asian America*, 61–64. See also R. Gregory Nokes, *Massacred for Gold, the Chinese in Hells Canyon* (Corvallis: Oregon State University, 2009).
13. Elmer Clarence Sandmeyer, *The Anti-Chinese Movement in California* (Urbana: University of Illinois Press, 1991), 97–98.
14. Donald T. Hata Jr., *"Undesirables": Early Immigrants and the Anti-Japanese Movement in San Francisco, 1892–1893* (New York: Arno Press, 1978), 122.
15. *Bulletin*, May 4, 1891.
16. Daniels, *Asian America*, 111.
17. Daniels, *Asian America*, 110.
18. Herbert B. Johnson, *Discrimination against Japanese in California: A Review of the Real Situation* (Berkeley, CA: Courier, 1907), 74–75.
19. Roger Daniels, The *Politics of Prejudice: The Anti-Japanese Movement in California, and the Struggle for Japanese Exclusion* (Berkeley: The University of California Press, 1962), 33.
20. Yuji Ichioka, "The 1921 Turlock Incident: Forceful Expulsion of Japanese Laborers," in *Counterpoint: Perspectives on Asian America*, ed. Emma Gee (Los Angeles: Asian American Studies Center, University of California, Los Angeles, 1976), 195–201.
21. *Bellingham Reveille*, September 5, 1907; Garald N. Hallberg, "Bellingham, Washington's Anti-Hindu Riot," *Journal of the West* 12 (1973): 163–175.
22. Sucheta Mazumdar, "Colonial Impact and Punjabi Emigration to the United States," in *Labor Immigration under Capitalism: Asian Workers in the United States before World War II*, ed. Lucie Cheng and Edna Bonacich (Berkeley: University of California Press, 1984), 316–336.
23. Sucheng Chan, *Asian Americans: An Interpretive History* (Boston: Twayne, 1991), 52.
24. H. Brett Melendy, "Filipinos in the United States," *Pacific Historical Review* 43, no. 4 (1974): 520–547; and Antonio T. Tiongson, Jr., Edgardo V. Gutierrez, and Ricardo V. Gutierrez, Positively No Filipinos Allowed: Building Communities and Discourse (Philadelphia: Temple University Press, 2006).
25. Daniels, *Asian America*, 125–126.
26. Bong-Youn Choy, *Koreans in America* (Chicago: Nelson-Hall, 1979), 87–88.
27. Coolidge, *Chinese Immigration*, 278–279.
28. Entry 135, "Chinese Smuggling File," RG 85, National Archives, Washington, DC.
29. Chinese Exclusion Cases Habeas Corpus Petitions, Case File 103, U.S. District Court for the Eastern District of Missouri, St. Louis, RG 21, National Archives–Central Plains Region, Kansas City, MO.
30. Betty Lee Sung, *Mountain of Gold: The Story of the Chinese in America* (New York: Macmillan, 1967), 97.
31. Erika Lee and Judy Yung, *Angel Island: Immigrant Gateway to America* (New York: Oxford University Press, 2010), 4, 328.

32. See Leslie Allen, *Ellis Island* (Liberty Island, NY: Evelyn Hill Group, 1995), 18–21; and Vincent J. Cannato, *American Passage: The History of Ellis Island* (New York: Harper, 2009).
33. H. Mark Lai, Genny Lim, and Judy Yung, *Island: Poetry and History of Chinese Immigrants on Angel Island* (San Francisco: Hoc Doi, 1980), 14–15.
34. Case 14284/4-4, RG 85, National Archives, Pacific Sierra Region, San Bruno, CA. In this case, the applicant's name was filed as Wong Shee, but the author used her maiden name, Wong Yee Gue, in the text in order to distinguish her from Wong Shee in case 19571/18-5 in the sidebar.
35. Connie Young Yu, "The World of Our Grandmothers," in *Making Waves: An Anthology of Writings By and About Asian Women*, ed. Asian Women United of California (Boston: Beacon, 1989), 36; George Anthony Peffer, *If They Don't Bring Their Women Here: Chinese Female Immigration before Exclusion* (Urbana: University of Illinois Press, 1999).
36. For more details about Chinese immigrants' experiences on Angel Island, see Lai, Lim, and Yung, *Island*; Huping Ling, *Surviving on the Gold Mountain: A History of Chinese American Women and Their Lives* (Albany: State University of New York Press, 1989); and Lee and Yung, *Angel Island*.
37. Case 10385/5799, RG 85, National Archives, Pacific Sierra Region.
38. Cases 10577, 10641, 10642, 10654, and 10666, Civil Case Files, 1871–1911; Huping Ling, *Chinese Chicago: Race, Transnational Migration, and Community since 1870* (Stanford, CA: Stanford University Press, 2012), 44–45.
39. "Highbinder" was the name given to members of certain oath-bound Chinese secret societies in American cities by American police and the press. It was believed that these secret societies had their origin in the Great Hung League, or *Hung-men*, a political organization aimed at overthrowing the Manchu Qing dynasty in China. The terms "highbinders" and "tongs" were often used interchangeably.
40. "75 Years Ago—Thursday, June 8, 1892," *Global-Democrat*, June 9, 1967, in Huping Ling, *Chinese St. Louis: From Enclave to Cultural Community* (Philadelphia: Temple University Press, 2004), 31.
41. Chinese Exclusion Cases Habeas Corpus Petitions; Ling, *Chinese St. Louis*, 32.
42. See John King Fairbank, *East Asia: Tradition and Transformation*, rev. ed. (Belmont, CA: Wadsworth, 1989); Immanuel Hsu, *The Rise of Modern China* (New York: Oxford University Press, 1990), 296–298.
43. Lo Hsiang-lin, *Liang Cheng de chushimeiguo* [Liang Cheng: The Chinese minister in Washington] (Hong Kong: Zhongguo wenhua yanjiusuo, 1977), 189 and 248.
44. *Congressional Documents* (1981–1982), s. n. 4268 and 4440.
45. Wu Ting Fang, *America, through the Spectacles of an Oriental Diplomat* (1914), http://www.gutenberg.org/files/609/609-h/609-h.htm.
46. Guanhua Wang, *In Search of Justice: The 1905–1906 Chinese Anti-American Boycott* (Cambridge, MA: Harvard University Press, 2001), 22.
47. Eiichiro Azuma, *Between Two Empires: Race, History, and Transnationalism in Japanese America* (New York: Oxford University Press, 2005), 35–60.
48. For impact on China, see, for example, Wang, *In Search of Justice*; Delber L. McKee, *Chinese Exclusion versus the Open Door Policy, 1900–1906: Clashes over China Policy in the Roosevelt Era* (Detroit: Wayne State University Press, 1977); and Zhang Cunwu, *Guangxu Sanshiyinian Zhongmei Gongyue Fengchao* [Agitation in 1905 against the Sino-American Exclusion Treaty] (Taipei: Institute of Modern Chinese History Research, Academia Sinica, 1965). For the impact on Chinese Americans, see, for example, Yong Chen, *Chinese San Francisco, 1850–1943: A Trans-Pacific Community* (Stanford, CA: Stanford University Press, 2000), 148–161.

49. Chen, *Chinese San Francisco*, 149, 308n4.
50. Wang, *In Search of Justice*, 15.
51. U.S. Congress, House, *Facts Concerning the Enforcement of the Chinese-Exclusion Laws*, 152–153.
52. Chen, *Chinese San Francisco*, 300n80.
53. Ling, *Chinese Chicago*.
54. *Takao Ozawa v. U.S.*, 260 U.S. 178 (1922).
55. *An Appeal of the Chinese Equal Rights League to the People of the United States for Equality of Manhood* (New York, 1892), 2.
56. Ling, *Chinese Chicago*, 44.
57. "Chinese Colony Indignant at the Plan for Detecting Chinamen," *Chicago Tribune*, August 10, 1892.
58. On November 5, 1940, the immigration station moved from Angel Island to 801 Silver Avenue due to a fire on the island that burned the administration building.
59. Case 41369/11-29, RG 85, National Archives, Pacific Sierra Region.

3. LABOR

1. Sucheng Chan, *Asian Americans: An Interpretive History* (Boston: Twayne, 1991), 35.
2. *Hawaiian Gazette*, June 27, 1877, as cited in Ronald Takaki, *Strangers from a Different Shore: A History of Asian Americans* (Boston: Little, Brown, 1989), 132.
3. Chan, *Asian Americans*, 26.
4. Chan, *Asian Americans*, 36.
5. Chan, *Asian Americans*, 36–37; Takaki, *Strangers from a Different Shore*, 137.
6. Clarence Glick, *Sojourners and Settlers: Chinese Migrants in Hawaii* (Honolulu: University of Hawai'i Press, 1980), 34–35.
7. Takaki, *Strangers from a Different Shore*, 142–155.
8. Wayne Patterson, *The Korean Frontier in America: Immigration to Hawaii, 1896–1910* (Honolulu: University of Hawai'i Press, 1988), 98, 115.
9. Takaki, *Strangers from a Different Shore*, 134–135.
10. Patterson, *Korean Frontier in America*, 4–9, 115; Chan, *Asian Americans*, 18, 36.
11. California State Mining Bureau, "Ninth Annual Report of the State Mineralogist" (San Francisco: State Office, 1890), 23.
12. Sue Fawn Chung, *In Pursuit of Gold: Chinese American Miners and Merchants in the American West* (Urbana: University of Illinois Press, 2011; Randall E. Rohe, "After the Gold Rush: Chinese Mining in the Far West, 1850–1890," *Montana: The Magazine of Western History* 32, no. 4 (Autumn 1982): 2–19. See also David V. DuFault, "The Chinese in the Mining Camps of California: 1848–1870," *Historical Society of Southern California Quarterly* 41 (June 1959): 155–170; Ping Chiu, *Chinese Labor in California 1850–1880* (Madison: State Historical Society of Wisconsin, 1963); and Liping Zhu, *A Chinamen's Chance: The Chinese on the Rocky Mountain Mining Frontier* (Niwot: University Press of Colorado, 1997).
13. E. L. Sabin, *Building the Pacific Railway* (Philadelphia, 1919), 110–111.
14. The above two paragraphs are drawn from Alexander Saxton, "The Army of Canton in the High Sierra," *Pacific Historic Review* 35, no. 2 (May 1966): 141–152. For a more detailed and recent account of the Chinese railroad workers, see Gordon H. Chang, *Ghosts of Gold Mountain: The Epic Story of the Chinese Who Built the Transcontinental Railroad* (Boston: Houghton Mifflin Harcourt, 2019), 121–128.

15. "Sikh Farmer in California," http://www.sikhpioneers.org/SikhFarmers.html.
16. Paul C. P. Siu, *Chinese Laundryman: A Study of Social Isolation* (New York: New York University Press, 1987), 46.
17. Sucheng Chan, *This Bitter-Sweet Soil: The Chinese in California Agriculture, 1860–1910* (Berkeley: University of California Press, 1986), 55, 63, 69, 74.
18. Wong Chin Foo, "The Chinese in New York," *Cosmopolitan* 5 (March–October 1888): 297–311, as cited in Renqiu Yu, *To Save China, to Save Ourselves: The Chinese Hand Laundry Alliance of New York* (Philadelphia: Temple University Press, 1992), 207n3.
19. Yu, *To Save China*, 9.
20. Siu, *Chinese Laundryman*, 27–31; Huping Ling, *Chinese Chicago: Race, Transnational Migration, and Community since 1870* (Stanford, CA: Stanford University Press, 2012), 32, and 78–81.
21. Huping Ling, *Chinese St. Louis: From Enclave to Cultural Community* (Philadelphia: Temple University Press, 2004), 35.
22. Ling, *Chinese St. Louis*, 37. See also Victor G. Nee and Brett de Bary, *Longtime Californ': A Documentary Study of an American Chinatown* (New York: Pantheon Books, 1972); Yu, *To Save China*, 9; Siu, *Chinese Laundryman*; and Victor Jew, "Broken Windows: Anti-Chinese Violence and Interracial Sexuality in 19th Century Milwaukee," in *Asian Pacific American Genders and Sexualities*, ed. Thomas K. Nakayama (Tempe: Arizona State University Press, 1999).
23. Siu, *Chinese Laundryman*, 58.
24. Kirksville City Directories, 1892–1992, Special Collection, Pickler Memorial Library, Truman State University, Kirksville, MO.
25. Maxine Hong Kingston, *The Woman Warrior: Memoirs of Girlhood among Ghosts* (New York: Knopf, 1977), 104–105.
26. Joseph Zheng and Gabriella Oldham, "Chinese American Restaurants and Cuisine," in *Asian American History and Cultures: An Encyclopedia*, ed. Huping Ling and Allen Austin (New York: Routledge, 2010), 226.
27. Iris Chang, *The Chinese in America: A Narrative History* (New York: Viking, 2003), 48.
28. Zheng and Oldham, "Chinese American Restaurants and Cuisine."
29. See Ling, *Chinese Chicago* and *Chinese St. Louis*; Lucy M. Cohen, *Chinese in the Post–Civil War South: A People without a History* (Baton Rouge: Louisiana State University Press, 1984).
30. See Renqiu Yu, "Chop Suey: From Chinese Food to Chinese American Food," in *Chinese America: History and Perspectives* (San Francisco: Chinese Historical Society, 1987), 87–99; Haiming Liu, *Journal of Transnational American Studies* 1, no. 1 (2009): 1–24; and Andrew Coe, *Chop Suey: A Cultural History of Chinese Food in the United States* (New York: Oxford University Press, 2009).
31. Coe, *Chop Suey*, 161–165.
32. Calvin B. T. Lee, *Chinatown, USA* (Garden City, NY: Doubleday, 1965), 57.
33. Mai liqian [Him Mark Lai], *Cong huaqiao daohuaren: Ershi shiji meiguuo huaren shehui fazhan shi* [From overseas Chinese to Chinese Americans: A history of twentieth-century Chinese American social and economic development] (Hong Kong: San Lian, 1992), 85 and 393.
34. "Chop Suey Resorts," *New York Times*, November 15, 1903.
35. Bayard Taylor, *Eldorado* (New York: Putnam, 1850), 116–117.
36. Andrew Coe has offered one of the best analyses of the relationship between Jewish immigrants and chop suey. See Coe, *Chop Suey*, 198–205; and Hanna Miller, "Identity Takeout: How American Jews Made Chinese Food Their Ethnic Cuisines," *Journal of Popular Culture* 39, no. 3 (2006): 446.

37. For upscale Chinese restaurants in New York, see "Chop Suey Resorts," *New York Times*, November 15, 1903; for Chicago, see Ling, *Chinese Chicago*, 72–74; for San Francisco, see Yong Chen, *Chinese San Francisco, 1850–1943: A Trans-Pacific Community* (Stanford, CA: Stanford University Press, 2000), 197. See also Coe, *Chop Suey*.
38. Ling, *Chinese Chicago*, 60–61. See also Yong Chen, *Chinese San Francisco*; and Madeline Y. Hsu, *Dreaming of Gold, Dreaming of Home: Transnationalism and Migration between the United States and South China, 1882–1943* (Stanford, CA: Stanford University Press, 2000).
39. Information for the above three paragraphs is based on cases 16135/5-11, 19938/4-11, 12017/36900, and 33610/7-1, RG 85, National Archives, Pacific Sierra Region, San Bruno, CA.
40. Ling, *Chinese Chicago*, 63–66, and 70.
41. Connie Young Yu, "The World of Our Grandmothers," in *Making Waves: An Anthology of Writings By and About Asian American Women*, ed. Asian Women United of California (Boston: Beacon, 1989), 37.
42. Lily Chan, "My Early Influences," October 25, 1926, William Carlson Smith Documents, MK-2, Special Collections, Main Library, University of Oregon, Eugene.
43. Case 10385/5799, RG 85, National Archives, Pacific Sierra Region; Huping Ling, *Surviving on the Gold Mountain: A History of Chinese American Women and Their Lives* (Albany: State University of New York Press, 1989), 64–70.
44. Case 9514/536, RG 85, National Archives, Pacific Sierra Region.
45. Cases 9514/537, 9514/538, and 9509/37, RG 85, National Archives, Pacific Sierra Region.
46. Rose Hum Lee, *The Growth and Decline of Chinese Communities in the Rocky Mountain Region* (Ph.D. diss., Department of Sociology, University of Chicago, 1947), 193–194.
47. Interview 7 by the author.
48. Case 19938/4-11, RG 85, National Archives, Pacific Sierra Region.
49. Interview 9 by the author.
50. See Xiaolan Bao, *Holding Up More Than Half the Sky: A History of Women Garment Workers in New York's Chinatown, 1948–1992* (Urbana: University of Illinois Press, 2001); Richard Kim et al., "A Preliminary Investigation: Asian Immigrant Women Garment Workers in Los Angeles," *Amerasia Journal* 18, no. 1 (1992): 71; and Miriam Ching Louie, "Immigrant Asian Women in Bay Area Garment Sweatshops: After Sewing, Laundry, Cleaning and Cooking, I Have No Breath Left to Sing," *Amerasia Journal* 18, no. 1 (1992): 11.
51. Roger Daniels, *Asian America: Chinese and Japanese in the United States since 1850* (Seattle: University of Washington, 1988), 78.
52. Lucie Cheng Hirata, "Chinese Immigrant Women in Nineteenth-Century California," in *Asian and Pacific American Experience*, ed. Nobuya Tsuchida et al. (Minneapolis: University of Minnesota Press, 1982), 38–55, 46.
53. *Chinese Digest*, July 1937, March 1938, and July 1938.
54. Jennie Matyas, *Jennie Matyas and the ILGWU* (Berkeley: University of California Institute of Industrial Relations, 1957), 192–193.
55. Daniels, *Asian America*, 156.
56. Edna Bonacich and John Modell, *The Economic Basis of Ethnic Solidarity: Small Business in the Japanese American Community* (Berkeley: University of California Press, 1980), 39.
57. John Modell, *The Economics and Politics of Racial Accommodation: The Japanese of Los Angeles, 1900–1942* (Urbana: University of Illinois Press, 1977), 94.

58. Daniels, *Asian America*, 156.
59. Bonacich and Modell, *Economic Basis of Ethnic Solidarity*, 38.
60. S. Frank Miyamoto, *Social Solidarity among the Japanese in Seattle* (Seattle: University of Washington Press, 1984), 70–71.
61. Quintard Taylor, "Blacks and Asians in a White City: Japanese Americans and African Americans in Seattle, 1890–1940," *Western Historical Quarterly* 22, no. 4 (November 1991): 401–429.
62. Eiichiro Azuma, "A History of Oregon's Issei, 1880–1952," *Oregon Historical Quarterly* 94, no. 4 (Winter 1993/1994): 315–367.
63. Barbara Yasui, "The Nikkei in Oregon, 1834–1940," *Oregon Historical Quarterly* 76, no. 3 (September 1975): 225–257.
64. Yamato Ichihashi, *Japanese in the United States* (Stanford, CA: Stanford University Press, 1932), 109.
65. Roger Daniels, "The Issei Generation," in *Roots: An Asian American Reader*, ed. Amy Takishi, Eddi Wong, and Franklin Odo (Los Angeles: Asian American Studies Center, University of California, Los Angeles, 1976), 139.
66. Chan, *Asian Americans*, 39–40; Yuji Ichioka, *The Issei: The World of the First Generation Japanese Immigrants, 1885–1924* (New York: Free Press, 1988).
67. H. A. Millis, *The Japanese Problem in the United States* (New York: Macmillan, 1915), 31.
68. Evelyn Nakano Glenn, *Issei, Nisei, War Bride: Three Generations of Japanese American Women in Domestic Service* (Philadelphia: Temple University Press, 1986), 109–123.
69. Chan, *This Bitter-Sweet Soil*, 1, 17, 122.
70. Daniels, *Asian America*, 156–157.
71. Eiichiro Azuma, *Between Two Empires: Race, History, and Transnationalism in Japanese America* (New York: Oxford University Press, 2005), 64.
72. Leonard Bloom and Ruth Riemer, *Removal and Return: The Socio-economic Effects of the War on Japanese Americans* (Berkeley: University of California Press, 1949), 85.
73. Modell, *Economics and Politics of Racial Accommodation*, 94.
74. Daniels, *Asian America*, 164.
75. Ling, *Surviving on the Gold Mountain*, 76.
76. Daniels, *Asian America*, 163.
77. See Sandy Lydon, *Chinese Gold: The Chinese in the Monterey Bay Region* (Capitola, CA: Capitola Book Company, 1985), 156–161; Eve Armentrout Ma, "Chinese in California's Fishing Industry, 1850–1941," *California History* 60 (1981): 142–157; and Jack Masson and Donald Guimary, "Asian Labor Contractors in the Alaskan Canned Salmon Industry, 1880–1937," *Labor History* 22 (1981): 377–397.
78. Miyamoto, *Social Solidarity among the Japanese in Seattle*, 70–82.
79. Chan, *Asian Americans*, 38–39,
80. Karen I. Leonard, *Making Ethnic Choices: California's Punjabi Mexican Americans* (Philadelphia: Temple University Press, 1992), 80–81.
81. Gary R. Hess, "The Forgotten Americans: The East Indian Community in the United States," *Pacific Historical Review* 43, no. 1 (1986): 45.
82. James Ciment, "The Filipino American Experience: History and Culture," in Ling and Austin, *Asian American History and Cultures*, 252.

4. DEFINING HOME AND COMMUNITY

1. Roger Daniels, *Asian America: Chinese and Japanese in the United States since 1850* (Seattle: University of Washington, 1988), 69, 127; Chan, *Asian Americans*, 109.
2. For recent studies on Asian women immigration and family, see Yen Le Espiritu, *Asian American Women and Men: Labor, Laws, and Love*, 2nd ed. (Lanham, MD: Rowman & Littlefield, 2007); Leonard, *Making Ethnic Choices*; Huping Ling, "Family and Marriage of Late-Nineteenth and Early-Twentieth Century Chinese Immigrant Women," *Journal of American Ethnic History* 19, no. 2 (Winter 2000): 43–63; Huping Ling, *Voices of the Heart: Asian American Women on Immigration, Work, and Family* (Kirksville, MO: Truman State University Press, 2007); Barbara M. Posadas, "Crossed Boundaries in Interracial Chicago: Filipino American Families since 1925," *Amerasia Journal* 8 (Fall 1981): 31–52; Barbara M. Posadas and Roland L. Guyotte, "Interracial Marriages and Transnational Families: Chicago's Filipinos in the Aftermath of World War II," *Journal of American Ethnic History* 25, nos. 2–3 (Winter–Spring 2006): 134–155; Eun Sik Yang, "Korean Women of America: From Subordination to Partnership, 1903–1930," *Amerasia Journal* 11, no. 2 (1984): 1–28; and Judy Yung, *Unbound Feet: A Social History of Chinese Women in San Francisco* (Berkeley: University of California Press, 1995).
3. Huping Ling, *Surviving on the Gold Mountain: A History of Chinese American Women and Their Lives* (Albany: State University of New York Press, 1989), 18–20, 25–39.
4. Huping Ling, *Chinese Chicago: Race, Transnational Migration, and Community since 1870* (Stanford, CA: Stanford University Press, 2012), 102–110; Paul Siu, "Chinese Family in Chicago" (EWB Papers, University of Chicago, ca. 1930s); and oral history interviews by the author.
5. Siu, "Chinese Family in Chicago."
6. Interviews conducted by the author.
7. Louis Chu, *Eat a Bowl of Tea* (Seattle: University of Washington Press, 1979); Ling, *Chinese Chicago*, 104.
8. Siu, "Chinese Family in Chicago."
9. For examples of the financial difficulties of Chinese immigrant men, see case 19571/18-5, RG 85, National Archives, Pacific Sierra Region, San Bruno, CA; "Survey of Race Relations," document 251, Hoover Institution on War, Revolution and Peace Archives, Stanford, CA; and Ling, *Surviving on the Gold Mountain*, 25–26. For examples of Chinese patriarchal control, see cases 19571/18-5, 14284/4-4, RG 85, National Archives, Pacific Sierra Region; Ling, *Surviving on the Gold Mountain*, 26–27; and Sucheng Chan, *Asian Americans: An Interpretive History* (Boston: Twayne, 1991), 104.
10. Case 3358d, entry 134, "Customs Case File No. 3358 Related to Chinese Immigration, 1877–1891," case 1355, entry 132, "Chinese General Correspondence, 1898–1908," RG 85, National Archives, Washington, DC.
11. Case 19571/18-5, RG 85, National Archives, Pacific Sierra Region; and Lin Yutang, *Chinatown Family* (New York: John Day, 1948), 196–197.
12. Case 3358d, entry 134, "Customs Case File No. 3358d Related to Chinese Immigration, 1877–1891," RG 85, National Archives, Washington, DC.
13. Case 1355, entry 132, "Chinese General Correspondence, 1898–1908," RG 85, National Archives, Washington, DC.
14. Mrs. C, interview by the author, 1992.
15. Lucy M. Cohen, *Chinese in the Post–Civil War South: A People without a History* (Baton Rouge: Louisiana State University Press, 1984), 147; James W. Loewen, *The Mississippi Chinese: Between*

Black and White (Cambridge, MA: Harvard University Press, 1971), 75; Sarah R. Mason, "Family Structure and Acculturation in the Chinese Community in Minnesota," in *Asian and Pacific American Experiences: Women's Perspectives*, ed. Nobuya Tsuchida (Minneapolis: Asian/Pacific American Learning Resource Center and General College, University of Minnesota, 1982), 160–171; and John Kuo Wei Tchen, "New York Chinese: The Nineteenth-Century Pre-Chinatown Settlement," in *Chinese America: History and Perspectives, 1990* (Los Angeles: Chinese Historical Society of America, 1990), 157–192.

16. Tenth Census, 1880, New Orleans, LA, population schedules, as cited in Cohen, *Chinese in the Post–Civil War South*, 147.
17. Tchen, "New York Chinese," 176–177.
18. Siu, "Chinese Family in Chicago."
19. Huping Ling, *Chinese St. Louis: From Enclave to Cultural Community* (Philadelphia: Temple University Press, 2004), 26–27, 65; Mason, "Family Structure and Acculturation," 163.
20. Siu, "Chinese Family in Chicago."
21. Siu, "Chinese Family in Chicago."
22. U.S. census, 1860–1920.
23. Yuji Ichioka, "Amerika Nadeshiko: Japanese Immigrant Women in the United States, 1900–1924," *Pacific History Review* 49, no. 2 (May 1980): 339–357. For more recent study on the topic, see Erika Lee and Judy Yung, *Angel Island: Immigrant Gateway to America* (New York: Oxford University Press, 2010), 117–127.
24. Taylor Sakamoto, "The Triumph and Tragedies of Japanese Women in America: A View across Four Generations," *History Teacher* 41, no. 1 (November 2007): 97–122.
25. Ibid., 99.
26. Ichioka, "Amerika Nadeshiko."
27. Information for the above five paragraphs is drawn from Choy, *Koreans in America* (Chicago: Nelson-Hall, 1979), 88–89, 111–114.
28. Elizabeth Jameson, "Imperfect Unions: Class and Gender in Cripple Creek, 1894–1904," *Frontiers* 1, no. 2 (Spring 1976): 89–117.
29. Karen I. Leonard, *Making Ethnic Choices: California's Punjabi Mexican Americans* (Philadelphia: Temple University Press, 1992), 66–72.
30. Nayan Shah, *Stranger Intimacy: Contesting Race, Sexuality and the Law in the North American West* (Berkeley: University of California Press, 2011).
31. Shah, *Stranger Intimacy*, 266–267.
32. Yen Le Espiritu, *Filipino American Lives* (Philadelphia: Temple University Press, 1995), 63–70.
33. Lucie Cheng Hirata, "Free, Indentured, Enslaved: Chinese Prostitutes in 19th Century America," *Signs* 5 (1979): 3–29, 23–24.
34. Mary R. Coolidge, *Chinese Immigration* (New York: Henry Holt, 1909; reprint, New York: Arno Press, 1969); and George Anthony Peffer, *If They Don't Bring Their Women Here: Chinese Female Immigration before Exclusion* (Urbana: University of Illinois Press, 1999).
35. Hirata, "Free, Indentured, Enslaved"; Marion S. Goldman, *Gold Diggers and Silver Mines: Prostitution and Social Life on the Comstock Lode* (Ann Arbor: University of Michigan Press, 1981), 96.
36. Ling, *Surviving on the Gold Mountain*, 54.
37. Alexander MacLeod, *Pigtails and Gold Dust* (Caldwell, ID: Caxton Printers, 1948), 180–181.

38. Lucie Cheng Hirata, "Chinese Immigrant Women in Nineteenth-Century California," in *Asian and Pacific American Experience*, ed. Nobuya Tsuchida et al. (Minneapolis: University of Minnesota Press, 1982), 38–55.
39. Records of Women's Occidental Board of Foreign Missions of the Presbyterian Church, 1873–1920, San Francisco; Carol Green Wilson, *Chinatown Quest* (San Francisco: California Historical Society with Donaldina Cameron House, 1974); Interviews conducted by Victor G. Nee and Brett de Bary, *Longtime Californ': A Documentary Study of an American Chinatown* (New York: Pantheon Books, 1972). For scholarly works, see Curt Gentry, *Madames of San Francisco* (New York: Doubleday, 1964); Goldman, *Gold Diggers and Silver Mines*; Hirata, "Free, Indentured, Enslaved" and "Chinese Immigrant Women in Nineteenth-Century California"; Mildred Crowl Martin, *Chinatown's Angry Angel: The Story of Donaldina Cameron* (Palo Alto, CA: Pacific Books, 1977); and Benson Tong, *Unsubmissive Women: Chinese Prostitutes in Nineteenth-Century San Francisco* (Norman: University of Oklahoma Press, 1994). See also Ruthanne Lum McCunn, *Thousand Pieces of Gold: A Biographical Novel* (San Francisco: Design Enterprises, 1981).
40. Hirata, "Free, Indentured, Enslaved."
41. Tong, *Unsubmissive Women*.
42. Chinese Mortuary Record of the City and County of San Francisco, National Archives, Pacific Sierra Region.
43. Goldman, *Gold Diggers and Silver Mines*, 95.
44. Judy Yung, *Chinese Women of America: A Pictorial History* (Seattle: University of Washington Press, 1986), 19.
45. Goldman, *Gold Diggers and Silver Mines*, 96–97.
46. Yung, *Chinese Women of America*, 19.
47. *Idaho Statesman*, December 11, 1875, c. 1–2, p. 2; Li-hua Yu, "Chinese Immigrants in Idaho" (PhD diss., Bowling Green State University, 1991), 210.
48. Joan Hori, "Japanese Prostitution in Hawaii during the Immigration Period," in *Asian and Pacific American Experiences: Women's Perspectives*, ed. Nobuya Tsuchida, 56–65.
49. Julie Roy Jeffrey, *Frontier Women: The Trans-Mississippi West 1840–1880* (New York: Hill & Wang, 1979), 121.
50. Ruth Rosen, *The Lost Sisterhood: Prostitution in America, 1900–1918* (Baltimore: Johns Hopkins University Press, 1982), xiv.
51. Ling, "Family and Marriage."
52. Yung, *Chinese Women of America*, 44.
53. Betty Lee Sung, *Mountain of Gold: The Story of the Chinese in America* (New York: Macmillan, 1967), 197–198.
54. Liu Bo-ji, *Meiguo Huaqiao Shi* [History of the overseas Chinese in the United States] (Taipei: Li Ming, 1981), 297.
55. Sue Fawn Chung, "Gue Gim Wah, Pioneering Chinese American Woman of Nevada," in *History and Humanities*, ed. Francis X. Hartigan (Reno: University of Nevada Press, 1989), 45–79.
56. Cases 16135/5-11, 19938/4-11, 12017/36900, 33610/7-1, RG 85, National Archives, Pacific Sierra Region.
57. Daniels, *Asian America*, 78.
58. Hasia R. Diner, *Erin's Daughters in America: Irish Immigrant Women in the Nineteenth Century* (Baltimore: Johns Hopkins University Press, 1983), 46.

59. "Life History," William Carlson Smith Documents, MK-12, Special Collections, Main Library, University of Oregon, Eugene.
60. "Life History," by a Chinese girl at McKinley High School, Honolulu, November 20, 1926, William Carlson Smith Documents, MK-12; "Life History," by a Japanese boy, MK-23; and interview 9 by the author.
61. For example, the Survey of Race Relation projects, directed by Robert E. Park and conducted by a group of scholars in the 1920s among the Chinese, Japanese, and other nonwhite residents along the Pacific Coast and in Hawaii, contains numerous oral history interviews with second-generation Chinese, Japanese, and Koreans. Survey of Race Relations, Hoover Institution, Stanford University, William Carlson Smith Documents.
62. Leonard, *Making Ethnic Choices*, 157.
63. William Hoy, *The Chinese Six Companies* (San Francisco: California Chinese Historical Society, 1942), 1–6; H. Mark Lai, "Historical Development of the Chinese Consolidated Benevolent Association / Huiguan System," in *Chinese America: History and Perspectives, 1987* (San Francisco: Chinese Historical Society of America 1987), 13–51.
64. Kuo-lin Chen, *Hua Ren Bang Pai* [The Chinatown gangs] (Taipei: Juliu, 1995).
65. Ling, *Chinese St. Louis*, 88; Huping Ling, "Governing 'Hop Alley': On Leong Chinese Merchants and Laborers Association, 1906–1966," *Journal of American Ethnic History* 23, no. 2 (Winter 2004): 50–84.
66. Ling, *Chinese St. Louis*, 89–92.
67. Chan, *Asian Americans*, 67.
68. The above four paragraphs are drawn from Yuji Ichioka, "Japanese Associations and the Japanese Government: A Special Relationship, 1906–1926," *Pacific Historical Review* 46 (1977): 409–437; Daniels, *Asian America*, 128–131.
69. The above two paragraphs are based on Chan, *Asian Americans*, 69–71.
70. Helen F. Clark, "The Chinese of New York Contrasted with Their Foreign Neighbors," *Century* 53 (November 1896): 110.
71. Ivan H. Light, *Ethnic Enterprise in America: Business and Welfare among Chinese, Japanese, and Black* (Berkeley: University of California Press, 1972), 28.
72. Ivan H. Light, Im Jung, and Deng Zhong, "Korean Rotating Credit Associations in Los Angeles," *Amerasia Journal* 16, no. 2 (1990): 35–54.
73. Choy, *Koreans in America*, 114.
74. Tim J. Watts, "Filipino American Association," in *Asian American History and Cultures: An Encyclopedia*, ed. Huping Ling and Allen W. Austin, 2 vols. (New York: M. E. Sharpe, 2009), 262.
75. The above four paragraphs are based on Choy, *Koreans in America*, 114–119; see also Richard S. Kim, *The Quest for Statehood: Korean Immigrant Nationalism and U.S. Sovereignty, 1905–1945* (New York: Oxford University Press, 2011).
76. Joan M. Jensen, *Passage from India: Asian Indian Immigrants in North America* (New Haven, CT: Yale University Press, 1988), 19–20.
77. Ira M. Condit, *The Chinaman as We See Him and Fifty Years of Work for Him* (Chicago: Missionary Campaign Library, 1900); Wesley Woo, "Chinese Protestants in the San Francisco Bay Area," in *Entry Denied: Exclusion and the Chinese in America, 1882–1943*, ed. Sucheng Chan (Philadelphia: Temple University Press, 1991), 213–245; and Fenggang Yang, *Chinese Christians in America*, 5.

78. Choy, *Koreans in America*, 254; David K. Yoo, *Contentious Spirits: Religion in Korean American History, 1903–1945* (Stanford, CA: Stanford University Press, 2010), 45–46; Chan, *Asian Americans*, 73–74.
79. Tim J. Watts, "Japanese American Religion," in Ling and Austin, *Asian American History and Cultures*, 456–458; Gayle K. Yamada and Dianne Fukami, *Building a Community: The Story of Japanese Americans in San Mateo County* (San Mateo, CA: San Mateo Chapter JACL, 2003), 38–41.
80. Louise H. Hunter, *Buddhism in Hawaii* (Honolulu: University of Hawaiʻi Press, 1971).
81. Harry H. L. Kitano, *Japanese Americans: The Evolution of a Subculture* (Englewood Cliffs, NJ: Prentice Hall, 1976), 59–60.
82. Tony Carnes and Fenggang Yang, eds., *Asian American Religions: The Making and Remaking of Borders and Boundaries* (New York: New York University Press, 2004); and Raymond Brady Williams, *Religions of Immigrants from India and Pakistan: New Treads in the American Tapestry* (New York: Cambridge University Press, 1988).
83. Brett H. Melendy, *Asians in America: Filipinos, Koreans, and East Indians* (Boston: G. K. Hall, 1977); Maria P. P. Root, ed., *Filipino Americans: Transformation and Identity* (Thousand Oaks, CA: Sage, 1997); and David K. Yoo, ed., *New Spiritual Homes: Religions and Asian Americans* (Honolulu: University of Hawaiʻi Press, 1999).
84. See Leonard, *Making Ethnic Choices*, 267; Ling, *Voices of the Heart*, 257–268; Yoo, *Contentious Spirits*.

5. WORLD WAR II

1. Sucheng Chan, *Asian Americans: An Interpretive History* (Boston: Twayne, 1991), 121; Roger Daniels, *Asian America: Chinese and Japanese in the United States since 1850* (Seattle: University of Washington, 1988), 187.
2. See Akira Iriye, *Power and Culture: The Japanese-American War, 1941–1945* (Cambridge, MA: Harvard University Press, 1981); John W. Dower, *War without Mercy: Race and Power in the Pacific War* (New York: Pantheon, 1987).
3. Harold R. Isaacs, *Images of Asia: American Views of China and India* (New York: Harper & Row, 1972), xviii–xix.
4. Ronald Takaki, *Strangers from a Different Shore: A History of Asian Americans* (Boston: Little, Brown, 1989), 359.
5. Chan, *Asian Americans*, 122; Thomas Chinn, *Bridging the Pacific: San Francisco Chinatown and Its People* (San Francisco: Chinese Historical Society, 1989), 147–150.
6. Richard Ho, letter to Huping Ling, July 24, 2001.
7. Judy Yung, *Unbound Feet: A Social History of Chinese Women in San Francisco* (Berkeley: University of California Press, 1995), 254.
8. *Chinese Nationalist Daily*, November 27, 1944; Huping Ling, *Surviving on the Gold Mountain: A History of Chinese American Women and Their Lives* (Albany: State University of New York Press, 1989), 120.
9. Yung, *Unbound Feet*, 257; Xiaojian Zhao, *Remaking Chinese America: Immigration, Family, and Community, 1940–1965* (New Brunswick, NJ: Rutgers University Press, 2002), 60–65; Wong, *Americans First*, 55–56.
10. Takaki, *Strangers from a Different Shore*, 359–360.

11. Bong-Youn Choy, *Koreans in America* (Chicago: Nelson-Hall, 1979), 173–174, 326.
12. Daniels, *Asian America*, 246–249.
13. Judy Yung, *Unbound Voices: A Documentary History of Chinese Women in San Francisco* (Berkeley: University of California Press, 1999), 473n1.
14. Zhao, *Remaking Chinese America*, 55–57.
15. Ling, *Chinese St. Louis: From Enclave to Cultural Community* (Philadelphia: Temple University Press, 2004), 121–122.
16. Choy, *Koreans in America*, 280.
17. Yen Le Espiritu, *Filipino American Lives* (Philadelphia: Temple University Press, 1995), 41–43.
18. Daniels, *Asian America*, 192.
19. Fred Warren Riggs, *Pressures on Congress: A Study of the Repeal of Chinese Exclusion* (New York: King's Crown Press, 1950), 113–116.
20. Act to Repeal the Chinese Exclusion Acts, to Establish Quotas, and for Other Purposes, 57 Stat. 600–601 (1943).
21. Roger Daniels, *Concentration Camps USA: Japanese Americans and World War II* (New York: Holt, Rinehart and Winston, 1972), 45–46.
22. Peter H. Irons, *Justice at War* (Berkeley: University of California Press, 1983), viii–ix.
23. Takaki, *Strangers from a Different Shore*, 387–389.
24. Roger Daniels, "Words Do Matter: A Note on Inappropriate Terminology and the Incarceration of the Japanese Americans," in *Nikkei in the Pacific Northwest: Japanese Americans and Japanese Canadians in the Twentieth Century*, ed. Louis Fiset and Gail Nomura (Seattle: University of Washington Press, 2005), 183–207.
25. Instructions to implement Civilian Exclusion Order No. 108, National Archives.
26. Chan, *Asian Americans*, 126.
27. Donald Teruo Hata and Nadine Ishitami Hata, *Japanese Americans and World War II: Mass Removal, Imprisonment, and Redress* (Wheeling, IL: Harlan Davison, 2011), 27–28.
28. This section is based on Valerie Matsumoto, "Japanese American Women during World War II," *Frontier* 8 (1984): 6–14; Hata and Hata, *Japanese Americans and World War II*, 23–38; Daniels, *Asian America*, 231–260; and Chan, *Asian Americans*, 128–131.
29. The most detailed study on MIS training and its graduates' services during the war is Kelli Y. Nakamura, "'They Are Our Secret Weapons': The Military Intelligence Service and the Role of Japanese-Americans in the Pacific War and in the Occupation of Japan," *The Historian* 70, no. 1 (Spring 2008): 54–74. It's.
30. See Franklin Odo, *No Sword to Bury: Japanese Americans in Hawai'i during World War II* (Philadelphia: Temple University Press, 2004).
31. Masayo Umezawa Duus, *Unlikely Liberators: The Men of the 100th and 442nd*, trans. Peter Duus (Honolulu: University of Hawai'i Press, 1987), 178–219.
32. Daniels, *Asian America*, 254.
33. This section is based on Jacobus tenBroek, Edward N. Barnhart, and Floyd W. Matson, *Prejudice, War and the Constitution: Causes and Consequences of the Evacuation of the Japanese Americans in World War II* (Berkeley: University of California Press, 1954); Peter H. Irons, *Justice at War* (Berkeley: University of California Press, 1983); Peter Irons, ed., *Justice Delayed: The Record of the Japanese American Internment Cases* (Middletown, CT: Wesleyan University Press, 1989); Hata and Hata, *Japanese Americans and World War II*, 35–38; and Chan, *Asian Americans*, 135–138.

34. The most recent detailed studies on the Japanese American resettlement, from which this section draws most its information, are Sandra C. Taylor, "Leaving the Concentration Camps: Japanese American Resettlement in Utah and the Intermountain West," *Pacific Historical Review* 60, no. 2 (May 1991): 169–194, and Allen W. Austin, "Eastward Pioneers: Japanese American Resettlement during World War II and the Contested Meaning of Exile and Incarceration," *Journal of American Ethnic History* 26 (Winter 2007): 58–84.
35. Hata and Hata, *Japanese Americans and World War II*, 41.
36. Taylor, "Leaving the Concentration Camps," 184–185.
37. Emily Hiramatsu Morishima, "Redress Movement," in *Asian American History and Cultures: An Encyclopedia*, ed. Huping Ling and Allan W. Austin (New York: M. E. Sharpe, 2010), 455–456; Roger Daniels, "Incarceration of the Japanese Americans: A Sixty Year Perspective," *History Teacher* 35 (2002): 297–310.

6. NEW WAVES OF IMMIGRANTS AND REFUGEES

1. U.S. Immigration and Naturalization Service, "Annual Report" (Washington, DC: Government Printing Office, 1945–1949).
2. U.S. Immigration and Naturalization Service, "Annual Report" (Washington, DC: Government Printing Office, 1945–1954).
3. U.S. Census Bureau, "The U.S. Census of Population, 1960" (Washington, DC: U.S. Department of Commerce, 1960).
4. U.S. Statutes at Large, vol. 66, 82nd Cong. (1952), 163–282.
5. Rogelio Saenz, Sean-Shong Hwang, and Benigno E. Aguirre, "In Search of Asian War Brides," *Demography* 31, no. 3 (August 1994): 549–559.
6. Caroline Chung Simpson, "'Out of an Obscure Place': Japanese War Brides and Cultural Pluralism in the 1950s," *Differences* 10, no. 3 (1998): 47–81.
7. Evelyn Nakano Glenn, *Issei, Nisei, War Bride: Three Generations of Japanese American Women in Domestic Service* (Philadelphia: Temple University Press, 1986), 58–63; Huping Ling, *Voices of the Heart: Asian American Women on Immigration, Work, and Family* (Kirksville, MO: Truman State University Press, 2007), 145–146.
8. Philip Q. Yang, *Asian Immigration to the United States* (Cambridge: Polity Press, 2011), 84.
9. Ling, *Voices of the Heart*, 209–226.
10. David Yoo and Ruth Chung, eds., *Religion and Spirituality in Korean America* (Urbana: University of Illinois Press, 2008), 3.
11. David Reimers, *Still the Golden Door: The Third World Comes to America* (New York: Columbia University Press, 1985), 24–25.
12. Paul Ong and Tania Azores, "The Migration and Incorporation of Filipino Nurses," in *The New Asian Immigration in Los Angeles and Global Restructuring*, ed. Paul Ong, Edna Bonacich, and Lucie Cheng (Philadelphia: Temple University Press, 1994), 164–195.
13. Bong-Youn Choy, *Koreans in America* (Chicago: Nelson-Hall, 1979), 42–45.
14. Ong and Azores, "Migration and Incorporation of Filipino Nurses," 172.
15. Choy, *Koreans in America*, 61–62.
16. Ong and Azores, "Migration and Incorporation of Filipino Nurses," 174.

17. *Public Papers of the Presidents of the United States: Lyndon B. Johnson, 1965*, vol. 2 (Washington, DC: Government Printing Office, 1966), entry 546, 1037–1040.
18. *Statutes at Large*, vol. 79 (Washington, DC: Government Printing Office, 1965), 912–913.
19. Immigration Reform and Control Act of 1986, Pub. L. No. 99–603 (1986).
20. Immigration Act of 1990, 104 Stat. 4978 (1990).
21. Yang, *Asian Immigration to the United States*, 111–117; Pyong Gap Min, "Korean Americans," in *Asian Americans: Contemporary Trends and Issues*, ed. Pyong Gap Min (Thousand Oaks, CA: Pine Forge Press, 2006), 230–259; Daisuke Akiba, "Japanese Americans," in Min, *Asian Americans*, 148–177; and Huping Ling, "The Rise and Fall of the Study in America Movement in Taiwan," *Overseas Chinese History Studies*, no. 4 (2003): 21–28.
22. Paoze Thao, "Cultural Transition and Adjustment: The Experiences of the Mong in the United States," in *Emerging Voices: Experiences of Underrepresented Asian Americans*, ed. Huping Ling (New Brunswick, NJ: Rutgers University Press, 2008), 34–51.
23. Rubén G. Rumbaut, "Vietnamese, Laotian, and Cambodian Americans," in Min, *Asian Americans*, 232–270. Among work on Indochinese refugees, Rumbaut's essay remains one of the best and most comprehensive contributions.
24. Rubén G. Rumbaut, "The Structure of Refugee: Southeast Asian Refugees in the United States, 1975–1985," *International Review of Comparative Public Policy* 1 (1989): 97–129.
25. Rumbaut, "Vietnamese, Laotian, and Cambodian Americans."
26. Ha, interview by the author, May 28 and June 14, 1999; see also Huping Ling, *Chinese St. Louis: From Enclave to Cultural Community* (Philadelphia: Temple University Press, 2004); and James M. Freeman, *Hearts of Sorrow: Vietnamese American Lives* (Stanford, CA: Stanford University Press, 1989), 369–373.
27. The above five paragraphs are drawn from Rumbaut, "Vietnamese, Laotian, and Cambodian Americans."
28. Mark E. Pfeifer, comp., "Hmong Population 2005 American Community Survey" (n.d.), http://www.hmongstudies.org/2005AmericanCommunitySurveyHmong.
29. Kou Yang, "Hmong American Contemporary Experience," in Ling, *Emerging Voices*, 236–253.
30. Rumbaut, "Vietnamese, Laotian, and Cambodian Americans."
31. Kou Yang, "Hmong American Contemporary Experience."
32. Half in Ten, "Restoring Shared Prosperity: Strategies to Cut Poverty and Expand Economic Growth" (October 2, 2011), 6, https://www.aecf.org/resources/restoring-shared-prosperity.
33. Rumbaut, "Vietnamese, Laotian, and Cambodian Americans."
34. R. L. Bach and R. Argiros, "Economic Progress among Southeast Asian Refugees in the United States," in *Refugee Policy: Canada and the United States*, ed. H. Adelman (Toronto: York Lanes, 1991), 322–343.
35. S. S. Forbes, *Adaptation and Integration of Recent Refugees to the United States* (Washington, DC: Refugee Policy Group, 1985).
36. B. Link and B. P. Dohrenwend, "Formulation of Hypotheses about the True Prevalence of Demoralization," in *Mental Illness in the United States: Epidemiological Estimates*, ed. B. P. Dohrenwend (New York: Praeger, 1980), 114–132; and Rubén G. Rumbaut, "Portraits, Patterns and Predicators of the Refugee Adaptation Process," in *Refugees as Immigrants: Cambodians, Laotians and Vietnamese in America*, ed. D. W. Haines (Totowa, NJ: Rowman & Littlefield, 1989), 138–182.

37. D. E. Lopez, "Language Diversity and Assimilation," in *Ethnic Los Angeles*, ed. R. Waldinger and M. Bozorgmehr (New York: Russell Sage Foundation, 1996), 139–164.
38. Min Zhou and Carl Bankston III, *Growing Up American: How Vietnamese Children Adopt to Life in the United States* (New York: Russell Sage Foundation, 1998); J. D. Vigil and S. C. Yun, "Vietnamese Youth Gangs in Southern California," in *Gangs in America*, ed. C. R. Huff (Newbury Park, CA: Sage, 1990), 146–162.
39. Alejandro Portes and Reben G. Rumbaut, *Immigrant American: A Portrait* (Berkeley: University of California Press, 1996), 189–198.
40. Zhou and Bankston, *Growing Up American*, 170.
41. Patrick Radden Keefe, "Snakeheads and Smuggling: The Dynamics of Illegal Chinese Immigration," *World Policy Journal* 26 (Spring 2009): 33–44.
42. Jack Herrera, "Most Undocumented Immigrants Are Not Mexican," *Pacific Standard*, June 13, 2019.
43. See, for instance, Miriam Jordan, "The Overlooked Undocumented Immigrants: From India, China, Brazil," *New York Times*, December 3, 2019.
44. "Indians Fastest-Growing Illegal Immigrants in U.S.," *Silicon India*, August 11, 2009, http://www.siliconindia.com/shownews/Indians_fastestgrowing_illegal_immigrants_in_US-nid-60255-cid-1.html?utm_source=clicktrack&utm_medium=banner&utm_campaign=mostcommented; Michael Hoeffer, Nancy Rytina, and Bryan C. Baker, "Estimates of the Unauthorized Immigrant Population Residing in the United States: January 2009" (Department of Homeland Security, 2009), 4, http://www.dhs.gov/xlibrary/assets/statistics/publications/ois_ill_pe_2009.pdf.
45. Jordan, "Overlooked Undocumented Immigrants," and Herrera, "Most Undocumented Immigrants Are Not Mexican."
46. See Peter Kwong, *Forbidden Workers: Illegal Chinese Immigrants and American Labor* (New York: New Press, 1997); Peter Kwong, "Forbidden Workers and the U.S. Labor Movement," *Critical Asian Studies* 34, no. 1 (2002): 69–88; Ko-lin Chin, *Smuggled Chinese: Clandestine Immigration to the United States* (Philadelphia: Temple University Press, 1999); Susie Ling, "Sex Slavery Then and Now," *Asian Week*, March 9, 2007; Keefe, "Snakeheads and Smuggling"; Patrick Radden Keefe, *The Snakehead: An Epic Tale of the Chinatown Underworld and the American Dream* (New York: Doubleday, 2009); and Xiaojian Zhao, *The New Chinese America: Class, Economy, and Social Hierarchy* (New Brunswick, NJ: Rutgers University Press, 2010).
47. U.S. Immigration and Naturalization Service, Office of Policy and Planning, "Estimates of the Unauthorized Immigrant Population Residing in the United States: 1990 to 2000" (2001), table B, "Estimated Unauthorized Resident Population, Top 15 Countries: 1990 and 2000," 9.
48. Kwong, "Forbidden Workers"; Ling, "Sex Slavery Then and Now."
49. This section is based on Lin Ying, interview by the author, August 18, 1998; *Lianhe bao* [United daily], August 7, 2000; Kwong, "Forbidden Workers"; Keefe, "Snakeheads and Smuggling"; and Keefe, *The Snakehead*.
50. Lin Ying, interview by the author, August 18, 1998; Zhao, *New Chinese America*, 133–134;《来美生子得不偿失，50月子中心被查》("50 Chinese Birth Centers inspected"),《世界日报》(*The World Journal*), March 4, 2015;《纽约华人月子中心人心惶惶》("The Chinese Birth Centers in New York are Under Attack"),《世界日报》(*The World Journal*), March 4, 2015.
51. Lin Ying, interview; Kwong, *Forbidden Workers*; Peter Kwong's film on prostitution in Chinatown broadcast by CBS, March 3, 1998; and *World Journal*, March 4, 1998.
52. Ling, "Sex Slavery Then and Now."

53. Zhao, *New Chinese America*, 118–123; Zeng Huiyan, "Changle ren zai meiguo," pt. 3 [Changle people in America], *Shijie zhoukan* [World journal weekly], October 5, 2003, 31.
54. Winnie Tam Hung, "Dowries and Debts: Fuzhounese Youth Geographies of Fear, Resentment, and Obligation," *Journal of Asian American Studies* 18, no. 1 (February 2015): 11–40.
55. Zhao, *New Chinese America*, 123; Zeng Huiyan, "Changle ren zai meiguo," pt. 1 [Changle people in America], *Shijie zhoukan* [World journal weekly], September 21, 2003, 13.
56. Long Chen, interview by the author, May 18, 2002.
57. Lin Ying, interview by the author, August 18, 1998; Mr. Wang, interview by the author, March 12, 2010.
58. Padma Wangaswamy, "South Asians in Dunkin' Donuts: Niche Development in the Franchise Industry," *Journal of Ethnic and Migration Studies* 33, no. 4 (May 2007): 671–686.
59. Herrera, "Most Undocumented Immigrants Are Not Mexican."
60. Michael Maher, "The Children of the Killing Fields," *Global Mail*, February 8, 2012, http://www.theglobalmail.org/feature/the-children-of-the-killing-fields/39/; and Max Shapira, "A Cambodian American Who Can Never 'Go Home,'" *BBC*, April 6, 2012, http://www.bbc.co.uk/news/magazine-17527030.
61. For international adoption, see R. H. Weil, "International Adoptions: The Quiet Migration," *International Migration Review* 18 (1984): 276–293; Richard M. Lee et al., "Cultural Socialization in Families with Internationally Adopted Children," *Journal of Family Psychology* 20 (2006): 571–580; Richard M. Lee and Matthew J. Miller, "History and Psychology of Adoptees in Asian America," in *Asian American Psychology: Current Perspectives*, ed. Nita Tewari and Alvin N. Alvarez (New York: Lawrence Erlbaum, 2009), 337–363; and Catherine Cenaza Choy, *Global Families: A History of Asian International Adoption in America* (New York: New York University Press, 2013). For transnational adoption from Korea, see Kim Park Nelson, "Mapping Multiple Histories of Korean American Transnational Adoption" (U.S. Korea Institute at SAIS, 2009), a good survey on transnational adoption; Jodi Kim, "An 'Orphan' with Two Mothers: Transnational and Transracial Adoption, the Cold War, and Contemporary Asian American Cultural Politics," *American Quarterly* 61, no. 4 (December 2009): 855–880; Eleana Kim, "Our Adoptee, Our Alien: Transnational Adoptees as Specters of Foreignness and Family in South Korea," *Anthropological Quarterly* 80, no. 2 (Spring 2007): 497–531. For transnational adoption from China, see Kay Johnson, Huang Banghan, and Wang Liyao, "Infant Abandonment and Adoption in China," *Population and Development Review* 24, no. 3 (September 1998): 469–510; Kay Johnson, "Politics of International and Domestic Adoption in China," *Law & Society Review* 36, no. 2 (2002): 379–396; Kristen E. Johnston et al., "Mothers' Racial, Ethnic, and Cultural Socialization of Transracially Adopted Asian Children," *Family Relations* 56 (October 2007): 390–402; Toby Alice Volkman, "Embodying Chinese Culture: Transnational Adoption in North America," *Social Text* 21, no. 1 (Spring 2003): 29–55. Information in this section is drawn from the above sources.
62. Yoo and Chung, *Religion and Spirituality in Korean America*, 1–17.
63. Ellen Herman, "Transracial Adoptions" (Adoption History Project, Department of History, University of Oregon, 2012), http://pages.uoregon.edu/adoption/topics/transracialadoption.htm.
64. Rita James Simon and Howard Altstein, *Adoption across Borders: Serving the Children in Transracial and Intercountry Adoptions* (Lanham, MD: Rowman & Littlefield, 2000), 2.
65. Johnson, "Politics of International and Domestic Adoption in China," 387.
66. Matthew Salesses, "What I Would Like to Tell Adoptive Parents (About Answers): A Letter from an Adoptee" (Good Men Project, August 11, 2012), http://goodmenproject.com/families/what-i-would-like-to-tell-adoptive-parents-about-answer-a-letter-from-an-adoptee/.

7. MOVING UPWARD

1. *San Francisco Chronicle*, December 1, 1983.
2. Terrance J. Reeves and Claudette E. Bennett, "We the People: Asians in the United States" (Washington, DC: U.S. Census Bureau, 2004), 12.
3. U.S. Census Bureau, "2012 American Community Survey," tables B15002D and S1501, http://factfinder2.census.gov/bkmk/table/1.0/en/ACS/10_1YR/B15002D and http://factfinder2.census.gov/bkmk/table/1.0/en/ACS/10_1YR/S1501.
4. Starting in 2005, data on Asian Americans have excluded Pacific Islanders, whose rate of educational attainment has also been below the national average.
5. Abundant works have studied the topic. See, for example, Harry Kitano, *Japanese Americans: The Evolution of a Subculture* (Englewood Cliffs, NJ: Prentice Hall, 1976); Stanford M. Lyman, *Chinese Americans* (New York: Random House, 1974); William Petersen, *Japanese Americans: Oppression and Success* (New York: Random House, 1971).
6. "Asian-Americans Blast UC Admissions Policy," Associated Press, April 24, 2009; "Diversity: Annual Accountability Sub-Report" (University of California, September 2010).
7. "Asian-Americans Question Ivy League's Entry Policies," *New York Times*, May 30, 1985, B1-4. One of the best discussions on the issue is in Dana Takagi, *Retreat from Race: Asian Admissions and Racial Politics* (Piscataway, NJ: Rutgers University Press, 1992).
8. Jesse Washington, "Some Asians' College Strategy: Don't Check 'Asian,'" Associated Press, December 3, 2011.
9. Peter Kiang, "Issues of Curriculum and Community for First-Generation Asian Americans in College," *New Directions for Community Colleges* 80 (1992): 97–113; J. Lew, J. Chang, and W. Wang, "UCLA Community College Review: The Overlooked Minority. Asian Pacific American Students at Community Colleges," *Community College Review* 33, no. 2 (2005): 64–84; "Pacific Islanders Lagging Behind in Higher Educational Attainment," *CrossCurrents*, Spring/Summer 2007, 12.
10. For general reviews, see Lyman, *Chinese Americans*; Petersen, *Japanese Americans*; and Jennifer C. Ng, Sharon S. Lee, and Yoon K. Pak, "Contesting the Model Minority and Perpetual Foreigner Stereotypes: A Critical Review of Literature on Asian Americans in Education," *Review of Research in Education* 31 (2007): 95–130; Shirley Hune and Kenyon Chan, "Special Focus: Asian Pacific American Demographic and Educational Trends," in *Minorities in Higher Education: Fifteenth Annual Status Report: 1996–1997*, ed. D. Carter and R. Wilson (Washington, DC: American Council on Education, 1997), 39–67.
11. William Caudill, "Japanese-American Personality and Acculturation," *Genetic Psychology Monographs* 45 (1952): 3–101; Francis L. K. Hsu, *The Challenge of the American Dream: The Chinese in the United States* (Belmont, CA: Wadsworth, 1971); Betty Lee Sung, *Mountain of Gold: The Story of the Chinese in America* (New York: Macmillan, 1967); Charles Hirschman and Morrison G. Wong, "The Extraordinary Educational Attainment of Asian-Americans: A Search for Historical Evidence and Explanations," *Social Forces* 65, no. 1 (September 1986): 1–27.
12. Hirschman and Wong, "Extraordinary Educational Attainment of Asian-Americans," 8; William L. Yancey, Eugene P. Ericksen, and Richard N. Juliani, "Emergent Ethnicity: A Review and Reformulation," *American Sociological Review* 41 (1976): 391–403.
13. Hirschman and Wong, "Extraordinary Educational Attainment of Asian-Americans," 9–10.
14. Harry H. L. Kitano and Roger Daniels, *Asian Americans: Emerging Minorities* (Upper Saddle River, NJ: Prentice Hall, 2001); Huping Ling, *Chinese St. Louis: From Enclave to Cultural Community*

(Philadelphia: Temple University Press, 2004); Gap Pyong Min, *Ethnic Solidarity for Economic Survival: Korean Greengrocers in New York City* (New York: Russell Sage Foundation, 2011).
15. Edna L. Paisano, "We the Americans: Asians" (Washington, DC: U.S. Census Bureau, 1993), 6.
16. Terrance J. Reeves and Claudette E. Bennett, "We the People: Asians in the United States" (Washington, DC: U.S. Census Bureau, 2004), 14.
17. U.S. Census Bureau, "2012 American Community Survey," table B24010D, http://factfinder2.census.gov/bkmk/table/1.0/en/ACS/10_1YR/B24010D.
18. U.S. censuses 1980 and 1990.
19. Robert W. Gardner, Bryant Robey, and Peter C. Smith, "Asian Americans: Growth, Change and Diversity" (Washington, DC: Population Reference Bureau, 1985).
20. Pyong-Gap Min and Andrew Kolodny, "Middleman Minority Characteristics of Korean Immigrants in the US," *Korean Journal of Population and Development* 23, no. 2 (December 1994): 179–202; Pyong Gap Min, *Caught in the Middle: Korean Communities in New York and Los Angeles* (Berkeley: University of California Press, 1996).
21. See Heeduk Bang, "The Self-Help / Mutual Aid Component in Small Business within the Korean-American Community" (PhD diss., University of Pennsylvania), 86; and Pyong Gap Min, "Korean Immigrant Entrepreneurship: A Comprehensive Explanation," in *Koreans in America: New Perspectives*, ed. Seong Hyong Lee and Tae-Hwan Kwak (Seoul: Kyungnam University Press, 1988), 160.
22. Ling, *Chinese St. Louis*, 155; Bernard P. Wong, *Patronage, Brokerage, Entrepreneurship and the Chinese Community of New York* (New York: AMS Press, 1988).
23. Peter S. Li, "Chinese Investment and Business in Canada: Ethnic Entrepreneurship Reconsidered," *Pacific Affairs* 66, no. 2 (Summer 1993): 219–243.
24. Linda Y. C. Lim, "Chinese Economic Activity in Southeast Asia," in *The Chinese in Southeast Asia*, vol. 1: *Ethnicity and Economic Activity*, ed. Linda Y. C. Lim and L. A. Peter Goaling (Singapore: Maruzen Asia, 1983).
25. Discussions in this section are based on Susan Eckstein and Thanh-Nghi Nguyen, "The Making and Transnationalization of an Ethnic Niche: Vietnamese Manicurists," *International Migration Review* 45, no. 3 (Fall 2011): 639–674; M. N. Federman, D. E. Harrington, and K. J. Krynski, "Vietnamese Manicurists: Are Immigrants Displacing Natives or Finding New Nails to Polish?," *Industrial and Labor Relations Review* 59, no. 2 (January 2006): 302–318; and Karen Grigsby Bates, "Nailing the American Dream, with Polish," National Public Radio, June 14, 2012, http://www.npr.org/2012/06/14/154852394/with-polish-vietnamese-immigrant-community-thrives?sc=fb&cc=fp.
26. Pawan Dhingra, *Life Behind the Lobby: Indian American Motel Owners and the American Dream* (Stanford, CA: Stanford University Press, 2012), 12.
27. Padma Wangaswamy, "South Asians in Dunkin' Donuts: Niche Development in the Franchise Industry," *Journal of Ethnic and Migration Studies* 33, no. 4 (May 2007): 671–686.
28. Sucheng Chan, *Asian Americans: An Interpretive History* (Boston: Twayne, 1991), 171; Pei-te Lien, *The Making of Asian America through Political Participation* (Philadelphia: Temple University Press, 2001); Leland Saito, "Asian Americans and Multiracial Political Coalitions," in *Asian Americans and Politics: Perspectives, Experiences, Prospects*, ed. Gordon H. Chang (Stanford, CA: Stanford University Press, 2001), 383–408; George Lipsitz, *The Possessive Investment in Whiteness: How White People Profit from Identity Politics* (Philadelphia: Temple University Press, 1998).
29. Chang, *Asian Americans and Politics*, 1.

30. Don T. Nakanishi and James S. Lai, eds., *2007–08 National Asian Pacific American Political Almanac* (Los Angeles: UCLA, Asian American Studies Center, 2008), 82–83.
31. See, for instance, AAPI Data, "State of AAPIs: Civic Participation and Democracy" (Center for American Progress and AAPI Data, 2014), https://aapidata.com/civic/voting/, and AAPI Data, "Asian American Electorate in California" (National Asian American Survey and AAPI Data, 2015), https://aapidata.com/civic/voting/.
32. See, for instance, AAPI Data, "State of AAPIs: Public Opinion" (Center for American Progress and AAPI Data, 2014), https://aapidata.com/civic/voting/.
33. Rufus P. Browning, Dale Rogers Marshall, and David H. Tabb, *Protest Is Not Enough* (Berkeley: University of California Press, 1984).
34. Katherine Underwood, "Process and Politics: Multiracial Electoral Coalition Building and Representation in Los Angeles' Ninth District, 1949–1962" (PhD diss., University of California, San Diego, 1992).
35. Lipsitz, *Possessive Investment in Whiteness*; Saito, "Asian Americans and Multiracial Political Coalitions"; and Browning, Marshall, and Tabb, *Protest Is Not Enough*.
36. *World Journal*, July 21, 1990; Huping Ling, *Surviving on the Gold Mountain: A History of Chinese American Women and Their Lives* (Albany: State University of New York Press, 1989), 133–145.
37. U.S. Department of Energy, "Dr. Steven Chu" (n.d.), http://energy.gov/contributors/secretary-energy-dr-steven-chu.
38. Washington State Office of the Governor, "Governor Gary Locke" (2004), http://www.digitalarchives.wa.gov/governorlocke/bios/bio.htm.
39. Judy Chu, "About Judy" (n.d.), http://chu.house.gov/about/index.shtml.
40. "US House 'Regrets' Chinese Exclusion," *Yahoo! News*, June 18, 2012, http://news.yahoo.com/us-house-regrets-chinese-exclusion-000917802.html.
41. Bobby Jindal, https://en.wikipedia.org/wiki/Bobby_Jindal.
42. For scholarly discussion on the model minority, see Bob H. Suzuki, "Educational and the Socialization of Asian Americans: A Revisionist Analysis of the 'Model Minority' Thesis," *Amerasia Journal* 4 (1977): 23–51, one of the earliest critiques of the model minority thesis; Keith Osajima, "Asian Americans as the Model Minority: An Analysis of the Popular Press Image in the 1960s and 1980s," in *Reflections on Shattered Windows: Promises and Prospects for Asian American Studies*, ed. Gary Y. Okihiro et al. (Pullman: Washington State University Press, 1988), 165–174; Lucie Cheng and Philip Q. Yang, "The 'Model Minority' Deconstructed," in *Ethnic Los Angeles,* ed. Roger Waldinger and Mehdi Bozorgmehr (New York: Russell Sage Foundation, 1996), 305–344; Paul Wong et al., "Asian Americans as a Model Minority: Self-Perceptions and Perceptions by Other Racial Groups," *Sociological Perspectives* 41, no. 1 (1998): 95–118; and Frieda Wong and Richard Halgin, "The 'Model Minority': Bane or Blessing for Asian Americans?," *Journal of Multicultural Counseling and Development* 34 (January 2006): 38–49.
43. William Petersen, "Success Story, Japanese-American Style," *New York Times Magazine*, January 9, 1966, 20–43; "Success Story of One Minority in the U.S.," *U.S. News & World Report*, December 26, 1966, 73–78.
44. President Ronald Reagan, speech to a group of Asian and Pacific Americans in the White House, February 23, 1984, reprinted in *Asian Week*, March 2, 1984.
45. U.S. Department of Health, Education, and Welfare, "A Study of Selected Socio-Economic Characteristics of Ethnic Minorities Based on the 1970 Census, vol. 2: Asian Americans" (Washington, DC: Department of Health, Education, and Welfare, 1974), 108 and 112.

46. Herbert R. Barringer et al., "Education, Occupational Prestige, and Income of Asian Americans," in *The Asian American Educational Experience*, ed. Don T. Nakanishi and Tina Yamano Nishida (New York: Routledge, 1995), 150.
47. Peter Kwong, *The New Chinatown* (New York: Hill & Wang, 1987), 62–65; Victor G. Nee and Brett de Bary, *Longtime Californ': A Documentary Study of an American Chinatown* (New York: Pantheon, 1972), 278–319; Bernard Wong, "The Chinese: New Immigrants in New York's Chinatown," in *New Immigrants in New York*, ed. Nancy Foner (New York: Columbia University Press, 1987), 243–271; and Min Zhou, *Chinatown: The Socioeconomic Potential of an Urban Enclave* (Philadelphia: Temple University Press, 1992), 159–182.
48. Barringer et al., "Education, Occupational Prestige, and Income of Asian Americans," 152.
49. Korn/Ferry International, "U.S. Glass Ceiling Commission", reprinted in Leadership Education for Asian Pacifics, Inc., *Newsletter* (October 1996): 5.
50. U.S. Department of Health, Education, and Welfare, "A Study of Selected Socio-economic Characteristics of Ethnic Minorities Based on the 1970 Census" (1972), 108 and 112.
51. "Labor Force Characteristics of Selected Asian and Pacific Islander Groups by Nativity, Citizenship, and Year," in *1990 Census of Population: Asians and Pacific Islanders in the United States* (Washington, DC: U.S. Census Bureau, 1993), 111–112.
52. *All Things Considered Weekend Edition*, National Public Radio, March 8, 1997.
53. Wong and Halgin, "'Model Minority.'"
54. Jennifer Epstein, "Obama: Asians Are More Than 'Model Minority,'" *Politico*, May 8, 2012, http://www.politico.com/politico44/2012/05/obama-asians-are-more-than-model-minority-122846.html.

8. NEW FORMATIONS OF ASIAN AMERICAN COMMUNITIES

1. Percentage computed according to U.S. Census Bureau, "U.S. Census of Population: 1950," vol. 4, Special Reports, 3B-19, and the U.S. census, 1940–2010.
2. Mary R. Coolidge, *Chinese Immigration* (New York: Henry Holt, 1909; reprint, New York: Arno Press, 1969), 402.
3. Rose Hum Lee, *The Chinese in the United States of America* (Hong Kong: Hong Kong University Press, 1960), 52; Bernard P. Wong, *A Chinese American Community: Ethnicity and Survival Strategies* (Singapore: Chopmen Enterprises, 1979), 18; Kay J. Anderson, *Vancouver's Chinatown: Racial Discourse in Canada, 1875–1980* (Montreal: McGill-Queen's University Press, 1991), 9; and David Lai, "Socio-economic Structures and the Viability of Chinatown," in *Residential and Neighborhood Studies in Victoria*, ed. C. Forward (Victoria: University of Victoria, Western Geographical Series no. 5, 1973), 101–129.
4. Yong Chen, *Chinese San Francisco, 1850–1943: A Trans-Pacific Community* (Stanford, CA: Stanford University Press, 2000), 58–62.
5. John Kuo Wei Tchen, *New York before Chinatown: Orientalism and the Shaping of American Culture, 1776–1882* (Baltimore: Johns Hopkins University Press, 1999), 225–226. For more works on New York's Chinatown, see Bernard P. Wong, *A Chinese American Community: Ethnicity and Survival Strategies* (Singapore: Chopmen Enterprises, 1979); Wong, *Chinatown: Economic Adaptation and Ethnic Identity of the Chinese* (New York: Holt, Rinehart & Winston, 1982); Wong,

Patronage, Brokerage, Entrepreneurship and the Chinese Community of New York (New York: AMS Press, 1988); Peter Kwong, *Chinatown, New York: Labor and Politics, 1930–1950* (New York: Monthly Review Press, 1979); Kwong, *The New Chinatown* (New York: Hill & Wang, 1987); Min Zhou, *Chinatown: The Socioeconomic Potential of an Urban Enclave* (Philadelphia: Temple University Press, 1992); Hsiang-shui Chen, *Chinatown No More: Taiwanese Immigrants in Contemporary New York* (Ithaca, NY: Cornell University Press, 1992); and Jan Lin, *Reconstructing Chinatown: Ethnic Enclave, Global Change* (Minneapolis: University of Minnesota Press, 1998).

6. Chen, *Chinatown No More*, 27–28.
7. Huping Ling, *Chinese Chicago: Race, Transnational Migration, and Community since 1870* (Stanford, CA: Stanford University Press, 2012).
8. Huping Ling, *Chinese St. Louis: From Enclave to Cultural Community* (Philadelphia: Temple University Press, 2004).
9. Roger Daniels, *Asian America: Chinese and Japanese in the United States since 1850* (Seattle: University of Washington, 1988), 157.
10. According to Milton Gordon's classification in *Assimilation in American Life* (New York: Oxford University Press, 1964).
11. Harry Kitano et al., "Asian-American Interracial Marriage," *Journal of Marriage and the Family* 46, no. 1 (February 1984): 179–190.
12. Bruna Mori Darini, "Little Tokyo," in *Asian American History and Culture: An Encyclopedia*, ed. Huping Ling and Allan Austin (New York: M. E. Sharpe, 2010), 434–435.
13. U.S. Immigration and Naturalization Service, "Annual Report" (Washington, DC: Government Printing Office, 1995).
14. Kyeyoung Park, *The Korean American Dream: Immigrants and Small Business in New York City* (Ithaca, NY: Cornell University Press, 1997), 9–13; Jae-Hyup Lee, *Dynamics of Ethnic Identity: Three Asian American Communities in Philadelphia* (New York: Garland, 1998), 39; and John Stephens and Sung-Ae Lee, "Diasporan Subjectivity and Cultural Space in Korean American Picture Books," *Journal of Asian American Studies* 9, no. 1 (February 2006): 1–25.
15. See, for example, Nancy Abelmann and John Lee, *Blue Dreams: Korean Americans and the Los Angeles Riots* (Cambridge, MA: Harvard University Press, 1995); Edna Bonacich, Ivan Light, and Charles C. Wong, "Small Business among Koreans in Los Angeles," in *Counterpoint: Perspectives on Asian America*, ed. Emma Gee (Los Angeles: Asian American Studies Center, University of California, 1976), 436–449; Illsoo Kim, *New Urban Immigrants: The Korean Community in New York* (Princeton, NJ: Princeton University Press, 1981); Kim, "The Koreans: Small Business in an Urban Frontier," in *New Immigrants in New York*, ed. Nancy Foner (New York: Columbia University Press, 1987), 219–242; Ivan Light and Edna Bonacich, *Immigrant Entrepreneurs: Koreans in Los Angeles, 1965–1982* (Berkeley: University of California Press, 1988); Gap Pyong Min, "A Structural Analysis of Korean Business in the United States," *Ethnic Groups* 6 (1984): 1–25; Min, *Ethnic Business Enterprise: Korean Small Business in Atlanta* (New York: Center for Migration Studies, 1988); and Min, *Caught in the Middle*.
16. Rodelen Paccial, "Koreatown (Los Angeles)," in Ling and Austin, *Asian American History and Culture*, 488–489.
17. Park, *Korean American Dream*, 20–21.
18. Pyong Gap Min, "A Structural Analysis of Korean Business in the United States"; Park, *Korean American Dream*; Jae-Hyup Lee, *Dynamics of Ethnic Identity*.

19. Illsoo Kim, *New Urban Immigrants*, 226.
20. Information for the above four paragraphs is based on Nazil Kibria. "South Asian Americans," in *Asian Americans: Contemporary Trends and Issues*, ed. Pyong Gap Min (Thousand Oaks, CA: Pine Forge Press, 2006), 206–227; V. Prashad, *The Karma of Brown Folk* (Minneapolis: University of Minnesota Press, 2000), 75–79; Ling and Austin, *Asian American History and Culture*, 311–367; and 2000 and 2010 U.S. censuses.
21. Pauline Agbayani-Siewert and Linda Revilla, "Filipino Americans," in Min, *Asian Americans*, 142.
22. U.S. censuses 2000 and 2010.
23. Sucheng Chan, *Asian Americans: An Interpretive History* (Boston: Twayne, 1991), 149.
24. Agbayani-Siewert and Revilla, "Filipino Americans," 143.
25. Yen Le Espiritu, *Home Bound: Filipino American Lives across Cultures, Communities, and Countries* (Berkeley: University of California Press, 2003), 11; Chan, *Asian Americans* 149.
26. Espiritu, *Home Bound*, 32; Chan, *Asian Americans*, 150; Huping Ling, *Voices of the Heart: Asian American Women on Immigration, Work, and Family* (Kirksville, MO: Truman State University Press, 2007).
27. Espiritu, *Home Bound*, 105–117.
28. Garbriella Oldham, "Little Manila," in Ling and Austin, *Asian American History and Culture*, 293–294; Linda Nueva Espana-Maram, *Creating Masculinity in Los Angeles's Little Manila: Working-Class Filipinos and Popular Culture, 1920s–1950s* (New York: Columbia University Press, 2006).
29. Colette Marie McLaughlin and Paul Jesilow, "Conveying a Sense of Community along Bolsa Avenue: Little Saigon as a Model of Ethnic Commercial Belts," *International Migration* 36, no. 1 (1998): 49–63.
30. U.S. census 2000.
31. McLaughlin and Jesilow, "Conveying a Sense of Community"; Linda Trinh Võ, "Transforming an Ethnic Community: Little Saigon, Orange County," in *Asian America: Forming New Communities, Expanding Boundaries*, ed. Huping Ling (New Brunswick, NJ: Rutgers University Press, 2009), 87–103; and U.S. census 2010.
32. Ling, *Chinese Chicago*, 222–226.
33. Cambodian American Heritage, http://www.cambodianheritage.org; Cambodian American League of Lowell, http://www.cambodianamerican.net; Cambodian American National Council, http://www.cancweb.org; Cambodian Mutual Assistance Association, http://www.cmaalowell.org
34. U.S. census 2010.
35. Kou Yang, "Hmong American Contemporary Experience," in *Emerging Voices: Experiences of Underrepresented Asian Americans*, ed. Huping Ling (New Brunswick, NJ: Rutgers University Press, 2008), 236–253; and Pamela A. DeVoe, "The Role Ethnic Leaders in the Refugee Community: A Case Study of the Lowland Lao in the American Midwest," in Ling, *Emerging Voices*, 52–70.
36. Wei Li, *Ethnoburb: The New Ethnic Community in Urban America* (Honolulu: University of Hawai'i Press, 2009), 100.
37. Yen-Fen Tseng, "Chinese Ethnic Economy: San Gabriel Valley, Los Angeles County," *Journal of Urban Affairs* 16, no. 2 (1994): 169–189. For other works on Chinese communities in suburban Los Angeles, see Joe Chung Fong, "Transnational Newspapers: The Making of the Post-1965 Globalized/Localized San Gabriel Valley Chinese Community," *Amerasia Journal* 22, no. 3 (1996): 65–77; John Horton, *The Politics of Diversity: Immigration, Resistance, and Change in Monterey Park, California* (Philadelphia: Temple University Press, 1995); Leland Saito, *Race and Politics: Asian and Latino and White in Los Angeles Suburbs* (Urbana: University of Illinois Press, 1998);

and Yu Zhou, "Ethnic Networks as Transactional Networks: Chinese Networks in the Producer Service Sectors of Los Angeles" (PhD diss., University of Minnesota, 1996).
38. Chen, *Chinatown No More*, 28–33.
39. Lin, *Reconstructing Chinatown*.
40. U.S. census 1990.
41. U.S. census 2000.
42. Ling, *Chinese Chicago*, 226–229.
43. Ling, *Chinese St. Louis*.
44. Ling, *Chinese Chicago*, 228–229.
45. Fujita and O'Brien, *Japanese American Ethnicity*, 4–5.
46. Park, *Korean American Dream*.
47. Angie Y. Chung, *Legacies of Struggle: Conflict and Cooperation in Korean American Politics* (Palo Alto, CA: Stanford University Press, 2007).
48. Linda Trinh Võ and Rick Bonus, eds., *Contemporary Asian American Communities: Intersections and Divergences* (Philadelphia: Temple University Press, 2002), 6.
49. Rick Bonus, *Locating Filipino America: Ethnicity and Cultural Politics of Space* (Philadelphia: Temple University Press, 2000).
50. Allyson Tintiangco-Cubales, "Building a Community Center: Filipinas/nos in San Francisco's Excelsior Neighborhood," in Ling, *Asian America*, 104–125.
51. Sanjoy Mazumdar, Shampa Mazumdar, Faye Docuyanan, and Colette Marie McLaughlin, "Creating a Sense of Place: The Vietnamese-Americans and Little Saigon," *Journal of Environmental Psychology* 20 (2000): 319–333.
52. Jerry Everard, *Virtual States: The Internet and the Boundaries of the Nation States* (New York: Routledge, 2000); Steven G. Jones, "Understanding Community in the Information Age," in *Cybersociety: Computer-Mediated Communication and Community*, ed. Steven Jones (Thousand Oaks, CA: Sage, 1995), 10–35; Jones, "The Internet and Its Social Landscape," in ed. Steven Jones, *Virtual Culture: Identity and Communication in Cybersociety* (Sage Publications, 1997), 7–35; and Yuan Shu, "Virtual Community and the Cultural Imagery of Chinese Americans," in Ling, *Asian America*, 179–197.
53. Shu, "Virtual Community."
54. Roy Wells, "41.6% of the US Population Has a Facebook Account," *Social Media Today*, August 8, 2010, https://www.socialmediatoday.com/content/416-us-population-has-facebook-account.
55. Mark Hachman, "Facebook Now Totals 901 Million Users, Profits Slip," *PCMag*, April 23, 2012, http://www.pcmag.com/article2/0,2817,2403410,00.asp. Note that the term "users" here does not necessarily equate "people," as one individual/organization/business can set up multiple accounts. Therefore the number of users is far greater than the number of people who are using Facebook.
56. Mark Zuckerberg, "Everyone Deserves to Be Connected on the Net," *CNN*, August 21, 2013.
57. "Facebook Is a Community," *ScienceDaily*, January 25, 2012, http://www.sciencedaily.com/releases/2012/01/120125091053.htm.
58. "State of the Media: The Social Media Report, Q3 2011," Nielsen, September 2011, https://www.nielsen.com/insights/2011/social-media-report-q3/.
59. "WeChat Now Has over 1 Billion Active Monthly Users Worldwide," *TechNode*, March 5, 2018, https://technode.com/2018/03/05/wechat-1-billion-users/.
60. Ronald Deibert, "Opinion/WeChat Users Outside China Face Surveillance While Training Censorship Algorithms," *Washington Post*, September 20, 2020.

61. Kiran Sharma, "Indian Apps Soar after Ban on China's TikTok, WeChat and Baidu: Relations Soured by Ladakh Clash Force Modi to Refocus Economic Struggle," *Nikkei*, August 4, 2020, https://asia.nikkei.com/Spotlight/Asia-Insight/Indian-apps-soar-after-ban-on-China-s-TikTok-WeChat-and-Baidu.
62. Tali Arbel, "Trump Bans Dealings with Chinese Owners of TikTok, WeChat," Associated Press, August 6, 2020, https://apnews.com/article/global-trade-ap-top-news-politics-asia-business-719d8c83f689929c9c9d8c9aa5593fc8.
63. Jeff Han, "Cover Story/COVID-19 Heavily Damaging American Chinatowns" (世界周刊《封面故事》新冠疫情 重創美國唐人街), *World Weekly*, June 28, 2020.

9. THEORIZING ASIAN AMERICA

1. Don T. Nakanishi and Russell Leong, "Toward the Second Decade: A National Survey of Asian American Studies Programs in 1978," *Amerasia Journal* 5, no. 1 (1978): 1–19.
2. Russell Endo and William Wei, "On the Development of Asian American Studies Programs," in *Reflections on Shattered Windows: Promises and Prospects for Asian American Studies*, ed. Gary Y. Okihiro, Shirley Hune, Arthur A. Hansen, and John M. Liu (Pullman: Washington State University Press, 1988), 5–15; Peter Nien-chu Kiang, "The New Wave: Developing Asian American Studies on the East Coast," in Okihiro et al., *Reflections in Shattered Windows*, 43–50; and William Wei, *The Asian American Movement* (Philadelphia: Temple University Press, 1993).
3. Based on author's study on the development of Asian American studies throughout the United States from 1968 to the 2010s.
4. The acronym LGBT later evolved into LGBTQIA+. It is an inclusive term covering people of all genders and sexualities, such as those who identify as lesbian, gay, bisexual, transgender, questioning, queer, intersex, asexual, or pansexual and their allies.
5. Huping Ling, "Editor's Preface," *Journal of Asian American Studies* 12, no. 2 (June 2009): v–x.
6. Nina Glick Schiller, Linda Basch, and Cristina Blanc-Szanton, eds., *Towards a Transnational Perspective on Migration: Race, Ethnicity, and Nationalism Reconsidered* (New York: New York Academy of Science, 1992), ix.
7. See, for example, Aihwa Ong, *Flexible Citizenship: The Cultural Logics of Transnationality* (Durham, NC: Duke University Press, 1999); and Alejandro Portes, Luis E. Guarnizo and Patricia Landolt, "The Study of Transnationalism: Pitfalls and Promise of an Emergent Research Field," *Ethnic and Racial Studies* 22 (1999): 224; and Philip Q. Yang, "Transnationalism as a New Mode of Immigrant Adaptation: Preliminary Evidence from Chinese Transnational Migrants," *Journal of Chinese Overseas* 2 (2006): 173–192.
8. For historical works with a transnationalism approach, see, for example, Renqiu Yu, *To Save China, to Save Ourselves: The Chinese Hand Laundry Alliance of New York* (Philadelphia: Temple University Press, 1992); Haiming Liu, *Transnational History of a Chinese Family: Immigrant Letters, Family Business, and Reverse Migration* (New Brunswick, NJ: Rutgers University Press, 2005); Yong Chen, *Chinese San Francisco, 1850–1943: A Trans-Pacific Community* (Stanford, CA: Stanford University Press, 2000); Madeline Y. Hsu, *Dreaming of Gold, Dreaming of Home: Transnationalism and Migration between the United States and South China, 1882–1943* (Stanford, CA: Stanford University Press, 2000); Adam McKeown, *Chinese Migrant Networks and Cultural Change* (Chi-

cago: University of Chicago Press, 2001); and Huping Ling, *Chinese Chicago: Race, Transnational Migration, and Community since 1870* (Stanford, CA: Stanford University Press, 2012).

9. Erika Lee, "Orientalism in the Americas: A Hemispheric Approach to Asian American History," *Journal of Asian American Studies* 8, no. 3 (October 2005): 235–256.

10. See, for example, Lisa Rose Mar, *Brokering Belonging: Chinese in Canada's Exclusion Era, 1885–1945* (New York: Oxford University Press, 2010); Lok C. D. Siu, *Memories of a Future Home: Diasporic Citizenship of Chinese in Panama* (Stanford, CA: Stanford University Press, 2007); and Lisa Yun, *The Coolie Speaks: Chinese Indentured Laborers and African Slaves in Cuba* (Philadelphia: Temple University Press, 2009).

11. http://www.aasp.illinois.edu/home.html.

12. Cynthia Boyd, "Asians Fastest-Growing Ethnic Group in Minnesota," *Minnpost*, June 18, 2013, http://www.minnpost.com/community-sketchbook/2013/06/asians-fastest-growing-ethnic-group-minnesota.

13. University of Minnesota, "Asian American Studies Program" (2022), http://aas.umn.edu.

14. Huping Ling, *Chinese St. Louis: From Enclave to Cultural Community* (Philadelphia: Temple University Press, 2004); Ling, *Chinese Chicago*; Ling, *Chinese Americans in the Heartland: Migration, Work, and Community* (New Brunswick, NJ: Rutgers University Press, 2022).

15. Sook Wilkinson and Victor Jew, eds., *Asian Americans in Michigan: Voices from the Midwest* (Detroit: Wayne State University Press, 2015).

16. David Eng and Alice Hom, eds., *Q & A: Queer in Asian America* (Philadelphia: Temple University Press, 1998), 2–3.

17. Dana Takagi, "Maiden Voyage: Excursion into Sexuality and Identity Politics in Asian America," *Amerasia Journal* 20, no. 1 (1994): 1–17.

18. Sean-Shong Hwang, Rogelio Saenz, Benigno E. Aguirre, "Structural and Assimilationist Explanations of Asian American Intermarriage," *Journal of Marriage and Family* 59, no. 3 (August 1997): 758–772.

19. Joan Walsh, "Asian Women, Caucasian Men," *Image*, December 2, 1990, 11–6.

20. Wendy Wang, "The Rise of Intermarriage: Rates, Characteristics Vary by Race and Gender" (Pew Research Center, February 16, 2012), http://www.pewsocialtrends.org/2012/02/16/the-rise-of-intermarriage/?src=prc-headline.

21. Milton Gordon, *Assimilation in American Life* (New York: Oxford University Press, 1964), 80. Other works with similar views include John N. Tinker, "Intermarriage and Assimilation in a Plural Society: Japanese Americans in the U.S.," in *Intermarriage in the United States*, ed. Gary A. Cretser and Joseph J. Leon (New York: Hayworth Press, 1982), 61–74; Harry Kitano et al., "Asian American Interracial Marriage," *Journal of Marriage and the Family* 46, no. 1 (February 1984): 179–190; and Betty Sung, *Chinese American Intermarriage* (New York: Center for Migration Studies, 1990).

22. Kingsley Davis, "Intermarriage in Caste Societies," *American Anthropologist* 43, no. 3 (July–September 1941): 376–395.

23. Davis, "Intermarriage in Caste Societies," 386–393.

24. Larry Hajime Shinagawa and Gin Yong Pang, "Intraethnic, Interethnic, and Interracial Marriages among Asian Americans in California, 1980," *Berkeley Journal of Sociology* 33 (1988): 95–114.

25. Paul Spickard, *Mixed Blood: Intermarriage and Ethnic Identity in Twentieth-Century America* (Madison: University of Wisconsin Press, 1989), 6–9.

26. Colleen Fong and Judy Yung, "In Search of the Right Spouse: Interracial Marriage among Chinese and Japanese Americans," *Amerasia Journal* 21, no. 3 (1995–1996): 77–98.
27. Huping Ling, *Surviving on the Gold Mountain: A History of Chinese American Women and Their Lives* (Albany: State University of New York Press, 1989), 174–177.
28. For examples of academic work on the Hmong, see Sucheng Chan, ed., *Hmong Means Free: Life in Laos and America* (Philadelphia: Temple University Press, 1994); Nancy D. Donnelly, *The Changing Lives of Refugee Hmong Women* (Seattle: University of Washington Press, 1994); Beth L. Goldstein, "Schooling for Cultural Transitions: Hmong Girls and Boys in American High Schools" (PhD diss., University of Wisconsin–Madison, 1985); Glenn L. Hendricks, Robert T. Downing, and Amos S. Deinard, eds., *The Hmong in Transition* (Staten Island, NY: Center for Migration Studies, 1986); Karen L. S. Muir, *The Strongest Part of the Family: A Study of Lao Refugee Women in Columbus, Ohio* (New York: AMS Press, 1988); and Vincent K. Her and Mary Louise Buley-Meissner, eds., *Hmong and American: From Refugees to Citizens* (Saint Paul: Minnesota Historical Society Press, 2012).
29. U.S. Census Bureau, "We the Americans: Asians" (Washington, DC: Government Printing Office, 1993), 2.
30. U.S. Census Bureau, "Census 2000 Brief: The Asian Population: 2000", https://www.census.gov/library/publications/2002/dec/c2kbr01-16.html#:~:text=Census%202000%20showed%20that%20the%20United%20States%20population,as%20well%20as%20one%20or%20more%20other%20races.
31. U.S. Census Bureau, "U.S. Asian Population" (2010), http://www.census.gov/prod/cen2010/briefs/c2010br-11.pdf.
32. U.S. Census Bureau, "U.S. Asian Population" (2010).
33. Clark E. Cunningham, "Unity and Diversity among Indonesia Migrants to the United States," in *Emerging Voices: Experiences of Underrepresented Asian Americans*, ed. Huping Ling (New Brunswick, NJ: Rutgers University Press, 2008), 90–108.
34. Haley Duschinski, "Community Identity of Kashmiri Hindus in the United States," in Ling, *Emerging Voices*, 126–142.
35. 2000 census; Todd LeRoy Perreira, "The Gender of Practice: Some Findings among Thai Buddhist Women in Northern California," in Ling, *Emerging Voices*, 160–182.
36. Yosay Wangdi, "'Displaced People' Adjusting to New Cultural Vocabulary: Tibetan Immigrants in North America," in Ling, *Emerging Voices*, 71–89.
37. U.S. Census Bureau, "U.S. Asian Population" (2010).
38. Asian American Justice Center, "A Community of Contrast: Asian Americans and Pacific Islanders in the United States, Demographic Profile" (Asian Pacific American Legal Center of Southern California, Asian Law Caucus, and Asian American Institute, 10.
39. 2000 and 2010 censuses.
40. Wangdi, "'Displaced People' Adjusting to New Cultural Vocabulary."
41. Cunningham, "Unity and Diversity."
42. Mary Somers Heidhues, *Southeast Asia: A Concise History* (London: Thomas and Hudson, 2000), 7–8.
43. Suzuko Morikawa, "Dynamics, Intricacy, and Multiplicity of Romani Identity in the United States," in Ling, *Emerging Voices*, 109–125.
44. Ibrahim Aoude, "Arab Americans and Ethnic Studies," *Journal of Asian American Studies* 9, no. 2 (2006): 141–155; Sanaina Maira and Magid Shihade, "Meeting Asian / Arab American Studies," *Journal of Asian American Studies* 9, no. 2 (2006): 117–140.

45. Jim Lobe, "Post-9/11 Immigrant Roundup Backfired—Report," Inter Press Service, June 27, 2003.
46. A. Bakalian and M. Bozorgmehr, *Backlash 9/11Middle Eastern and Muslim Americans Respond* (Oakland, CA: University of California Press, 2009).
47. Nadine C. Naber, "So Our History Doesn't Become Your Future," *Journal of Asian American Studies* 5, mo. 3 (October 2002): 217–242.
48. Yen Le Espiritu, *Asian American Panethnicity: Bridging Institutions and Identities* (Philadelphia: Temple University Press, 1992), 6–7.

10. THE FUTURE OF ASIAN AMERICA UNDER GLOBALIZATION

1. For instance, Beijing University sponsored a lecture series titled "The Rise of Big Powers" in the 2000s.
2. World Bank, Development Research Center of the State Council, People's Republic of China, "China 2030: Building a Modern, Harmonious, and Creative High-Income Society" (World Bank, 2012).
3. High-speed rail refers to any commercial train service in China with an average speed of 200 km/h (124 mph) or higher.
4. Jonathan Kaiman, "Chinese Company Builds 30-Story Building in 15 Days," *Los Angeles Times*, March 7, 2012.
5. OECD, "PISA 2009 Results: Executive Summary (2010).
6. John Hechinger, "U.S. Teens Lag as China Soars on International Test," *Bloomberg*, December 7, 2010, http://www.bloomberg.com/news/2010-12-07/teens-in-u-s-rank-25th-on-math-test-trail-in-science-reading.html.
7. D. Michael Lampton, *Three Faces of Chinese Power: Might, Money and Mind* (Berkeley: University of California Press, 2009); Andrew Leonard, "No Consensus on the Beijing Consensus: Neoliberalism with Chinese Characteristics? Or the Long-Lost Third Way?" *Salon*, September 15, 2006; James Mann, "A Shinning Model of Wealth without Liberty," *Washington Post*, May 20, 2007; and Susan Shirk, *China: Fragile Superpower: How China's Internal Politics Could Derail Its Peaceful Rise* (New York: Oxford University Press, 2008).
8. World Bank, "United States" (2022), http://data.worldbank.org/country/united-states.
9. World Bank, "Comparing United States and China by Economy," *Statistics Times* May 15, 2021, https://statisticstimes.com/economy/united-states-vs-china-economy.php.
10. Bureau of Economic Analysis of the U.S. Department of Commerce, "U.S. Economy at a Glance: Perspective from the BEA Accounts" (2021), http://www.bea.gov/newsreleases/glance.htm.
11. http://www.treasurydirect.gov/NP/BPDLogin?application=np; http://www.whitehouse.gov/sites/default/files/omb/budget/fy2013/assets/tables.pdf.
12. Bureau of Labor Service, Current Population Survey, "Household Annual Average Data, 1. Employment Status of the Civilian Noninstitutional Population, 1940 to Date", http://www.bls.gov/cps/cpsaat1.pdf.
13. See, for example, Chalmers Johnson, "Japan in Search of a 'Normal' Role," *Daedalus* 121, no. 4 (Fall 1992): 1–33.
14. "Niall Ferguson: Empire on the Edge of Chaos" *U.S. News*, Nov. 17, 2010, https://www.huffpost.com/entry/niall-ferguson-empires-on_n_721761, http://fora.tv/2010/07/28/Niall_Ferguson_Empires

_on_the_Edge_of_Chaos#chapter_02; Niall Ferguson, *Colossus: The Rise and Fall of the American Empire* (New York: Penguin, 2005), 28.

15. "What Percentage of the U.S. Federal Budget Is Spent on Entitlements?," *Answers* (2012), http://wiki.answers.com/Q/What_percentage_of_the_U.S._federal_budget_is_spent_on_entitlements.
16. World Bank Database, http://databank.worldbank.org/databank/download/GDP.pdf.
17. Klaus Schwab, "The Global Competitiveness Report, 2010–2011" (World Economic Forum, 2010), http://www3.weforum.org/docs/WEF_GlobalCompetitivenessReport_2010-11.pdf.
18. Joe Weisenthal, "FORGET THE BRICs: Citi's Willem Buiter Presents The 11 "3G" Countries That Will Win The Future," *Insider*, February 22, 2011, http://www.businessinsider.com/willem-buiter-3g-countries-2011-2?slop=1#vietnam-11.
19. For the positive impact of globalization, see, for example, Thomas L. Friedman, *The Lexus and the Olive Tree: Understanding Globalization* (New York: Anchor Books, 2000), and Friedman, *The World Is Flat: A Brief History of the Twenty-First Century* (New York: Farrar, Straus and Giroux, 2005). For the negative impact of globalization, see Amy Chua, *World on Fire: How Exporting Free Market Democracy Breeds Ethnic Hatred and Global Instability* (New York: Anchor Books, 2004).
20. Niall Ferguson, "What 'Chimerica' Hath Wrought," *American Interest Online*, January–February 2009, http://www.the-american-interest.com/article.cfm?piece=533.
21. Immanuel Wallerstein, "China and the United States: Rivals, Enemies, Collaborators?" (January 15, 2012), http://www.iwallerstein.com/commentaries/.
22. Fareed Zakria GPS, "A GPS Tour of the World's Hotspots" (February 26, 2012).
23. Amy Chua, *Day of Empire: How Hyperpowers Rise to Global Dominance—and Why They Fall* (New York: Anchor Books, 2007), 341.
24. Friedman, *Lexus and the Olive Tree*, 7–14.
25. Friedman, *Lexus and the Olive Tree*, 440–444.
26. Wang Wangbo and Zhuang Guotu, eds., *A Brief Characterization of the Chinese Overseas in 2008* (Beijing: World Knowledge, 2010), 12.
27. Jon Clifton, "150 Million Adults Worldwide Would Migrate to the U.S." (Gallup, April 20, 2012), http://www.gallup.com/poll/153992/150-Million-Adults-Worldwide-Migrate.aspx.
28. Wang and Zhuang, *Brief Characterization*, 12.
29. Philip Q. Yang, *Asian Immigration to the United States* (Cambridge: Polity, 2011), 231.
30. Wei Li and Lucia Lo, "New Geographies of Migration? A Canada-U.S. Comparison of Highly Skilled Chinese and Indian Migration," *Journal of Asian American Studies* 15, no. 1 (February 2012): 1–34.
31. H. J. Holzer, "Immigration Policies and Less-Skilled Workers in the United States" (Washington, DC: Migration Policy Institute, 2011), http://www.migrationpolicy.org/pubs/Holzer-January2011.pdf; Migration Policy Institute, "Side-by-Side Comparison of 2006 and 2007 Senate Legislation and 2009 CIR ASAP Bill" (2009), http://www.migrationpolicy.org/pubs/CIRASAPsidebyside.pdf; and D. M. West, *Creating a "Brain Gain" for U.S. Employers: The Role of Immigration* (Washington, DC: Brookings Institution, 2011), http://www.brookings.edu/~/media/Files/rc/papers/2011/01_immigration_west/01_immigration_west.pdf.
32. "House Gives Go-Ahead on Green Card Plan," Associated Press, November 30, 2012, http://www.ksby.com/news/house-gives-go-ahead-on-green-card-plan/.
33. http://www.changjiang.edu.cn/news/10/10-20090715-247.htm.
34. "Chinese Students Studying Abroad Exceed 1.39 Million," *People's Daily Online*, March 26, 2009, http://english.people.com.cn/90001/90776/90882/6622888.html; Zhongguo tongjiju, *Zhongguo tongji nianjian* (Beijing: Zhongguo tongji chubanshe, 2010), 757.

35. Lisong Liu, "Return Migration and Selective Citizenship," *Journal of Asian American Studies* 15, no. 1 (February 2012): 35–68.
36. Aihwa Ong, *Flexible Citizenship: The Cultural Logics of Transnationality* (Durham, NC: Duke University Press, 1999), 2; Liu, "Return Migration and Selective Citizenship," 55–56.
37. Jose C. Moya and Adam McKeown, "World Migration in the Long Twentieth Century," in *Essays on Global and Comparative History*, ed. Michael Adas (Washington, DC: American Historical Association, 2011), 39.
38. Huping Ling, *Chinese Chicago: Race, Transnational Migration, and Community since 1870* (Stanford, CA: Stanford University Press, 2012); Peter Li, *Destination Canada: Immigration Debates and Issues* (Toronto: Oxford University Press, 2003); and Manying Ip, ed., *Transmigration and the new Chinese: Theories and Practices from the New Zealand Experience* (Hong Kong: Hong Kong Institute for Humanities and Social Sciences, University of Hong Kong, 2011); Li Anshan 李安山, *Feizhou huaqiao huarenshi* 非洲華僑華人史 [A history of Chinese overseas in Africa] (Beijing: Zhingguo huaqiao chubanshe 中國華僑出版社 [Chinese overseas publishing company], 2000); Li Minghuan 李明歡, *Dangdai haiwai huaren shetuan yanjiu* 當代海外華人社團研究 [Contemporary overseas Chinese community organizations] (Xiamen, China: Xiamen daxue chubanshe 廈門大學出版社 [Xiamen University Press], 1995).
39. Moya and McKeown, "World Migration."
40. Yinglin Chen and Rong Li, "Chinese Immigrants Make Waves for Returning to Taiwan," *World Journal*, July 5, 2011.
41. R. A. Chiang, "Chinese American Undergraduates' Choice of College Major: A Social-Structural Analysis Using Blau's Occupational Choice Model" (PhD diss., New York University, 1994); S. E. Park and A. A. Harrison, "Career Related Interests and Values, Perceived Control and Acculturation of Asian American and Caucasian College Students," *Journal of Applied Social Psychology* 25 (1995): 1184–1203.
42. http://factfinder2.census.gov/faces/tableservices/jsf/pages/productview.xhtml?pid=DEC_00_SF4_QTP29&prodType=table, http://factfinder2.census.gov/faces/tableservices/jsf/pages/productview.xhtml?src=bkmk, and http://factfinder2.census.gov/faces/tableservices/jsf/pages/productview.xhtml?pid=ACS_10_1YR_S2405&prodType=table.
43. D. D. Guttenplan, "Critics Worry about Influence of Chinese Institutes on U.S. Campuses," *New York Times*, March 4, 2012; Confucius Institute, https://baike.baidu.com/item/%E5%AD%94%E5%AD%90%E5%AD%A6%E9%99%A2/812632.
44. Manlin, "Luban Workshop: A New Seed Sewed by the Chinese Government within Developing Countries," *Liberty Times Net*, November 9, 2022, https://talk.ltn.com.tw/article/breakingnews/4117433.
45. Huping Ling, *Voices of the Heart: Asian American Women on Immigration, Work, and Family* (Kirksville, MO: Truman State University Press, 2007); author's interviews with Asian American students between 1992 and 2012.
46. Yinglin Chen and Qing Yang, "Transmigrant Families Pay High Prices for the Life Style," *World Journal*, August 22, 2011.
47. *World Journal*, August 12, 2010; July 4, 2011; July 5, 2011; November 6, 2011; Lcosguy, posting to Haiguinet, February 20, 2009, http://www.haiguinet.com/forum/viewtopic.php?p=1470671.
48. Kirk Semple, "Soldier's Death Raises Suspicions in Chinatown," *New York Times*, October 31, 2011; *World Journal*, July 20, 2012.
49. See news reports in *World Journal*, May 9, 10, 17 and 18, 2020.
50. See news reports in *World Journal*, June 5, 11, 2020.

51. Peter Romeo, "Prejudice and Irrational Fears Are Key Factors, the Research Found," *Restaurant Business Online*, April 13, 2020, https://www.restaurantbusinessonline.com/operations/half-nations-chinese-restaurants-have-closed-study-finds.
52. See reports in *World Journal*, June 27, July 5, and August 6, 2020.
53. On March 19, 2020, in response to increased racially motivated violence against Asian peoples in the United States as a result of the COVID-19 pandemic, three organizations, including the Asian Pacific Planning and Policy Council (A3PCON), Chinese for Affirmative Action (CAA), and the Asian American Studies Department of San Francisco State University, launched the Stop AAPI Hate reporting center. This nonprofit social organization tracks incidents of discrimination, hate, and xenophobia against Asian Americans and Pacific Islanders (AAPIs). See the organization's press release of February 9, 2021, https://secureservercdn.net/104.238.69.231/a1w.90d.myftpupload.com/wp-content/uploads/2021/02/Press-Statement-re_-Bay-Area-Elderly-Incidents-2.9.2021-1.pdf.
54. Jenny Manrique, "Ethnic Communities Unite to Combat Anti-Asian Violence," *Ethnic Media Services*, February 23, 2021, https://ethnicmediaservices.org/immigration/ethnic-communities-unite-to-combat-anti-asian-violence/.
55. Mark Berman, Brittany Shammas, Teo Armus, and Marc Fisher, "The Atlanta Spa Shooting Suspect's Life before Attacks," *Washington Post*, March 19, 2021, https://www.washingtonpost.com/national/atlanta-shooting-suspect-robert-aaron-long/2021/03/19/9397cdca-87fe-11eb-8a8b-5cf82c3dffe4_story.html.
56. See, for example, Ellen Moynihan and Clayton Guse, "'A Lifetime of Anti-Asian Hate': New Yorkers Rally Against Hate Crimes Targeted at Asian-Americans," *New York Daily News*, March 21, 2021, https://www.nydailynews.com/new-york/ny-asian-american-hate-crime-rally-nyc-20210322-7cdsltljxzaoxk5oqidl7qg3xu-story.html; Dragon Eagle TV, "Resisting Hate Crimes Against Asians Summit," YouTube, March 20, 2021, https://www.youtube.com/watch?app=desktop&v=N2pglGlGk88&feature=youtu.be&fbclid=IwAR2HqsdcDyogmrzYznTEBasjV5dC3dlJ4Lt9bj5dyVKK4_EDMW0e9bFbJtA.
57. *World Journal*, May 2, 2020.
58. Jenny Manrique, "Ethnic Communities Unite to Combat Anti-Asian Violence."
59. Mimi Lau, "Chinese Students Weigh Overseas Options as COVID-19 and US Visa Limits Take Toll: Report," *South China Morning Paper*, March 3, 2021.
60. See the organization's press release of February 9, 2021, https://secureservercdn.net/104.238.69.231/a1w.90d.myftpupload.com/wp-content/uploads/2021/02/Press-Statement-re_-Bay-Area-Elderly-Incidents-2.9.2021-1.pdf.
61. "New Docuseries Unpacks More Than 150 Years of Asian American History," *PBS*, May 11, 2020.
62. See *World Journal*, September 23, 2020.
63. For example, Facebook and other social media had significant posts/announcements on lectures, panel discussions, and roundtables during the pandemic given by various academic specialists in Asian American studies, including the author's several public Zoom presentations in 2020–2021.
64. See *World Journal*, February 11, 12, 13, and March 1, 2, 3, 2021.
65. Shanon Maglente, "Why Some Asian Americans Are Staying Silent about the Ongoing Hate Crimes," *Good Housekeeping*, March 2, 2021.
66. *World Journal*, April 22, 2021.

67. Min Liu, telephone interviews by the author, April 26, 2020, March 12 and 17, 2021. See also numerous posts on WeChat.
68. *World Journal*, May 2, 2020.
69. Min Liu, telephone interview by the author, April 26, 2020.
70. *World Journal*, February 7 and 12, March 2, 2021.
71. *World Weekly*, June 28, 2020.

INDEX

Note: The letter *f* following a page number denotes a figure; *s* denotes a sidebar; *t* denotes a table.

Act to Repeal the Chinese Exclusion Acts, to Establish Quotas, and for Other Purposes, 139
adoptees, 164
Adoption. *See* transnational and transracial adoption
"agent orange," 174
Ahn Chang-ho, 121
Alien Registration Act, 141
Allen, Horace N. 23. *See also* patterns of Asian migration
Amerasia Journal, 281, 293
American Civil Liberties Union (ACLU), 154
"Americanization" of Filipino culture, 244
American Pacific expansions, 12–14; acquisition of Samoa, 14; annexation of Hawaii, 13–14; motivations, 12–13; open door to China, 14
Angel Island immigration station, 43–48, 337n58, 45f; cross-interrogation, 44–48, 46s, 48f, 49f; plaque, 44f
Ansei Treaties, 20
anti-Chinese violence in: Chico (1877), 36; Denver (1880), 37; Los Angeles (1871), 36; Rock Springs (1885), 37. *See also* physical violence against Asian immigrants
anti-Vietnam War movement, 272
Aoki, Kazue, 102
Aqua DC gaysian–DC Gay Pride Parade 2012, 281f
Asian American businesses, commercial square, 252f
Asian American employment, dual structure of, 213

Asian American lesbian/gay organizations in metropolitan centers, 280
Asian American movement, 272–274; Asian American, 271, 274; contents of, 273–274; identity construction, 273–274; origins, 272–273; pen-ethnic identity, 271; service-oriented community activism, 274; significance, 274; student activism, 272–273; Yellow Identity Conference, 273
Asian American Political Alliance (AAPA), 272
Asian American population change, in southern and midwestern states, 278t
Asian American representation, 2007: by state, 223–224t; totals, 313t
Asian Americans for Action (Triple A), 273
Asian American Studies (AAS), institutionalization of, 274–275; AAS program in Midwest and South, 277–280; Truman State University, 279; University of Illinois Urbana-Champaign, 277–278; University of Minnesota, 279; University of Texas at Austin, 279
Asian Community Center, 274
Asian Indian agricultural workers, 87; Asian Indian railroad workers, 69; working conditions, 69
Asian laborers in Hawaiian sugar plantations, 62–66; female laborers, 66; Filipino laborers, 66; Korean laborers, 65–66; laborer resistance, 65; living conditions, 63; move to the mainland, 66; racial and class hierarchy, 65–66; wages, 64–66; work song, 63s; working conditions, 63–64

Asian laborers in mining, 66–69; Chinese miners' contributions, 68; gold mining methods, 67–68
Asian Legal Services, 274
Asian migration, global context for, 10–14
Asian population, by number of detailed groups, 2010, 287t
Asian trade, 10–12, 11s; American trade in China, 11–12; British trade in China, 11; British trade in India, 10–11; Canton system (1760–1842), 11
Association for Asian American Studies (AAAS), 263, 279–280
asylum seeker crossing U.S.-Canadian border, 186f
Azuma, Eiichiro, 52, 86

"bachelor society," 93–110
Balcony of Golden Joy and Delight (restaurant), 74
Baojia system, 264, 319
Basement Workshop, 274
Bhagat Singh Thind v. U.S. (1923), 54
Black Power movement, 271–272
Bloom, Leonard, 86
Bornales, Marie, 168
Buddhism, 7–8
Burlingame, Anson, 51

California Gold Rush, 12; and Chinese gold miners, 67f
Cambodia, the children of the killing fields, 195s
Cambodian American Heritage, Inc. (CAHI), 251
Cambodian American National Council (CANC), 251
Cambodian Humanitarian Organization for Peace on Earth (C-HOPE), 251
Carr, Ralph Lawrence, 155–156
Central Pacific Railroad Company (Big Four—Leland Stanford, Charles Crocker, Mark Hopkins, and C. P. Huntington), 68–69
challenges of Asian American identities, 275–276; "the Great Third Coast," 277–280; growth of AAS academic programs in the Midwest and South, 277–280; hemispheric approach, 276–277; interracial marriages, 282–284; neo-exclusionism, 290–293; queer Asian America, 280–282; transnationalism, 275; underrepresented Asian American groups, 284–290
Chan, Charlie, 273
Chan, H, 100
Chan, Lily, 79
Chan, Sucheng, 144
Chan, T, 100
Chao, Elaine, 226
Chen, Danny, 314
Chen, Steve, 214s
Chen, Yong, 53
Chin, F. Foin, 76–77, 77s; and wife, 76f
Chin, Vincent, 225, 314
"China Lobbies," 164–165
China rise, 299–301, 303; Beijing-Shanghai High-Speed Railway, 300; Broad Sustainable Building Company (BSB), 300; duality of Chinese economy, 301; high-speed rail (HSR), 300, 361n3; Organization for Economic Cooperation and Development (OECD), 300–301; Shanghai Maglev Train, 300; "socialism with Chinese characteristics," 301; state monopoly, 301
Chinatowns, 238–240, Chicago, 230; New York, 239; San Francisco, 239, 247f; St. Louis, 240. *See also* urban enclaves
Chinese agricultural workers, 85–86, 112
Chinese Consolidated Benevolent Association (CCBA or Zhonghua Huiguan), 53, 116–117
Chinese contract laborers, on a sugar plantation in nineteenth-century Hawaii, 64f
Chinese Exclusion Act (1882), 40–41; repeal of, 139, 164
Chinese folk song, on gold mountain men, 4s
Chinese garment shops, 80–82; Chinese Ladies Garment Workers Union, 81–82; "flexibility," 81; unionization, 81–82
Chinese grocery stores, 76–80, 78f; characteristics, 76–77; Henry Company, 78–79; Kong Wo Sang Co., 78; multiple functions, 79; operation, 77–80; Sun Fat Company (Chinese

Bargain Store); 77–78; Tong Sang Company, 78; unpaid family members, 79, 111
Chinese laundries, 70–74; in Chicago, 71; development pattern, 71–72; in New York, 71; operation methods, 72–74; portrayals of Chinese laundries, 72s; in San Francisco, 71; in St. Louis, 71; wife of a laundryman, 73–74, 111
Chinese marriage patterns, 95–101; interracial marriage, 99–101; love union, 99–101; polygamy, 96–97; rarity of interracial marriages among early Chinese women, 101; traditional marriage, 97–99, 98f; transnational split marriage: Taishanese "widow" and American "concubine," 95–97
Chinese Progressive Association, 274
Chinese railroad workers, 68–69; working conditions, 69
Chinese restaurants, 74–76, in East Coast, 74; in Midwest, 74, 217f; in New York, 74; pioneers of Chinese fine dining, 76–77; in San Francisco, 74; in South, 74, wives, 111
Chinese Six Companies, 118; officers of the Six Companies, San Francisco, ca. 1900, 117f. *See also* Chinese Consolidated Benevolent Association (CCBA or Zhonghua Huiguan)
"Chinkie, Chinkie, Chinaman," 32s
Cho, John, 317s
Choe, Sara, 103
Choi, Roy, 218f
chop suey, 74–76; flexibility, 75; modest price, 75
Chow Tar, 55
Choy, Bong-youn, 136
Christianity, 9, 124
Chu, Judy, 227–228
Chu, Louis Chu, *Eat a Bowl of Tea*, 96
Chu, Steven, 226, 312
Civil Liberty Act of 1988, 156, 157f
civil rights movement, 271–272
Commission on Wartime Relocation and Internment of Civilians (CWRIC), 156
community organizations for mutual aid and self-governing, 116–121; guilds, 117; rotating credit association, 119; *tong* (tang), 116
concubinage, 96

Confucianism, in China, 3–4; in Japan, 5–6; in Korea, 5; Three Obediences and Four Virtues, 4; in United States, 124; in Vietnam, 5
Confucius Institutes, 312
Congressional Asian Pacific American Caucus (CAPAC), 228
containment policy, 174
coolie and slave trade, 19s
coronavirus, and conditional belonging, 317s
COVID-19 pandemic, 314–319; economic loss, 315; hate crimes, 315–316, 316s; impacts, 315–317; mutual aid, 319; psychological trauma, 316–317; responses from Asian American communities, 317–319; Stop AAPI Hate, 318–319; vigil against Asian hate, 318f
cultural community, 256–260; applicability, 258–260; Chicago, 257–258; definition of, 256; Filipino, 260; Japanese, 259; Korean, 259; St. Louis, 256–257
cultural heritage of Asian migrants, 3–9
cyber communities through social networks, 260–264; China News Digest (CND), 260; definition, 260–261; Facebook, 261–263; WeChat, 263–264

Daniels, Roger, 112
Daoism, 3, 124
Dennis, William, 156
Department of Labor, 169
deportation of Cambodian Americans, 193–195
Devon Avenue (an Indian American neighborhood in Chicago, 2012), 249f
DeWitt, General John L., 140–142, 152–154
Dhingra, Pawan, 220–221
Dien Bien Phu, 174
Displaced Persons Act, 164
distribution of spouse's ethnicity for six groups of Asians by gender (percentage), 1980, 283t
Diversity Immigrants Program (the Green Card Lottery program), 172–173
Dunkin' Donuts outlets, 221–222

East Coast AAPA, 273
Ebens, Ronald, 225

economic sanctions against Asian immigrants, 32–35; alien land laws, 34–35, 238; Foreign Miners' License Tax, 32–34, 238

educational achievements, 207–211; American socioeconomic conditions, 212–213; Asian values, 212; causes, 211–213; discriminatory admissions policies and practices, 209–211, 210s; disparity, 211; higher school enrollment rates, 208–209

educational attainment, by race, 1970–2010, 209t

Eisenhower, Milton, 145

Ellis Island immigration station, 44

emerging economies in Asia, 304

employment patterns, 213–222; occupational monopolies, 214; overrepresentations in small-businesses, 214; professionals, 213–216

Endo, Mitsuye, 153

ethnic community building, 116–124

ethnic suburban communities, 254–255; American-educated professionals, 255; Chicago suburbs, 255; "global town," 254; Monterey Park, 254; San Gabriel Valley, 254; "satellite city," 254, 251f

exclusion acts, 40–42

exclusion enforcement at, entry ports, 43–48; local level, 48–50

Executive Order 9066, 142

family life: Asian Indians, 104–106; Filipinos, 106–107; Japanese, 102–103; Koreans, 103–104

Ferguson, Niall, 303–304

Ferrara, Emilio, 262

Filipino agricultural workers, 87

Filipino mutual aid organizations, 120–121; Caballeros de Dimas-Alang, 120–121; Great Filipino Lodge, 120; Legionairios del Trabajo, 121

Filipino national dresses, 1998, 259f

Filipino nurses, influx of, 166–169, 245; causes, 166–169; Exchange Visitor Program (EVP), 167–169; Marie Bornales, 168s; nursing education in Philippines, 166–167

Filipino population, 87

Fong, Colleen, 284

Friedberg, Aaron L., 305

Friedman, Thomas, 306–307

Fu Manchu, 273

Geary Act, 48–49, 54–55

Gee, Emma, 272

Gee, Maggie, 136

Gee Quock Shee, 47–48, 79–80

gender role changes, 110–113; co-decision makers, 112–113; joint heads of households, 110–111; providers of families, 111–112

Gentlemen's Agreement, 41, 101, 103, 118

geographical concentration of Japanese migration, 21

G.I. Fiancées Act, 164

glass ceiling, 207

globalization, "Chinmerica," 305; collaboration of multilateral powers, 306; competition for highly skilled immigrants, 309–310; consequences, 304–305; "constrained competition," 305; distinctions between travel and migration, 311; "flexible citizenship," 311, 314; immigration destinations, 307–308; immigration sources, 308–309; importance of, 305; new opportunities and challenges, 311–314; new patterns of residence and citizenship, 311; new trends, 307–314; three balances theory, 306–307; transmigrants, 313–314

Gordon, Milton, 282

Great Proletarian Cultural Revolution, 272

Guam, tent city, 176f

Gue Gim Wah, 111

Gujarat, 220

gun-owner clubs, 319

Gupta, Sanjay, 216s

H-1B visa, 309–310

Hakka (or "guest people"), 17

Hamada, James, 222

hate crimes, 291

Hedren, Tippi, 219

Highbinder murder case, 50

Hinduism, 7, 124; caste system, 7

Hirabayashi, Gordon, 153, 156

Hirabayashi v. United States, 153

Hirata, Lucie Cheng, 81, 107
Hmong American communities, 252–254, 360n28; three stages of development, 252–254
Hmong people, in the U.S., 180f, 285s
Ho, Richard, 134
home front, 137–138; defense industry, 137–138; reasons to work, 137–138; shipyards, 137
Hop Alley, 50, 134, 256

Ichioka, Yuji, 101, 272
Iijima, Kazu, 273
Immigrant Act of 1917 (Asiatic Barred Zone Act), 42
Immigration Act of 1990, 172–173
Immigration and Nationality Act of 1965, 146f,164, 169–173, 244; causes of, 169; effects of, 169–173; preference quotas, 170–171
Immigration and Naturalization Services (INS), 167–168, 291
immigration population, 172–173, patterns of, 172–173
Immigration Reform and Control Act of 1986 (IRCA), 171–173
Indian American motel, 220–221, 221s; high-budget motels, 221; low-middle-budget franchise motels, 220–221; middle-budget franchise motels, 221
Indian bride, 258f
Indian Square, Jersey City, New Jersey, 250f
International Hotel Tenants Association, 274
interracial homosocial relationships and homosexual intimacies, 105
interracial marriage, 99–101, 104–106, 165, 241, 282–284, 257f; and assimilation, 284; assimilation theory, 282; hypergamy theory, 282–283
Irons, Peter, 141
Irwin, Robert Walker, 21. *See also* patterns of Asian migration
Islam, 8, 124
IT industry, 312

Japanese agricultural workers, 86–87, 112; economic upward mobility, 86–87; land ownership, 86–87; types of crops, 86
Japanese American Citizens League (JACL), 149, 153, 156
Japanese American community, federal government searches of, 142s
Japanese community organizations for mutual aid and self-governing, 117–119; American Magazines and Books Association, 119; Art Goods and Nations Commercial Association, 118–119; Central Japanese Agricultural Association of California, 119; Japanese Chamber of Commerce, 119; Japanese Shoemakers' League, 118; Nihonjin-kai (Japanese association), 117–118; San Francisco Japanese Cloth Dye Trade Association, 119; United Northwestern Japanese Association, 118
Japanese Community Youth Center, 274
Japanese domestic services, 84–85; day workers, 85; Issei women, 85; Nisei women, 85; "schoolgirls," 85; types, 84–85; wages, 84–85; wives as, 85
Japanese green businesses, 82–84, 83f; operation, 82–83
Japanese internment, 140–156; demography and race, 141–142; Executive Order 9066, 142; generation conflict, 146; housing in, 146f; killing of internees, 147; life in the internment camps, 145–150, 145s, 147f; mass evacuation, 142–145, 143f; mass protests, 149–150; military necessity, 140–141; public and political pressure, 141, 134s; reasons behind Japanese internment, 140–142; redress movement, 155–156; release and resettlement, 154–155; relocation centers, 145; second executive order 9106, 145; temporary detention camps, 144s
Japanese picture brides, 101–102, comparison between Japanese picture brides and Korean picture brides, 104
"Japanese schoolboys," 84
Japanese urban population centers, 82–84; Los Angeles, 82; Portland, 84; San Francisco, 82; Seattle, 84
Japantowns, 240–241. *See also* urban enclaves
Jindal, Bobby, 228

Journal of Asian American Studies (JAAS), 271
J-Town Collective, 274
Justice Department, 141–142

Kang Youwei, 122
Kanghwa Treaty, 22. *See also* patterns of Asian migration
Kearny Street Workshop, 274
Khmer Rouge, 249–250
Kim, Jeong H., 215
Kim, Willyce, 281
Kingston, Maxine Hong, *The Woman Warrior*, 74
Korean agricultural workers, 87, 112
Korean picture brides, 102–104
Korean self-governing community organization, 120; *dong-hoe* (village council), 120
Korean small businesses, 216–218; "caught in the middle," 217–218; ethnic and kinship networks, 217–218; middleman minority, 216–217
Koreantowns, 241–242; Los Angeles, 242; New York, 242; separation of commercial and residential lives, 242. *See also* urban enclaves
Korean War orphans, 166
Korematsu, Fred, 153, 156

Lee, Alla, 240. *See also* Chinatowns: St. Louis
Lee, Choua, 252
Lee, Hazel Ah Ying, 135–136
Lee, Rose, 138
Lee, Wah, 71
Legend of Miss Sasagawara, 148s
Leonard, Karen Isaksen, 87, 104–105
LGBTQIA+, 281, 358n4; population, 281–282
Li Hongzhang, 75
Li Jiacheng (Li Ka-shing), 310
Liang, Cheng, 51
Lipsitz, George, 225
Little Indias and other South Asian communities, 242–243; immigration waves, 242–243. *See also* urban enclaves
Little Manilas, 244–246; Filipino population, 244; Historic Filipinotown (Hi-Fi), 245; Los Angeles, 245; New York, 246; San Diego, 245; San Francisco, 245–246; Stockton City, 246. *See also* urban enclaves

Little Saigon, 219, 247–249, 253; in Chicago, 248–249; in Orange County, California, 247–248, 253s; population, 247–248
Little Tokyo, 241
Locke, Gary, 226–227, 312; official portrait of the U.S. secretary of commerce, 2009, 227f
Loo, Ming Hai, 225
Low How See, 80
Low, Joe (Chinese merchant), and his wife, Chan Shee, 1916, 98f
Luce-Celler Act of 1946, 140

Ma, Huateng, 263. *See also* Tencent
Macao and Woosung Restaurant, 74
Mahan, Admiral Alfred T., 12–13
map, of sending places for emigration from five Asian countries, 15f
Matsuda, Minn, 273
McCarran-Walter Act of 1952, 165
Meiji Restoration, 20–21, 133
Mexican-American War, 12
middleman minority theory, 216–218
military services, 134–137; Army Nurse Corps, 134–135; Army Training Program, 136; Asian Indians, 136–137; Chinese, 134–135; Filipinos, 134, 136; First Filipino Infantry Regiment, 136; Japanese Nisei, 137; Koreans, 136; mass naturalization ceremonies, 134; Second Filipino Infantry Regiment, 136; WAC (Women's Army Corps), 135; war experience, 134–135; WASP (Women Airforce Service Pilots), 135–136; WAVES (Women Accepted for Volunteer Emergency Service), 135
Modell, John, 83, 86
Model Minority, 229–232, 353n42; myth, 229–230, 230s; reality, 229–232, 232t
Moore Dry Dock Company, 137
Moy Dong Chow, 55, 239
Moy Dong Hoy, 55
Mrs. C, 97–99
Muslim immigrants, 291; American Muslim organizations, 291; Asian American activism, 293
Myer, Dillon S., 145

National Committee for Redress (NCR), 156
National Council for Japanese American Redress (NCJAR), 156
Native Hawaii and Other Pacific Islander (NHOPI), 277
Native Sons of the Golden West, 154
network communities, decoding of, 262s
Nguyen, Diem, 219
Nguyen, Kien, 219
Nihonmachi, or Japantown, 84
Nisei soldiers, 150–152; the 442nd Regimental Combat Team, 152; Military Intelligence Service Language School (MISLS), 150; the 100th Battalion, 151; Presidential Distinguished Unit Citations, 152
Nitz, Michael, 225
Noda, Barbara, 281
No-No Boy, 151s
nursing, in the Philippines, 167s

Olmstead, Lanya, 210
Onyett, Helen Pon, 135
Opium War (1839–1842), 14–15; impact of, 16
"Oriental," 273–274
"overseas returnees," 310

Page Law, 40
Pang, Gin Yong, 283
Park Yong-man, 121
patterns of Asian migration, 14–25; Asian Indian migration, 24–25; Canton, 17; Chinese coolie trade, 18; Chinese in Guangdong, 16–17; credit-ticket system, 17–18; Filipino migration, 23–24; Japanese migration, 18–21; Korean migration, 21–23; "push and pull," 14
Pearl Harbor attack, 132
pensionados (students), 244
Perry, Commodore Matthew C, 20, 133
Petersen, William, 229–230
physical violence against Asian immigrants, 35–40; anti-Filipinos, 40; "anti-Hindu" riots, 39–40; anti-Japanese, 38–39; anti-Koreans, 40; Chico incident in 1876, 36–37; Los Angeles massacre in 1871, 36; *People v. Hall*, 36

Piche, Robert and Lloyd (brothers), 225
"picture brides," 85
points system, 309
political incorporation, 222–228; characteristics, 222–225; coalition politics, 225; high-profile positions, 225–228, 312–313; mass protest, 225
political parties, 121–122; Dong-Ji Hoi (Comrade Society), 121; Emperor Protection Society (Baohuang Hui), 122; Indo-American Association, 122; Korean National Association (KNA), 121; Korean Women's Association, 122; Korean Women's Patriotic League, 122; Korean Women's Society, 122; Nationalist Party (Guomindang), 122; Pan Aryan Association, 122; Sin-Min-Hoi (New People's Society), 121; Women's Friendship Association, 122
population increase in Hawaii, 62–63
Program for International Student Assessment (PISA), 300–301
prostitution, 107–110; comparison between Asian and Euro-American prostitutes, 110; comparison between Japanese and Chinese prostitutes, 109–110; composition, 107; living conditions, 108–110; resistance, 109; "slave girls," 108; smuggling, 107–108
protests against exclusion and discrimination, 50–56; boycotts of American goods, 53; legal battles, 54; official protests by Asian governments, 51–52; public protests and debate, 54–55; suicides, 56
public mood, changes during WWII toward Chinese, Filipinos, and Japanese, 132–134; reasons of, 132
Punjab, 24–25
Punjabi farmers, 87
Punjabi-Mexican families, 87, 104–106, 243
Punjabi-Mexican marriages, examples of, 105s

racial prejudice against Asian immigrants, 31–32; by American merchants, American diplomats, and American missionaries, 31–32; existing racial problems, 32
Refugee Act of 1980, 171, 252

refugee experience, 178–180, 178–179s; Refugee Relief Act, 164; Vietnamese, 176–177f
religious organizations, 122–124; Buddhist temples, 123; Chinese Christian churches, 123; Filipino religious organizations, 124; Hawaiian Mission of the Methodist Episcopal Church, 123; home shrines, 124; Japanese Christian churches, 124; Korean Christian churches, 123; Korean Evangelical Society, 123; Korean Methodist Church, 123; Shin Buddhism, 124; Sikhs temples, 124
Rhee Syngman, 121
Riemer, Ruth, 86
Roh Shin-tae, 103–104
Rostow, Eugene, 153–154
Roybal, Edward, 225
Rumbaut, Rubén G., 177, 180–181

Saito, Leland, 225
Sam Wah Laundry, St. Louis, 73s
Santos, A. B., 138
scholarly work on the Midwest, 280
school attendance, by race and sex for the United States, 1910–1940, 114t
Scott Act, 41, 97
second-generation "dilemma," 113–116; generational and cultural conflicts, 113–115; racism and limited opportunities, 115–116, 115s
September 11 terrorist attacks, 290–291
sex ratio among Asian immigrants, 94, 102, 104, 165
Shima, George, 118
Shinagawa, Larry Hajime, 283
Shintoism, 8, 124
Sikh immigrants, 24s
Sikhism, 8, 124
Sikh self-governing community organization, 120; Khalsa Diwan (Free Divine) Society, 120
Singh Sodhi, Balbir Singh, 291–292
Sit, Hong, 134–135; wartime experience of Hong Sit, 135s
Snake River Massacre of 1887, 37
Sodhi, Balbir Singh, the murder of, 292s
South Chinatown, Chicago, 248f
Southeast Asian Americans, 174–184; bi-cultural and generational conflicts, 184; causes of refugees, 174–175; challenges, 183–184; economic progress, 182; ethnic network, 177–180; government refugee policies and settlement patterns, 177–180; mental health issues, 183; population concentrations, 177–179; problems at schools, 183; refugee experience, 175, 178–179; social and economic characteristics, 180–182; waves of refugees, 175–177
Spanish-American War, 13
Spickard, Paul, 283
STEM Jobs Act of 2012, 310
St. Louis Globe-Democrat, 50
Sun Yat-sen, 122
Sun Fat Company, 80–81
Supreme Court cases, 152–154
Swami Vivekananda, 124

Tael, 333n15
Taishan, 95–96
Takagi, Dana, 281
Takaki, Ronald, 63s
Takao Ozawa v. U.S. (1922), 54
Tayama, Fred, 149
Taylor, Quintard, 84
Tchen, John Kuo Wei, 11s
Tencent, 263
Thai New Year celebration, 261f
Third World Liberation Front (TWLF), 273
Third World Liberation Strike at San Francisco State College (SFSC), 273
Third World strikes, 273
Tibetan refugees, 286s
Tinikling Dance (native folk dance in the Philippines), 1999, 260f
Tirona, Connie, 106–107, 115
Tokugawa Shogunate (1600–1868), 20, 133
tong (tang), 116; Chih Kung (Zhigong), 116; Hip Sing (Xiesheng), 116; On Leong (Anliang), 116
Tonghak (East Learning) movement, 22
transcontinental railroad, 68–69, 70f
transnational and transracial adoption, 194–200; causes, 196–198; comparisons of Korean and Chinese adoptions, 198–200, 200f; domestic transracial adoption, 196; Families with

Children from China (FCC), 199; fees and expenses, 198; Holt Agency, 196; Korean Adoptee/Adoptive Family Network (KAAN), 199; one-child policy in China, 197; relationships with the Asian American community, 199–200; socioeconomic and demographic changes in the United States, 197
Treaty of Nanjing (1842), 15
Treaty of Paris (1898), 244
Tsui, Kitty, 281
Tydings-McDuffie Act, 42

Ueno, Harry Y., 149
underrepresented Asian Americans, 284–290; Asian Americans as a dynamic and evolving concept, 285–286; definition, 285; immigration and American foreign policy, 289; meaning, 290; numbers, facts, and beyond, 286–289; old labeling and new consciousness, 289–290
undocumented immigrants, 164, 185–193; causes of, 185–187; domestic workers, 190; Fujianese, 185–186; Fuzhou–Hong Kong–Bangkok–South America pattern, 187; *Golden Venture*, 188–189; mechanisms of smuggling, 187–189; "out of state," 192–193; "photo-sub" passports, 187–188; plights of, 189–191, 191s; population, 185; potentials of, 191–193; prostitution, 190–191; smuggling fees, 187; "snake heads," 186–89; South Asians, 193; "spirit of Changle," 191–192; wage-withholding period, 190; wholesaling passengers, 188–189
Union Pacific Railroad Company, 68
United Farm Workers movement, 273
University of Illinois Urbana-Champaign, 277–278
Uno, Edison, 156
urban enclaves, 238–254; Cambodian American communities, 249–251; Chinatowns, 238–240; commercial and residential centers, 238–246; commercial/tourist Centers, 246–249; Japantowns, 240–241; Koreantowns, 241–242; Little Indias and other South Asian communities, 242–243; Little Manilas, 244–246; Little Saigons, 247–249; race riot in 1992, 242

urban niche economy, 69–85
USA Department of Homeland Security, 291
USA PATRIOT Act, 291
U.S.-China relations, importance of, 305s
US decline, 302–204; Cold War, 303; Fukushima Daiichi nuclear crisis, 303; historical cycle, 302–304; Japan, 303; Libyan Revolution, 302; "Obama Doctrine," 302, 302s; "red scare" mentality, 303

Vietnamese in nail care service, 219–220; Advanced Beauty College (ABC), 219; causes, 219–220; government regulations, 220; "McNailing of America," 219–220
Vietnam War, 174–175
Vivekananda, Swami. *See* Swami Vivekanada

Wallerstein, Immanuel, 306
War Brides, 164–166
War Brides Act, 164
War Department, 141
War Relocation Authority (WRA), 145, 150, 152–155
Wartime Civil Control Authority, 144
Women's liberation movement, 271
Wong, Chi Foo, 33, 55, 71; fight against anti-Chinese prejudice, 33s
Wong, Helen Hong, 110–111
Wong, Shee, 45
Wong, Shee (who committed suicide), 56
Wong, Susie, 273
Wong Yee Gue, 47
Woo, Merle, 281
World's Columbian Exposition of 1893, 49
Wu, Ting Fang, 52

Yang, Philip Q., 172
Yangtze River Scholar Award Program, 310
Yasui, Minoru, 152–153, 156
Yung, Judy, 284
Yurie systems: high-tech hot rod, 215s

Zengakuren student movement, 272
Zhao, Xiaojian, 191–192
Zheng, Cuiping (Cheng Chui Ping), 188–189
Zuckerberg, Mark, 261

ABOUT THE AUTHOR

HUPING LING, professor emerita of history at Truman State University in Kirksville, Missouri, served as the executive editor in chief for the *Journal of Asian American Studies* from 2008 to 2012. A prize-winning author, she has authored or edited over thirty books and published over two hundred articles on Asian American studies.